Henry Reginald Buckler

The perfection of man by charity

A spiritual treatise

Henry Reginald Buckler

The perfection of man by charity
A spiritual treatise

ISBN/EAN: 9783741175602

Manufactured in Europe, USA, Canada, Australia, Japa

Cover: Foto ©Andreas Hilbeck / pixelio.de

Manufactured and distributed by brebook publishing software
(www.brebook.com)

Henry Reginald Buckler

The perfection of man by charity

THE PERFECTION OF MAN BY CHARITY.

Nihil obstat.

FR. PHILIPPUS LIMERICK, O.P.,
Censor deputatus.

Imprimatur.

HENRICUS EDUARDUS,
CARD. ARCHIEP. WESTMONAST.

In festo S. Dominici, 1889.

THE

PERFECTION OF MAN

BY

CHARITY.

A SPIRITUAL TREATISE.

BY

FR. H. REGINALD BUCKLER, O.P.

"Principaliter et per se consistit perfectio in caritate, quæ est radix omnium virtutum." (S. THOM. QUODL. DE CARIT. ART. XI., AD 5.)

LONDON: BURNS & OATES, LD.
NEW YORK: CATHOLIC PUBLICATION SOCIETY CO.

APPROBATIO ORDINIS.

Nos, infrascripti librorum revisores, opus R. P. F. Reginaldi Buckler, Ord. Præd., cui titulus "The Perfection of Man by Charity," attente perlegimus, nihilque in eo animadversione dignum reperimus, quin potius animarum saluti proficuum fore judicamus.

Datum LONDINI, *die* 22 *Julii*, 1889.

FR. RAYMUNDUS PALMER, O.P.
FR. PHILIPPUS LIMERICK, O.P.

Imprimi permittimus.

FR. ED. GREGORIUS, KELLY, O.P.,
Provincialis.

PREFACE.

THE following Treatise has been written mainly for Religious persons, in view of placing briefly before them what may be termed the science of their profession, as contained in the inspired Word, proposed by our Divine Master, and handed down from the early ages of Christianity through the Fathers of the Desert, and the Church, the Doctors of the Middle Ages, and the Saints and Spiritual writers of later date, to our own times. For, although it be certain that "not the hearers of the law are just before God, but the doers of the law shall be justified,"[1] we are none the less admonished that "he that hath looked into the perfect law, and continued therein, not becoming a forgetful hearer, but a doer of the work, this man shall be blessed in his deed".[2]

In consideration, therefore, of our need of looking "into the perfect law," the present Treatise has been compiled, as an aid in presenting to the minds of those professing Religious life, a compendious view of the perfection of their state, by

[1] Rom. ii. 13.   [2] S. James i. 25.

endeavouring to show wherein that perfection consists, and how it may be attained : in order that
by being "hearers of the law," they may afterwards
be "doers of the work" : remembering how God
Himself accounts for the defection of His people,
by their want of knowledge : "Therefore is My
people led away captive, because they had not
knowledge ".[1]

It is hoped, at the same time, that the general
principles and plan of the work may be accept-
able to Ecclesiastics generally, and Pastors of
souls more especially, who, as the *perfectores
aliorum*, aspire themselves to the knowledge and
practice of Christian perfection ; and who, in the
labours of their active life, seek the support and
refreshment of the contemplative element.
Further, it is trusted that much of the volume, as
touching on the inmost spirit of Christianity,
namely, the highest love of which man is capable,
and for which, indeed, he has been made—will be
found suitable to many of the faithful in general,
who, while not being called to the Religious state,
wish to realise, in some degree, the perfection of
Christian life.

The principal scope of the Treatise is to show
that the whole work of our perfection is reduced
to the development of the one central virtue of

[1] Isaias v. 13.

LOVE, namely, the habit of Divine Charity, as being the spring of our actions, and the soul of the virtues in the supernatural order; on which all the laws of God rest,[1] wherein they are all contained,[2] and to the perfection of which they all tend.[3] And, further, to bring forward the important and practical teaching of S. Thomas,[4] and S. Bonaventure,[5] that the Spirit of God works in us through the medium of His own virtue of love; *mediante habitu caritatis:*[6] thus governing us according to our nature, which moves by means of love, freely, readily, and sweetly.

Moreover, no small consolation comes to souls anxious to advance in the ways of Christian and Religious life, when they understand that the work of their perfection lies in the development of their love. For, as S. Jerome says :—" In other works a man may bring excuse ; but from *love* no one may excuse himself. One might say, ' I cannot fast ' ; but who could say : ' I cannot love '? We are not told, ' Go to the East, and seek for Charity ' ; ' Cross to the West, and you shall find love '. Our

---

[1] "Universa lex pendet et prophetæ." (S. Matt. xxii. 40.)

[2] "Plenitudo legis est dilectio." (Rom. xiii. 10.)

[3] "Finis præcepti est Caritas." (1 Tim. i. 5.)

[4] S. Thom., 2 2, Q 23, Art. 2.

[5] S. Bonav., "In Sent.," D 17, P 1, A 1, Q 1.

[6] "Dilectio est quasi medium inter amantem et amatum." (S. Thom., 2 2, Q 27, A 5.)

treasure is within us; in the heart, whither we are commanded by the Prophet to return: 'Return transgressors, to the heart'.[1] For that which is asked of us is not to be got from afar."[2]

While this is drawn out in view of presenting to the mind a knowledge of what the will has to embrace, and carry into effect—since nothing is willed but that which is known[3]—it is understood that much here expressed in the abstract, and exhibited from the writings of the Fathers and the Saints, is to show loving souls rather what they are to *tend to* by a gradual and steady progress, and "preparation of heart,"[4] than what they can hope at once to do: as S. Augustine and S. Thomas say in regard to the great precept itself, "Thou shalt love the Lord thy God, with thy whole heart, and with thy whole soul, and with thy whole strength".[5] And, in-

---

[1] Isaias xlvi. 8.

[2] "In reliquis operibus bonis interdum potest aliquis qualemcunque excusationem praetendere. Ad habendam vero dilectionem nullus se poterit excusare. Potest mihi aliquis dicere, non possum jejunare. Nunquid potest dicere 'non possum amare'? Non nobis dicitur, Ite ad orientem, et quaerite Caritatem. Navigate ad occidentem, et invenietis dilectionem. Intus, in nostro corde est, ubi redire jubemur, dicente Propheta, 'Redite praevaricantes ad cor'. Non enim in longinquis regionibus invenitur, quod a nobis petitur." (S. Jerome, in Matt., C 5.)

[3] "Nil volitum, nisi praecognitum."

[4] "Thy ear hath heard the preparation of their heart." (Ps. ix. 17.)

[5] S. Aug. "de perfec. justitiae," C 8. S. Thom., 2 2, Q 44, Art. 6, and "Quodl. de Carit," Art. 10, ad 1.)

deed, it may be said that the present Treatise aims at nothing more than a drawing out of this law of love, in its due dimensions, and happy results.

And as the law of love proceeds upon the laws of nature, seeing that we are creatures of habit, and that habits of some sort *will* be forming according to our repetitions of act, the irresistible conclusion forces itself upon us, that if we choose the formation of lower habits, there is no reason why we should not choose the formation of the higher, and the highest, which are those of Divine knowledge and love, adapted, as they are, to our highest capacities of mind and heart. Nor is it easy to see how, by doing otherwise, we should be in harmony with our principles, and loyal to our highest convictions.

Doubtless, the tendency of our day is rather to extroversion than introversion. But seeing that the operations of man follow his nature, according to the well-received adage of the schools, " operatio sequitur esse "—if the outer works of life are to be done " according to God,"[1] must not the inward springs of action in mind and heart be first formed according to Him, by means of His

[1] " Not fashioned according to the former desires of your ignorance, but according to Him that hath called you, who is holy, be you also in all manner of conversation holy: because it is written, ' You shall be holy, for I am holy'." (1 Peter i. 14.)

Divine wisdom and love? Let it not, therefore, be said that attendance to the interior is incompatible with the requirements of outer life. Rather let it be acknowledged that human life is lamentably disordered—out of order to its end—and that souls must be made to return again (as the Prophet of old cried) to the inmost heart, the spring of spiritual life and action;—" Return, transgressors, to the heart ".[1] If the exterior is to be reformed, the interior must be reformed : nor is there any better way of securing right order, justice, fidelity to duty, and Charity to God and to men, than by going to the root of action, which is love. As the spring of the watch regulates the movement of the hands, so the love of God regulates the works of life : and orders the soul securely to its eternal life : since Charity, affective and effective, is God's own life, and the everlasting life of the Blessed in heaven ; and is begun in time, to be consummated in eternity.

[1] " Redite prævaricantes ad cor." (Isaias xlvi. 8.)

CONTENTS.

BOOK I.—THE STUDY OF PERFECTION.

BOOK II.—THE LIFE OF CHARITY.

"When thou shalt have read, and shalt know many things, thou must always return to one principle." ("Imit. of Christ," B iii., C 43.)

THE PERFECTION OF MAN BY CHARITY.

BOOK I.

THE STUDY OF PERFECTION.

CHAPTER I.

THE CONSIDERATION OF THE END.

"ANTE OMNIA CONSIDERANDUS EST FINIS: ET SECUNDUM FINEM DIRIGENDUS EST CURSUS."

"BEFORE ALL THINGS THE END IS TO BE CONSIDERED: AND ACCORDING TO THE END OUR COURSE HAS TO BE DIRECTED."

So deeply-set is this principle in man's natural intelligence, that we adopt it without reflection, and act upon it without effort, in all our rational undertakings. If we walk into the country, our first thought is of the end. *Where* are we going? This being decided, we know the way to take, and bend our steps accordingly. If we read a book, or write a letter, or work, or paint, or play music, we form to ourselves, more or less consciously, an object to be attained; and the wish to gain this, whatever it may be, causes us to move ourselves in a way that will secure it. If we forget our chief end, the probability is that other objects have drawn us from our course, and will effectually hinder us in gaining our point, unless we make a fresh start and put ourselves again in order to our end.[1] Thus, a letter, well begun, is discontinued for some passing attraction : it may be resumed ; but if the attraction be too great, it is neglected, forgotten, and finally perishes. So of the rest. It is the view of the *end* that throws a light upon the different means ; that enables us to judge concerning them ; that shows us the need of using them, and finally urges us to undertake and pursue our work. Hence the apparent paradox of Aristotle, so consistently adopted by S. Thomas : " Finis est principium " :[2] Our end is the beginning, or first principle of action.

How well was this truth grasped, and applied to the spiritual life in the early days of the Fathers of the Desert ! The Abbot Moses, about the end of the fourth century, thus speaks to Cassian : " Every art and profession has its proper end or object, and the appropriate means for the attainment of that end. The student, anxious to excel in any art or science, directs to this end all the dangers he may encounter, the labours he endures, and the expense which he may incur in this pursuit. The husbandman tills his ground, at one time under a burning sun, at another amidst frost and snow ; by frequently ploughing and harrowing it, and cutting up the weeds, he brings it into cultivation,

[1] " In ordine ad finem."
[2] " Finis est principium in operabilibus ab homine." (S. Thom., 1 2, Q 1, A 1, sed c.)

so that the soil may be clean and well prepared for the seed. But his object or end in all this labour is to reap an abundant harvest, wherewith to provide for his subsistence, or to augment his present store. In like manner, merchants do not dread the perils of the sea or the fatigues of a long journey, so long as they have before them the prospect of an adequate remuneration. The aspirants to military fame fear no dangers, no inconveniences, shrink from no assault or enterprise, so long as glory and honour are to be the reward of their valour. And as archers trained to warfare endeavour, when they wish to show their dexterity in the presence of kings, to shoot their arrows within the circle of the target on which the prize is painted ; so if they can catch a clear view of their object, and give a right direction to their shaft, they feel confident of winning the reward, which was the *end* they proposed to themselves in their practice. But if anything distracts their attention, or clouds their view, or turns their weapon from its direct course, however trifling this may be, their arrow will fly wide of the mark through their unskilfulness. Their unpractised and unsteady sight did not permit them to take the right aim, and so their shaft missed the target."[1] Now, if in natural things men are wise enough to move according to the end which they propose ; if the prospect of glory, riches, and earthly rewards exercise a prompt influence on the mind of the student, the

[1] Cassian, Conf. i., C 2 and 5.

soldier, the merchant, the husbandman, and the
archer, so as to move them effectually to select and
to use the means to gain their respective ends, how
can we account for Christians and Religious having
the prospect of eternal blessedness before them as
their end, and yet living and moving heedlessly of
this glorious aim ?   How little of the care and
vigilance of the husbandman do they show !   How
little of the interest and energy of the merchant !
How little of the industry of the student, of
the courage of the soldier, of the steady aim
of the archer !   Sad, indeed, it is for us to
have less interest and care in spiritual things than
worldlings have in things temporal !   S. Bernard
felt this, when he addressed his brethren in Religion
as follows : " Would, O brothers, that we were as
desirous of spiritual goods as seculars are of temporal !   We ought, indeed, to desire them more, by
how much the more precious they are.   Would
that we might but equal them ! for it is a great, a
very great confusion to us to find that they desire
pernicious things more ardently than we do things
so beneficial. ·They run quicker to death than we
do to life."[1]   As S. Gregory said, long before :
" They are dull to heavenly things, in which they
ought to have been ardent ; and they are ardent
in earthly things, to which they might have laudably been dull".[2]   "That which is of little or no

---

[1] S. Bern., Serm. 36 de Divers.   ·

[2] " Torpent a cœlestibus, ad quæ flagrare debuerant, et flagrant
terrenis rebus, a quibus laudabiliter torpuissent." (S. Greg.,
" Moral.," Lib. xxxi., C 7.)

profit takes up our thoughts ; and that which is above all things necessary is negligently passed over."[1] " We have eyes, and see not."[2] " We are all hot in earthly things, and all cold in heavenly things."[3]

"Verily it is a wonder to me" (says Walter Hilton), " seeing grace is so good and profitable, that a man when he hath but little thereof, yea, so little that he can scarce have less, should say, ' Ho ! I will have no more of this, for I have enough !'. When yet I see a worldly man, though he have of worldly goods much more than he needeth, yet will he never say, ' Ho ! I have enough ; I will have no more of this !' but will covet more and more, and bestir all his wits and might, and never set a stint to his covetousness to get more.   Much more, then, should a chosen soul covet spiritual good, which is everlasting, and which maketh a soul blessed, and never should cease from coveting to get what he might.   For he that coveteth most shall have most."[4]

Let us learn, then, from the children of the world, since our Lord tells us that they are "wiser in their generation than 'the children of light".[5] They choose ·a profession, and give themselves to it ; they undertake a work, and they do it.   What is the secret of their success ?   It is the view they

[1] " Imit.," B iii., C 44.
[2] Ps. cxiii. 13.
[3] " Ferventissimi in terrenis, frigidissimi in cœlestibus sumus." (Epist. ad Demetr., in Append. Epist. S. Aug., Ep. 17.)
[4] Hilton, "Scale of Perfection," 2nd pt., C 2, S 1.
[5] S. Luke xvi. 8.

have of the *end*, and the care they take to move
according to it. "What man, having a mind to
build a tower, does not first sit down and reckon
whether he have wherewithal to finish it ; lest,
having laid the foundation, all that see it say,
"This man began to build, and was not able to
finish'."[1]

We have a work to do which belongs to the
state we have chosen. By taking the state, we take
the work which belongs to it.[2] "If you are the
children of Abraham, do the works of Abraham."[3]
If you are the children of Religion, do the works
of Religion. Our work in the Religious state
is the work of our perfection.[4] And it may well
be compared to the building of an edifice ; for
our souls have to be built up in spiritual perfection in order to become the fit habitation of God,
wherein He may dwell as in His own abode
and home on earth,[5] our rightful Master[6]—yes ;
and our Divine Lover, drawing us to Himself
as our one Love,[7] communicating His gifts, and
using us for His own ends and interests here
below. "You are the temple of the living God ;

---

[1] S. Luke xiv. 28.

[2] "Quilibet tenetur servare spectantia ad statum suum."

[3] S. John viii. 39.

[4] "Finis status Religionis est perfectio Caritatis." (S. Thom., 2
2, Q 186, A 2.)

[5] "We will come to him, and make our abode with him." (S.
John xiv.)

[6] "You call Me Master and Lord, and you say well, for so I am."
(S. John xiii. 13.)

[7] "My Beloved to me, and I to Him." (Cant. ii. 16.)

as God saith, I will dwell in them and walk among them ; and I will be a Father to you, and you shall be My sons and daughters, saith the Lord Almighty."[1]

" Do not suppose the work is done because you have become a Religious. For it will not serve you to be a Religious unless you *do* the things for which you entered Religion."[2]

How forcibly and repeatedly, both in the Old and the New Testament, is the necessity of *doing*, as distinct from knowing and hearing, impressed upon us ! " Hear, O Israel, and observe *to do* the things which the Lord hath commanded thee."[3] " Which if a man *do*, he shall live in them."[4] " Be ye doers of the Word, and not hearers only."[5] " Why call you Me Lord, and do not the things that I say ? "[6] " If you know these things, you shall be blessed if you *do* them."[7] For " not the hearers of the law are just before God, but the doers of the law shall be justified ".[8] " Everyone that heareth My words, and *doth* them, shall be likened to a wise man, who built his house on a rock. . . . But he that heareth My words, and *doth them not*, shall be like a foolish man, who built his house on the sand : and the rain fell, and the floods came, and the winds blew, and beat upon that

---

[1] 2 Cor. vi. 16, 18.
[2] Rodriguez, "Christian Perfection". (T i., C 15.)
[3] Deut. vi. 3.   [4] Ezech. xx. 11, 13, 21.
[5] S. James i. 22.   [6] S. Luke vi. 46.
[7] S. John xiii. 17.   [8] Rom. ii. 13.

house ; and it fell, and great was the fall thereof." [1]
Thus we are taught by the Divine Master that our
wisdom lies not in *knowing* our work, but in
doing it.

But the house is not built because it is begun.
We have yet to consider, as our Lord tells us,
" the charges that are necessary—whether we have
wherewithal to finish it " ; lest it be said of us,
" This man began to build, and was not able to
finish ".[2] " Do not suppose the work is done because you have become a Religious."   Have you
yet calculated the cost of the tower?   Are you
prepared to give all that is necessary to become a
finished and perfect Religious ?   Are your foundations as those of the rock, against which the stream
may beat vehemently, and you will yet stand
securely ?   If we know, and hear, and say, but *do*
not, we have the words of Eternal Truth that we
are as the unwise man, building on the sand.   We
may show a fair appearance externally, and stand
for a while ; but in the day of trial, our virtue, for
want of consistency and stability in *doing*, quickly
collapses.

" Do not, therefore, suppose the work is done because you have become a Religious.   For it will not
serve you to be a Religious unless you *do* those
things for which you entered Religion.   Now you
have come to Religion to aspire continually after
perfection.   If this be not the thing we aim at,
what is it we do?   And what have we done all

---

[1] S. Matt. vii. 24.   [2] S. Luke xiv. 28.

this while if we have not done this? What art or profession could I have chosen wherein I should not have rendered myself perfect during the same time I have been in Religion? I have made choice of the profession of a Religious, and hitherto I have advanced little or nothing in it. So many years are now passed since I was admitted into this school of virtue, and I have not yet learnt the first rudiments of it. Others become good philosophers and divines in seven years' space ; and I, after so many years, have not yet learnt to be a good Religious. How easy were it notwithstanding for us to be so, if we would but give the same care and labour to acquire true virtue which we take to become eminent in learning," or to succeed in the business of this life.[1]

Let us at least be as wise in spiritual things as we are in temporal matters. If we conceive ardent desires and take bold resolutions, and bring ourselves to act accordingly, in the things of this life, why are we not equally provident of the higher goods of the spiritual order? Is it to be said of us that we take much care to please men, and to please ourselves, and but little pains to please God? "I have loved you, saith the Lord, and you have said, wherein hast Thou loved us? The son honoureth the father, and the servant his master. If, then, I be a Father, where is My honour? If I be a Master, where is My fear, saith the Lord of hosts? And now, if you will not hear, and if you

[1] Rodriguez, "Christian Perfection". (T i., C 15.)

will not lay it to heart and give glory to My name, saith the Lord, I will send poverty upon you, because you have not laid it to heart."[1]

"The God of glory, the King of kings seeks to gain our hearts and to be loved by us. Is He not a Lóver infinitely worthy of love? Since He is a Spouse infinitely amiable, infinitely wise, infinitely rich, infinitely beautiful, infinitely perfect. Is there a man with a spark of reason who, seeing himself pursued by this adorable Majesty, can close to the loving God the door of his heart?"[2]

[1] Malach. i. 2-6 ; ii. 2.
[2] Saint-Jure, "Knowledge and Love of our Lord". (B i., C 8.)

CHAPTER II.

UNION WITH GOD, OUR ULTIMATE END.

"THERE is one God, of whom are all things, and we unto Him."[1] God alone is the One, Essential, and Eternal Good : infinite in His perfection, and self-sufficient in His happiness ; the only Good :[2] the ever-flowing and over-flowing Fountain of all goodness : "of whom, and by whom, and in whom are all things".[3] Creatures are not good, but the recipients of God's goodness. He stood in no need of them, but lived in His own eternity, in happiness ineffable. Yet He willed to communicate Himself ; for such is the nature of goodness that it seeks to diffuse itself. *Bonum est diffusivum sui.* He surrounded Himself with a glorious creation. "He made His Angels Spirits, and His ministers a flaming fire."[4] "The heavens declare the glory of God, and the firmament showeth the work of His hands."[5] He made man to His own image and likeness, thus fitting him for union with Him-

---

[1] 1 Cor. viii. 6.
[2] "None is good but God alone." (S. Luke xviii. 19.)
[3] Rom. xi. 36.   [4] Ps. ciii. 4.   [5] Ps. xviii. 1.

self.[1] This likeness is in the soul, and is found in a certain resemblance of our faculties to the adorable Trinity; that inasmuch as God is Spirit, Intelligence, and Love, so the soul of man is spiritual, intelligent, and loving. The intellect and the will are the two great capacities of our spiritual nature; and they each want filling, the intellect with knowledge, and the will with love. Thus they tend to their perfection, to the fulness of knowledge, and the fulness of love; which tells us that they are made for God: for certain it is that no creature can supply such fulness; since creatures are but limited recipients themselves, and like us seeking to be filled. Hence the Angelic Doctor tells us that "man's desires can be satisfied by none but God alone; since from the visible things of creation, he is moved to search into their cause; nor is that desire satisfied, till he come to the First Cause, which is God".[2] Indeed, "our great avidity, our unquiet eagerness, our insatiable curiousity to see, to hear, to know, and possess something new, are evident marks that created things are not our end; since it is the property of the end to calm the heart and appease the desires of the soul".[3]

How strong is this tendency to our end! S.

---

[1] "Similitudo est causa amoris, et ratio unionis." (Denis Carthus., "de vita inclusar," Art. 18.)

[2] "Naturale hominis desiderium in nullo alio quietari potest, nisi in solo Deo; innatum est enim homini ut ex causatis desiderio quodam moveatur ad inquirendum causas: nec quiescit illud desiderium quousque perventum fuerit ad Primam Causam, quæ Deus est." (S. Thom., Quodl. "de Virtutib.," Art. 10.)

[3] Saint-Jure, "Spiritual Man," Vol. ii., C 3, S 3.

Thomas tells us that all our desires for good things of any sort are so many declarations of our tendency to God Himself, as the Fountain of all goodness. " All things," says the Holy Doctor, " tend to God, by tending to good, whether intellectual, sensible, or natural ; because nothing is truly good or desirable, except as participating the Divine likeness."[1]

Look at the tendency of the intellect, how it thirsts for knowledge ! It begins its activity at the dawn of reason, and where shall we say that it stays it ? It continues to expand by impressions daily received ; by a succession of apprehensions, reflections, and deductions. It observes, enquires, considers, reasons, and concludes. It continues this course day by day, and year by year ; and, after all, how little it acquires ! How limited is the supply of knowledge, even in the wisest man ! for if he knows many things, how many more there are of which he is ignorant ! He comes to the last day of his life : and then, does the intellect rest ? Ah, no ! " unfound is the boon, unslaked the thirst ". It carries away its desire for knowledge into the next world : and it rests not until it rests in the knowledge of God. There is the end ; and it finds the fulness of knowledge in its source ; its wants are now satisfied ; and it lives in the posses-

---

[1] " Omnia appetunt Deum ut finem, appetendo quodcunque bonum, &c. quia nihil habet rationem boni, et appetibilis, nisi secundem quod participat Dei similitudinem." (S. Thom., 1, Q 44, Art. 4 ad 3.)

sion and enjoyment of its everlasting beatitude.[1]
In the same way the faculty of the will is ever
tending to love. We have only to consider a little
to see that our desires and affections are constantly
seeking for objects on which to engage themselves.
We may love God, or creatures, or ourselves ; but
we must love something, since love as well as intelligence belongs to our nature. Have we not felt
its power from our earliest years? How often
has it drawn us to one thing, urged us to another,
withheld us from a third? Love is our moving
power; "pressing the soul on by its own force,"
says S. Augustine, "so that good or bad *loves* make
good or bad *lives*" :[2] love being, according to S.
Thomas, the root of both appetites and passions :
seeing that, as a man loves, so he desires, so he
wills, so he acts. "If we love a thing, we desire it
when it is absent, we rejoice when it is present, we
grieve when it is removed from us, and show our
anger to those who deprive us of it. So that
every act proceeding from a passion proceeds also
from love, as from its cause."[3] "Hope, fear, joy,

---

[1] " Cum intellectiva virtus creaturæ non sit Dei essentia, relinquitur quod sit aliqua participativa similitudo ipsius, qui est primus
intellectus." (S. Thom., i., Q 12, Art. 2.)

[2] "Animus velut pondere amore fertur quocunque fertur. Nec
faciunt bonos vel malos mores, nisi boni vel mali amores." (S.
Aug., Epist. 157 and 155, ad Hilar. et Maced.)

[3] "Amor est communis radix omnium appetitivarum opera-
tionum. Et ideo oportet quod omnis operatio appetitus ex amore
causetur. Et quia omnis operatio uniuscujusque rei ex appetitu
causatur, sequitur quod omnis actio cujuscunque rei ex amore
causetur. Ex hoc enim quod aliquid amamus, desideramus illud
si absit, gaudemus cum adest, tristamur cum ab eo impedimur ; et

sorrow, wishes, endeavours, expectations, cares, disappointments, career wildly through the human heart, like the waves of the sea, rising, falling, and rising again, and filling it with a burning desire for some good, the acquision of which is to bring rest ; and, as soon as it is attained, fresh restlessness begins."[1]

This reminds us again that we are made for God. For we go on seeking, and desiring, and loving. Our lives pass onwards, the last day comes, and we have to leave all we have loved in this world. But the capacity for loving ! we cannot leave that. We carry it with us still unsatisfied. We are wanting more than ever to love and be loved ; and we rest not until we rest in the love of God. "Thou hast made us for Thyself, O Lord ; and our heart rests not until it rests in Thee."[2] There is our end. There we find beauty, and goodness, and love, in their source : and we see that all the separate goods that so attracted us here below were but small participations of the Divine Goodness. Now, we have the Essential Good ; and the will is replete with love. Its wants are now satisfied, and it rejoices for ever in its end.

It is clear from this that we shall not attain to the perfection of our being, till we are in possession

---

odimus quæ nos ab amato impediunt ; et irascimur contra ea." (S. Thom., Opusc. "de Div. Nom." C 4, l 9, and "Cont. Gentes," L 4, C 19.)

[1] Hahn-hahn, "Lives of Fathers of the Desert" ; "Paul of Thebes."

[2] S. Aug., "Confess." i. 1.

of our end; and if not to the perfection of our
being, neither to the perfection of happiness.   So
that man's end, perfection, and beatitude meet in
one and the same point, according to the teaching of
S. Thomas.[1]   Further, as our end is our perfection,
it follows that we shall not be able to attain our
end, until the soul has *attained its relative perfection.*
The realising this is of vast importance to us.   It
shows us the necessity of undertaking the work of
our perfection.   God is our ultimate end.   The
attainment of perfection may be called our *proximate* end, as being the necessary and immediate
disposition that fits us for union with God.   "You
have been made by God"; (says Lewis of Granada)
"but you are not yet finished.   And none but He
that began the work can rightly finish it.   This is
why all effects have an inclination and tendency to
the causes that produced them : that they may
receive from them their last perfection."[2]

---

[1] " Beatitudo est bonum perfectum.   Et unumquodque dicitur
perfectum inquantum attingit proprium finem."   (S. Thom., 1 2,
Q 2, Art. 8 and 2 2, Q 184, Art. 1.)

[2] Lewis de Gran., "Sinner's Guide".   (C 2, S 1.)

CHAPTER III.

THE ATTAINMENT OF PERFECTION, OUR PROXIMATE END.

THE attainment of our ultimate end will be impossible until the soul is in the proximate disposition for uniting with God. And this disposition can be nothing less than the soul's perfection. We know that God will not admit imperfect souls to the eternal union of heaven. Otherwise how would "all things be subdued to Him, that God may be all in all?"[1] And how would heaven be the all-happy and perfect place that it is? "What fellowship hath light with darkness?"[2] and what agreement has perfection with imperfection? Does not the whole doctrine of purgatory rest upon this truth? How could the poor soul endure the unclouded blaze of God's overwhelming majesty, conscious of the stains and shades of its own dark misery? Would it not hide its face, and seek to flee from the unutterable purity of the Divine light?

In the life of heaven we see no longer "in a dark manner, but face to face".[3] God Himself shines

---

[1] 1 Cor. xv. 28.   [2] 2 Cor. vi. 14.   [3] 1 Cor. xiii. 12.

2

within the souls of the Blessed, by the effulgence
of His Divine light and love. And as pure crystals
before the shining sun reflect unimpeded the
splendour of the sun's brightness, and retain the
likeness of its image within them, so the souls of
the glorified in the beatific vision stand before the
Face of God, and reflect the Divine similitude, by the
participation of God's own life, and light, and love,
and happiness.[1] " We know that when He shall
appear we shall be like to Him, because we shall
see Him as He is. And everyone that hath this
hope in Him sanctifieth himself, as He also is
holy." [2]

Perfect purity of soul is therefore the proximate
and immediate disposition for union with God ;
since by means of this alone we become capable of
reflecting purely the Divine likeness. It is this
Divine impression and reflection that at once
sanctifies and perfects the soul. For God alone is
Holiness and Perfection ; and we can only be called
holy and perfect by participation when this Divine
resemblance shines within us. But as the sun's
reflection would be impeded in a crystal dimmed
with spots and shades, so the brightness of God's
light and love would never be able to reflect itself
purely in a soul darkened with imperfection. It is
only in perfect purity that the light of Divine glory
shines.   Therefore it is written, " Be ye holy,

---

[1] "Tunc perfecta erit Dei similitudo, quando Dei perfecta erit
visio." (S. Aug., "de Trin." Lib. xiv., C 17.)
[2] 1 John iii. 2.

because I the Lord your God am holy ".[1]   " Be ye
perfect, as your Heavenly Father is perfect." [2]
Hence the necessity of attaining to perfection,
before we can attain to God.   As then perfection
is our end, it follows that we are all obliged to *tend*
to perfection ; just as in making a journey we are
obliged to advance, if we mean to reach the
journey's end.   We are not bound at once to be
perfect; because the work of perfection is a gradual
process.   But all, both Christians and Religious, are
called upon to tend, each in his own state and way,
to perfection ; for the very reason that we are all
obliged to tend to God as our ultimate end.

Did we not learn in the first chapter of the
catechism that we were made to know and to love
God, and to prepare ourselves to be happy with
Him hereafter, and that we had to give Him our
homage by believing in Him, hoping in Him, and
loving Him with our whole heart ?   If what we
have learnt since our childhood has tended to
make us forget this first lesson, which tells us that
our business here below is to lead a spiritual life,
is it not necessary that we should return again to
our elementary instruction ?   " Unless you become
as little children, you shall not enter the kingdom of
heaven." [3]

Let it be said, however, for the tranquillity of
consciences, that souls *tend* to perfection very easily,
and, as it were, naturally, without adverting to the
fact that they are doing so ; and this on account of

---

[1] Levit. xix. 2.   [2] S. Matt. v. 48.   [3] S. Matt. xviii. 3.

the law of perfectibility in our nature.[1]   That is to
say, they tend "*aliquo modo*," in some way. Whether
they are progressing quickly or safely are further
questions.   Many Christians, and even Religious,
may think little about perfection, and yet, strictly
speaking, tend to it, though with slow and tottering
steps.   Certainly every soul maintaining itself in
grace, is in some way tending to perfection, because,
if it persevere in that disposition, it will infallibly
reach perfection sooner or later.   Grace is glory
begun : and glory is grace perfected.   But if it
only *thought more* of its perfection, how much
quicker would it be able to advance !   And these
very ones who think so little of the great work
awaiting them,[2] bestow indefinite time and pains
upon the cultivation of lower things, and the
perishable satisfactions of this passing life.   If it
is a question of learning a worldly profession, of
acquiring a particular science or art, what interest
do we see !   Hour upon hour, day after day, and
year after year are given to careful consideration,
and diligent application.   The mind is trained, the
memory stored, heart and soul are engaged in the
pursuit.   In time, by dint of care and practice, the
habit of the art or science is acquired : difficulties
have vanished ; exercise and action are now easy,
pleasant, and natural.   Men become eminent in

[1] The law, namely, by which we naturally tend to, or wish for,
perfection; as S. Thomas says, "Unumquodque appetit suam
perfectionem." (Sum. i., Q 6, Art. 1.)   By marking what is imperfect, we thereby show the wish for what is perfect.

[2] "Hesitating to die to death, and to live to life." (S. Aug.,
"Confess.," Lib. viii., c. 11.)

their state, perfect in their art ; fit to communicate to those around them ; to lead, influence, and govern their fellow-creatures.

If only our faith were more vivid, and our love of God more fervent, we might give the same attention and care to spiritual things that these children of the world give to temporals, and as they attain perfection in their profession, we might at least aim at it in ours.[1] Would not the work be easy, and even pleasant, did we but take the same pains over it that we take to become good men of business, or accomplished in literature and art?

And what we must lament is, that if we do not undertake here the work of our perfection, which we might do with such great glory to God, such benefit to others, and so much happiness and merit to ourselves, it will have to be done *for* us in Purgatory, without this glory to God, benefit to others, and merit to ourselves. There in Purgatory we shall be passive ; and the everlasting merit of having sought with heart and soul, striven for, and attained to union with the Sovereign Good in this life, will not be ours for all eternity. How sad then to content ourselves with a low aim and a slow pace in so vastly important a work ! We have heard of the archer who shoots with a slack bow. If he but just points the arrow at the mark, he will miss it. His only plan, if he wish to hit it, will be to take a high aim. Now the possession of God must be the aim of every true Christian. But let

[1] "Cui Deus portio est, nihil debet curare nisi Deum." (S. Ambr., "de fuga Sæculi," C 2.)

it not be forgotten that our bow is slack. Human nature is weak. If then we desire to attain to the possession of God, let us not be contented with just providing for our necessary sanctification. Let our aim be perfection ; and then with all the weakness that encompasses us, we may at least succeed in attaining what is necessary.

Why should we not advance quickly, if the end is to be gained ? Why not labour industriously if the work is to be done ? People of the world are not so heedless of their common interests as we are of our eternal gains. Do we see them contented on a journey with walking lamely along the way? And what would they say to one who satisfied himself with crawling about ?[1] We know that their desire to gain the end prompts them to take the means of advancing rapidly. They are far too much alive to their needs to wish to loiter on the road. So in the way of perfection, some may be said to walk slowly, and some just creep along the way. Others find means of going forward quickly, while others run rapidly along, making great advances day by day. All these *tend* to perfection in different ways and degrees, even those who creep, since creeping is, absolutely speaking, tending. But what a slow tendency ! How far from anything like a rational progress ! How little would they dream of such folly in worldly business ! How much wiser would they be ! And the chances are

---

[1] S. Teresa says : "We must take care that our Director be one who does not teach us to crawl like toads ". ("Life by herself," C 13.)

that those who content themselves with going so slowly will find life slipping away and their work not half done, if indeed they do not stop altogether or die on the way, and so never reach the wished-for end.[1]

" Delay not," says the " Spiritual Combat," " the spinning of the wool for thy nuptial robe, till the marriage-day be come, when thou shouldst be ready-arrayed to go before thy Spouse. Remember that God who gives thee the morning does not promise thee the evening."[2] And to all such torpid souls the words of the Psalmist would seem to apply: "They have eyes, and see not. They have ears, and hear not. They have hands, and feel not. They have feet, and walk not."[3] That is, in spiritual life, they have great powers—many capabilities and opportunities; but they use them not. They work naturally, and not spiritually. Will not the talent which they neglect to use be taken from them? " For to everyone that hath, shall be given, and he shall abound. But from him that hath not, that also which he seemeth to have shall be taken away."[4]

Shall we not then make up our mind for our work—the great work of going forwards till we attain to God ? Can we possibly hesitate to advance

---

[1] " The just walk, the wise run, the loving fly towards God. You ought always to advance in the paths of holiness. You will do wrong to walk if you can run, and to run if you can fly; because time is short." (B. Battista Varani, "Life," Suppl., C 2.)

[2] " Spiritual Combat," C on Sloth.

[3] Ps. cxiii. 13.   [4] S. Matt. xxv. 29.

day by day, and to advance quickly ? for in spiritual
life the quicker we go, the more easily we go, says
S. Bernard. [1]   Think of the Psalmist, who says,
" I have run in the way of Thy commandments,
when Thou didst enlarge my heart ".   He was not
content with a slow space.   He runs with an en-
larged heart.   And, doubtless, if we offer our hearts
to God by true love, He will enlarge them, and
enable us to run forward in His way, imitating the
Divine Lover, who " rejoiced as a giant to run His
course ".[8]

Let us henceforth then consider the work of our
perfection as the main business of life—the distinct
object of our profession ; as people of the world
profess the sciences and the arts, and aim at perfection therein.   " In everything much is lost if we
do not advance," says S. Teresa.   Moreover, let us
strive to reach perfection, even in this life, though it
be but a quarter of an hour before we die, as S.
Francis of Sales said.   How insufficient will be our
love of God, and how wanting shall we be in
appreciating our opportunities and consulting our
best interests, if we let life slip by, wasting our time
and energies on perishable gratifications, instead of
devoting them to the grand work for which our
powers have been made ; the work that will bring
such glory to God, such good to our fellow-creatures,
such merit and happiness to our own souls.   " Woe "

---

[1] " In via vitæ, quo citius, eo facilius curritur." (S. Bern.,
Epist. 385.)
[8] Ps. cxviii. 32.   [8] Ps. xviii. 6.

(says S. Bernard) " to this unhappy generation, that suffices itself with such insufficiency!"[1]   If the work of perfection is to be done, why not do it in this life, and have the benefit and the merit of it? Why should we be content to live and to die imperfect, leaving our work undone, and not having gained to God the glory, and to ourselves the merit of it? If the work is ours, let us do it, and do it while we can. "Work while it is day; for the night cometh when no man can work.[2]   " It is astonishing to see with what love God engages Himself with us, and yet how few souls occupy themselves with Him."[3]   Further, if we neglect our perfection, or take but little heed of it, may we not fear to incur the rebuke of the Master to His steward, that he had "wasted His goods"?[4]   We have the power to advance, and the means, and the time, and the opportunities.   Shall we not use our powers, our time, our means, and our opportunities? and if we neglect to use them, shall we not waste them?

"Trade till I come," was the injunction of the Master in the parable of the pounds.[5]   How many talents are committed to us ! We have vast powers of working for God, both internally and externally : and of making His gifts fructify to His glory, and to our own and others' benefit. We are able to love

---

[1] "Væ generationi huic miseræ ab imperfectione sua, cui sufficere videtur insufficientia, imo inopia tanta!" (S. Bern., Serm. 27, "de Divers".)

[2] S. John ix. 4.   [3] Surin., Lett. ix., Vol. ii.
[4] S. Luke xvi. 1.   [5] S. Luke xix. 13.

Him generously, to turn to Him frequently, to think of Him lovingly, to give ourselves to Him unreservedly, to labour for Him zealously, to suffer for Him patiently. We are able to be "all" for Him. "Trade till I come." Are we good traders ? Are we turning our talents to account, in the way our Divine Master intends they should serve both Him and us ?

Doubtless, in the way of perfection, it is of the greatest advantage to start upon the right track in early years ; in order that habits of mind, heart, and action may be formed accordingly. Hence the Divine admonition : "The things thou hast not gathered in thy youth, how shalt thou find them in thy old age ?"[1] We are creatures of habit ; and it is of the utmost consequence that our early habits should be the right ones. "The form a man first takes he hardly changes."[2] Consequently, if the higher habits of Divine knowledge and love are not duly formed, lower habits quickly get the entrance, gather strength, and become unmanageable. To unform old habits, and form new ones late in life, is an acknowledged difficulty. This made Lallemant say that (in the ordinary course) "no one will give himself to the interior life in his old age who has not done so in his youth,"[3] although even here Divine Grace may supply, and will, if a soul be loving, courageous, and consistent.

[1] Ecclus. xxv. 5.

[2] "Formam quam primo quis recipit, vix deponit." (S. Bonav., "Spec. discipl.," prol.)

[3] Lallemant, "Spir. Doctrine". (P 5, C 2, A 3, § 3.)

It concerns us then at once to know where our work lies. What is perfection? And in what precisely does our own perfection consist? The first step to success in any work is to ascertain what the work really is. If it is to be done, it must first be known. " Therefore is My people led away captive, because they had not knowledge." [1]

Perfection may be described differently, and yet its reality be ever one and the same. Beginners might open a number of spiritual books, in view of learning the way of perfection, and think that one says one thing, and another another. It is, indeed, true that there are different ways of doing the same work, as there are different roads that lead to the same end. We must not complain of this variety, which is suitable to the varied wants of different souls. It is quite certain that the *end* of all is the same. " The Holy Spirit," says Blosius, " leads us by different ways to the wine-cellar of His love." [2] And, therefore, when spiritual writers seem to say many things, we must own that it is rather their *ways* that are different than their *end*. Moreover, if we had more light, it would be easy to see that they are all in agreement together.

Still, it *is* a benefit to each one's soul to be able to find the central point to which the varied teaching of Doctors and Spiritual men is known to be directed, or from which it may be said to radiate. If we find that point, it is like eyesight, enabling us to see things, which before, for want of a certain

---

[1] Isaias v. 13.   [2] Blosius, " Spec. Monach," C. 5.

deep, inward, general principle, we failed to recognise.[1]   In the case of many who appear to content
themselves with creeping along the way of perfection (as though the Divine Loveliness were not
sufficient to induce them to go quickly,) it is likely
that they would have but little method in their
spiritual life.   " I pray to God," they would say :
" I go to the Sacraments ;   I do not want to commit
mortal sin :   I try to do the duties of life."   All
this is certainly good.   But, perhaps, they do not
remember that their bow is slack.   Human nature
is weak, and the enemies of our salvation are strong.
If they aim no higher than this, do they not run the
risk of missing the mark?   Anyhow, if they are
contented in creeping to heaven, it is their own
look-out.   In worldly business they are usually
wiser.   " If you offer the blind, and the lame, and
the sick for sacrifice, is it not evil ?   Offer it to thy
prince, if he will be pleased with it, or if he will
regard thy'face, saith the Lord of Hosts.   If you will
not hear, and if you will not lay it to heart, to give
glory to My name, saith the Lord, I will send poverty
upon you ; because you have not laid it to heart." [2]

To others, however, who wish to advance more
securely to their end, it will be of great advantage
to adopt some method of proceeding in spiritual
things, which will involve their having a definite
aim in view, and bringing its influence to bear on
the works of daily life.

---

[1] "Ubi amor, ibi oculus." (Rich. of S: Vict., "de præp. ad
Contempl.," C 13.)
[2] Malach. i. 8 and ii. 2.

Now it may well happen to souls who strive to
serve God in earnest—who say with the Psalmist,
" show me, O Lord, Thy ways, and teach me Thy
paths,"¹ to find themselves strongly drawn in some
particular direction.   Such drawing, indeed, may be
well regarded as an assured sign of God's working
in the soul : for in this work God is the principal
Worker, and the soul has to respond to the Divine
call.   Let it, therefore, say again with the Psalmist,
" I will hear what the Lord God shall speak within
me ".²

One, for instance, might be deeply impressed with
the conviction that the simple will of God was the
compendium of all he needed ; and day by day he
would endeavour to recognise that Divine will
in each duty and occurrence, and strive to do it as
faithfully as he could.   Another might be drawn to
the exercise of conformity to Christ our Lord as
the model of perfection. He would have the Divine
Master constantly in view, meditating on His life
and virtues, as it were walking with Him, and striving to imitate Him in the perfection of His Sacred
Humanity.   A third would make the presence of
God the one thought of his life, endeavouring to
realise the Sovereign Wisdom and Love, as sustaining and pervading all things ; " in whom we live,
and move, and have our being " :³ and this thought
would be made to sanctify his life, for it would
gradually lead to the love of God, as the only good ;
and more love would bring more light, and more

¹ Ps. xxiv. 4.   ² Ps. lxxxiv. 8.   ³ Acts xvii. 28.

light more love; and thus life and actions would be ordered by the light and strength of love, according to God. Another would make his work lie in putting off "the old man" by mortification, and putting on the "new man" by living according to the spirit. This seems to be S. Paul's idea of Christian perfection, which is no small recommendation. Others would feel less definite attractions; trying to live always in God's grace, praying daily, and offering the works and trials of life to the Divine glory.

It must be said that all these views of spiritual life are good. God's graces are manifold. "There are diversities of graces, but the same spirit. And there are diversities of operations, but the same God, who worketh all in all." [1] "The Spirit breatheth where He will:" [2] and God deals differently with different souls, and with the same soul at different times. How different have the Saints been! God seems to delight to manifest Himself in great variety, in the order of grace, as in that of nature. As the flowers, and fruits, and trees are all beautiful in their variety, so are the saints of God and holy souls; and so are the works of the saints and the writings of spiritual men; all different, and all good; and the Divine Spirit, their common principle, working "all in all".

Let those, therefore, who have any particular attraction in spiritual life, whether it be to one plan or another, so long as it is good, and influences

[1] I Cor. xii. 4.   [2] S. John iii. 8.

them rightly, follow such attraction as long as it
may last, as the Divine call in their regard. If, as
time goes on, new lights are received and higher
aspirations arise, let them, as the Apostle says, " be
zealous for the better gifts," and ready to follow
the " more excellent way ";[1] remembering that our
life here below is to be a constant progress ; that
when one step is made we must be ready for the
next ; when one height is gained we have to com-
mence another ; for "the path of the just, as a
shining light, goeth forwards, and increaseth to perfect day ";[2] remembering also S. Paul's persuasion
that he had still to go onwards to perfection : " not
as though I had already attained, or were already
perfect : but I follow after, if by any means I may
apprehend. Forgetting the things that are behind,
and stretching forth myself to those that are before,
I press towards the mark."[3]

It may happen, however, that some souls have
desires for perfection, and yet feel none of the
attractions named, but would gladly find means of
gaining a clear idea of their work—such as would
at once enlighten them to undertake it, and aid
them to accomplish it. It is for these more
especially that the present treatise is designed.

Let all such know that they have within them the
germ of their own perfection, which only awaits
development. Thus they need not seek their treasure from afar. They have it deep within their own
souls. It "is not above thee, nor far off from thee ;

[1] 1 Cor. xii. 31.   [2] Prov. iv. 18.   [3] Philip. iii. 12.

nor is it in heaven, that thou shouldst say, Which of
us can go up to heaven, to bring it to us?   Nor is it
beyond the sea, that thou mayest excuse thyself, and
say, Which of us can cross the sea, and bring it unto
us?   But it is very nigh to thee, in thy heart, that
thou mayest do it, that thou mayest love the Lord
thy God, and walk in His ways, and adhere to
Him ; for He is thy life."[1]

The state of grace places the soul even now in
union with God, elevating it to the Divine friendship, and making it a participator in Divine
knowledge and love by the theological virtues,
which belong essentially to the life of grace.   The
germ of our perfection is in the theological virtue
of charity, as being love of the highest order, and
therefore the animating and moving principle in
the will, commanding through the will the other
virtues, thus ordering and regulating the soul, and
gradually perfecting the whole man in his life and
actions.[2]   For even in the natural order love is the
principle of action and perfection.   " Each one lives
according to his love, for good or for bad," says S.
Augustine.[3]   As a man loves, so he wills and
moves.   Love is the spring of his actions.   So in

---

[1] Deut. xxx. 11.

[2] " Caritas est virtus dignissima, cæterarum virtutum regina, imperatrix, motrix, forma, vita, et finis ; quia per caritatem maxime ac
propinquissime conjugimur, conformamur, adhæremusque Deo.   Et
sicut in naturalibus forma movet, ornat, perficitque materiam, sic
in intellectualibus atque moralibus, caritas cæteras movet, perficit,
ornat, actuatque virtutes." (Denis Carthus., "de Profess. Monast."
A I, and "de Regul. vitæ Christianæ," L i., A 8.)

[3] " Ex amore suo quisque vivit, vel bene, vel male.   (S. Aug.,
" Cont. Faust." L v.)

the spiritual order, Charity or Divine love is the principle of action.[1]   Hence the Holy Fathers speak of it as the root of good things, and the source and mother of the virtues.[2]   This queen of virtues resides within us as a *habit*, or permanent quality of soul (the property of sanctifying grace, by which God loves the soul and the soul loves God ;[3] God abides in the soul and the soul abides in Him);[4] the habit of Divine Charity, uniting the soul (according to the nature of love) with the beloved object ; subduing and likening it thereto, and finally transforming it ; according to the words of the Apostle, " He who is joined to the Lord is one spirit ".[5]   Here we find the reason for placing our perfection in Charity.[6]   God alone is perfection.

[1] "Caritas est principium omnium bonorum operum, quæ in finem ultimum ordinari possunt." (S. Thom., 1 2, Q 65, Art. 3.)

[2] "Caritas est radix bonorum." (S. Aug., "de Gratia Christi," Lib. i.) "Caritas radix est, fons, materque cunctorum bonorum." (S. John Chrys., "Hom. 2 in die Pentec.".)

[3] S. John xiv. 23.

[4] 1 John iv. 16.

[5] 1 Cor. vi. 17.

[6] The definition of perfection is given as follows by Bouix : " Perfection is Charity so habitual and intense, as proximately to dispose a man to act ordinarily and easily according to the Divine precepts and counsels ". (" De jure Regul.," P i., C 3, P 4.)   "I infer with Suarez " (says Scaramelli) "that perfection consists in the formation of the habit of Charity; and in rendering it easy, ready, and prompt in the exercise of full and fervent acts of love towards God and our neighbour." (Scaramelli, " Direct. Ascet.," Vol. i., S 1, A 1, C 2.)   This reducing the work of our perfection to the development of the one great habit of habits rests upon a simple law of nature, viz., that love is the spring of our actions. Hence our Lord tells us that on Charity "dependeth the whole law and the prophets". (S. Matt. xxii. 40.) As though He would teach us that all the laws of God, and the doctrine of inspired men, are comprised in one Charity; this being the inward life and principle, moving the soul to the observance of all the rest.   In this

3

Our perfection is but relative, and must therefore
consist in resembling Him.   But how is our nature,
divided and darkened by so many imperfect habits,
to be brought to that oneness and perfect purity
that likens it to God, and enables the Divine light
to shine unimpeded within it?   It is by "the operation whereby He is able to subdue all things to
Himself"[1] that God will effect this ; the operation
of His Divine love, which enkindles its fire within
the soul, and gradually communicates its virtue to
the faculties, senses, and even bodily members ;
expelling all contrary elements ; changing, subduing, refining, spiritualising the nature, and finally
transforming it to the Divine likeness ;[2] much as
in material things the fire acts upon the wood, consuming all dissimilar qualities, and changing it into
its own form.   "Our God is a consuming fire."[3]
So He dwells within us, and by the fire of His
Charity works in our souls, eliminating the human
spirit and substituting the Divine.   But "while the
Divine fire consumes, it afflicts not," says S. Bernard.
"It burns sweetly, and lays waste happily.   While it
subdues the imperfections of the soul, it diffuses
therein the sweetness of its unction."[4]   How this is

way the other virtues become the different operations of the one
Charity : "love always working in a thousand different ways," as
says S. Teresa. ("Int. Castle," M 6, C 9.)

[1] Philip. iii. 21.

[2] "In eandem imaginem transformamur." (2 Cor. iii. 18.)

[3] Heb. xii. 29.

[4] "Ignis, qui Deus est, consumit quidem, sed non affligit.
Ardet suaviter, desolatur feliciter.   Est enim vere carbo desola-
torius ; sed qui sic in vitia exerceat vim ignis, ut in anima vicem
exhibeat unctionis." (S. Bern., Serm. 57 "in Cantic.".)

done, and how the life of Divine Charity thus unites in itself all other plans of perfection, and so may be considered a short and compendious way to our end, we will endeavour to see in the chapters which follow.

CHAPTER IV.

OUR NEED OF HUMILITY.

IT is evident that the Charity which gives us our perfection and beatitude by union with our End must be *perfect Charity* as distinguished from Charity simply possessed, which is compatible with imperfection and venial sins. As already said, the simple possession of Charity common to all in the state of grace is a germ that awaits its development, and must attain its perfection before it is capable of this Divine union ; inasmuch as God, who is Infinite Perfection, could never take imperfection into the eternal union of heaven ; "for the vileness of the creature" (says S. John of the Cross) "is much less capable of the dignity of the Creator than darkness is of light ".[1]

The work of bringing Charity to its perfection will require us to devote ourselves to this one project only. It must be our exclusive work ;[2] that is, the various duties and trials of life must

---

[1] S. John of the Cross. ("Ascent of M. Carm.," B i, C 4.)

[2] "Caritas est principium omnium bonorum operum, quæ in finem ultimum ordinari possunt." (S. Thom., 1 2, Q 65, Art. 3.)

be made to enter into it, by proceeding in them from the principle of Divine love, instead of our own natural love.[1]   For as the fruits of a tree depend on the sap rising from the root and spreading its virtue through all the branches ; so the fruits of our life, which are our daily works, need vivifying by the sweet virtue of Divine love, rising in the soul from the root of sanctifying grace, and spreading its influence through our lives and actions.

And as when we see a tree bringing forth bad fruits we know that the cause lies in the defective virtue of the root, so when we see the imperfect produce of our lives we know that the root of self-love is entwining itself with that of Divine love, and spreading its influence in our powers, which in their turn bring forth evil fruits.[2]   In either case the cause is at the root, and the remedy too.   If we wish the whole tree to flourish, and its fruits to be ever sweet and abundant, the virtue of the root and the sap must be uniformly and exclusively good. So if our souls are to live a perfect life, and bring forth sweet and abundant fruits to God, they must be under the full influence of the Divine principle which lies at the root of the spiritual life.   And as a change at the root would change the fruits, so to leave the Divine for the natural principle would affect us in the like way spiritually.   If, therefore, we wish to succeed in the work of our perfection, we

---

[1] " Ut cuncta nostra operatio a Te semper incipiat."
[2] "Amor sui est causa omnis peccati." (S. Thom., 1 2, Q 77, A 4.)

must go to the root of the matter.   Take in hand
the perfecting principle, which is the habit of Charity,
as a moving power, opposed to self-love, and keep
consistently under its influence through life, until
its work within us is complete.   Then the Divine
Lover will no more complain that after all the care
He has had of us we bring forth " wild grapes ".[1]

The influx of Charity into our actions may be
either actual or virtual.   Actual, when the mind
and heart are engaged with the thought and
love of God affectively, or when the habit of
Charity moves us to action effectively.   Virtual,
when the principle of Divine love practically though
imperceptibly influences us, in virtue of former acts
and the habitual attitude of the soul.   By offering
ourselves to God for the one project of perfect
Charity, and keeping thus consistently to its principle, we might possibly attain our perfection as
life is drawing to a close : whereas if we divide
ourselves on other projects not entering into the life
of Charity, we can never, in this disposition, get to
perfection.   Oneness, simplicity, perfect purity of
soul—this is what Charity needs for its perfection,
as bringing the soul to the Divine resemblance.
Multiplicity, therefore, and division are necessarily
impediments.[2]   Even Seneca's teaching is that " a

---

[1] " What is there that I ought to do more to My vineyard that
I have not done to it ?   Was it that I looked that it should bring
forth grapes, and it hath brought forth wild grapes ? " (Isaias v. 4.)

[2] " Deus unus et simplicissimus est.   Nunquam poterit anima
unioni apta esse, nisi una et simplicissima efficiatur." (Card. Bona.,
" Manuduc." fin.)

virtuous life must be all of a piece ".[1] Hence
S. Francis of Sales tells us that those who aspire
to heavenly love withdraw their thoughts from
worldly things, and reduce all their projects to
one—that of loving God only.[2] All their exertions are not too great for the execution of such a
design.

In view, then, of providing for the safety and
durability of our work, let us know that if we
are to ascend above ourselves to the union of
perfect Charity with God, it is very necessary
that we should first descend into ourselves by
true self-knowledge and humility, in order to
realise what we are of ourselves ; that thus the
gifts and operations of Divine Charity may be
preserved intact to God, whose property they are ;
and lest from error and ignorance of the mind
we should be hindered in our course onwards,
or altogether diverted from it, by the troublesome
seductions and subtleties of pride and self-com-
placency.

How clearly the Fathers and Saints of the
Church instruct us in this method of descending
downwards before we venture to rise upwards.
" Descend, that you may ascend," says S. Augustine.[3] And the Abbot Nesteros advises Cassian to
apply himself to humility, as the way of attaining
to perfect Charity. " Establish in your heart,"

[1] Seneca, Epist. 21.

[2] S. Fran. of Sales., "Love of God," B xii., C 3.

[3] " Descendite, ut ascendatis." (S. Aug., "Confess.," Lib. iv.,
C 12.)

he says, "a profound humility, which by degrees
will conduct you to perfect charity."[1]   S. Bernard also tells us to begin with the consideration
of ourselves, lest our progress to further things be
in vain ; "for without self-knowledge," says he,
"we are as one building without a foundation, and
preparing rather a ruin than an edifice".[2] We remember, too, the sentence of the "Imitation":
"By so much the higher a man ascends into
God, by how much the lower he descends into
himself".[3]

How impressive, again, is our Lord's instruction
to S. Catherine of Siena on this point : "Daughter,
knowest thou what thou art, and what I am? If
thou have a perfect knowledge of these two points,
thou art blessed.   For by means thereof thou
shalt easily escape the snares of the enemy, and
be able to attain to all grace, all truth, all charity,
without any great difficulty or hardness.   Thou
art she that is not: I am He who is.   This is a
brief doctrine, by the which a man may, without
reading many books, be made blessed, and unite
himself with God."[4]

"In the beholding of God we fall not, and
in the beholding of ourself we stand not." "It
is full profitable to us that we see these both

[1] Cassian, Conf. 14, C 10.

[2] "A te tua consideratio inchoet, ne frustra extendaris in alia.
Si te nescieris, eris similis aedificanti sine fundamento, ruinam non
structuram faciens." (S. Bern., "de Consid.," Lib. ii., C 3.)

[3] "Imit.," B iii., C 42.

[4] S. Cath. Sien., "Life," by Caterinus, P 1, C 17.

at once. For the higher beholding keepeth us in ghostly joy in God ; and the lower beholding keepeth us in dread. But our good Lord willeth ever that we hold ourselves much more in the beholding of the higher, and yet not leave the knowing of the lower."[1]

" Neither angel nor man hath aught of himself, but God alone. And this truth maketh the soul to be poor (for she seeth that she hath nothing), and as she seeth the good of poverty, she loveth it. "Afterwards it maketh her see the Divine Goodness, and thus she loveth God, since she accounteth that she hath nothing of her own to love. And as she loveth, so she worketh."[2]

In order the better to see ourselves before God, and realise more our nothingness before His Immensity, our poverty and misery before His Grandeur and Loveliness, and so gain a knowledge of the work that has to be done within our souls to bring them to perfection, let us place the following diagram, representing the imperfect and the perfect soul before God, and the process of purification that has to be undergone before the soul attains its perfection.

Fig. 1 shows the imperfect and unpurified soul, containing, however, the germ of its perfection in Charity, awaiting its development by the full formation of the habit.

Fig. 2 shows the soul purified and perfect, by the

[1] M. Juliana of Norw., "Revel," C 82.
[2] B. Angela of Folig., "Visions and Instr.," C 55.

development of its Divine life, in the formed and finished habit of Charity, disposed to its acts.

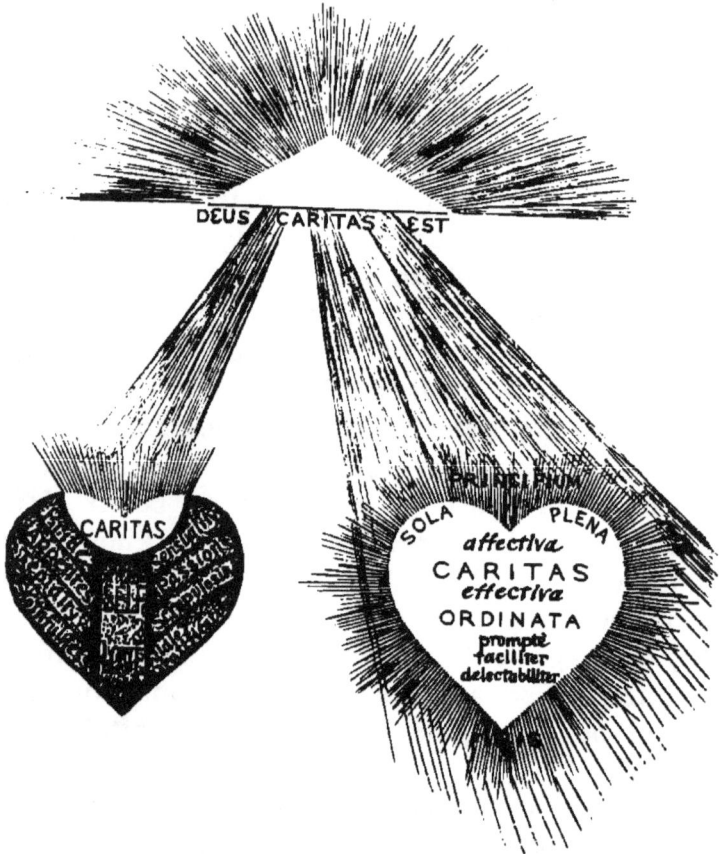

1. The Imperfect Soul.   2. The Perfect Soul.

"Quanto magis regnum cupiditatis destituitur, tanto caritatis augetur."[1]

"Thou must give all for all, and be nothing of thine own."[2]

[1] S. Aug., "de doctrina Christiana," Lib. iii., C 10.
[2] "Imit.," B iii., C 27.

God Himself is the Fountain of life. "With
Thee there is the fountain of life."[1]   The Divine
life is the life of Charity, because "God is Charity,"[2]
and His love is the life of the soul.[3]   God sheds the
light and love of His Charity upon every soul in
grace.[4]   But its brightness is reflected in a greater
or lesser degree, according to the soul's inward
purity, in proportion to which it is enabled to participate more or less the Divine quality.

Fig. 1 represents the soul as yet unpurified, and
so darkened with its sins and miseries, yet living in
the state of grace.   Divine Charity is therefore at a
low degree; its life and operations being impeded
by the dark activity of the natural man.   Fig. 2
shows the soul purified, and therefore radiant with
God's own life.   Having eliminated its miseries by
mortification, the Divine light and love flow into
it unimpeded, communicating to it the fulness of
Charity, thus raising it to the Divine assimilation,
and placing it in a state of perfection.   Of the soul
thus purified we may say, in the words of Wisdom:
"She is the brightness of eternal light, and the
unspotted mirror of God's majesty, and the Image
of His goodness.   Being one, she can do all things;
and remaining the same, she reneweth all things.

---

[1] "Apud Te est fons vitæ." (Ps. xxxv. 10.)

[2] "Deus Caritas est." (1 John iv. 16.)

[3] "Recte dicitur Caritas et Deus, et Dei donum. Itaque Caritas dat caritatem, substantia accidentalem. Ubi dantem significat,
nomen substantiæ est, ubi donum, qualitatis." (S. Bern., "de dilig.
Deo," C 12.)

[4] "The Charity of God is poured forth in our hearts by the Holy
Ghost, who is given to us. (Rom. v. 5.)

She conveyeth herself into holy souls, and maketh
friends of God, and prophets; yea, and the Lord of
all things hath loved her."[1]

The rays from above signify the communication
of Himself which God makes to the soul by His
Divine Charity.

In Fig. 1 Charity is seen to be at a low degree,
being hindered from fully occupying the soul, by a
number of venial sins, unruly habits, and imperfect
dispositions, which souls retain to the great prejudice of their spiritual life. All these miseries appear
as so many ramifications of cupidity or self-love,
the direct antagonist of Charity.[2] Hence the soul,
instead of reflecting to the full the brightness of
Divine Charity, lives on in its dark activity; thus
hindering the communications of God's light and
love. Fig. 2 shows the soul under the full influence
of Charity; when from having been a germ,
Charity has been allowed to extend itself, and
strengthen, and spread within; and so eliminate
the evil and imperfect habits of the natural man:
thus gaining full possession and command of the
kingdom of God within the soul;[3] becoming hereby
the moving and ruling principle ("principium") of
the soul in all its acts,[4] as well as the end ("finis")
of all the virtues and exercises undertaken in the

---

[1] Wisdom vii. 26.

[2] "Caritas est amor rectus. Cupiditas est amor pravus; cum
propter se amatur creatura." (S. Aug., "Enar. in Ps. 9," and "de
Trinit.," L ix., C 8.)

[3] "The kingdom of God is within you." (S. Luke xvii. 21.)

[4] "Caritas est principium omnium bonorum operum, quæ in
finem ultimum ordinari possunt." (S. Thom., 1 2, Q 65, Art. 3.)

work of our perfection : [1] à Charity which is offered
to God as "sola et plena"; that is, we recognise no
other moving principle in all our deliberate acts,
but this only. And we desire that its life within
us should be full, unimpeded by lower principles of
action ; lest it be said of us, " I find not thy works
full before God".[2] And, though this unreservedness be not yet attained, we are, nevertheless, tending to it, and offer it to God in " preparation of
heart". A Charity which is at once " affective " and
"effective". Affective, by occupying the inmost
heart, with the love of God and divine things :
effective, by moving us to action in accordance
with our love : which Charity is rightly ordered
("ordinata") by Discretion, the light of love,[3]
shining in the mind, as it burns in the heart,[4]
enabling the soul to discern between the movements of the Divine Spirit, and those of the
human or evil spirit ; leading it onwards, till
it operates in all things promptly, easily, and
sweetly : (" prompte, faciliter, delectabiliter : ")
since a perfect habit produces perfect acts : as
" every good tree brings forth good fruits ":[5] and
a good man, from a good treasure, bringeth forth
good things".[6]

---

[1] "The end of the commandment is Charity." (1 Tim. i. 5.)

[2] Apoc. iii. 2.

[3] "Ordinavit in me caritatem." (Cant. ii. 4.)

[4] "Love is a fire burning and shining: when it burns in the
will, it shines in the understanding." (Card. Bona., "Via compend.," C 9.)

[5] S. Matt. vii. 17.

[6] S. Matt. xii. 35.

We learn from this 'the great lesson of self-knowledge and humility, so necessary to have deeply impressed on us for life.[1] We distinguish once for all our own property from that which is God's. Our being itself belongs to God. He has made it for Himself, in order to possess it, to live within it as His own abode,[2] enjoying Himself,[3] and working therein according to His will:[4] so that everything we have in nature and grace is to be regarded as the Divine production and property ; and whatever esteem and love is bestowed on the gifts we thus hold is to be at once referred to God alone. Whatever powers of advancing further in good, or of benefiting others we hold, are to be regarded as the powers of God, entrusted to us for His own purposes, and the interests of His glory. Whatever graces, lights, gifts, and virtues we have, or may have, are to be considered not our own, but God's : *in* us, but not *of* us. He is the proprietor of them, we the recipients. If others admire and

[1] " The knowledge of ourselves is the bread we have to eat with all the meats, however delicate they may be, in the way of Prayer. Without this bread life cannot be sustained, though it must be taken in measure. But when a soul clearly understands that there is no goodness in it, when it feels itself abashed in the presence of God, why should it be necessary for it to waste its time on this subject? Why should it not rather proceed to other matters which our Lord places before it ? " (S. Teresa, " Life, by herself," C 13.)

[2] " We will come to Him, and make our abode with Him." (S. John xiv. 23.)

[3] " When I shall be all Thine, Thou enjoyest Thyself in me, and I enjoy myself in Thee; and Thou givest me Thyself, to be mine whole and undivided, if I give myself to Thee, whole and undivided." (" Fiery Soliloquy of the Soul," C 15.)

[4] "It is God who worketh in you, both to will and to accomplish." (Philip. ii. 13.)

love them, the admiration and love pass on to God : for " none is good but God alone " :[1] and " if a man think himself to be something, whereas he is nothing, he deceiveth himself ".[2] Thus we claim nought for ourselves but nothingness, misery, and sin. Let this be our " intrenchment," outside which all belongs to God.[3] " Of a truth," says B. Angela of Foligno, " the soul can have no better knowledge than to see her own nothingness, and to stand in her own intrenchment " :[4] that is, in as far as the knowledge of our nothingness brings the Divine light and presence to the soul.

Seeing then our wretchedness, apart from God, and the lamentable development of evil habits, and imperfect dispositions, which have taken place within us (as seen in Fig. 1 of the Diagram), the soul, as S. Catherine of Siena says, " conceives a certain holy hatred of her own inclinations, and a desire to kill the root of them, which is self-love. And because the root of this self-love lies so deep that it cannot utterly be removed, but something will still remain which from time to time will molest her, therefore there daily grows in her this holy hatred and contempt of self, which increases her desire to advance nearer to God : and for His love she is ready to endure the sharpest discipline that may

[1] S. Luke xviii. 19.
[2] Gal. vi. 3.
[3] " Let this be an intrenchment that thou never quit." (" Sp. Combat," C 32.)
[4] B. Angela of Folig., "Vis. and Instr.," C 55.

subdue that proneness to sin, which keeps her back
from her desired joy."[1]

As, therefore, this misery is the cause of our
separation from God, we are moved to "holy hatred"
thereof:[2] and resolve to renounce ourselves, to
subdue the activity of our natural powers, which
have wrought so much evil within us, to the Divine
principle of Charity, whereby God may govern us.
We see that the senses, imagination, memory,
intellect, and will, left to their natural movements,
are springs of evil to the soul, drawing us away
from God. We, therefore, renounce our natural use
of them, leaving them void of their objects, that
God may occupy them.[3] This is the self-denial
which our Lord establishes in the Gospel, carried to
a perfect issue.[4] It may be called the love of God,
by the sacrifice of self:[5] and is expressed in the fol-

[1] S. Cath. Sien.: "All her disciples noticed how frequently she
dwelt on this lesson of 'holy hatred'. It lay at the root of her
whole interior life. She saw in the disorder of self-love the great
antagonist of the love of God. And she understood that it was the
business of a loving soul to make war on this great rebel, and to
deliver it to death by the relentless practice of mortification."
(Hist. of S. Cath., A. T. Drane, C 4.)

[2] "Si bene oderis, tunc amasti." (S. Aug., Tract. 51 in Epist.
Joan.)

[3] "No created thing can serve as a proximate means of union
with God, because creatures bear no proportion of similitude to
Him. To attain to Divine union, it is necessary to release the
faculties, empty them, and make them renounce their natural
operations, in order that God may fill them, seeing that the ability
of them cannot compass so great a matter, but rather prove a
difficulty in the way." (S. John of the Cross, "Ascent of M.
Carm.," B ii., C 8.)

[4] "If any man will come after Me, let him deny himself." (S.
Matt. xvi. 24.)

[5] "Amor Dei, ad contemptum sui." (S. Aug., "de Civ. Dei,"
Lib. xiv., C 28.)

lowing chosen words of S. Catherine of Siena's Dialogue on Perfection : " The more thou dost empty thy heart of that which is thine own, the more abundantly will I fill it with that which is Mine ".[1]

Then by the ruling power of His love, God forms, governs, and moves the soul according to Himself. Gradually, under the consuming and absorbing influence of His Charity, the miseries of the natural man lose their hold, and yield their sway ; and our powers are occupied and directed by the Spirit of God. Thus the soul attains to its perfection by losing its natural life, and finding one which is Divine ; and the words are verified, " He that shall lose his life . . . shall find it ".[2]

[1] S. Cath. Sien., " Dial. on consummate perfection ".
[2] S. Matt. xvi. 25.

CHAPTER V.

THE PRECEPT OF PERFECTION.

" THOU shalt love the Lord thy God with thy whole heart, and with thy whole soul, and with thy whole strength." [1]   This is undoubtedly the precept of perfection ; and that in a twofold way.   First, inasmuch as it points to the aim we have to take, namely, the plenitude of Divine Charity, affectively and effectively, which is the very essence of perfection, as shown at length in the next chapter. Secondly, in as far as it prescribes even now, as " the greatest and first commandment," [2] a "totality" of love, as S. Thomas expresses it,[3] which implies, in some sense, perfection, according to the saying of philosophy, " totum et perfectum idem sunt". This view of the great law of love is recognised by S. Augustine.   " Let us hear," he says, "the precept of perfection, lest we neglect to run to the plenitude of Charity." [4]   Here he speaks of it as commanding rather whither we should tend, than what we should

[1] Deut. vi. 5.
[2] S. Matt. xxii. 38.
[3] S. Thom. 2 2, Q 27, Art. 5.
[4] "Audiamus præcepta perfectionis, ne currere negligamus ad plenitudinem Caritatis." (S. Aug., "de perfect. justitiæ," C 8.)

do.[1] And "why," he asks, "should not such perfection be commanded, even though no man reach it in this life? Because no one runs rightly, if he know not whither he runs. But how would he know the aim to take, if no precept pointed it to him. Let us, therefore, so run that we may obtain."[2] Here the Saint is evidently taking the former sense of the precept, prescribing the aim we have to take, namely, perfect Charity, or Christian perfection. So clearly does he feel that the plenitude of Charity and perfection is rather to be aspired to as an end, than attained in this life, that he tells us that the fulness of this law of love is reserved for the life of heaven. "When that which is perfect shall come, that which is in part shall be done away; in the plenitude of which Charity the precept shall be fulfilled, 'Thou shalt love the Lord thy God with all thy heart, and soul, and strength'. For as long as there remains anything in us of carnal concupiscence, God is not in every way loved with the whole soul. For the flesh lusteth not without the soul. Then shall the just man be altogether without sin, when there shall be no law in his members fighting against the law of his mind; but he shall love God entirely with all his heart and soul."[3] "But now you see

---

[1] "Indicatur per hoc, non quid faciendum sit, sed potius quo tendendum sit." (S. Thom., "Quodl. de Carit.," Art. 10 ad 1.)

[2] "Cur ergo non præciperetur homini ista perfectio, quamvis eam in hac vita nemo habeat? Non enim recte curritur, si quo currendum est, nesciatur. Quomodo autem sciretur, si nullis præceptis ostenderetur? Sic ergo curramus ut comprehendamus." (S. Aug., "de perfect. justitiæ," C 8.)

[3] "Cum venerit quod perfectum est, quod ex parte est, destruetur. In qua plenitudine caritatis præceptum impletur, Diliges

not God.   You cannot fully love what you do not
see." [1]   Here we must carefully observe the Saint is
speaking of the *perfect* fulfilment of the precept.
He does not say that it cannot in any way be fulfilled here below.   His words are, " omni modo
diligere " ; " plene amare," which denote the fulness
and perfection of Charity.   Still, he says, the precept
is given to us now, in terms expressive of perfection,
in order that we may know what aim we have to
take, and what end we have to reach.

It must not, however, be supposed that the great
commandment of Charity points *only* to perfection
as an end to be attained.   It is well, indeed, to be
convinced that it does so ; because this conviction
tells us that we must never say the word " enough "
in the love and service of God : but that we are
always to be aspiring to something higher.   " Always
add, always advance ; stay not on the way ; turn
not back ; turn not aside ; if you say, ' enough,' you
are lost." [2]   Even the glorious Apostle, who was a
vessel of election, and able to say, " I live, not I,
but Christ liveth in me," [3] is yet persuaded that he
must still be striving onwards.   " Not as though I

Dominum Deum tuum ex toto corde tuo.   Nam cum est adhuc
aliquid carnalis concupiscentiæ, non omni modo ex tota anima
diligitur Deus.   Non enim caro sine anima concupiscit.   Tunc
erit justus sine ullo omnino peccato, quando nulla lex erit in
membris ejus repugnans legi mentis ejus, sed prorsus toto corde,
tota anima diligit Deum." (S. Aug., "de perfect. justitiæ," C 8.)

[1] " Nondum vides Deum ; non potes amare plene, quod nondum
vides."   (S. Aug., "Enar. in Ps. cxlv. 12.")

[2] " Semper adde, semper profice, noli in via remanere, noli retro
redire : noli deviare.   Si dixeris, sufficit, periisti." (S. Aug., Serm.
169 de Verb Apost. Phil. 3.)

[3] Gal. ii. 20.

had already attained, or were already perfect ; but I follow after, if by any means I may apprehend : forgetting the things that are behind, and stretching forth myself to those that are before, I press towards the mark."[1] Hence the Angelic Doctor teaches that our Charity here below is capable of indefinite increase ; and that, as it increases, the capacity for receiving it further enlarges ; so that no limit can be placed to its increase in this life.[2]

Thus we are to be constantly going forwards, not thinking so much on what has been done, but on what remains to be done. The highest point we can reach in this life is still short of our ultimate end : and we must still say with the Apostle, " Not as though I had already attained ". I forget the past, I follow on, I stretch forth : I press towards the mark.

It would seem then that God has named the highest perfection in the precept, in order to oblige us to go on constantly advancing, however great our progress may be ; so that we may never set bounds here below to our advancement in the ways of love and perfection, but keep ourselves in continual movement towards the end.

Yet with all this, there is a mode proper to our present life, in which the great commandment is to

---

[1] Philip. iii. 12.

[2] " Semper caritate excrescente, superexcrescit habilitas ad ulterius augmentum. Capacitas creaturæ rationalis per caritatem augetur, quia per ipsam cor dilatatur; secundum illud, ' Cor nostrum dilatatum est ' (2 Cor. vi. 11), unde relinquitur quod caritatis augmento nullus terminus præfigatur in hac vita." (S. Thom., 2 2, Q 24, Art. 7, in c. and ad 2.)

be embraced, and carried into effect. For that God does not command impossible things is an article of Faith, defined by the Council of Trent.[1] And let us bear in mind once more that S. Augustine, when considering the precept as expressing a perfection rather to be aimed at than attained in this life, is speaking of its *perfect* fulfilment. And S. Bernard and S. Thomas are both in agreement with him.[2]

S. Augustine indeed speaks in words of singular impressiveness of the mode of fulfilling the precept in this life ; which go far to show us the standard of perfection to which we are called even now. He says : "When our Lord commands us to love Him with all our heart, and soul, and mind, He leaves no part of our life unclaimed, giving place, as it were, for the enjoyment of things apart from Himself. But whatever offers itself to be loved is carried on in the full-flowing tide of love to God alone. Whoever therefore rightly loves his neighbour, ought to strive to get him also to love God with his whole heart, soul, and mind. Thus loving him as he loves himself, he refers all the love of himself and others to the love of God, which suffers not the smallest ripple to turn aside, that would diminish the fulness of its flow onwards to God."[3]

---

[1] Conc. Trid., Sess. 6, Can. 18.

[2] S. Bern., " de dilig. Deo," C 10; S. Thom., 2 2, Q 44, Art. 6.

[3] " Cum Dominus ait, toto corde, tota anima, tota mente, nullam vitæ nostræ partem reliquit, quæ vacare debeat, et quasi locum dare, ut alia re velit frui. Sed quidquid aliud diligendum venerit in animum, illic rapiatur quo totus dilectionis impetus currit. Quisquis ergo recte proximum diligit, hoc cum eo debet agere, ut

Here we get some idea of what the true Christian life should be. The greatest and first commandment regulates everything. It "leaves no part of our life unclaimed, giving scope, as it were, for the enjoyment of things apart from God," but carries on everything to Him, in the mighty tide of love. If the excellencies of God's creatures attract us, we are not to divide our love upon them, but include them in the one deep flow of love that goes onward to God alone : loving them as we love ourselves ; that is, helping them to love God, as we also ought to love Him, with the whole heart, and soul, and strength ; since Divine Charity cannot suffer the smallest ripple of its love to turn aside ; for that would diminish its full flow onwards to God.[1]

If, then, the fulfilment of the precept in its perfection is to be our aim, the goal to which we are to be constantly advancing through life, it is equally true that, according to our capacity, we are bound to its observance even now, though in our own imperfect way. We cannot but notice the forcible terms in which the commandment was given, and reiterated to the people of the old law :—
" Hear, O Israel, and observe to do the things which

etiam ipse toto corde, tota anima, tota mente diligat Deum. Sic enim eum diligens tanquam seipsum, totam dilectionem sui et illius refert in illam dilectionem Dei, quæ nullam a se rivulum duci extra patitur, cujus derivatione minuatur." (S. Aug., "de doctr. Christiana," L i., C 22.)

[1] S. Gregory also speaks as follows of the unreservedness to which the law of love calls us : " Notandum est quod Divinus sermo, cum Deum diligi præcipit, non solum narrat *ex quo*, sed etiam informat *ex quanto*, cum subjungit ' ex toto' ; ut videlicet qui perfecte Deo placere desiderat, sibi de se nihil relinquat." (S. Greg., " Moral.," Lib. x., C 4.)

the Lord hath commanded thee. Thou shalt love
the Lord thy God with thy whole heart, and with
thy whole soul, and with thy whole strength. And
these words which I command thee this day shall
be in thy heart; and thou shalt tell them to thy
children; and thou shalt meditate upon them,
sitting in thy house, and walking on thy journey,
sleeping and rising. And thou shalt bind them as
a sign on thy hand; and they shall be, and shall
move between thine eyes; and thou shalt write
them in the entry, and on the doors of thy house."[1]
"What doth the Lord thy God require of thee,
but that thou walk in His ways, and love and serve
Him with all thy heart, and all thy soul?"[2]
Observe attentively, and in work fulfil the
commandment, that you love the Lord your God,
and walk in all His ways, and keep all His
commandments, and cleave to Him, and serve Him
with all your heart and soul."[3] "Cleave ye unto
the Lord your God. This only take care of with
all diligence, that you love the Lord your God."[4]
"With all thy strength love Him that made thee."[5]

Our present state indeed is one of imperfection;
and with all our desires for perfect Charity, we are
constantly falling short. As our knowledge of
God by faith is imperfect, for "we know in part";[6]
so our love is imperfect also. "You do not yet see
God; you cannot fully love what you do not see."[7]

[1] Deut. vi. 3.   [2] Deut. x. 12.   [3] Josue xxii. 5.
[4] Josue xxiii. 8.   [5] Ecclus. vii. 32.   [6] 1 Cor. xiii. 9.
[7] S. Aug., "Enar. in Ps. cxlv.".

We therefore receive and observe the precept in our own imperfect way, while our desires and aspirations are for perfection. And in this let us be consoled with S. Bernard's teaching, that the constant endeavour to advance to perfection is reputed to us for perfection :[1] knowing that God accepts the preparation of our heart : as the Psalmist says, " Thy ear hath heard the preparation of their heart ".[2]

The great commandment then is observed in this life, truly, though imperfectly ; in some way, but not every way ;[3] when a man loves God as far as he is able ; "ex toto posse suo ".[4] This is explained as follows by S. Thomas : " A precept may be observed in two ways, perfectly and imperfectly. It is observed perfectly, when the end which is designed is attained. It is observed imperfectly, when, although the end is not attained, the right order thereto is not departed from. As, for instance, when a general commands his soldiers to fight, those observe the order perfectly, who conquer the enemy, which was the end intended. But the others fulfil the command, yet imperfectly, whose fighting does not end in victory, provided they act not against military discipline. So God intends by this precept of love, that man should be closely united with him ; which will be accomplished in

---

[1] " Indefessum proficiendi studium, et jugis conatus ad perfectionem, perfectio reputatur." (S. Bern., Épist. 254.)

[2] Ps. ix. 17.

[3] " Aliquo modo, non omni modo." (S. Thom., 2 2, Q 44, Art. 6 ad 1.)

[4] S. Thom., 2 2, Q. 27, Art. 5.

heaven, when God will be 'all in all'; and therefore
the precept will be perfectly fulfilled there. In this
life it is fulfilled, but imperfectly ; those observing
it the more perfectly, who approach nearer to the
perfection of heavenly life." [1]

The question now remaining is, in what manner
is this imperfect observance of the precept to be
carried out? In heaven indeed, says S. Thomas,
the intellect and will, with all our thoughts,
affections, and operations, are ever directed actually
to God. But in this life it is impossible, on account
of human infirmity, to be always thus intent on
Him ; although we ought to strive, as far as may
be, to approach to this perfection ; and herein
consists the perfection of this life. [2]

S. Augustine has already given us his mind on
this point, by saying that "when our Lord commands us to love Him with all our heart, and soul,
and mind, He leaves no part of our life unclaimed,
to give place, as it were, for the enjoyment of things
apart from Himself; but whatever offers itself to
be loved is carried on in the full-flowing tide of love
to God alone ". [3]   And S. Thomas follows him, by

---

[1] " Dicendum quod praeceptum aliquod dupliciter potest impleri.
Uno modo perfecte; alio modo, imperfecte.   Perfecte quidem
impletur praeceptum, quando pervenitur ad finem quam intendit
praecipiens.   Impletur autem, sed imperfecte quando etsi non per-
tingat ad finem praecipientis, non tamen receditur ab ordine ad
finem. Sicut si dux exercitus praecipiat militibus, &c." (S. Thom.,
2 2, Q 44, Art. 6.)

[2] " Æmulari tamen debemus, ut in similitudinem perfectionis
illius, quantum possibile est, nos trahamus: et in hoc perfectio
hujus vitæ consistit." (S. Thom., Opusc. " de perfect. vitæ Spir.,"
C 6.)

[3] S. Aug., " de doctr. Christiana.," L i., C 22.

saying that although we cannot here below be always in actual union with God, yet we ought to tend to this perfection, by striving to love God as far as we can, and referring to His love whatever we have to do.[1] Both the great Doctors then agree in assigning a definite mode of fulfilling the precept in this life, namely, by the *reference* to God, "ex toto posse," of the whole heart, soul, mind, and strength: so that all these are used in accordance with the Divine Will, and not in opposition to it. Let us once more follow the lead of the Angelic Doctor. Having spoken of the perfect love of God in the next life, when souls are always in the actual Divine union, he proceeds: "In another way we may love God with all our heart, soul, mind, and strength: by referring everything to Divine love, actually or habitually. And to this perfection the precept binds us. First, that man should refer all to God, as to his end; as the Apostle says: 'Whether you eat or drink, or whatsoever else you do, do all to the glory of God'; which is fulfilled when a man orders his life to the service of God: so that all he does is consequently ordered to God, excepting things which lead us from Him, such as sin. Secondly, that man should subject his intellect to God, believing those things that are revealed by Him, as it is said, 'bringing into captivity every understanding to the obedience of Christ'. Thus,

---

[1] "Déus totaliter diligi debet; quia ex toto posse suo homo debet diligere Deum; et quidquid habet, ad Dei amorem ordinare; secundùm illud, "Diliges Dominum Deum tuum ex toto corde tuo," &c. (S. Thom., 2 2, Q 27, Art. 5.)

God is loved with the whole mind. Thirdly, that whatever a man loves, he should love in God, and refer all his affections to Him; as the Apostle says : 'Whether we be transported in mind, it is to God; or whether we be sober, it is to you ; for the Charity of Christ presseth us'. Thus is God loved with the whole soul. Fourthly, that all our externals—words and works—should rest firmly on Divine Charity, according to the words, ' Let all your things be done in Charity'. Thus is God loved with all our strength. This, therefore, is a mode of perfect love, to which all are bound in virtue of the precept." [1]

It concerns us, then, to order our lives to the love of God : to fix in our minds the term to which we are bound, which is perfect Charity. Then to offer ourselves, and our operations, inward and outward, to the Majesty of God, to be expended according to the Divine Will : and so to live and act that, " ex toto posse," we may not revoke what we have once tendered to God's love, but that in all things, actually or virtually,[2] Charity may be our ruling and moving principle ;[3] keeping us habitually under the influence of the Divine Spirit ;[4] making us re-

---

[1] S. Thom., Opusc. " de perfec. vitæ Spir." C 5.

[2] The influx of Charity into our actions may be either actual or virtual : actual, when the mind and heart are engaged with the thought and love of God affectively, or, when the habit of Charity moves us to action, effectively. Virtual, when the principle of Divine love practically, though imperceptibly, influences us, in virtue of former acts and the habitual attitude of the soul.

[3] " Caritas est principium omnium bonorum operum, quæ in finem ultimum ordinari possunt." (S. Thom., 1 2, Q 65, Art. 3.)

[4] " Whosoever are led by the Spirit of God, they are the sons of God." (Rom. viii. 14.)

sponsive to the Divine call ;[1] establishing its virtue as the habit of habits within us:[2] leading us onwards ; purifying and fortifying the soul through life ; prompting, regulating, and perfecting the operations of the entire man, until "we all, beholding the glory of the Lord with open face, are transformed into the same image, from glory to glory, as by the Spirit of the Lord ".[3]

[1] " Bene sequentes instinctum Divinum." (S. Thom., 1 2, Q 68, Art. 2.)
    " Regard thy call; that's all in all." (D. Gert. More.)

[2] " Caritas est universalis motor et principalis inter omnes et super omnes habitus in anima, per respectum ad finem ultimum, ad quem ipse dirigit et movet. Sic est omnium habituum et actuum meritoriorum ad vitam æternam radix, forma, et finis; cui conjunctus est Divinus amor Increatus, illabens animæ, purificans eam, illuminans, et perficiens." (Gerson, " Tract. sup. Cantic. i. de amor. grat.".)

[3] 2 Cor. iii. 18.

CHAPTER VI.

OUR ESSENTIAL PERFECTION.

THERE is a twofold perfection, as S. Thomas teaches, essential and accidental.[1] The essential perfection of a thing consists in its answering perfectly the end for which it was made.[2] Accidental perfection lies in the possession of additional qualities, subserving the main purpose, and contributing beauty, adornment, and finish to the whole. Thus, the essential perfection of a watch consists in its keeping accurate time : this being the purpose for which it was made, and without time it is no watch at all, however much it may have the appearance of one. Its accidental perfection is found in its outer material, its shape, size, elegance of design, jewelry, and fineness of detail and workmanship in all its parts : which things, being accidental, may vary in kind and degree, without affecting the essential nature of the watch. So in man, his essential perfection is placed in Charity, that is, the habit of Divine love, the bond of union with God, this being the end of his existence—a Charity which is at once affective and effective, that is, a habit of love disposed to its acts,

[1] S. Thom., 2 2, Q 184, Art. 3 ; and Quodl. de Carit., Art. xi. ad 5 ; and Opusc. "de perfec. vitæ Spir.," C 1.

[2] "Unumquoque dicitur perfectum, inquantum attingit proprium finem." (S. Thom., 2 2, Q 184, Art. 1.)

or an operative habit.[1] The accidental perfection of man consists in the assemblage of virtues that cluster around Charity, and help him to serve God in his particular state of life, adorn his soul with a varied beauty, and aid him to accomplish his daily works promptly, easily, and sweetly.

That Charity is the essential constituent of our perfection is clear beyond a doubt, since without it nothing else can possibly unite us with our end. Whereas it alone contains radically all other goods of the spiritual order that the human soul can hope or wish for. It is by Charity that we love God, and God loves us ; by Charity we give ourselves to Him, and He gives Himself to us ; by Charity we abide in Him, and He abides in us ;[2] by Charity we enjoy ourselves in Him, and He enjoys Himself in us ; by Charity we work in Him, and He works in us ; by Charity we live in Him, and He lives in us. Truly this is our *all.* And love itself forms the whole man according to God, and thus gains the perfection which is the end of our existence.[3]

How emphatically does S. Paul proclaim its praises, and tell us that apart from Charity the highest virtues reckon for nothing, but that with it

---

[1] " Uniuscujusque perfectio præcipue consideratur in ordine ad suum finem. Finis autem potentiæ actus est. Unde potentia dicitur esse perfecta, secundum quod determinatur ad suum actum." (S. Thom., 1 2, Q 55, Art. 1.)

[2] "He that abideth in Charity abideth in God, and God in him." (1 John iv. 16.)

[3] " In Caritate clauditur collectio mandatorum, et comprehensio omnium Scripturarum : et Caritas ipsa est radix, forma, et finis virtutum, quæ jungit omnes cum ultimo fine, et ligat omnia ad invicem, simul, et ordinat." (S. Bonav., " Breviloq.," P 5, C 8.)

all virtues follow in its train : " If I speak with the tongues of men and angels, and have not Charity, I am become as a sounding brass, and a tinkling cymbal. And if I should have prophecy, and should know all mysteries, and all knowledge ; and if I should have all faith, so that I could remove mountains, and have not Charity, I am nothing. And if I should distribute all my goods to feed the poor, and if I should deliver my body to be burned, and have not Charity, it profiteth me nothing." [1] So far he speaks of the absence of Charity, and declares that without it the most glittering appearances of virtue are as nothing ; the reason of which is, that Charity is the vivifying principle or *soul* of all the virtues in the supernatural order,[2] by which, unless they are animated, they are as body without soul.[3] But only let Charity live and work, and see how the other virtues at once spring into action. " Charity is patient, is kind, envieth not, dealeth not perversely, is not puffed up, is not ambitious, seeketh not her own, is not provoked to anger, thinketh no evil ; beareth all things, believeth all things, hopeth all things, endureth all things. Charity never fall-

---

[1] 1 Cor. xiii. 1.

[2] " Sicut in naturalibus forma movet, ornat, perfecitque materiam, sic in intellectualibus atque moralibus Caritas cæteras movet, perficit, ornat, actuatque virtutes, intantum quod sine ea nihil est meritorium et Deo acceptum ; dicente Apostolo, ' Si linguis hominum et angelorum loquar, Caritatem autem non habeam, nihil sum' ; quoad esse gratiæ, non naturæ." (Denis Carthus., "de Regul. Vitæ Christianæ," L i., A 8, Reg. 3.)

[3] " Effectus exterior non pertinet ad Caritatem, nisi inquantum *ex affectu* procedit, in quo primo est Caritatis actus. Unde oportet quod ex affectu in effectum procedat." (S. Thom., 3 Sent. Dist. 29, Q 1, Art. 2.)

eth away."[1] And elsewhere the same Apostle, after naming various Christian virtues, exhorts us above all to "have Charity, which is the bond of perfection"[2]—called the bond of perfection, as uniting the soul with God, in whom our perfection is found.[3] S. John epitomises our perfection when he says "God is Charity, and he that abideth in Charity, abideth in God, and God in Him. In this is the Charity of God perfected with us."[4] And S. Paul speaks of love as the fulfilment and the end of the law. "The end of the commandment is Charity."[5] "Love is the fulfilling of the law."[6]

It is apparent then, from these testimonies, that the highest gifts of God—the tongues of men and angels, faith to remove mountains, prophecy, knowledge of all mysteries, the sacrifice of goods to the poor, and even martyrdom, if these be separated from Charity, will not suffice for man's perfection. Nay, in the spiritual order, without Charity he is reckoned, even with all these noble powers and acts, as nothing. The reason of this is, that the soul, as the principal part of our nature, being inward life and spirit, cannot possibly be perfected by any number of external works which are but accidental to it. It is only as recipients of God's Divine knowledge and love that we are made "partakers," by grace, "of the divine nature,"[7] and so attain to the

---

[1] 1 Cor. xiii. 4.   [2] Col. iii. 12.
[3] "Caritas, ex natura sua est vinculum, quia est amor uniens amatum amanti." (S. Thom. in Pauli Epist. ad Coloss., C 3, Lec. 3.)
[4] 1 John iv. 16. [5] 1 Tim. i. 5. [6] Rom. xiii. 10. [7] 2 Pet. i. 4.

5

perfection of which, in virtue of the Divine likeness within us, we are capable. But in the life of grace the link of union is *love*, because in its nature love is a unitive virtue,[1] uniting the lover with the Beloved ; and because, also in its nature, it is a ruling and moving power, capable of forming both interior and exterior life according to itself.[2] Whereas let there be any amount of external appearances, without the virtue of unitive love, the soul cannot attain to the Divine life within, which is the essence and principle of its perfection, because the bond of union is wanting. On the other hand, let there be no great wealth of external perfections, yet simple Charity within, there is the " bond of perfection ". The soul reflects the Divine life and likeness, and is united with its origin and its end. Thus it reaches its perfection. Not that the work of its perfection is complete, but that the essential constituent of its perfection exists. So that the development of Charity in the soul is the development of the soul's spiritual life and perfection.

It has to be constantly borne in mind, that Charity being the Divine life of the soul, is a principle of supernatural operation,[3] becoming the motive cause

---

[1] " Amor est virtus unitiva."

[2] " Manifestum est quod caritas, inquantum ordinat hominem ad finem ultimum, est principium omnium bonorum operum quæ in finem ultimum ordinari possunt. Et quia habet pro objecto ultimum finem humanæ vitæ, scilicet beatitudinem æternam, ideo extendit se ad actus totius humanæ vitæ per modum imperii." (S. Thom., 1, 2, Q 65, Art. 3 & 2 2, Q 23, Art. 4 ad 2.)

[3] " Operatio sequitur esse."

of our actions.[1]   The reason of this is, that Charity
is love; and love in its nature is the spring of action.
" Everyone lives by his love, whether for good or
for evil," says S. Augustine.[2]   As then the spring of
Divine love moves in the soul, it gradually communicates its virtue to the faculties, and even the
senses and bodily members, leavening them with its
Divine influence, purifying and regulating their
operations, calling forth the different virtues as they
are needed, and stirring the various powers to action,
conformably to the dictates and movements of the
Spirit of God.   For although, as Constantine Barbanson remarks, " Divine love is the consummation
of all good, nevertheless it is also its fountain and
origin ".[3]   " As therefore the soul begins with love,
and finishes with it, the whole way to God becomes
a certain sweet exercise of love, so that by referring
all things to this, they are changed into love, and
become love's progress to greater perfection.   Thus
the soul has love for its end, and strews it in its way
as means to the end, by the frequent repetition of

[1] " Caritas est causa motiva omnium aliarum virtutum, Per
modum imperii in omnibus nos dirigat quæ ad rectam vitam pertinent." (S. Thom., " Quodl. de Carit.," A 5 ad 1 & 9.)

[2] " Ex amore suo quisque vivit vel bene, vel male." (S. Aug.,
" Cont. Faust.," L 5.)

[3] Let it be remembered that Charity is twofold—the Increated
and created.   The Increated Charity is God Himself, who is the
" consummation of all good".   The created Charity is the habit of
Divine love, infused and diffused within man's soul : to which is
ever joined the " communication of the Holy Spirit " to man's
spirit.   Thus the " fountain " of our spiritual good flows within us,
and the habit of Charity becomes the soul and moving-principle of
the other virtues.   Hence, says S. Bernard, " Recte dicitur Caritas
et Deus, et Dei donum ".   (S. Bern., " de dilig. Deo," C 12.)

its acts. And although God gives many lights to
the soul, He imbues it so much with this love that
the other things are made to serve love, so that the
soul may rest here and nowhere else. If therefore
you will advance to a happy, tranquil, and spiritual
life, see that Divine love is your principal exercise,
and that in all your actions, movements, and desires
the love of God be your moving principle, and
desire nothing but what may be referred to its increase and full development within you." [1]

All this is the work of perfection progressing, and
of Charity operating. The words of our Lord leave
no room for doubting this force of His love. He
says, " If anyone love Me, he will keep My word.
And My Father will love him, and We will come to
him and make Our abode with him, and I will manifest Myself to him ".[2] Here the keeping of God's
word, or the doing of His will, is shown to flow from
our love. And love merits love. "Amorem meretur amor." God loves the soul in return for its
love, comes to it as His own abode, and manifests
Himself to it. "We will come to him, and make
Our abode with him, and I will manifest Myself
to him." What is all this but Charity working for
the Beloved, and bringing the soul to union and contemplation ? Is not this the soul's perfection, and
all the offspring of its love?

Further, how weighty is the declaration of our
Divine Master, that on Charity depend "all the

[1] Constant. Barbanson, O.S.F., "Hidden Ways of Divine
Love," P 2, C 15, and P 1, C 5.

[2] S. John xiv. 23, 21.

law and the prophets"!¹ Is not everything comprised there, where "universa lex pendet"? And
justly so : because if our love is true, it moves us
by its own principle to the observance of every law.
Who is more obedient to law than a loving soul ?
A true lover is ever ready to do the will of the
Beloved, and that in the most perfect way : anxious
for its outward acts to respond to its inmost love.²
So that Charity thus becomes perfect justice to
God, to others, and to ourselves, according to S.
Augustine's emphatic sentence : "Caritas est
verissima, plenissima, perfectissimaque justitia".³
So convinced is this great Father that Charity is
our *all*, that he does not hesitate to consider it as
the *only* virtue in the Christian life, and regards the
other virtues as different aspects of Charity. He
says : " I would affirm that virtue is nothing whatever but the supreme love of God. For the four
great virtues, as I understand, are but named from
the various affections of love itself. I hesitate not,
therefore, to define them as follows : Temperance,
as love maintaining itself in integrity to God.
Fortitude, as love readily enduring all things for
God. Justice, love serving God, and placing things
in due order among men. Prudence, love rightly
discerning between things helping us on to God,
and those impeding our advancement to Him." ⁴

¹ " Universa lex pendet et prophetæ." (S. Matt. xxii. 40.)

² " Ut cuncta quæ coram hominibus rutilant, flamma intimi
amoris accendat." (S. Greg., " de Cura Past.," P 2, C 3, fin.)

³ S. Aug., " de Natura et Gratia," C 42.

⁴ " Nihil omnino virtutem affirmaverim, nisi summum amorem
Dei. Nam illud quod quadripartita dicitur virtus, ex ipsius amoris

Hence, the same Father concludes that "Holy Scripture commands nothing but Charity, and blames nothing but cupidity":[1] that "Charity, therefore, is the highest wisdom";[2] and that "all our good works are, consequently, the many operations of the one Charity".[3] S. Gregory treats the same subject in admirable words : "The precepts of our Lord," he says, "are many, yet one. Many, as prescribing different works : one, in the principle of love from which they spring. For, as many branches of a tree spring from one root, so many virtues proceed from one Charity."[4] "Well, therefore, is the law of God said to be 'manifold'": (Job xi.) "because, when Charity" (which is God's law) "has well taken possession of the soul, it spurs us on to innumerable good works".[5] Then,

vario quodem affectu, quantum intelligo dicitur. Itaque illas quatuor virtutes sic etiam definire non dubitem ; ut temperantiam dicamus esse amorem Deo sese integrum servantem ; fortitudinem, amorem omnia propter Deum facile perferentem ; justitiam, amorem Deo servientem, et bene imperantem cæteris quæ homini subjecta sunt ; prudentiam, amorem bene discernentem ea quibis adjuvetur in Deum, ab iis quibus impediri potest." (S. Aug., "de Morib. Ecclesiæ," L i., C 15.

[1] "Non præcipit Scriptura nisi caritatem, nec culpat nisi cupidatem." (S. Aug., "de doctr. Christiana," L iii., C 10.)

[2] "Summa sapientia est Caritas Dei." (S. Aug., Epist. 140 ad Honorat., C 18.)

[3] "Omnia bona opera nostra unum opus est caritatis." (S. Aug., in Ps. lxxxix.)

[4] "Præcepta 'Dominica et multa sunt, et unum. Multa per diversitatem operis ; unum, in radice dilectionis. Ut enim multi arboris rami ex una radice prodeunt, sic multæ virtutes ex una caritate generantur." (S. Greg., Hom. 27 in Evang.)

[5] "Bene ergo lex Dei multiplex dicitur ; quia cum una eademque sit Caritas, si mentem plene ceperit, hanc ad innumera opera multiformiter accendit. Cujus diversitatem breviter exprimimus, si in electis singuli bona illius numeremus. Hæc namque primum per

passing in review the Patriarchs and Prophets of the old law, and the Saints of the New Testament, he recognizes in their various virtues so many different forms of one and the same Charity. "Manifold, therefore, is the law of God, which adapts itself to so many changing circumstances, yet remains unchanged itself." [1]

If we turn to those masters of the spiritual life, the Fathers of the Desert, we find them in perfect agreement with the Doctors of the Church, and upholding the same great principles in forcible words to their disciples. The Abbot Moses, about the end of the fourth century, speaking on S. Paul's words, "If I distribute all my goods to feed the poor, and have not Charity, it profiteth me nothing," says : "It is evident that perfection does not consist in the mere privation of earthly goods, &c., but in the possession of Charity unfeigned ".[2] He then proceeds to say that the development of Charity must be our one great aim, and all our other exer-

---

Abel electa Deo munera obtulit. Hæc Enoch inter homines spiritaliter vivere docuit. Hæc Noe, despectis omnibus solum Deum placibilem ostendit. Hæc Abrahæ dexteram, quia ad mortem filii obediendo extulit, hunc prolis innumera gentium patrem fecit. Hæc Isaac mentem, quam semper ad munditiam tenuit, ad videnda longe post ventura dilatavit. Hæc Jacob compulit, &c. Hæc Joseph docuit, &c. Hæc Moysen per zeli studium erexit, &c. Hæc Josue exploraterem docuit, &c. Hæc Samuel in principatu humilem præbuit, &c. Hæc David, &c. Hæc Eliam vivere spiritaliter docuit. Hæc Eliseum magistri spiritu dupliciter implevit. Hæc in Petro, hæc in Paulo, &c."

[1] " Multiplex ergo ista lex Dei est, quæ singulis rerum articulis non permutata congruit, et causis se variantibus, non variata conjungit. Cujus legis multiplicatem bene Paulus enumerat, dicens, ' Caritas patiens est, benigna est, non æmulatur,' &c." (S. Greg., " Moral.," L x., C 4.)

[2] Cassian, "Conf.," 1, C 6 and 7.

cises be made subservient to it. " It becomes us,
therefore, to practise fasting, watching, retirement,
and meditation, *with reference to our object, which is
purity of heart, or Charity.*[1] To this end should be
referred our solitude, our daily employments, yea,
every penitential exercise and every virtue : that by
these means our hearts may be preserved in calm,
and thus ascend to the perfection of Charity." [2]

The Abbot Abraham also speaks as follows : " A
religious should centre all his thoughts upon *one
object.* He should imitate the builder erecting an
arch, who has the centre always before his mind,
that he may regulate his work accordingly. Our
souls should, in like manner, regard Divine Charity
as their only centre. This Divine rule should regulate all our thoughts, and all the movements of our
heart, that it may keep them in due order and proportion, and reject whatever is uneven and irregular." [3]

S. Thomas, applying his angelic mind to the
consideration of this subject, plainly sets forth the
distinction between essential and accidental perfection ; and teaches in precise terms that our essential
perfection is to be placed in Charity, as uniting man
with his end, and that the other virtues make up
accidental or instrumental perfection, as being
either the effects of an already existing Charity, or
means used towards its more perfect attainment

---

[1] " Charity, or purity of heart ; " of which the ancient Fathers
of the Desert made so much. It may be well to note that they are
identical. Purity of heart is purity of love ; purity of love is pure
love ; and pure love is Charity.

[2] Cassian, "Conf.," 1, C 6 and 7.

[3] Cassian, "Conf.," 24, C 6.

and development.[1] " It is evident," he continues,
" that the perfection of the Christian life principally
consists in the love of Charity to God ; and with
reason, for the perfection of a thing stands in the
attainment of its end ; but the end of the Christian
life is Charity, to which all things are to be directed :"
as the Apostle says, " the end of the commandment
is Charity ".[2]   In fine, he teaches with S. Augustine,
that our perfection lies simply in the great law of
love : " Thou shalt love the Lord thy God with thy
whole heart, and soul, and strength," and all other
particular precepts and counsels he regards as
ordained to the formation, exercise, and perfection
of Charity. " The form of the precept," he says,
" expresses perfection, and all other precepts and
counsels are ordained to Charity : precepts to
remove things contrary to Charity, counsels to
remove impediments to the acts of Charity."[3]

[1] " Dicendum quod perfectio dicitur in aliquo consistere dupliciter. Uno modo, per se et essentialiter. Alio modo, secundario
et accidentaliter. Per se quidem et essentialiter consistit perfectio
Christianæ vitæ in Caritate ; principaliter quidem secundum dilectionem Dei ; secundario, secundum dilectionem proximi. Accidentaliter consistit in aliis virtutibus, inquantum per ea subtrahuntur
homini impedimenta, quibus remotis, meus liberius fertur in Deum ;
et inquantum hæ virtutes sunt perfectæ caritatis effectus."   (S.
Thom., 2 2, Q 184, A 3, and " Quodl. de Carit.," A 11 ad 5.)

[2] " Patet quod præcipue in affectu Caritatis ad Deum perfectio
Christianæ vitæ consistit ; et hoc rationabiliter. Cujuslibet enim
rei perfectio in assecutione sui finis consistit. Finis autem Christianæ vitæ est Caritas, ád quam sunt omnia ordinanda ; secundum
illud, ' Finis præcepti est Caritas '. (S. Thom., Opusc. " Cont.
retrah. a Relig.," C 6.)

[3] " Forma præcepti perfectionem demonstrat. Consilia autem
omnia, sicut et præcepta, ordinantur ad Caritatem ; præcepta, ad
removendum ea quæ sunt Caritati contraria. Consilia, ad remo-
vendnm impedimenta actus Caritatis." (S. Thom., 2 2, Q 184,
Art. 3.)

S. Bonaventure treats of Divine Charity in various
works, which have merited for him the title of the
Seraphic Doctor.   He regards it as " the root, the
form, the end, the bond of perfection, to which all
the laws of God are reduced ".[1]   He considers it also
as the one virtue which brings the soul to perfection,
and secures the perfection of all the other virtues.[2]
For that " it unites man with his ultimate end," and
by " rectifying his will, rectifies his life ".[3]   " Love
the one Good," he exclaims, "in which are all
goods, and it is enough."[4]   S. Teresa also grasps
the great principle, when she says : " Let us remember, my daughters, that true perfection consists in
the love of God and our neighbour.   The more
perfectly we observe these two precepts, the more
perfect shall we be.   Our whole rule and constitu-
tions serve for nothing else but as so many means
for enabling us to do this with more perfection."[5]
From S. Catherine of Siena we learn the same, in
the Dialogue on Perfection, where she is thus
divinely instructed : "This is My Will, that thou

[1] " Sciendam quod radix, forma, finis, complementum et vinculum perfectionis, Caritas est; ad quam Magister omnium Christus
legem et prophetas, et per consequens universa Dei documenta
reducit." (S. Bonav., "Apol. paup.," R 1, C 3.)

[2] " Caritas sola ducit hominem ad perfectionem.   Ad mortifi-
candum enim vitia, ad proficiendum in gratia, ad consequendum
omnium virtutum perfectionem summam, nihil potest dici melius,
nihil excogitari utilius Caritate potest." (S. Bonav., " de perfectione Vitæ," C 7.)

[3] " Caritas est regula rectificans voluntatem : qua rectificata tota
anima recte vivit." (S. Bonav., " Centiloq.," P 3, S 40.)

[4] "Ama unum bonum, in quo sunt omnia, et sufficit." (S.
Bonav., " de perf. Vitæ," C 8.)

[5] S. Teresa, " Int. Castle," M 1, C 2.

shouldst love Me always, and above all, as I have commanded thee, with thy whole heart, and soul, and strength. In the fulfilment of this precept stands thy perfection, for love is the fulfilling of the law." [1]

S. Francis of Sales, as we know, has written a "Treatise on the love of God," wherein, at great length, he sings the praises of Divine Charity. He says that "those who are animated by Charity possess a perfection which contains the virtue of all perfections and the perfection of all virtues". [2] Elsewhere the Saint tells us that "a perfect life means perfect Charity, for Charity is the life of the soul". [3]

Lewis of Granada has left a sublime work on the "perfection of the love of God," admirably adapted to enlighten and inflame souls desirous of advancing in the ways of perfection. Among many beautiful things relating to Divine love, he says: "Charity is the end of all precepts, counsels, and virtues, they being as means and steps by which to attain to it. As the end of the Christian life is Charity, so its perfection is perfect Charity. Charity is the life and the sum of all virtues, and the plenitude of all perfection. Whatever is contained in Holy Scripture, or the writings of the Saints, is either Charity or belongs to it." [4]

"Hence," says Denis the Carthusian, "to advance

---

[1] S. Cath. Sien., " Dial. on cons. perfection."
[2] S. Fran. of Sales, " Love of God," B 11, C 8.
[3] " Letters," B 6, L lii.
[4] Lewis de Gran., " de perfec. amor. Dei," C 1.

in Charity is to advance in all the virtues, and in the gifts of the Holy Ghost. For of all virtues Charity is the form, the life, the summit, the queen, the mover: since it unites the soul most closely with God, conforming the human will to the Divine, so urging it to will and to do the things that please God, and to reject and avoid those which displease Him. And thus all the Gospel precepts and counsels are ordained to the perfection of Charity."[1]

"Love God therefore, choose Him, run to Him, take, possess, enjoy Him. It is by Charity you choose the way, by Charity you run along the way, by Charity you gain the end, by Charity you grasp it and enjoy it. O good Charity, by which we love God, we choose God, we advance to God, we attain to God, we possess God! What more shall I say of thee, O Charity? Thou art the *way*. ' I show you yet,' says S. Paul, 'a more excellent way. Thou art the super-excellent way, the chief of all right ways, for all right ways proceed from thee and meet in thee. For the laws of God are His ways, which all depend on thee. Thou art the way, therefore, O Charity! the way of men to God, and of God to men. Thou bringest God to men,

[1] "In Caritate proficere est in omni virtute incrementum accipere, atque in septem donis Sancti Spiritus augmentum sortiri. Caritas namque est cæterarum virtutum regina, motrix, forma, vita, et finis; quia per caritatem maxime ac propinquissime conjungimur, conformamur, adhæremusque Deo. Et cum Caritas conformet voluntatem hominis voluntati Creatoris instigat eum ad volendum et agendum ea quæ placent Deo, et ad vitandum ea quæ displicent ei. Hinc præcepta et consilia universa ordinantur ad Caritatis perfectionem." (Denis Carthus, "Inflammat. Div. amoris," 1, and "de profess. Monast.," A 1.)

and thou leadest men to God. Neither He nor we can pass to one another but by thee! O dear Charity! come upon us, and enlarge our hearts, that they may become the abode and dwelling-place of God. May He pour thee forth in our hearts by the Holy Ghost, and so vouchsafe to come to us, and make His abode within us; who liveth and reigneth for ever and ever. Amen."[1]

[1] "Dilige ergo Deum, elige Deum, curre, apprehende, posside, fruere. Per viam Dei curritur ad Deum. Cito pergere est ardenter amare. Vide ergo quomodo totum bonum tuum ex Caritate pendet; per Caritatem viam eligis, per Caritatem viam curris, per Caritatem ad patriam pervenis, per Caritatem apprehendis et frueris. O bona Caritas! per quam Deum diligimus, Deum eligimus, ad Deum currimus, ad Deum pervenimus, Deum possidemus. Quid amplius dicam de te, Caritas? Tu *via* es. 'Adhuc,' inquit Paulus, 'viam excellentiorem vobis demonstrabo.' Tu es namque via super-excellens, vias rectas ostendens, vias distortas dirigens. Tu es caput viarum rectarum. Omnes viæ rectæ a te exeunt, et in te recurrunt. Nam præcepta Dei viæ sunt ejus, quæ omnia a te pen-dent,* et in te consistunt. Tu es plenitudo justitiæ, perfectio legis, consummatio virtutis, agnitio veritatis. Via igitur es, O Caritas, via hominis ad Deum, et Dei ad homines. Tu Deum ad hominem deducis; tu hominem ad Deum dirigis. Nec ille, nec nos, nisi per te ad alterutrum transire possumus. O cara Caritas! illabere nobis, et dilata cor nostrum, ut capere possit hospitem et mansorem Deum. Infundat et diffundat te in cordibus nostris per Spiritum sanctum suum Redemptor noster Jesus Christus Filius Dei, ut Ipse cum Patre ad nos venire dignetur, et mansionem in nobis facere; qui cum eodem Patre et Spiritu Sancto vivit et regnat Deus per omnia seculorum sæcula. Amen." (Hugo a. S. Vict., "de laude Caritatis.")

* "Universa lex pendet." (S. Matt. xxii. 40.)

CHAPTER VII.

THE essential perfection of a watch, as we have seen, consists in its keeping accurate time, this being the purpose for which it was made. But in order thus to answer its end, it stands in absolute need of a carefully-formed and well-adjusted interior mechanism, in which one part moves another, each remaining true to its place and work, and all combining together in due measure and order to mark the perfection of time. If a spring be injured or a chain loosened, the movement of the various parts is at once checked, and the time becomes irregular or ceases to be shown altogether. It is evident, therefore, that the works of the watch are absolutely indispensable to the keeping of the time. They are the necessary instrumental means by which the end is attained. But if, in addition to this inner workmanship, we suppose the watch to be carefully finished throughout, adorned with jewels, encased in gold, and surrounded with the delicate designs of art, all such additional properties and embellishments would make up its accidental perfection. It would be a true watch independently of these extra qualities, because of the accuracy of its time, but for lack of surroundings, it could not be called perfect; nor would it be nearly so valuable or useful to the owner. Thus the watch has a threefold perfection, essential, instrumental, and accidental. So also in man. The first perfection which he needs is that which is essential to his spiritual life, namely, Charity, which unites him with God; this being the end of his existence.[1] Charity, however, must be sustained; and more than this, it has to grow, strengthen, and develop, in its life and action, until it yields its fruits to God, in all sweetness and abundance. But in order to do this it is absolutely requisite that we use the instrumental means ordained by God for this end,[2] which in the Christian life are the commandments of God, prayer and mortification, the sacraments, the moral virtues, the works and trials of life, and in the Religious State further comprise the three vows, and the proper rules of the Order professed. In the faithful use of these various means is to be found our instrumental perfection. To our souls they are what the wheels and works are to the watch—indispensable to the attainment of the end. Thus the Christian will not attain Christian perfection without the means provided for this end in the Christian life. Nor will the religious attain to religious perfection without the means proper to the religious life. For the same reason, the individual Christian finds his individual instrumental perfection in the duties and opportunities of

---

[1] " Dilectio est quasi medium inter amantem et amatum." (S. Thom., 2 2, Q 27, Art. 5.)

[2] " The end of the commandment is Charity." (1 Tim. i. 5.)

his particular calling in life ; and each religious finds his own instrumental perfection in the vows which he has taken, the rule according to which he has made his profession, the duties of his particular office, and the occasions and opportunities of his daily life.   Thus a Carthusian would not gain his perfection by using the means provided for Dominicans and Franciscans.   Nor would these aim rightly at perfection by taking the instrumental means proper to Jesuits or secular priests.   Neither would Christians in married life tend properly to the perfection of their state by adopting the means peculiar to priests or religious.[1]   Charity indeed is the common end, as it is the essential perfection of all.   But nstrumental perfection varies according to states and circumstances.   Hence the Apostle speaks of the variety of works in the Christian life, but the one spirit or principle animating all.   "There are diversities of graces, but the same spirit.   And there are diversities of ministries, but the same Lord. And there are diversities of operations, but the same God, who worketh all in all."[2]

The Abbot Moses, about the end of the fourth century, as Cassian tells us, pointed to this distinction between essential and instrumental perfection ; and it is pleasing to be able to receive even now, the instruction of these enlightened

[1] To those neglecting their own instrumental means of perfection, while busying themselves in things external to their profession, might be applied the words, "They run well, but out of the way". "Bene currunt; in via non currunt." (S. Aug., Serm. 141 de verb. Joan.)

[2] 1 Cor. xii. 4.

masters of the spiritual life, the Fathers of the Desert. " Fasting, watching, meditation, poverty, and privation," says he, " are not themselves perfection, but the instruments by which we may acquire perfection. They are not the object of our profession, but the means by which we may obtain it. It becomes us therefore to use these means with reference to our end, which is purity of heart, or Charity. What will it avail us to perform with punctuality our ordinary exercises, if the main purpose for which we perform them is eluded ? To this end therefore should be referred our solitude, our fasts, our daily employments, yea, every penitential exercise, and every virtue : that by these means our hearts may be preserved in calm, and thus we may ascend to the perfection of Charity."[1]

S. Thomas gives us in clear terms the threefold distinction in reference to perfection, when he says that a thing may appertain to perfection essentially, instrumentally, or consequently : and applying it to Christian perfection, he assigns the perfect observance of the laws of Charity as essential perfection ; other virtues, poverty, chastity, abstinence, and the like, as instrumental perfection ; and the effects of a holy life as the result or consequence hereof.[2] When he says that " the counsels, as well

---

[1] Cassian, " Conf.," I, C 7.

[2] " Dicendum quod ad perfectionem aliquid pertinent tripliciter. Uno modo, essentialiter, sicut perfecta observantia præceptorum Caritatis. Alio modo, consequenter ; sicut illa quæ consequuntur ex perfectione Caritatis. Tertio modo, instrumentaliter, sicut paupertas, continentia, abstinentia, et alia hujusmodi." (S. Thom., 2 2, Q 186, Art. 2).

as particular precepts, are ordained to Charity,"[1] he
speaks of instrumental perfection, as residing in particular virtues, the exercise of which leads on to the
essential perfection of Charity, developed as a
habit, and disposed to its acts : as he expresses in
the following :—" The counsels are ordained to
Charity as to their end ; that by their means the
precepts may be more easily and perfectly observed ;
and we may thus attain to the perfect love of God
and our neighbour".[2]   " The counsels therefore
belong to the perfection of life, not as though perfection principally consisted in them ; but inasmuch
as they are the way, or the instruments by which
we may reach to the perfection of Charity."[3]

From all this it appears that the different virtues,
exercises, and opportunities afforded in the
Christian and Religious life, are to be regarded as
the instrumental means of developing the habit of
Charity within the soul ; since "the end of the
commandment is Charity,"[4] as bringing to our
nature its essential perfection.   So that day by day
we have a set purpose in hand, to which we are
constantly applying ourselves, whether it be by

---

[1] " Consilia, sicut et præcepta, ordinantur ad Caritatem." (S.
Thom., 2 2, Q 184, A 3.)

[2] " Consilia ordinantur ad Caritatem, sicut ad finem ; ut per
ea præcepta facilius et perfectius custodiantur.   Sic per hujusmodi
consilia perveniatur ad perfectionem dilectionis Dei et proximi."
(S. Thom., Opusc. " Cont. Retrah. a Relig.," C 7.)

[3] " Patet quod consilia ad vitæ perfectionem pertinent, non quia
in eis principaliter consistit perfectio, sed quia sunt via quædam,
vel instrumenta ad perfectionem Caritatis habendam." (S. Thom.,
Opusc. sup., C 6.)

[4] 1 Tim. i. 5.

engaging in prayer or meditation, by receiving the Sacraments, fasting, silence, mortification ; or by the faithful endeavour to practise our vows, keep our rules, discharge the duties of our office, and meet the trials and emergencies of daily life.[1] This purpose is the attainment of perfect Charity, which by uniting the soul with God, and ordering its operations according to Him, becomes hereby our essential perfection. Let therefore the exercises of Christian and Religious life be used as *means to the end*—as the instruments for accomplishing our work. Let us keep the end in view as the archer keeps his eye on the target, the builder on his edifice, and the husbandman on his crops. Thus, in examination of conscience and Confession, we labour to purify the soul from its faults and imperfections. Why? To free ourselves from the impediments to Charity.[2] In Mental Prayer we approach to God, as the Fountain of Charity,

---

[1] "Certum est exteriores observantias regulares, abstinentia, jejunia, disciplinas, silentium, separationem a mundo, clausura, ad interiorum reformationem, ornatum, et perfectionem principaliter ordinari. Quo ergo fugient, qui diu fuerunt in Ordine, et tamen adhuc proni ad impatientiam, ira, ac proprii sensus immansionem? Nunquid tales suis satisfaciunt votis? Non utique. Imo perversi et stulti sunt ; et similes illis qui navem habent aut scalam, nec tamen eis utuntur, navigando aut ascendendo." (Denis Carthus., ": de profess. Monast.," A 7.)

[2] Self-examination and Confession, being among the instruments of perfection, care must be taken to use them wisely, not unwisely ; for sometimes a good instrument may not be well used. To those walking in the way of perfection, and aspiring to the union of love with God (more especially if there be in them a tendency to undue fear or scrupulosity), a sparse use of examen and Confession would be often far more profitable than a frequency of these exercises, which sometimes have the effect of drawing souls from God into themselves ; instead of which let them be taught to

opening our souls to the inflowing streams of His love. Or we look to our Lord as the model of perfect Charity, recognizing the Divine virtue in the fulness of its perfection, whether in His joyful, sorrowful, or glorious mysteries. Or we consider our faults as so many deficiencies of Charity ;[1] and the various virtues as different exercises of it.[2]

Coming to mortification, the natural man is subdued by self-denial and penance. Why? To tame the appetites and passions, which by warring against the spirit, hinder the reign of Charity within the soul. We take the vows of Religion, all in reference to the same end ;[3] Poverty, to free

transcend their faults and fears, by the higher exercises of Divine love, which of their own virtue suffice to cleanse the soul ; thus " getting out of the habitation of nature," and living in the bright sphere of Divine Charity. Let the teaching of the Council of Trent be well remembered, viz. that venial sins may without fault remain unconfessed, and be expiated by other remedies. "Venialia, quanquam recte in confessione dicantur, taceri tamen citra culpam, multisque aliis remediis expiari possunt." (Conc. Trid., Sess. 14, cap. 5.) And let S. Thomas' teaching be known, that Divine Charity itself purifies the soul from venial sins. "Caritas tollit per suum actum peccata venialia." (S. Thom., 3, Q 97, Art. 4 ad 3.) This is the doctrine of "transcension," so insisted on by F. Baker, and taught before him by Blosius, Suso, S. Greg. (Hom. 22 in Ezech.), and others.

[1] Omnis imperfectio est Caritatis defectio.

[2] "Omnia opera bona nostra unum opus est Caritatis." (S. Aug., Enar. in Ps. lxxxix.)

[3] "Ista tria vota Sancti Patres et Ordinum Institutores ordinaverunt a cunctis Religiosis esse promittenda ad hoc, ut per eorum adimpletionem ad Caritatis perfectionem velocius et expeditius queant pertingere. Ideo certum est quod religiosæ quæ in Caritatis sinceritate et profectu non crescunt, præfata vota inaniter promiserunt. Omnis ergo religiosa persona penset quotidie diligenter, imo omni die frequenter, hæc tria vota, et cur ea promiserit, recogitet, utpote quatenus per eorum impletionem crescat in caritate ; sicque indefesse conetur vota sua implere, atque per hæc in caritate proficere ac perfici." (Denis Carthus., " de profess. Monast.," A 1.)

us from attachments that would occupy our time and efforts to the detriment of Charity; Chastity, to reserve our affections and energies for Charity; Obedience, that our natural will may be controlled, and ruled by a higher principle, viz., the love of God, moving us to action through obedience. We live under rule and discipline, recognizing here so many manifestations of the Divine will in our regard; thus renouncing the will and ways of the natural man, in view of disposing ourselves for the higher life of Divine Charity. Charity is the end to be gained, because it unites the soul with God; and all the other virtues and exercises are the means to gain it. "The end of the commandment is Charity."[1] Let us not forget it. In this way the observance of the least rule, and the exercise of the smallest good work, will have their meaning. We are aiming at perfect Charity; and all that helps us to it we readily embrace.

We come now to the consideration of accidental perfection; and a short sentence from S. Thomas will prepare the way to its clear understanding. He says that Charity commands all the virtues, as the will commands all the powers:[2] the reason being that Charity is love; and love in its nature is the spring of action, proceeding from the will through which it operates. So that as the will moves the different powers to their respective virtues, Charity, by ruling the will, rules also the

---

[1] 1 Tim. i. 5.

[2] "Caritas imperat omnibus virtutibus sicut voluntas omnibus potentiis." (S. Thom., 2, Sent. D. 40, Q 1, A 5.)

powers subordinate to it. We suppose now that by the use of instrumental perfection, the habit of Charity is being gradually developed and strengthened in the soul. It becomes in time the ruling-principle of the spiritual man, and the motive-cause of his actions. Yet it is clear that notwithstanding this residence of Charity in the will, considering our complex nature, many of our powers are likely to be but very imperfectly under the sway of Divine love: it being so much a matter of time, and habit, and practice, before the thoughts and affections within, and the senses and members without, move in all things according to God. Here, then, is the need of accidental perfection, by which the various powers of soul and body are brought into right order and movement under Charity. For, as S. Gregory says: "Charity takes care to extend itself to acts of all the virtues".[1] Herein lies the arduous work of the spiritual life, in bringing the habit of Charity to that degree of development, whereby it is readily and easily disposed to its acts:[2] energizing freely, and extending

[1] "Studiosa sollicitudine Caritas ad cuncta virtutum facta dilatatur." (S. Greg., "Mor.," L x., C 4.)

[2] "The perfection of virtues is found not in the *habit*, but in the *acts*, according to the unanimous teaching of philosophers and theologians; because the habits of virtue do not give the highest perfection to the powers in which they repose: that is reserved for the acts, to which the habits refer as to their end and perfection. A man is not virtuous because he *can* live virtuously, but because he *does* live so. Habits are like a good sword in the scabbard: and acts like the sword drawn, and used valiantly. The sword is not made to lie hid in the sheath, but to be employed according to its purpose. If it be not used, it rusts. Habits of virtue are to produce acts of virtue as frequently and perfectly as possible." (St. Jure, "Knowl. and Love of our Lord," V i., B 2, C i.)

its influence to the entire man ; calling forth every virtue as it is needed, until the soul becomes clothed in spiritual beauty: " Desiring," says S. Paul, "to be clothed upon with our habitation that is from heaven : that we be found clothed, not naked ".[1] Thus it is that Charity weaves her own nuptial garment, in which to appear when the Bridegroom comes. " Ecce Sponsus venit, exite obviam Ei."[2] Accidental perfection then gives to each particular power and sense moving under the will its own proper virtue at the right time, and in the right manner and measure, causing the several operations to proceed according to God.

All this is brought about by Charity extending her power from the will, and permeating the various faculties, senses, and operations with her life, gaining over them such an ascendency as to eliminate their carnal and natural desires, and substitute instead her own sweet life and love, refining and spiritualizing the nature, vivifying and prompting its operations, and causing them to proceed readily, easily, and sweetly. In this way the essential perfection uses the instrumental, and in course of time gains the accidental.

Let us hear S. Thomas on this subject[3] " Per-

---

[1] 2 Cor. v. 2.

[2] S. Matt. xxv. 6.

[3] " Principaliter et per se consistit perfectio in caritate, quæ est radix omnium virtutum. Secundario et per accidens consistit in aliis virtutibus, inquantum per ea subtrahuntur homini impedimenta occupationum, quibis remotis, mens liberius fertur in Deum : et inquantum hæ virtutes sunt perfectæ caritatis effectus. Qui enim perfecte diligit Deum, ab his se retrahit quæ eum retrahere possunt a Deo. Sic igitur in his quæ principaliter et per se ad

fection," he says, " principally and in itself consists
in Charity, which is the root of all virtues ; secon-
darily and accidentally it consists in the other
virtues, inasmuch as by them impediments are
removed from the soul, thus enabling it to go with
greater freedom to God, and in as far also as these
virtues are the effects of perfect Charity. For a
perfect lover of God withdraws himself from those
things which withdraw him from God. Thus in the
things which principally and in themselves belong
to perfection, greater perfection exists where these
abound the more. But in things which belong to
accidental perfection, one having more would not
necessarily be more perfect. ·Greater poverty, for
instance, would not necessarily imply greater perfection. But perfection in such is measured by the
degree in which the accidental bears on the essential,
so that he will be the more perfect whose poverty
detaches him the more effectually from earthly
things, thus enabling the soul with greater freedom
to give itself to God." [1]

Elsewhere the Angelic Doctor treats in profound
language of the necessity of attending to this accidental perfection in order to secure the perfection

perfectionem pertinent, sequitur quod sit major perfectio ubi hæc
inveniuntur magis ; sicut quod perfectior est qui majoris est Caritatis. In his autem quæ consequenter et accidentaliter ad perfectionem pertinent, non sequitur magis simpliciter, ubi magis inveniuntur ; unde non sequitur quod magis pauper sit magis perfectus : sed mensuranda est in talibus perfectio per comparationem
ad illa in quibis consistit perfectio simpliciter; ut scilicet ille di-
catur perfectior cujus paupertas magis sequestrat hominem a terrenis, ut facis liberius Deo vacare." (S. Thom., " Quodl. de Carit.,"
Art. 11 ad 5).

[1] S. Thom., " Quodl. de Carit.," Art. 11 ad 5.

of our works. And this is a vastly practical and important point. For be it ever remembered that the perfection of man is determined by the perfection of his *acts*, not of his habits, as such.[1] Thus a high degree of Divine habitual Charity will not suffice to perfect the soul, if the Charity pass not from habit to act ; that is, if it become not operative.[2] For to what purpose does a man possess virtue if he use it not? He is not virtuous because he *can* live virtuously, but because he *does* live so. Hence the well-known doctrine, that perfection resides in ordinary acts.

Now, this bringing of the habit of Charity into action, and that with readiness and delight—this it is that demands the accidental perfection of the soul. For although Charity resident in the will be the prime mover, yet if the movement also of the secondary powers and the senses be not in prompt accordance with it, imperfect action will ensue. But this accordance is the result of accidental perfection. An artisan using a tool will not be able to work perfectly if the instrument is not rightly adapted and tempered to the work, no matter how capable he himself may be. So for the perfection of our actions not only must the will be rightly ordered by Charity, but the subordinate powers, senses, and members working instrumentally under

---

[1] "Unumquodque intantum perfectum est, inquantum est actu : nam potentia sine actu imperfecta est." (S. Thom., 1 2, Q 3, A 2.)

[2] "Ratio potentiæ est, ut sit principium actus. Unde omnis habitus, qui est alicujus potentiæ principaliter importat ordinem ad actum." (S. Thom., 1 2, Q 49, A 3.)

Charity, must be in proper dispositions; that is, they need the habits of their respective virtues in order to move easily and sweetly in concert with Charity. Otherwise they hinder her work, as an imperfect instrument hinders a perfect workman.[1] But let it be observed that these habits of the different virtues making up accidental perfection are themselves rooted in the one Divine habit of habits. Charity contains and connects in itself all the other virtues.[2] This it does from its very nature, as being love of the highest order, since it is the property of love to actuate the will, and through the will to move the other powers to its own end ; thus calling forth the virtues which the exercise of the different powers involves. S. Paul tells us this when he says : " Charity is patient, is

---

[1] " Dicendum quod ad hoc quod actus inferioris potentiæ sit perfectus, requiritur quod non solum adsit perfectio in superiori potentia, sed etiam in inferiori. Si enim principale agens debito modo se haberet, non sequeretur actio perfecta, si instrumentum non esset bene dispositum. Unde oportet ad hoc quod homo bene operetur in his quæ sunt ad finem, quod non solum habeat virtutem qua bene se habeat circa finem, sed etiam virtutes quibus bene se habeat circa ea quæ sunt ad finem. Nam virtus quæ est circa finem se habet ut principalis et motiva respectu earum quæ sunt ad finem. Et ideo cum Caritate necesse est etiam habere alias virtutes morales." (S. Thom., 1 2, Q 65, Art. 3 ad 1.)

[2] " Dicendum quod cum Caritate simul infunduntur omnes virtutes morales. Cujus ratio est, quia Deus non minus perfecte operatur in operibus gratiæ, quam in operibus naturæ. Sic autem videmus in operibus naturæ, quod non invenitur principium aliquorum operum in aliqua re, quin inveniantur in ea quæ sunt necessaria ad hujusmodi opera perficienda. Manifestum est autem quod Caritas, inquantum ordinat hominem ad finem ultimum, est principium omnium bonorum operum quæ in finem ultimum ordinari possunt. Unde oportet quod cum caritate simul infundantur omnes virtutes morales, quibus homo perficit singula genera bonorum operum." (S. Thom., 1 2, Q 65, Art. 3.)

kind, envieth not, seeketh not her own, thinketh no evil, beareth all things, believeth all things, hopeth all things, endureth all things".[1] Here we see the different virtues flowing from the one Charity. Hence the repeated expressions of the Holy Fathers pointing to this truth. Charity is named as the root, the fountain, the mother, the mistress, the form, the soul, the mover of the virtues.[2] Truly, then, of this Divine virtue of virtues we may say, in the words of Wisdom, "All good things came to me together with her."[3]

Owing, however, to the long-standing imperfections and miseries of the natural man, the Divine principle of Charity is hindered from gaining sufficient power within the soul to awaken and apply to action these many subsidiary virtues which she needs in order to act perfectly ; and the consequence is that we live on with our spiritual resources undeveloped—deprived in a vast measure of the Divine light and love we should otherwise gain; lacking sadly our accidental perfection, and, as a consequence, given to our own imperfect modes of thinking, judging, and acting. For, as the Angelic Doctor has taught us, although the principal agent be perfect, yet if the instruments used be not rightly

---

[1] 1 Cor. xiii. 14.

[2] " Caritas est radix bonorum." (S. Aug., " de gratia Christi.," L i.) "Caritas radix est, fons, materque cunctorum bonorum." (S. Chrys. Hom. 2 in die Pent.). " Magistra bonorum omnium Caritas." (S. Greg. Epist. 108, Lib. 9.) " Caritas est virtus dignissima, cæterarum virtutum regina, imperatrix, motrix, forma, vita, et finis." (Denis Carthus., "de profess. Monast.," A 1.)

[3] " Venerunt autem mihi omnia bona pariter cum illa." (Sap. vii. 11.)

disposed, imperfect action must ensue.[1] Now, the
Spirit of God, moving the soul by Charity, is the
"agens principale"; and our faculties, senses, and
members are as the instruments acting under the
influence of Charity. But if they are not set in
order by their own proper virtues, what can be
expected but an ill-regulated disposition and unruly movement, that will serve as a constant
impediment to Charity's operations, and so effectually hinder the work of our perfection. Essential
perfection, therefore, without accidental, means
Charity deprived of many works and virtues, and
the tree without its flowers and fruit. In attaining to
this accidental perfection, as already said, lies the
arduous work of spiritual life, because Charity will
not be able thus to gain her place, and order the
virtues with the readiness and sweetness she needs,
until the opposing elements of the natural man are
subdued by a consistent practice of mortification.
"Mortificatus carne, vivificatus spiritu."[2] "When
I am weak, then I am strong."[3] When I am weak
according to the natural man, then I am strong
according to the spiritual man. The spiritual man
strengthens on the weakness of the natural man.
As S. Gregory says: "The virtue of the Divine
Spirit daily strengthens in us, as our own human
spirit weakens; and then it is that we attain to God,

---

[1] "Si principale agens debito modo se haberet, non sequeretur
actio perfecta, si instrumentum non esset bene dispositum." (S.
Thom., 1 2, Q 65, A 3 ad 1.)

[2] 1 Pet. iii. 18.

[3] 2 Cor. xii. 10.

when we altogether die to ourselves ".[1]   " But when thou shalt think thyself consumed, thou shalt rise as the day-star."[2]   " Whereunto you do. well to attend as to a light that shineth in a dark place : until the day dawn, and the day-star arise in your hearts."[3]   The natural light and love go down within us, and the Divine light and love arise in their place.[4]   And as the mortification of the natural man proceeds, Charity gradually gains her position, and puts forth her power ; and thus the soul advances to its accidental perfection.   " Set, therefore, your hearts upon your ways ; go up to the mountain ; bring timber, and build the house."[5]   Let us offer ourselves to the Divine Lover for " Caritas, sola, plena, ordinata," since hereby God reigns within the kingdom of our souls.   When His love becomes our one governing love, and is fully developed and diffused, moving easily and sweetly to its acts— rightly ordered and perfected by its own proper light (the light of discretion)—then the Holy Spirit of God finds a happy abode within the human soul,[6] and delights to display His grandeur in our nothing- ness, His omnipotence in our weakness.   Then

---

[1] " Quanto in nobis quotidie de Dei spiritu virtus crescit, tanto noster spiritus deficit. Tunc vero in Deo plene proficimus, cum a nobisipsis funditus defecerimus." (S. Greg., " Moral.," L xxii., C 14.)

[2] Job xi. 17.

[3] 2 Pet. i. 19.

[4] " Quando lux creata evanescit, lux increata exoritur." (Blo- sius, " Instit. Spir.," C 12, § 4.)

[5] Aggæus, 1 7.

[6] " We will come to him, and make our abode with him, and I will manifest myself to him." (S. John xxiii. 21.)

shine forth His Divine gifts and fruits, and then He uses the soul for His own purposes and interests here below. Let us offer ourselves for the one light, the one love, the one principle that regulates all : making us responsive to God's movement, and prompt in doing His justifications ("ad faciendas justificationes Tuas in æternum ") ; breaking down the barriers of " fleshly loves and fears "—all for His own great ends, and the vast needs of souls.

And let the development of this love be our one project, as S. Francis of Sales would say.[1] Anything less than this is insufficient. Sad would it be to content ourselves with an insufficiency in spiritual things which we could not endure in things temporal. " Woe," says S. Bernard, " to this generation for its imperfection, which suffices itself with such insufficiency ! For who is there now-a-days that even aspires to the perfection to which Holy Scripture points ? Let them see what excuse they have ! for since we profess Apostolic life, we pledge ourselves to Apostolic perfection."[2]

A constant, uniform, undivided, yes and *exclusive* spirit is what we need for our work. Our complex nature—the time and practice we require to form its various habits, and bring its different parts and powers under the prompt and easy management of Charity ;

---

[1] S. Fran. of Sales, " Love of God," B xii., C 3.

[2] " Væ generationi huic miseræ ab imperfectione sua, cui suffi-cere videtur insufficientia, imo inopia tanta ! Quis enim ad perfectionem illam quam Scripturæ tradunt, vel aspirare videtur ? Ipse viderint quid excusationis possint afferre; quoniam Apostolicam omnes nos vitam professi sumus, Apostolicæ perfectioni nomina dedimus universi." (S. Bern., Serm. 27 " de Divers.")

the counter-movements of our self-love, so quick at making claims and playing tricks : all this tells us that we cannot afford to divide ourselves between two spirits ; remembering, moreover, our Lord's words, that " no man can serve two masters ".[1] We must take our principle, and stand by it. If we grasp not the higher love, of necessity we fall upon the lower.[2] Let Charity, therefore, be our only acknowledged moving principle, and let it energize in the works and trials of daily life, till it brings to our nature its full measure of accidental perfection. Whatever aids us to this end, we use ; whatever hinders us, we avoid. Thus, day by day, the work progresses, till we attain to " the perfect man, unto the measure of the age of the fulness of Christ, that we be no more as children, tossed to and fro ; but doing the truth in Charity, we may in all things grow up in Him who is the head, Christ ".[3] From being as children in Charity, weak and unstable, we must grow into perfect men, after the pattern of Christ our Lord, strong in our powers, able in our operations. " In all things growing up in Him—- not in one thing only, but in all things : that is, growing in all good,"[4] which points to our full accidental perfection.

---

[1] S. Matt. vi. 24.

[2] " Quicunque avertitur a fine debito, necesse est quod aliquem finem indebitum sibi præstituat : quia omne agens agit propter finem." (S. Thom. 2 2, Q 45, Art. 1, ad 1.)

[3] Eph. iv. 13.

[4] " Crescamus in Illo per omnia, non in uno tantum, sed per omnia, id est, in omni bono crescentes." (S. Thom., "In Pauli Epist. ad. Ephes. 4.")

CHAPTER VIII.

RELIGIOUS PERFECTION.

LET all who enter the religious state clearly understand at the outset that they enter the *School of perfection*. " The mercy of God has not only numbered us with the elect, but called us to the school of the perfect," said S. Bernard to his religious brethren.[1] And S. Thomas distinctly teaches the same, when he says that the religious life is " a certain discipline, or exercise for the attaining of perfection ".[2]   Those who go to school are supposed as yet to be unlearned; but they wish to become learned, and so enter the schools with this set purpose, and with the determination of using consistently and perseveringly the means appointed for gaining their end.   Many are found who begin well ; yet in course of time they appear either to lose sight of the end they first proposed, or to be drawn aside by counter attractions, which causes them to relax their first endeavours, and to divert their energies and interests into other channels.·

---

[1] " Misericordia Dei nos non solum in electorum recepit numerum, sed vocavit ad collegium perfectorum." (S. Bern., Serm. 27, " de Divers.".)

[2] " Status Religionis est quædam disciplina vel exercitium ad perfectionem perveniendi." (S. Thom., 2 2, Q 186, Art. 2.)

In like manner, those who join the religious state are supposed as yet to be imperfect, but they wish to become perfect, and with this intent enter the school of perfection, " not as professing themselves perfect " (says S. Thomas), " but as labouring for the attainment of perfection ".[1] They lay aside their secular garments and receive instead the habit of religion, which tells them in the words of the Apostle, that they are to " put off the old man, with his deeds, and put on the new man, created according to God ".[2] Here, too, we find those who begin well, and yet, as time goes on, it would seem as though they had either never grasped the *end* of the religious state, or else that they had afterwards, by engaging themselves with other things, lost sight of their first aim.   Indeed, in the way of perfection, S. Jerome's saying seems often but too true, that " many make a beginning, but that few persevere," [3] that is, in anything like a steady progress.[4] The words of the Prophet might be addressed to them, " You have sown much and brought in little. You have clothed yourselves, but not been warmed.

[1] " Non profitentes se esse perfectos, sed adhibere studium ad perfectionem consequendam." (S. Thom., 2 2, Q. 186, Art. 2 ad 1.)

[2] Eph. iv. 22 ; Col. iii. 9.

[3] " Incipere plurimorum est, perseverare paucorum." (S. Jerome, "Adv. Jovinian," Lib. i.)

[4] "It is certain," says Denis the Carthusian, "that unless a Religious learn daily to subdue himself, and attend to his vocation, he becomes much worse in Religion than he was in the world. Hence we see some Religious harder, more unbending, and unconverted than worldly men. Let a Religious therefore give himself daily to the work of his own interior reformation." (Denis Carth., " de profess. Monast.," A 7.)

7

Thus saith the Lord, set your hearts upon your ways."[1]   Have they as yet set their hearts upon learning the ways of perfection?   Do they understand that perfection is the *end* of the religious life? " The end of the religious life," says S. Thomas, "is the perfection of Charity.   For the religious state has been formed for the attainment of perfection, by means of exercises which remove the impediments to perfect Charity.   Now it is clear that those who work for an end, while they are not obliged at once to reach the end, are bound in some way to tend thereto.   And therefore he who gives himself to religion is not obliged at once to have perfect Charity, but he is bound to tend to and labour for perfect Charity."[2]   See here the plain teaching of the Angel of the schools, that the end of the religious life is the attainment of perfection.   If perfection is the end of the religious life, it follows that religious life is a tendency to that end, and by taking the state of religion, we thereby take the duties of the state.[3]   By taking perfection for our end, we hereby accept the obligation of tending thereto.   Hence, says the Angelic Doctor, a religious binds himself

[1] Aggeus i. 6.

[2] " Finis status Religionis est ipsa perfectio Caritatis.   Religionis enim status principaliter est institutus ad perfectionem adipiscendam per exercitia quibus tolluntur impedimenta perfectæ caritatis. Manifestum est autem quod ille qui operatur ad finem, non ex necessitate convenit quod jam assecutus sit finem, sed requiritur quod per aliquam viam tendat ad finem.   Et ideo ille qui statum religionis assumit, non tenetur habere perfectam caritatem, sed tenetur ad hoc tendere, et operam dare, ut habeat caritatem perfectam."   (S. Thom., 2 2, Q 186, Art. 2, & Art. 1 ad 4.)

"[3] Quilibet tenetur servare spectantia ad statum suum."

for life to the study of perfection.[1]   He lives in the
School of Christ, to which the Apostles and the
Saints belonged.   He is not required to be perfect,
but to advance in the way of perfection.   If he
neglect this, he is unworthy of his Divine Master.
"Whoever," says S. Bernard, "advances not in the
school of Christ, is unworthy of His Mastership.
But the disciple who advances is the glory of the
Master."[2]   Let us bring glory to the Master of the
school.   Let us share the spirit of our profession
with those whose fellowship we enjoy.   What will
the habit and tonsure, and all outward appearances
and observances avail, if we have not the right spirit
within ?   "Religion is not in the habit, but in the
heart."[3]   The heart and mind, and the whole soul
and strength, are what God chiefly desires and commands.   External observances are to subserve the
internal life, and from it to receive their value, their
merit, their spirit, "that our name may answer to
our life, and our life answer to our name, lest our
name be vain, and our crime shame".[4]

Exterior observances make the exterior man a
religious, but not as yet the interior.   But "he that
renounces his own thoughts and affections," and

---

[1] "Religiosus totam vitam suam obligat ad perfectionis studium."
(S. Thom., 2 2, Q 184, A 8.)

[2] "Quisquis in schola Christi non proficit, ejus indignus est
magisterio.   Discipulus vero proficiens gloria est magistri." (S.
Bern., Epist. 385.)

[3] "In habitu non est religio, sed in corde." (S. Bern., Apol.
ad Gulielm., C 10.)

[4] "Ut nomen congruat actioni, actio respondeat nomini : ne sit
nomen inane, et crimen immane." (Int. Op. S. Ambr., "de dign.
Sacerd.," C 3.)

cleaves to Divine love, "hath truly made the interior man a religious also. A small desire makes the outward man a religious, but it is a task of no small labour to make the interior man so too."[1] The outward observances of religious life, as grave authors tell us, are ordained to the formation of the interior man. " As the kernel is to the shell, so is interior virtue to outer observances."[2] " Those therefore," says Cardinal Bona, " are much to be pitied, who, contenting themselves with external things, neglect the inner fund of the soul, and holy union with God. For even though the soul abound in spiritual goods, it can never be fully satisfied till it attain to God, by the contact of love and inward union."[3]

"The principal thing intended in a religious profession is the formation of the interior, the union of the spirit with God, to the attaining which Divine end all things practised in religion do dispose."[4]

And, as S. Paul says, " he is not a Jew that is one outwardly, nor is that circumcision which is outward in the flesh ; but he is a Jew that is one inwardly, and the circumcision is that of the heart ".[5] So we may say, he is not a religious that is one out-

---

[1] Hesychius, monach.

[2] " Omnia quæ ad Religionis observantiam exterius videmus, ad interioris hominis reformationem Spiritus sancti inspiratione ordinata sunt : quod qui nondum intelligit, ipsa instrumenta portare reputat. Sicut nucleus in testa, sic est virtus interior cæteris observantiis in Religione. Unde qui istis exterioribus contentus, interiora postponit, sic est quasi qui corticem sine nucleo habet." (Int. Op. S. Bonav., "de profect. Religios,"L i., C 4 ; L ii., C 22.)

[3] Card. Bona, "Via Compen.," C 7.

[4] F. Baker, " S. Sophia," T. i., S 3, C 4.

[5] Rom. ii. 28.

wardly, nor is that detachment which is outward, but he is a religious that is one inwardly, and the detachment is that of the heart. " For be thou well assured," says Walter Hilton, " that a *bodily* turning to God, without the *heart* following, is but a figure of virtues, and not the truth in itself. Wherefore wretched men and women are they, who, neglecting the care of their interior, show only exteriorly a form of holiness, in habit, speech, outward carriage, and works. Do not thou so, but together with thy body, turn principally thy *heart* to God, and frame thy interior to His likeness, by Humility and Charity. Then art thou truly turned to Him." [1]

But long before these holy writers, the Fathers of the desert had explained to their disciples the need of attending to perfection, as the proper end of the religious life. " Sad it is to make profession of a state, and never to become perfect in it," said the Abbot John. " If he who enters the religious state does not attain his proper end, he seeks the religious life in vain, for he does not acquit himself of the principal duty of his profession." [2] " It is better to be fervent in a state less perfect than to be lukewarm in one more exalted." [3] " It becomes us," said Abbot Moses, " to practise fasting, watching, retirement, meditation, *with reference to our object*, which is Charity. To this end should be referred

[1] Hilton, " Scale of Perfection," C 1.
[2] Cassian, " Conf.," 19, C 5 and 8.
[3] *Ibid.*, C 3.

our solitude, our fasts, our daily employments, yea, every penitential exercise and every virtue, that by these means our hearts may be preserved in calm, and we may thus ascend to the perfection of Charity."

" The artisan does not provide himself with tools that they may remain idle. He does not hope to derive profit from the mere possession of them. No ; he seeks by their means to make himself master of his art or trade."

" It is the same with us in our profession. Consequently, fasting, watching, meditation, and privation are not themselves perfection, but the instruments of perfection. They are not the object of our profession, but the means by which we may obtain it. He, therefore, who so rests his heart in these exercises as not to direct them to their proper end, performs them in vain. He has indeed the tools requisite for his trade, but he knows not how to use them." [1]

How truly important it is to all professing the religious life to be well impressed with this salutary teaching ! And these words come to us from the desert, fifteen hundred years ago ! These eminent Fathers are as the bright lights of religious life, and our models in the way of true perfection. And the Angelic Doctor, true to his work, has caught their spirit, and handed it down to us in his immortal Summa. What can be clearer than their united teaching on this point, that the various exercises of

[1] Cassian, " Conf.," i, C 7.

religious life are but means to an end ? They are not perfection, but the instruments of perfection. They are as the tools which the artisan uses to make himself master of his trade. This even applies to the vows of religion. They are also the instruments of perfection. " It is evident," says S. Thomas, " that the counsels belong to the perfection of life, not that perfection principally consists in them, but because they are the way, or the instruments, towards gaining the perfection of Charity." [1] " The vows are ordained to perfect Charity, as to their end, and all other observances of religion are ordained to the vows." [2]

To this let us add some words of S. Francis of Sales, telling us how Divine Charity is the common end of the Religious life ; and how the particular spirit of each Order lies in the different means used to attain it. He says : " All Religious Orders have a spirit in common together ; and each Order has a spirit peculiar to itself. The common spirit is the intention they all have of aspiring to the perfection of Charity, which is the general end of the Religious life. The individual spirit is the means they possess of attaining to perfect Charity ; one aiming at this end by action, another by contemplation," &c.[3]

---

[1] " Patet quod consilia ad vitæ perfectionem pertinent, non quia in eis principaliter consistit perfectio; sed quia sunt via quædam vel instrumenta ad perfectionem Caritatis habendam." (S. Thom., Opusc. " Cont. retrah. a Relig.," C. 6.)

[2] " Votum religionis ordinatur sicut in finem ad perfectionem Caritatis ; et omnes aliæ Religionum observantiæ ordinantur ad tria vota." (S. Thom., 2 2, Q 186, Art. 7 ad 1 & 2.)

[3] S. Fran. of Sales, " Sp. Conferences," C 13, " Spirit of the rules ".

It concerns all Novices in Religion therefore, and all beginners in spiritual life, to look before all things at the *end* of their profession. " Ante omnia considerandus est finis." [1] As the artisan diligently considers the object of his trade ; as the archer fixes a steady eye on the point of the target : as the former uses his tools to effect his work ; and the latter clears his view of distracting objects, and thus directs his shaft straight to the centre ; so we must fix our minds upon the object of our profession as Religious. This object is union with God by perfect Charity ; that is, the perfect love of God, which gives perfection to our nature, by uniting it with its Origin and its End.   In this we see that the *ultimate* end of the Religious is not different from that of the ordinary Christian life ; since God alone is the common end of all, and Charity is the only bond of union with Him.   A religious vocation does not change the end of our creation.   The difference between the ordinary Christian and the Religious life lies in the means to be used in each state for gaining the common end.   The Christian life provides *sufficient* means for attaining to perfect Charity. The Religious state provides the *perfect* means. It is therefore called a state of perfection, because of the perfect means it possesses for attaining the end, and the obligation it imposes on those who join it to use those means permanently in progressing to their end.   This being the case, we must see how mistaken those are who, having

---

[1] " Finis est potissimus in unoquoque.   Et defectus circa finem est pessimus." (S. Thom., 2 2, Q. 47, Art. 1 ad 3.)

chosen the Religious state, and finding within their
reach in the Convent a variety of pleasing occupations, suitable to their own natural tastes, begin to
amuse themselves therewith, without making them
instrumental to. the main purpose of Religion.
They play with their tools like children.[1] Would
that their superiors might remember to instruct them
carefully on this point, at the very commencement
of their career. Should it not be the first lesson of
every Novitiate ?[2] For who does not know the
readiness with which young souls receive their first
impressions of Religious life? How generously have
they left the world behind them ! How willingly
have they parted with their possessions and their
friends, in order to secure the riches of heaven, and
the friendship of God ! How readily they bid adieu
to their Christian home, as they responded to the
call of the Divine Lover to be " all " for Him ! And
did they not look at their prospects of a life of
happiness and usefulness among their fellow-
creatures ? They gave a look—but it was the look
of sacrifice. With what simple confidence did they
pass the threshold of the cloister, and entrust themselves to the hands of the Superior, representing the
authority of God ! O what a precious charge is
that of souls aspiring to perfection ! Who shall say
how ready they are now to receive, and be impressed ? and how lasting will their first impressions

[1] " Do not become children in sense. But in malice be children,
and in sense be perfect." (1 Cor. xiv. 20).

[2] " Woe to the shepherds of Israel, who fed themselves. Should
not the flocks be fed by the shepherd ? " (Ezech. xxxiv. 2.)

be ! [1]   May they find a leading hand!   May they continue day by day to be well impressed!   May no scandal or disedification cause their aspirations to suffer a collapse !   May they begin a series of good, fervent, religious acts, inward and outward, that will develop the corresponding habits !   Who shall say what the fruits of such a life will be ?   But when were the seeds sown, if not in the spring-time of Religious life ?

Let those, therefore, who hold in keeping the souls of others, be mindful of their charge. Surely the entrance to the Religious life must be regarded in the light of a contract.   Souls give themselves to Religion, that Religion may be given to them.   They leave the world, to find God. They forsake the life of the flesh, to attain to that of the spirit.   They renounce human loves, and human lovers, to find the Divine love, and the Divine Lover.   They flee from the ways of imperfection, to enter the way of perfection.   But who are those to receive them, as they enter the house of God ?   Who to take their anxious minds and loving hearts, and direct them straight to the Divine Object of their choice ?   O for the moment of entrance into the Religious life !—for the first day spent within the cloister !—for the first week within the hands of a Religious Superior !   How ready are these souls now to receive, and be im-

---

[1] " 'The form a man first receives, he with difficulty changes. And he who neglects discipline in the early years of his conversion, will hardly give himself to it in after life." (S. Bonav., " Spec. discipl.," prol.)

pressed! and how lasting will their first impressions be!

It is no small matter to live an enclosed life : and souls do not enclose themselves to endure a spiritual starvation.[1] If they withdraw their minds and hearts from worldly knowledge and love, is it not for the very purpose of giving them to the knowledge and love of God and Divine things? How then will they be justly repaid for leaving all things, if they are not fairly introduced by those above them, to the ways of Divine knowledge and love ; and taught and encouraged to walk therein, as the sweetest privilege of their vocation? O for a leading hand, and a few loving souls! And what is it to be a leader? Surely a leader is one who knows the way, who goes the way, and who shows the way. And are not Religious Superiors the leaders of their subjects? And what is the way they have to know, to go, and to show? Assuredly the way of perfection. "The end of the Religious state is the perfection of Charity," says S. Thomas.[2] And does not the common definition of Religious life, as given in handbooks of Theology, familiar

[1] Dame Gertrude More, O.S.B., seems to have experienced something in this way, as appears from the following colloquy in her "Confessions": "O that some who live wholly to Thee, and experience the infinite desire Thou hast to impart Thyself, would come out of their solitude, and declare the *way of* Love to hungry and even starved souls! O how many would then be as tractable lambs, who now live as stiff-necked souls! Verily Thou knowest that before I met with such a servant of Thine, my heart seemed to me, and also to others, to be grown, living yet in Religion, harder as to any good, than a stone." (Dame Gertrude More, "Confessions," 7.)

[2] "Ipsa perfectio Caritatis est finis status religionis." (S. Thom., 2 2, Q 186, A 2.)

to all the Clergy, tell us exactly the same? "The Religious state," say our Divines, " is a stable institution, approved by the Church, wherein the faithful, by means of the three vows, and a certain rule, tend to perfection."[1]   The work of perfection, or. the bringing on the soul towards the perfect love of God and our neighbour, is therefore the business of every Religious.   It is the distinct object of his profession.   As law is the object of the lawyer, as health is the object of the physician, as cultivation is the object of the husbandman, as government is the object of the statesman, so perfection is the object of the Religious.

We come then to Religion with the grand object in view of attaining our perfection by perfect Charity. The way in which the Religious life helps us to accomplish this purpose is clear.   As S. Thomas says, it supplies us with means which remove the impediments to perfect Charity.[2] " All the counsels," says the Holy Doctor, " by which we are invited to perfection, are directed to this, that the soul of man may be withdrawn from the love of earthly things ; and so be enabled the more freely to tend to God, by contemplating Him, loving Him, and doing His will."[3]   We know well how the three vows of

[1] S. Alph. Gury, &c., Theol. moral. "de Statu Relig.".

[2] "Per exercitia quibus tolluntur impedimenta perfectæ Caritatis." (S. Thom., 2 2, Q. 186, A 1 ad 4.)

[3] "Omnia igitur consilia quibus ad perfectionem invitamur, ad hoc pertinent, ut animus hominis ab affectu rerum temporalium avertatur, ut sic liberius mens tendat in Deum, contemplando, amando, et voluntatem Ejus implendo." (S. Thom., Opusc. "de perfectione vitæ Spirit," C 6.)

Religion free us from three distinct impediments to perfect Charity ; and thus become the most effectual instruments of perfection. "Hence," says Denis the Carthusian, "the Holy Fathers and Founders of Religious Orders have prescribed the three vows to all Religious, that by their means souls may be able to attain more easily and quickly to perfect Charity. And, therefore, it is certain that Religious who advance not in the way of Charity have made their vows in vain. Let them frequently consider why they made their vows ; and be careful by means thereof to advance to, and finally gain the perfection of Charity." [1]

First, the vow of poverty aids us powerfully towards this desired end, by releasing us from the embarrassments and distractions of temporal possessions. For it is easy to see that if our Charity is to be perfect, the affections must not cleave to anything apart from God. Now, if we are surrounded by the goods of earth, by numberless commodities that gratify the natural man, and enable him to feed his senses with a variety of engaging and exciting objects, it is evident that it will be ordinarily very difficult in the midst of all this to hold the affections disengaged and free for the exercise of Divine Charity. As the Angelic Doctor says, " It is difficult to have riches, and not be tied by affection to them ".[2] S. Augustine speaks of the love of holding

---

[1] Denis Carthus., "de profess. Monast.," Art. 1.

[2] "Difficile est affectum divitiis possessis non alligari." (S. Thom., " de perfect vitæ Sp., "C 7.)

earthly goods as the poison of Charity.[1]   And their
baneful effects on the soul are forcibly expressed by
S. Bernard, when he says that "the possession of
worldly things burdens us, the loss of them troubles
us, and the love of them defiles us".[2]   Hence S.
Thomas concludes that our souls are borne onwards
the more perfectly to love God, in proportion as they
are withdrawn from the love of earthly things.[3]

Let every Religious, therefore, study to make
Poverty an effectual instrument towards perfect
Charity.   In view of this, he must not only keep
the letter of his vow, by renouncing all temporal
possessions ; he must aim in right earnest at poverty
of spirit, by detaching the *heart* from its affection
to earthly things.   For to what purpose do we leave
the things of earth as to our hands, if we still hold
them in our hearts ?   It is the genuine, inward love
of the heart that God chiefly desires and asks of us.
"My Son, give Me thy heart."[4]   Can we imagine
that any amount of outward renunciation will satisfy
the Divine Lover, without the corresponding inward
renunciation of the heart ?   Love is the preference
of the heart.

"How, then, will you be poor?" asks Blosius.
"Be poor in *things*, but poorer still in *affection* for

---

[1] "Venenum Caritatis est spes adipiscendarum aut retinendarum
temporalium rerum."   (S. Aug., "de div. Quæst. Oct. tr.," Q 36.)

[2] "Possessa onerant, amissa cruciant, amata inquinant."   (S.
Bern., Epist. 103.)

[3] "Sic igitur tanto perfectius animus hominis ad Deum diligendum fertur, quanto magis ab affectu temporalium revocatur."
(S. Thom., ut sup.)

[4] Prov. xxiii. 26.

things—poor in spirit. If you still love things with a selfish love, you are not truly poor ; you cannot yet say, "Behold, we have left all things. Leave all things. Let not your heart cleave to anything. Be free from everything but God."[1] " If we desire to obtain true perfection," said Abbot Paphnutius, " we must hasten our steps, so that having abandoned in body our relations and possessions, we may *renounce also in heart* all things visible, and return no more to what we have once left ; lest we imitate the Israelites, who, after they had tasted the heavenly manna in the desert, sighed again for the goods of Egypt. They were a figure of what happens daily in persons of our profession."

" Hence we should not delay to follow the example of the few who are virtuous ; for ' many are called, but few are chosen '. The mere external renunciation of the world, the mere departure from Egypt, will profit us nothing without the inward *renunciation of the heart*, which is the one that is meritorious and profitable. For what will it profit me to despise the substance of the world, if I do not at the same time eradicate from my heart all depraved affections, and plant in their place Divine Charity ? "[2]

Moreover, let us remember that impressive point of spiritual doctrine handed down to us by Cassian, viz., that the mere renunciation at our conversion of all things is but a small matter, except we persevere

---

[1] Blosius, " Spech. monach., Cap de Mortif.".
[2] Cassian, " Conf.," 3, " Three Renunciations," C 7.

in this disposition, and renounce them every day.
"Parum est semel renuntiasse." " It is little matter
for a Religious to have renounced all things at the
commencement of his conversion, if he does not
persevere in that disposition, and renounce them
every day."[1]   How easily we return to what
we have left!   As the "Imitation" says, "Some
at first offer all, and then return again to what
they left ".[2]   How easily, again, we renounce
great things, and remain attached to small ones!
We leave the world, and our property, and
friends ; and by living under obedience, resign to a
considerable extent the dominion of our own wills.
Thus we renounce many things.   But do we
seriously aim at renouncing *all things?*   Our
Lord's sentence is firm : " Every one of you that
doth not renounce all that he possesseth, cannot be
My disciple ";[3] as though He would tell us that if
we will follow Him in the way of perfection, we
must resolve to give up all things that are less than
Him.   "A soul that loves God despises all things
that are less than Him."[4]   " We must renounce all
perishable creatures, and remove them from our
inmost soul, if we wish to attain to the surpassing
goodness of God."[5]   Who will be found to renounce
all things "ex animo," both without and within ?
Yet such is the price of perfect Charity.   This is the

---

[1] Cassian, "Conf.," 24, " Mortification," C 2.

[2] "Imit.," B iii., C. 37.   [3] S. Luke xiv. 33.   [4] "Imit.," B ii., C 5.

[5] "Omnes creaturas instabiles relinquere, et ex animo removere
oportebit, si præstantissimum Bonum, quod Deus est, suscipere
volemus." (Thauler, Serm. Dom. 5 p. Pasc.)

"goodly pearl," to gain which we must part with all we have.[1] "Leave all, and thou shalt find all."[2] "The price of Charity is yourself;"[3] that is, you must reserve absolutely nothing, but give your very inward life, by the denial of its natural operations, to gain the life that is Divine. "He that shall lose his life shall find it."[4] Leave the natural life, and you shall find the Divine life. But, as the "Imitation" says, "Seldom do we find anyone so spiritual as to be stripped of all things. For who shall be able to find the man that is truly poor in spirit, and divested of all affection to things created? If a man give his whole substance, it is yet nothing; and if he do great penance, it is yet little. And if he attain to all knowledge, he is far off still. And if he have great virtue, there is still much wanting to him; to wit, one thing which is chiefly necessary. And what is that? That having left all things else, he leave also himself, and wholly go out of himself, and retain nothing of self-love. Then may he say with the prophet, 'I am alone and poor'. Yet no one is richer than such a man, none more powerful, none more free, who knows how to leave himself and all things."[5]

It is just because we do not give all to God that we do not receive all from Him. This was what S.

---

[1] "Caritas est pretiosa margarita, sine qua nihil tibi prodest, quodcunque habueris; quam si solam habeas, sufficit tibi." (S. Aug., Tract 5 in Joan. Epis.

[2] "Imit.," B iii., C 32.

[3] "Pretium Caritatis, tu." (S. Aug., Serm. 34 de vers. Ps. cxlix., C 4.)

[4] S. Matt. xvi. 25.   [5] "Imit.," B ii., C 11.

8

Teresa felt. "O Lord," she says, "how is it that when a soul is determined to love Thee, she does not at once attain to perfect Charity? The fault is ours in not immediately enjoying this love with perfection. We are so fond of ourselves, and so slow in giving ourselves entirely to God, that as His Divine Majesty will not allow us to enjoy so great a treasure without paying the price for it, so we should never cease disposing ourselves to receive it. If we did what we could to prevent ourselves clinging to things of earth, and if all our care and conversation were in heaven, I am confident that very speedily this blessing would be given us. But the truth is, we think we give all, whereas we offer only the produce, keeping the land for ourselves. We resolve to be poor, and yet carefully see that we want nothing. We renounce our honour, and yet when it is touched forget that we gave it to God; and so it is in the rest. A strange way this of seeking the love of God: to desire to possess it entirely, and yet to retain our old affections; to wish for spiritual delights, and yet cling to earthly desires. We are seeking things that are incompatible. And therefore, because we do not give ourselves entirely to God, this treasure of perfect love is not given entirely to us."[1]

Let us remember, then, that we cannot have two *alls* in the heart together. We must leave one, to gain the other. "God listeth not to work in thy will, unless He be alone with thee. He is a jealous

---

[1] S. Teresa, "Life by herself," C 11.

lover, and may abide no fellowship. He asketh none other help, but only thyself. He will have thee only look upon Him, and let Him alone." [1] " If thou desirest to have peace and true union, thou must set all the rest aside." [2] " Let all things therefore be forsaken by me, so that, being poor, I may be able in great inward breadth to suffer the want of all things, out of and except God Himself. Most rich the while, and at the same time most poor. Most rich, in seeking nothing ; most poor, in having nothing. And if only I am able to attain to this, namely, to stand in the sight of our Lord, having all things in common with Him, within a pure heart, what is there more that I can desire? If thou shalt abide in Me (saith God within me), thou wilt be able to do without everything, and yet thou shalt want for nothing." [3]

Thus let Poverty work to the full within us. Let it bring us to nudity of spirit, detaching the inmost heart from creatures, natural and spiritual. For " man can only be Divine when he has put off all that is human," says an ancient philosopher.[4] And we know well the teaching of the " Imitation," that we are to rise to God and rest in Him alone, above all His goods and gifts.[5] " Give me, O God, to repose in Thee, above all things created ; above all the gifts that Thou canst give, and above all that is

---

[1] " Divine Cloud," C 2.
[2] " Imit.," B ii., C 5.
[3] " Fiery Soliloquy of the Soul," C 1 and 2.
[4] Hierocles.
[5] " Super omnia bona et dona." (" Imit.," B iii., C 21.)

less than Thee; because my heart cannot rest, till it rest in Thee, and rise above all Thy gifts, and all things created."[1]   In this way Poverty becomes what it ought to be—the instrument of perfection, by aiding the soul most effectually to its end, which is perfect Charity.

It is easy to see how powerful a means the vow of chastity becomes towards the same end.   For as S. Gregory says, "the more a man has of lower delectation, the more is he severed from heavenly love".[2]   The renunciation of external goods by poverty frees us indeed from the immense hindrances that encompass our path, and fetter our steps, on the way of perfection.   But even, when we are delivered from these, there remain within us a number of desires and tendencies that go quickly to the creatures around us, inclining us strongly to give ourselves to the things of the flesh, and withdrawing us from the higher aspirations of the spirit.   Chastity, therefore, becomes the means of severing us from these "carnal desires that war against the soul".[3]   "For," says S. Thomas, "it is evident that carnal love darkens and divides the soul."[4]   And as the energy of love is limited, it follows that, if we sink it downwards

[1] "Omnia dona, omnemque creaturam transcendat." ("Imit.," B iii., C 21.)

[2] "Tanto quisque a superno amore disjungitur, quanto inferius delectatur." (S. Greg., Hom. 30 in Evang.)

[3] 1 Pet. ii. 11.

[4] "Manifestum est quod carnales affectus intentionem mentis diverberant, ejusque faciem obscurant." (S. Thom., Opusc. "de perfectione Vitæ Sp.," C 8.)

to the things of the flesh, we impede it from rising upwards to the pure love of the spirit. So that "Chastity," continues the Angelic Doctor, "has a certain close connection with the work of our perfection : for that the soul of man is hindered from giving itself freely to God, not only by the love of external things, but much more by the impulses of interior passion. Now, among these none so absorbs the reason as the concupiscence of the flesh. And, therefore, the way of continence is more especially requisite for the attaining of perfection." [1]

This holy vow then is meant to detach us from the love of creatures, and the desires of the flesh, in order that our affections and energies may be consecrated wholly to God, in view of attaining to His perfect love. Let us see, therefore, that it serves its purpose to the full, by becoming instrumental to Charity ; leading us onwards by means of external disengagement and purity, to true inner detachment and purity of heart, the immediate disposition to perfect Charity. Let us aim at this in earnest, for it is Charity's own work in the soul. It will doubtless require great courage and fidelity. But for the pearl of great price we must part with all we have. And for the Divine love, and the Divine Lover, it is not too much to sacrifice earthly loves, and earthly lovers. For we are not to live without love, and without a lover ; but we leave human loves for

---

[1] " Habet castitas aliquam idoneitatem ad perfectionem adipiscendam, &c." (S. Thom., Opusc. " de perfect. Vitæ Sp.," C 8.)

Divine love, and human lovers for the Divine Lover.

Mind the word—detachment. "By this," says S. John of the Cross, "is not meant the absence of things, for absence is not detachment, if the desire of them remain. Detachment consists in suppressing desire and avoiding pleasure. It is this that sets the soul free."[1]

Let us have no desire then for fond attachments and idle gratifications, which are "according to the flesh":[2] since the heart must "never waste its affections, even for a moment".[3] "What blindness is this," says S. Francis of Sales, "to play away at hazard the principal power of our souls. Alas! we have not nearly so much love as we stand in need of. I mean to say that we fall infinitely short of having sufficient wherewith to love God. And yet, we lavish it away foolishly on vain and frivolous things, as though we had some to spare. Ah! this great God, who has reserved to Himself the whole love of our souls, will exact a strict account of the deductions we make from it. For, if He make so rigorous an examination into our idle words, how strictly will He not examine into our foolish and pernicious loves."[4] Let us, therefore, be in love with God alone. "My Beloved to me, and I to Him."[5] And let our desires and pleasures be for

---

[1] S. John of the Cross, "Ascent of M. Carm.," B i., C 3.
[2] "Who walk not according to the flesh, but according to the spirit." (Rom. viii. 1.)
[3] S. John of the Cross, "Maxims," 202.
[4] S. Fran. of Sales, "Devout Life," P 3, C 18.
[5] Cant. ii. 16.

things alone that appertain to Him ; looking not
" at the things which are seen, but at the things
which are not seen " :[1] for "whatever is not God, or
of God, love endureth not," says the enlightened
Thauler.[2]

We come now to obedience. " To attain
the perfection of Charity," says the Angelic
Doctor, " it is not only necessary that a man renounce external things, but, in a certain way, he
must leave himself also."[3] Divine Charity draws
the soul from itself to God ; " not suffering a man
to be his own, but His whom he loves ".[4] As S.
Paul said, " I live, not I, but Christ liveth in me ".[5]
The perfection, then, of the soul is to be attained
by renouncing not only external goods, not only
natural attachments, and carnal desires, but by
giving up the inmost life of the natural man to the
dominion of the Spirit of God ; so that faculties,
senses, and members may be occupied and governed
by the Divine in place of the human spirit ; may
move from the Divine principle instead of the
natural one. For " he who is joined to the Lord is
one spirit ".[6] But to attain to this, as S. John of
the Cross says, "he must die to all that lives in his

---

[1] 2 Cor. iv. 18.

[2] " Quidquid aut Deus, aut divinum non est, non patitur amor."
(Thauler, Serm. inf. Oct. Epiph.)

[3] " Non solum necessarium est ad perfectionem Caritatis consequendam, quod homo exteriora abjiciat, sed etiam quod quodammodo
seipsum derelinquat." (S. Thom., Opusc. " de perfec. Vitæ Sp.,"
C 10.)

[4] " Non sinens hominem suiipsius esse, sed ejus quod amatur."
(S. Thom., Opusc. " de perfec. Vitæ Sp.," C 10.)

[5] Gal. ii. 20.   [6] 1 Cor. vi. 17.

soul, whether great or small ".[1]   He must " release
the faculties, empty them, and make them renounce
their natural operations, in order that God may fill
them : seeing that the ability of them cannot compass so great a matter, but rather, unless suppressed, prove a difficulty in the way.   Hence, it
follows of necessity, that if we are to draw near
to God, it must be by denying to the utmost all
that may be denied, &c.   The soul, to attain to
Divine union, must be empty of all that is not
God."[2]

It is not difficult to see how the vow of obedience
helps us most effectually to this change of life and
principle.   For instead of choosing for ourselves,
moving ourselves, determining ourselves, the choice,
movement, and determining power come to us from
the Superior, representing the authority of God.[3]

---

[1] S. John of the Cross, "Ascent of M. Carm.," B i., C 11.

[2] *Ibid.*, B ii., C 8, and B iii., C 1 and 6.

[3] *Note to Superiors.*   It is most desirable that subjects should
understand from the very commencement of their Religious life,
that their obedience is exercised *to God;* according to the very terms
of their profession, " I promise obedience *to God* ".   For to what
purpose would they give up their own wills, to find only another
human will exercised over them ?   They do not leave " all things " to
love and obey a creature, but to love and obey God.   Should not
Superiors always make a point of letting them feel this, by governing them " according to God," not " according to man " ?   As
Superiors represent the authority of God, so they have to represent also the presence and mind of God; as the Apostle says, " Let
this mind be in you, which was also in Christ Jesus " (Philip. ii. 5).
Otherwise the governance of souls easily becomes human instead of
spiritual ; and the unhappy result is, that subjects are found suffer-
g from their superiors ; being impeded by their influence, in a
ritual course, rather than encouraged and furthered in it.   And
ereas when they began they were " ready for anything," and
the principle of Divine love might have been governed at a mere
k, and with a guiding hand would have made happy advances in

Obedience, therefore, secures to us the Divine principle. And oftentimes it will be found to confront the human principle; and thus oblige us to subdue it by subjection and humiliation. All this is the work of our perfection progressing ; for, if the Spirit of God is to gain possession of our souls by perfect Charity, it will be by the gradual inflow of the Divine principle, and the gradual outflow of the natural : the Divine operations supplanting the human. "He must increase, but I must decrease."[1] This is what obedience helps us to. It marks out our duties, decides our offices, appoints our time and place. The natural man would often like one thing, when he must do another. He would wish to rest, when he has to work. He would prefer to live here, when he is sent there. How efficacious a means is this—and that during the course of one's life—for eliminating the natural principle, and substituting the Divine ; provided always, that both on the part

the way of perfection ; now, for lack of light, and not being put into due "relation with God" by those above them, they are found to have deteriorated and degenerated in spirit; and there is a marked decay even in their natural virtues they brought with them from the world. So true it is that in the way of God, not to advance is to go back ; for if we take not the higher principle of love to live and move by, of necessity we fall upon the lower love of self and creatures. By the higher we advance to God, by the lower we recede from Him. Ah ! how important it is to point out these laws of grace to young souls entering on their Religious career ! How gladly will they then be taught and led ! Only let them be taught and led the right way, "according to God," not "according to man," by means of the one light, the one love, the one principle, that contains the "All" for which they leave "all". "Show me, O Lord, Thy ways, and teach me Thy paths." (Ps. xxiv. 4.)

[1] S. John iii. 30.

of superiors and of subjects, all is done in
"relation to God". Superiors govern by the principle of His love, and subjects obey from the same
principle. Superiors govern for God, and according
to Him ; and subjects obey for God, and according
to Him. O, what a paradise on earth would religious life then become! Would it not then be
easy to govern, and sweet to obey?

May the human spirit cease to move so much
among us! May souls be trained from the beginning to look to God alone as their one object,
their chosen friend, their best beloved, and "dear
delight". Then external obediences will find their
meaning. Not for their own sake are they exercised, but to aid in bringing the soul to true interior
obedience to God ; the full and perfect obedience
of the spirit ; whereby the natural man, divested
of his deeds and movements, is in total subjection
to the Spirit of God, living and acting by His
Divine principle, after the example of our Lord ;
"That as He," says S. Thomas, "renounced His
human will, subjecting it to the Divine, so we also
may subject our wills wholly to God, and to those
put over us in the place of God".[1]

In what chosen words does the author of the
"Imitation" tell us to renounce the movement of the
natural man, if we wish to gain the higher guidance
of the Divine Spirit. "Son, leave thyself, and thou

[1] " Ut sicut Ipse, suam voluntatem humanam abnegabat, suppo-
nendo cam Divinæ ; ita et nos, nostram voluntatem Deo totaliter
supponamus, et hominibus qui nobis præponuntur tanquam Dei
ministri." (S. Thom., Opusc. " de perfec. Vitæ Sp.," C 10.)

shalt find Me." [1]   Leave thyself, that is, renounce
the natural operations of thy will, thy intellect, thy
memory, imagination, senses, and members.   Use
not these powers for thine own selfish gratification.
Resign them, leave them free, empty, disengaged,
and "thou shalt find Me".   God will occupy our
faculties, if we leave them to Him : as He says,
" Behold, I stand at the door and knock: if any man
shall hear My voice, and open to Me the door, I will
come in to him ".[2]   The disciple then asks, " Lord,
how often shall I resign myself; and in what things
shall I leave myself ? "   And notice how unreserved
the renunciation is to be : " Always, and at all
times ; as in little, so in great.   I make no excep-
tion ; but will have thee to be found in all things
divested of thyself : otherwise how canst thou be
Mine, and I thine, unless thou be both within and
without, freed from all self-will ?   I have often said
it, and I repeat it now again, forsake thyself, resign
thyself, and thou shalt enjoy great inward peace.
Give all for all, and call for nothing back ; and
thou shalt possess Me."[3]   Hence, we are told in S.
Catherine's Dialogue, that " it is certain that everything depends on the perfect abnegation of self ".[4]
" Because," says S. Teresa, "when for the love of God
we empty our souls of all affection for creatures, that
great God immediately fills them with Himself." [5]
" For when a man perfectly forsakes himself, God

---

[1] " Imit.," B iii., C 37.   [2] Apoc. iii. 20.   [3] " Imit.," B iii., C 37.
[4] S. Cath. Sien., " Dial. on Consum. Perfection ".
[5] S. Teresa, " Int. Castle," M 7, C 2.

enters into him, governing and perfecting all he does."[1]
And "the. more we cast away that which is our own,
the more we shall receive that which is of God".[2]

Besides the three vows, which appertain to Religious life in general, each Order holds certain
particular instrumental means of perfection in the
rules proper to itself. And here, again, we must
be careful to keep the *end* in view. What can be
the meaning of so many minute regulations? and
is it necessary that we should be constantly mindful of observing them, especially when we are told
that they do not bind under sin? Now, remember,
our end is perfection. If this be lost sight of, what
wonder if the means are not felt to be necessary?
If the archer's eye is not upon the target, will he
care to stretch his bow? If the sculptor have no
object, will he want to use his tools? So when a
Religious forgets that his end is perfection, when
he no longer fixes his aim on perfect Charity, his
rules easily become a matter of indifference to him;
because the thought of the end no longer urges him
to use the means to gain it. Why should he care
to lift his instruments, if no work has to be done?
Why be anxious about the means, when the end is
not before him?

But, on the other hand, let perfect Charity be
our end in view, and all the exercises of Religious
life, down to the smallest rule, find their meaning.

---

[1] Thauler, Serm. 4 p. Oct. Epiph.
[2] "Quo diligentius ejecerimus quod nostrum est, eo abundan-
tius recipiemus quod Dei est." (Blosius, "Sacellum animæ," P 1,
S 4.)

Each duty to be done, each work to be attended to, from the order of a Superior to the first sound of the bell,[1] all become means for exercising the soul's love, and so gradually developing the Divine habit within us; thus enabling us to be constantly carrying on the work of our perfection, and so pro- gressing steadily to our end. And the more earnestly we are set upon gaining the end, the more deeply do we value, the more truly do we love, the more faithfully do we use, the means pro- vided for its attainment. We do not coldly enquire if we are bound under sin to keep our rules, and constantly seek excuses for breaking or evading them. Are we so desirous to tarry on the way to heaven? so willing to keep ourselves estranged from the Divine Lover? so fond of living in the darkness of our misery? What man of business is not wiser in his profession than these Religious are in theirs? Does the merchant ask if he is bound to take all the gold that comes in his way? Does the artisan complain that his tools are too numerous, his instruments too fine? How then shall we explain the attitude of those who wear the Religious habit, yet feel the rules of their state as burdensome: find means of explaining them away, or even habitually neglect or break them? What shall we say but that they do not realise the *end* of their profession, or that they are lamentably indifferent about gaining it? How truly has our Lord said that "the children of this world are

---

[1] The bell rings—the Master calls.

wiser in their generation than the children of light ".[1]   " Alas ! " says Blosius, " how many now-a-days deceive themselves, who take the Religious habit, and make their vows, and yet think but little or nothing of their perfection. They cling to creatures, seeking external comforts, pouring themselves out, wandering in their minds, careless in their habits, unguarded in their senses, frivolous in their conversation, and persevering in negligence till the end. I exhort thee, therefore, that thou frequently and seriously consider *why* thou camest to Religion, namely, to die to the world, and to thyself, and live to God alone. Strive then in earnest to do that which you have come to do. Your state requires it of you. You are called a Religious. See that you are truly what you are called. Do the work of a Religious. If you labour not for your perfection, you are no Religious. For although you are not bound to be perfect, you are bound by your profession to strive for your perfection. Thus it is, and not otherwise." [2]

The fact is, that the rules of the Religious life are the chosen instruments in God's hands for forming the Religious man, and aiding him daily and most effectually to his end of perfect Charity. As in the formation of a fair statue, the rough stone must be cut away, by many a hard knock of the hammer, and then be gradually and carefully brought into shape by repeated strokes of the chisel ; and as

---

[1] S. Luke xvi. 8.

[2] Blosius, " Regula tyron. Spir.," Præf., and " Spec. Monach.," C. 1.

the sculptor must then use a number of smaller, finer, and sharper instruments, each contributing to bring on the statue to its perfection; so in Religion, we are engaged in the formation of the Divine Image of perfect Charity in the soul. The departure from the world and the early exercises of Religious life serve for taking off the roughness of our former habits: but the soul as yet is far from its due resemblance to the Divine Model. A great deal of careful work remains to be done before it reaches anything like its proper perfection. The hammer and chisel of mortification and prayer must do their work, cutting away, paring down, subduing, refining, and re-fashioning the habits and dispositions of the natural man, and making the various powers and senses surrender to the influence and movement of the Spirit of God. God Himself is doing the work. But He has His appointed instruments by means of which He works the desirable change within us. These instruments are the very rules we are now considering. "All the external observances of Religious life," says an ancient author, "are ordained to the formation of the interior man. If a Religious understand not this, he is as one having instruments, and not using them."[1] As, then, the statue stands to the sculptor, so let a Religious stand to his Rule. We are undergoing a process of formation in the

---

[1] "Omnia quæ ad Religionis observantiam exterius videmus, ad interioris hominis reformationem ordinata sunt. Quod qui nondum intelligit, ipsa instrumenta portare reputat." (Int. Op. S. Bonav., "de profectu Relig.," L i., C 4.)

hands of God : the formation of perfect Charity, which likens us to Himself. But for the attainment of this, we must resign the thoughts, affections, and imperfect habits of the natural man, in order that the Spirit of God may replace them by His own Divine life, light, love, and movement.[1] But how is this to be accomplished, but by giving up our natural self-moving principle, and yielding ourselves to the Divine principle, being moved to action by it, instead of receiving our impulse from the natural man? Here the rules of Religion are seen to be the instruments of God upon our souls. Their principle is "ab extra" to ourselves; and representing as they do the mind and will of rightly-constituted authority, they represent the Divine mind and will to us ; for "there is no power but from God, and those that are, are ordained of God".[2] This gives us the assurance that whenever we follow our rules in the true spirit, we are moving according to a Divine principle. And if their observance is sometimes trying to the natural man, and puts his desires under restraint, and thwarts his affections, and diminishes his cupidity, and subdues his activity, and hinders the free flow of his tastes and manners, do we not see that all this is the work of our perfection progressing? God's hand is upon us. The roughness of the old man is

---

[1] "We ought unreservedly to allow God to work within us, to do with us what He wills, when He wills, as He wills ; even though He lead us to the shadow of death, and the shades of hell." (Blosius, "Instit. Spirit.," C 7.)

[2] Rom. xiii. 1.

disappearing, and the features of the new man are gradually coming into form. " Lose not, brother, thy confidence of going forward to spiritual things."[1] " It is hard, indeed, to leave off our old customs, and harder to go against our own will. But if thou dost not overcome things that are small and light, how wilt thou overcome greater difficulties ? "[2]

Here is what may be called the " rationale " of the many small rules of Religious life. They are the instrumental means of contradicting the little wills and ways of the natural man, teaching him a ready subjection, a prompt obedience, accustoming him to yield his mind and heart easily and sweetly, to remain quiet and passive in God's hands, until the Divine Will moves him to action. All this is in small things. But each act goes to the formation of the corresponding habit, in preparation for greater things in the future. God is not going to give us the joys of the Divine life of perfect Charity, except on condition of our leaving *all*. The pearl of great price cannot be purchased for less than this. " Forsake all and thou shalt find all."[3] As, then, the life of the Spirit gains possession of the soul, in lieu of the natural life, God demands the utter sacrifice from us. " Everyone of you that doth not renounce all that he possesseth cannot be My disciple."[4] " My son, thou must give all for all, and be nothing of thine own."[5] And the shortcomings of our renunciation the Divine Lover

---

[1] "Imit.," B i., C 22.   [2] "Imit.," B i., C 22.
[3] "Imit.," B iii., C 32.   [4] S. Luke xiv. 33.   [5] "Imit.," B iii., C 27.

Himself supplies. It may be that He will send us bodily sufferings, or mental trials ; or He will sever us from persons and occupations that we like, and place us where we have little to suit our natural tastes ; or He may allow misrepresentation and prejudice to rise against us, so that confidence in us is lost, or our honour and reputation are questioned. "That which is pleasing to others shall go forward. That which thou wouldst have shall not succeed. That which others say shall be hearkened to : what thou sayest shall not be regarded. Others shall be great in the esteem of men ; but of thee no notice shall be taken. To others this or that shall be committed ; but thou shalt be accounted fit for nothing. In these and many such-like things, the faithful servant of the Lord is used to be tried how far he can renounce himself and break himself in all things."[1] If, now, we are to remain faithful to our work, under these sharp instrumental means (by which God is bringing on to its perfection the Divine Image of perfect Charity in the soul), it is clear that we need a readiness in subduing our natural desires and ways, which are so apt to assert themselves in times of trial. But is it not true that such readiness will depend upon the habit of soul we have formed within us? If we have accustomed ourselves to self-control, discipline, and renunciation, and from the repetition of such acts have developed corresponding habits, our acts follow now in accordance

---

[1] "Imit.," B iii., C 49.

with the habits gained.[1] We renounced ourselves in smaller things, and now we are able to overcome in greater. But by what means did we gain this habit of renunciation? Truly by means of the repeated *acts* of self-renunciation involved in keeping our rules. And as we disposed ourselves to be faithful in small things, so now we are found faithful in those that are greater; according to our Lord's words, "He that is faithful in that which is least, is faithful also in that which is greater".[2] Whereas, look at those Religious who make but little account of their Rules; who seek excuses to evade them, and scruple not to break them, under plea of their not binding under sin. Have not their acts been forming their habits? If they are not given to renounce themselves in small things, is it to be expected that they will renounce themselves in greater? Will they not consider that such renunciation does not bind under sin? If they have not formed a disposition to respond faithfully to the clearer manifestations of the Divine Will, can we expect that they will yield themselves readily to the more secret invitations of grace, on which so much of their future spiritual life will depend? We want more *spirit;* more genuine love of God; a love of preference and affection; a sovereign love, worthy of the great and only Good, the infinite Beauty and Loveliness, our Origin and our End. This it is that spurs us on

---

[1] " Per operationes acquiritur habitus: et per habitum acquisitum perfectius aliquis operatur." (S. Thom., 2 2, Q 182, Art. 4 ad 2.)
[2] S. Luke xvi. 10.

to the desire of perfection, as bringing us nearer to
God, assimilating and uniting us to Him ; and the
desire for perfection urges us to use the means for
attaining it.

Would that all Religious would see this as their
own proper work ! As "the proper study of mankind is man," so the proper study of Religious is
perfection. How necessary it is that we should
realise it ! How happy a thing it is to dwell together in unity !—"the unity of the spirit," having
a common aim, viz., our perfection by perfect
Charity, and using all together, day by day, the
instrumental means of Religion in reference to
this end ! How it reminds us of the early Christian life, when "the multitude of believers had
but one heart and one soul ; continuing with
one accord in the temple, praising God, and
having favour with the people ".[1]

What then shall we say of those Religious who
are heedless of their Rules, except that a habit of
mind has not been formed in them of aiming consistently at perfect Charity ? As a consequence, they
are not accustomed to see in their Rules a means
for attaining this end. The result is, that the natural
man, not sufficiently held in check by the higher
principle, of necessity asserts himself, and, by a
repetition of his own imperfect acts, develops the
corresponding habits. Small things lead to greater.
As S. Gregory says, "We begin with little things ;
our defects multiply ; and we come to graver

---

[1] Acts iv. 32 and ii. 46. .

things ".[1] Thus imperfect Religious are developed, instead of perfect. And who shall say what the Church, and souls, have to suffer herefrom? Will imperfect Religious be likely to train others in perfection? And the evil that will follow in time, and the good that will be left undone, who shall estimate? What if the salt lose its savour? and "if the light that is in thee be darkness, the darkness itself how great shall it be?"[2]

Let us strive, therefore, to gain the *spirit* of our profession. The spirit of our profession is to be in love with the Divine Lover, and to let love work within us the work of our perfection. "Do you imagine," says Thauler, "that God has placed you in Religion to be His singing-birds, and praise Him outwardly? Nay, but He would have you to be His friends and lovers. How often shall I tell you not to cleave to appearances? How long shall we be childish? Shall we never realise *why* we have come to Religion? But you will say, 'We are in a holy Order: we pray, we study, we have Religious Society'. Nay, the Order does not make us holy. Neither my habit, nor tonsure, nor my convent, nor Religious Society, all together, can make me holy. But I must have a *holy interior*, an interior detached and free, if I wish to be Religious."[3] "The kingdom of God is within you;" that is, it consists "not in outward things, but in the virtues of the inward

---

[1] A minimis incipitur; et succrescentibus defectibus, ad graviora pervenitur." (S. Greg., "Moral.," L xxxi., C 9.)
[2] S. Matt. vi. 23.   [3] Thauler, ex lib. P. Denifle.

man ".[1] " Religion is not in the habit, but in the
heart."[2] " If you neglect your interior, and care
only for externals, moving your body to the works
of religion, but not your heart, you are no Religious."[3]

" Not that spiritual duties are to lessen our care
of external observances ; no, but that the former
must necessarily be done, and yet the latter not be
omitted. For by how much the spirit is more excellent than the body, by so much are spiritual
exercises more profitable than bodily works."[4]

" These things considered, if God so earnestly
protested to the Jews, saying, ' My soul hateth
your solemnities ; I am weary of bearing them.
The festivals I will not abide ; nor are your sacrifices pleasing to Me. Wash yourselves, and be
clean. Cease to do perversely. Learn to do well ;
and then come, saith the Lord : '[5] " which yet
were observances ordained by God Himself : and
this because those that practised them with all
exactness, rested in the outward actions, and ne-

<hr>

[1] " Regnum Dei intra vos est ; hoc est, non exterius in vesti-
mentis aut alimentis corporis, sed in virtutibus interioris hominis.
Unde Apostolus, Regnum Dei non in sermone, sed in virtute," &c.
(S. Bern., " Apol. ad Gulielm.," C 6.)

[2] " In habitu non est Religio, sed in corde." (S. Bern., " Apol.
ad Gulielm.," C 10.)

[3] Blosius, " Spec. Monach.," C 1.

[4] " Quid ergo, inquis ?   Sic ne illa spiritualia persuades, ut
etiam hæc quæ ex Regula habemus, corporalia, damnes ?   Nequaquam, sed illa oportet agere, et ista non omittere.   Quanto enim
spiritus corpore melior est, tanto spiritualis quam corporalis exer-
citatio fructuosior.   Hinc labor corporis ad modicum valet, pietas
autem ad omnia." (S. Bern., " Apol. ad Gulielm.," C 7.)

[5] Isa. i. 13, 18, and Jerem. vi. 20.

glected inward purity of heart, typified by them : much more will God despise and detest an exact performance of regular observances commanded by man, when the practisers of them do not refer them to the only true end regarded by the Institutor, which was by them to dispose and fit souls to Divine light and grace, internal solitude, and contemplative prayer ; without which a Religious state would be no better than a mere outward occupation or trade. And if only so considered, it is perhaps less perfect than one exercised in the world, by which much good commodity may be derived to others also."[1] " Perfection of soul cannot consist in external observances, which do not penetrate into the interior. They cannot without great danger be rested in, but must needs be directed to a further and nobler end—to wit, the advancement of the spirit."[2]

It seems but too often true, that the externals of Religious life are attended to, to the sad neglect of the interior spirit. Much is thought of building fine churches and convents, and adorning them with all care.[3] Great pains are taken to please people with attractive services and entertainments. Study,

---

[1] F. Baker, " S. Sophia," T i., S 3, C 4.

[2] *Ibid.,* T i., S 3, C 5 and 4.

[3] " Omitto sumptuosas depolitiones, curiosas depictiones ; quæ dum orantium in se detorquent aspectum, impediunt affectum. Patiamur hæc fieri in Ecclesia ; quia etsi noxia sunt vanis et avaris, non tamen simplicibus et devotis. Cæterum, in claustris quid facit illa formosa deformitas ? Tam multa formarum varietas apparet, ut magis libeat totum diem occupare ista mirando, quam in lege Dei meditando." (S. Bern., " Apol. ad Gulielm.," C 12.)

literature, politics, society, recreation, all find a
place. But where are the souls who are all for
God? Where is a true interior man?[1] Shall we
be less fervent in the love of God than others are
in perishable love? Shall we go with ease to the
things of the flesh, and with difficulty to those of
the spirit? "Did not He who made that which is
without, make also that which is within?"[2] Not
that externals are to be undervalued or neglected;
no, but that they are to be used in subservience to
the interior. Not to be rested in; but "directed to
a further and nobler end, to wit, the advancement
of the spirit; by doing them all in a spiritual
manner, for the advancement of our souls in God's
Divine love".[3]

Let all Religious, therefore, be taught at the out-
set to give their thoughts and affections to the
great work, the work of their perfection, by perfect
Charity; and to use all else in reference to it. This
will bring them a certain solidity and stability of
spirit, the result of oneness of principle, which is
the best guarantee for a due attendance and fidelity
to externals. Thus will they blend together, as
they should, the contemplative and the active
elements of Religious life, and so find and enjoy
the true benefit, merit, and sweetness of their
state.

[1] "Ubi forma hæc? In libris cernimus eam, sed non in viris."
(S. Bern.,."Vita S. Malach.," Præf.)

[2] S. Luke xi. 40.

[3] F. Baker, "S. Sophia," T i., S 3, C 4, and S 2, C 9.

BOOK II.

THE LIFE OF CHARITY.

"Ponite corda vestra in virtute ejus."—Ps. xlvii. 14.

CHAPTER I.

THE NATURAL AND THE SPIRITUAL MAN.

PHILOSOPHY teaches us that things which are contrary act and re-act on one another; one remaining passive while the other is active, and contrariwise.[1] The Apostle recognises this in our fallen nature, when he says, "The flesh lusteth against the spirit, and the spirit against the flesh; for these are contrary one to the other".[2] "The spirit and the flesh," says Lewis of Granada, "are as the scales of a balance. When one rises the other necessarily falls."[3]

In the work of our perfection we have to deal with this twofold principle: the "flesh," which signifies the natural life; and the "spirit," which denotes the Divine life. One prompts us to live

---

[1] "Contraria inter se vicissim agunt, patiunturque." (Arist., "de Gen. and Cor.," L i., C 7.)

[2] Gal. v. 17.

[3] Lewis of Gran., Serm. Dom. 4 Adv.

"according to man"; the other, "according to
God": as S. Augustine says, "living according to
the spirit, not according to the flesh, that is, according to God, not according to man".[1]

Both of these, however, cannot rule the soul
together. As one rises, the other falls. "No man
can serve two masters: for either he will hate the
one, and love the other; or he will sustain the one,
and despise the other."[2] Hence we must choose
our principle, and live by it consistently. "Put off
the old man, who is corrupted; and put on the new
man, according to God, created in justice and holiness."[3] The natural man must die, that the
spiritual man may live. "Whosoever will save his
life shall lose it. And he that shall lose his life
shall find it."[4] If we renounce the lower and
natural life, we attain to the higher and Divine
life. "Mortificatus carne, vivificatus spiritu."[5]

Here, doubtless, may be found some explanation
of the rarity of true perfection; which we find, as
S. Bernard says, "in books, but not in men".[6]
Souls are divided between the two principles; instead of choosing the higher one, and abiding by
it consistently, and bringing the natural man into
order under it. It stands to reason that two
opposing energies, each counteracting the other,

---

[1] "Viventes secundum spiritum, non secundum carnem, hoc
est secundum Deum, non secundum hominem." (S. Aug., "de
Civ. Dei, L xiv., C 9.)

[2] S. Matt. vi. 24.   [3] Eph. iv. 22.
[4] S. Matt. xvi. 25.   [5] 1 Pet. iii. 18.

[6] "In libris cernimus eam, sed non in viris." (S. Bern., "Vita
S. Malach.," Præf.)

should both be prevented from acquiring force. If, then, the Divine life of Charity be established within the soul, and yet the natural man reserves to himself the right of moving independently, what is to be expected? The two principles are there, but one gathers force, while the other loses it. And so life passes away, between gaining and losing. The powers of the soul have not been given to the *one project* that needed all their energy. They have been divided on many projects; and so the work of perfection failed.[1]

In order to avoid the misery and the losses of such a failure, let us at once yield ourselves to the Divine Spirit, and beg of Him to undertake the work of subjecting our souls to Himself.[2] Doubtless, God

---

[1] The biographer of Sister Benigne, lay-sister of the Visitation, speaking of her in the beginning of her Religious life, says: " It was evident, on all occasions, that she allowed nothing to nature, and refused nothing to grace." "God taught me" (she says) "that to Infinite love I owe love without limit; Benigne must be governed and led by love, and by love alone. She must do nothing but for God, and the good of her neighbour; for which she shall lavish her life." "I learnt that by love everything is sanctified; and that in all we do God loves only what is done for love. O how much I gain by losing myself, when I lose myself in love!" (Life of Sister Benigne de Gojos, by M. de Leyni, P 3, C 2 and 5.)

[2] Those familiar with the writings of F. Baker and Dame Gertrude More will be able to see in the present and following chapter the corresponding teaching to what they speak of as the "Divine call". It would seem that by taking the higher principle of love, which is "Caritas," as our Divine movement, instinct, or "call," the soul will find a clearer way, and, so to say, a more practical mean, wherein to proceed, in recognising these inward intimations of the good Spirit; remembering the words of the beloved disciple, that "Charity is of God". (1 John iv. 7.) When a soul has given itself to God, to be "all" for Him by love, it is not so difficult to detect the impulse of the Divine love, and so to separate the precious from the vile, and order ourselves accordingly. And thus we may say with Dame Gertrude More, " Regard thy call; that's all in all".

desires to possess us. For what king does not desire
to reign in his own kingdom ? " The kingdom of
God is within you." [1]   But if God is to give Himself
entirely to us, we shall have to give ourselves entirely
to Him (as S. Teresa was so fond of saying), that
He may occupy us, and move us by His Divine
Spirit ; since " He who is joined to the Lord is one
Spirit ".[2]   " My Beloved to me, and I to Him." [3]
Thus the soul will be rather passive than active, as
regards itself ; for when God moves it (by His love),
it is active ; but under Him.   He is the principal
Mover ("Agens principale "), and the soul is His
willing instrument, subject to His movement.   But,
although moved by Him, the soul still freely moves
itself, under Him, and with Him.[4]   Such is the fitting position of a creature in the hands of the
Creator ; and our Lord teaches us as much, by the
example of His Sacred Humanity, in loving subjection to the Divinity ; as where He says : " I do
nothing of Myself".[5]   " I came not to do My own
will." [6]   " The Father who abideth in Me, He doth
the works." [7]

This attitude of the soul before God may be
explained in a measure by the example of a crystal
under the influence of a bright light.   The crystal
represents the soul reflecting the Divine likeness.
The light is God, who shines upon every soul in
grace.   But the crystal is not yet perfectly pure.

---

[1] S. Luke xvii. 21.   [2] 1 Cor. vi. 17.   [3] Cant. ii. 16.

[4] " Per hoc quod movetur ab alio, non excluditur quin moveatur
ex se."   (S. Thom., 1, Q 105, Art. 4 ad 3.)

[5] S. John iv. 28.   [6] S. John vi. 38.   [7] S. John iv. 10.

It has dark spots and shades within it, which signify the venial sins and imperfect habits of the soul. When it brings itself before the Divine light, the soul is not found to be wholly dark, like one in mortal sin. It reflects the beauty of God's grace and love. But the Divine light makes all the more evident the dark misery of its nature. The memory is seen constantly occupied with a number of useless images. The intellect engages itself with a variety of objects merely according to the natural man. The affections are easily drawn aside, and held captive by the allurements of creatures. The senses move to and fro in quest of satisfaction. The bodily members seek for indulgence. The operations of the various powers betoken the yet unformed habits of the spiritual man. Now when the soul, thus darkened with its natural misery, gives itself up to God, offering its entire being, faculties, senses, members, with all its future life to Him, leaving itself and the arrangement of all things utterly in His hands, resigning the natural use of its powers, and seeking to be passive,[1] in order to undergo the purification from its dark misery, the Divine Spirit then takes it as His own, brings it under the influence of His heavenly light and love, and becomes life of its life, and soul of its soul ;[2] and by applying it to a series of actions and sufferings which He Himself prepares, He causes its darkness gradually to

[1] "Magis in Deum homo potest tendere per amorem passive ab Ipso Deo attractus, quam ad hoc eum propria ratio possit ducere." (S. Thom., 1 2, Q 26, Art. 3 ad 4.)

[2] "Tu amor meus, tu vita es animarum, vita vitarum, vita animæ meæ." (S. Aug., "Confess.," L iii., C 6.)

diminish, and infuses in its place the light and fire of His Charity.[1] It may be that the misery of the natural man will often assert itself actively, and want to take back what it had yielded to God, by resuming its own desires and pleasures. If it does so, its darkness intensifies, and overcasts the heavenly light.[2] Then the soul has to stir the fire of its Charity, by short, ardent acts of love and contrition:[3] renouncing itself again, casting its miseries into the sea of God's mercies ; offering itself anew, and resting once more on the strength of the Eternal Truth.[4] Thus it regains what it had lost; and, "although the outward man is corrupted, yet the inward man is renewed day by day ".[5] If, however, on the whole, it keeps faithfully passive, allowing the Divine Spirit to be its active principle,[6] in course of time its dark

[1] " A seipso deficiens, a Spiritu Divino feliciter agatur." (Harphius, "Theol. Myst.," iv. 2, 62.)

[2] " Not only our sins and unmortified habits hinder God from working in us, but the activity of our own minds, and the impressions of the senses, which perpetually traverse and weaken the operations of God." (Rigoleu, " Way of Perf.," C 4.)

[3] " When we fall by frailty or blindness, then our courteous Lord, touching us, stirreth and keepeth us. Then willeth He that we see our wretchedness. But he willeth not that we abide there, nor that we busy ourselves greatly about our accusing, or be too dejected. But He willeth that we hastily attend to Him : for He standeth all alone, waiting till we come, hasting to have us with Him: therefore He willeth that we readily attend to His gracious touching ; more rejoicing in his whole love, than sorrowing in our often fallings. For it is the best homage we may give to Him, to live gladly and merrily for His love." (M. Juliana of Norwich, " Revel.," C 79 and 81.)

[4] " Nec in despiciendis his immoratur et residet ; sed ascendit ad æterna et invisibilia, puro sensu piæ mentis se attolens." (S. Ambr., "de Isaac et Anim.," C 4.)

[5] 2 Cor. iv. 16.

[6] " Qui Spiritu Dei aguntur, ii sunt filii Dei." (Rom. viii. 14.)

misery is gradually dispelled, and finally supplanted by the light and love of the Spirit of God.[1]

This simile of the crystal agrees with the Abbot Theodore's instruction to Cassian, where he says : " The soul of the just man must not be compared to the soft wax, or other yielding substance. No ; it is like the adamant, that, retaining inviolable the bright image and likeness of God, it may not be changed by the accidents of life, but may transform them into its own firmness and stability." [2]

We are reminded, too, of our Lord's words: " Take heed that the light which is in thee be not darkness. If, then, thy whole body be lightsome, having no part of darkness, the whole shall be lightsome, and, as a bright lamp, shall enlighten thee." [3] And S. Paul : " You were heretofore darkness, but now light in the Lord. Walk, then, as children of light ; having no fellowship with the unfruitful works of darkness : but be ye filled with the Holy Spirit." [4]

Thauler also adopts a similar comparison, telling us how free and detached the soul must be, in order to reflect the purity of the Divine light : " Know for certain," says he, " that in whatsoever soul this Divine Sun shines, the same must be utterly free, and stripped of all images ; for, if one only image were to appear in this mirror, the soul

---

[1] Denis the Carthusian tells us that " as often as the soul turns itself with its whole heart to love God, resigning its own will, sub- jecting and conforming itself to the Divine good pleasure, and pouring itself forth to the Majesty of God, so often it obtains the full remission of all its sins." (Denis Carthus., " de profess. Mon- ast.," Appen.)

[2] Cassian, " Conf.," 6, C 12.

[3] S. Luke xi. 35.   [4] Eph. v. 8, 11, 18.

would be hindered by means thereof from the all-pure image of God Himself ".[1]

. This work of subjecting the soul to the Spirit of God, in order that He may purify, illuminate, and unite it with Himself, will doubtless require much time and great constancy of purpose before it is anything like complete. " We shall scarce meet with anyone," says S. John of the Cross, " who in all things is under the direct influence of God ; whose union with Him is so continuous, that his faculties are ever divinely directed. Still there are souls who, for the most part in their operations, are under the Divine guidance ; and these are not souls who move themselves. This is the sense of S. Paul, when he says that ' the sons of God are led by the Spirit of God '." [2] Indeed if we hope to succeed in such a work, we must, without doubt, make it the one project of our life ; as S. Francis of Sales says, " Those who aspire to heavenly love withdraw their thoughts from worldly things, and reduce all their projects to one, that of loving God only ".[3]

But let it be constantly borne in mind that the love of God is both affective and effective, or a habit disposed to its acts : so that in the life of Charity, while our principle is unalterably *one*, it moves us to action "in a thousand different ways," as S. Teresa says.[4] For as in the natural life the one

---

[1] Thauler, Serm. Dom. 4 p. Oct. Epiph.

[2] S. John of the Cross, " Ascent of M. Carm.," B iii., C 1.

[3] S. Fran. of Sales, " Love of God," B xii., C 3.

[4] " It is the property of love to be always working in a thousand different ways." (S. Teresa, " Int. Castle," M 6, C 9.)

soul moves the many powers and members to their respective functions, so in spiritual life the one love moves the various virtues to their manifold operations. Oneness of principle, therefore, in spiritual life, is not opposed to a life of activity. Rather, love itself is the strongest of moving powers ; and "spurs us on to do great things ".[1] If there be "one spirit," there are "diversities of operations".[2] Indeed the oneness of love induces a consistent activity, according to the words of Wisdom ; "being one, she can do all things ".[3] Whereas souls that divide themselves between the two principles, as though they would make a compromise between the old and the new man, soon lapse into inconstancy and instability—the results of inconsistency, leading to double-mindedness and double-heartedness. Hence, says S. James, "a double-minded man is inconstant in all his ways ".[4] And Ecclesiasticus warns us, " Come not to the Lord with a double heart ".[5] However flexible, therefore, discretion may bid us be in a thousand matters of detail, in principles it demands of us an uncompromising inflexibility. The *one* work in hand requires us to keep unalterably to *one* principle of action. The many details of daily life have to be set " in order to the end,"[6] as best they may, by the light of the one principle that alone answers to the end.[7] Hence the principle never changes, as the end never changes.[8] But

[1] " Imit.," B iii., C 5.   [2] 1 Cor. xii. 4.   [3] Wisd. vii. 27.
[4] S. James i. 8.   [5] Ecclus. i. 36.   [6] " In ordine ad finem."
[7] " Secundum finem dirigendus est cursus."
[8] " Principium respondet fini."

10

details of operation, which are means to the end, change according to the requirements of true discretion.

The very nature of our work demands this exclusiveness. For Charity is an absorbing and transforming principle, by which the Spirit of God possesses and governs the whole man with his entire life. "The fiery dart of love" (says Richard of S. Victor) "penetrates the mind, and transfuses the affections. Receding, and with greater force returning, it gradually leavens the soul, and empties its powers, till the whole spirit is subdued to its influence, and none but the one love is remembered or relished."[1]

But this undoubtedly calls for a full oblation of ourselves to God. For to allow the natural man to retain his ownership, and be his own mover, even in one thing, independently of the Divine Spirit, would be to retain so much darkness in the crystal, and put so much hindrance to the light of God. "What fellowship hath light with darkness?"[2] Hence S. Teresa was so fond of telling her daughters that "God does not give Himself entirely to us, till we give ourselves entirely to Him".[3] Which agrees with the repeated teaching of the

---

[1] ' Igneus ille amoris aculeus mentem penetrat, affectumque transverberat: sæpe recedens, semperque major rediens, paulatim animur emollit, viresque exhaurit ; donec plene animum sibi subigat, j que sui memoria totum occupat. Tunc nihil omnino satisface ꞏ praeter unum ; nihil sapere nisi propter unum ; nil dulcescit, fiil sapit, nisi hoc uno condiatur." (Rich. a S. Vict., " de quat. grad. viol. Car.".)

[2] 2 Cor. vi. 14.   [3] S. Teresa, " Way of Perf.," C 28.

" Imitation ": " Thou must give all for all, and be nothing of thine own ". " Leave thyself, and thou shalt find Me."[1]

We are therefore to make a full offering of ourselves to God for time and eternity. And what more appropriate time for making and renewing this oblation than the time of Holy Mass, when our Lord is making the great oblation of Himself, for love of God and men? "As I willingly offered Myself to God on the Cross, so that nothing remained in Me that was not turned into a sacrifice, so must thou willingly offer thyself to Me daily in the Mass, for a pure and holy oblation, together with all thy powers and affections. As it would not suffice thee, if thou hadst all things but Me, so neither can it please Me, whatever thou givest, as long as thou offerest not thyself. Give thy whole self for God, and thy offering will be accepted."[2] Let us, therefore, offer all, soul and body, faculties, senses, and members ; life, death, actions, sufferings, operations, intentions : all for the love of God, alone and full ; "Caritas, sola et plena"; as being both the principle and the end of our life and actions :[3] since Charity is union with God, by which He loves us, and we love Him ; He lives and works in us, and we in

---

[1] " Imit.," B iii., C 27 and 37.

[2] " Imit.," B iv., C 8.

[3] " Dicendum quod Caritas ad omnes alias virtutes comparatur et ut motor, et ut finis. Ut motor, secundum quod facit eas operari propter finem suum. Similiter etiam finis; quia actus omnium aliarum virtutum ordinantur ad actum caritatis, sicut ad finem ; et propter hoc dicitur Caritas finis praecepti." (S. Thom., 3 Sent., Dist. 27, Q 2, Art. 4, q 3.)

Him [1]—all in union with our Lord in His Divine life on earth, and in the Blessed Sacrament; in union with Mary Immaculate, with the Angels and Saints of heaven, the holy souls in Purgatory, and the faithful upon earth—all for God's own great ends, and the vast needs of souls: leaving the entire arrangement of all things in His hands, thus making over to Him all we have and hold; and coming ourselves to that poverty of spirit, which brings the kingdom of heaven into our souls.[2] "Most rich the while, and at the same time most poor. Most rich in seeking nothing; most poor in having nothing."[3]

After making the oblation, and renewing it daily in the Mass, our endeavour must be to keep all in God's hands; living and acting under the Divine influence and movement:[4] finding in the actions and sufferings of daily life the appointed means of exercising Divine Charity, remaining ourselves through all receptive and instrumental in God's hands;[5] receptive of Divine light and love; instrumental in acting under God.[6] Thus we live

---

[1] " He that abideth in Charity abideth in God, and God in Him." (1 John iv. 16.)

[2] " Blessed are the poor in spirit, for theirs is the kingdom of heaven." (S. Matt. v.)

[3] " Fiery Soliloquy of the Soul," C 1.

[4] " His qui moventur per instinctum divinum, non expedit consiliari secundum rationem humanam, sed quod sequantur interiorem instinctum; quia moventur a meliori principio, quam sit ratio humana." (S. Thom., 1 2, Q 68, Art. 1.)

[5] " Homo sic movetur a Deo ut instrumentum, quod tamen non excluditur quin moveat seipsum per liberum arbitrium." (S. Thom., 1 2, Q 21, Art. 4 ad 2.)

[6] " A soul that hath the *gift of love* seeth that God is all, and doth all. Therefore she asketh nought but love, that God would

in subjection, willing and loving, to the First Cause, renouncing the life of the natural man, lest by our dark misery we impede and obscure the shinings of the Divine light.[1] Not that this subjection means inactivity, but acting under God, from a Divine instead of a human principle; as S. Thomas explains by saying that, "when the principal agent is perfect, and the instrument not defective, the action of the instrument is always in accordance with the principal agent".[2] Now, in the spiritual life, God is the principal Agent; and the faculties of the soul are as the instruments in His hands, moving under Him freely and lovingly.[3] When they are purified from their miseries, they will offer no resistance to the Divine Spirit. Unpurified, they place constant impediments to God's work within us. This is why they must yield their natural activity, in order to live by the Divine

touch her with His gracious presence. And so cometh the gift of love, which is God, into a soul. And the more a soul noughteth itself, the nearer it approacheth to this blessed gift; for then is love master, and worketh in the soul, and maketh it forget itself, to see only how love worketh. Then is the soul more suffering than doing [*i.e.*, more passive than active], and that is pure love." (Hilton, "Scale of Perfection," P 3, C 5.)

[1] "Inter omnia bona hominis, Deus maxime acceptat bonum humanæ animæ ut hoc sibi in sacrificium offeratur." (S. Thóm., 2 2, Q 182, Art. 2 ad 3.)

[2] "Quando agens principale est perfectum, et non est aliquis defectus in instrumento, nulla actio procedit ab instrumento, nisi secundum dispositionem principalis agentis." (S. Thom., 4 Sent., D 44, Q 2, A 1, q 1 ad 3.)

[3] "Homo sic movetur a Deo ut instrumentum, quod tamen non excluditur quin moveat seipsum per liberum arbitrium." (S. Thom., 1 2, Q 21, Art. 4 ad 2.)

principle.[1] "Except the grain of wheat, falling into
the ground, die, itself remaineth alone, but if it die,
it bringeth forth much fruit."[2]   And "he who has
the True Good needs nothing more".[3]   It is not
therefore too hard to give our natural life, to
gain a Divine life: as it would not be hard for a
man to exchange a house of earth for a palace of
gold. Who would not hasten to make the exchange?

In thus resigning ourselves to the dominion of the
Spirit of God, we shall have to accept the trials that

[1] This dying to ourselves is the denying ourselves, which our
Lord prescribes to all wishing to follow Him in the perfect way :
" If any man will come after Me, let him deny himself ". (S. Luke
ix. 23.) It consists in willingly renouncing the natural use of our
faculties and powers, and resigning them into God's hands, so as
to move by the principle of His love, instead of by that of self-love.
The Divine love of Charity thus becomes the active principle of the
soul in the will ; the other powers remaining instrumental and
passive in God's hands ; that is, not moving independently for their
own pleasure, but living in silence and sweet service ; receiving in
the silence of prayer the Divine impressions ; ready, when Charity
calls, to serve the Divine behests.   Thus by renouncing our natural
operations, we become the recipients of Divine ones.   By leaving
all, we find all.   This substitution of the new life for the old one
is explained by S. John of the Cross as follows: "The intellect,
which previous to its union with God understood but dimly, by
means of its natural light, is now under the influence of another
principle, and of a higher illumination of God.   The will, which
previously loved but weakly, is now changed into the life of Divine
love; for now it loves deeply with the affections of Divine love,
moved by the Holy Ghost, in whom it now lives.   The memory,
which once saw nothing but the forms and figures of created things,
is now changed, and keeps in mind the ' Eternal years '.   Finally,
all the motions and acts of the soul, proceeding from the principle
of its natural life, are now changed into movements Divine.   For
the soul, as the true child of God, is moved by the Spirit of God ;
as it is written, ' Whosoever are led by the Spirit of God, they are
the sons of God ' (Rom. viii. 14)."   (S. John of the Cross, " Living Flame of Love," St. 2, li. 5.)

[2] S. John xii. 24.

[3] " Qui habet Verum Bonum, despuit cætera, nec requirit." (S.
Ambr., " de Jacob et b. vita," L i., C 7.)

accompany the period of transition. It is to be
expected, when we begin to relinquish our natural
habits and modes of action, and, on the other hand,
have not yet attained to the habits and operations
of the spiritual man, that we should betray a certain
weakness in mind and heart, which would be likely
to affect our outward bearing, and be remarked un-
favourably by others.[1]

This is but the natural result of unforming the
old man, and not having yet formed the new man.
Let us remember, however, the words of the
Apostle : " If any man seem to be wise in this
world, let him become a fool, that he may be wise".[2]
"For the foolishness of God is wiser than men; and
the weakness of God is stronger than men."[3]   Let
us be willing to become fools, in order to attain to
true wisdom.[4]   Let us become weak, in order to
become strong.   " Power is made perfect in infirmity."[5]   As time advances, the spiritual man
will strengthen on the weakness of the natural man.
" For which cause we faint not : for though our
outward man is corrupted, yet the inward man is
renewed day by day."[6]   We have to see things in
the light of God ; to live, love, judge, and act
according to Him.   In order to attain to this, we forego the loves and the ways of the natural man.   Thus
our old nature is made weak and foolish, because its
former aliment is withdrawn from it; and we become

---

[1] " Spiritualis a nemine judicatur." (1 Cor. ii. 15.)
[2] 1 Cor. iii. 18.   [3] 1 Cor. i. 25.
[4] " Nos stulti propter Christum." (1 Cor. iv. 10.)
[5] 2 Cor. xii. 9.   [6] 2 Cor. iv. 16.

(as S. Gregory says of S. Benedict) "knowingly unknowing, and wisely ignorant".[1] "We who live are always delivered unto death." But why? "That the life of Jesus may be manifest in our mortal flesh."[2] We lose the natural life to gain the Divine life. We leave that which is "according to man," to attain to that which is "according to God".

"All this doth the love of God" (says Walter Hilton) "when He giveth Himself to us. And we do right nought but suffer Him, and assent to Him. For that is the most that we do, to assent willingly to His gracious working in us. And this love cleanseth us from sins, and stirreth us to forsake fleshly loves and fears, and worketh in our souls all that is good, and all that belongeth to goodness; and it maketh us to love God. Afterwards this love doth more. For He openeth the eye of the soul, and showeth to the soul the sight of God wonderfully, as well as the soul can suffer it, little by little; and by that sight He ravisheth all the affections of the soul to Himself. And then beginneth the soul to know Him spiritually, and to love Him burningly. Then seeth the soul somewhat of the nature of the Divinity; how that He is All, and that He worketh all, and that all good deeds and good thoughts are only of Him, and He alone shall have the worship and thanks for them, and none but Him. This love reformeth the soul in feeling, bringing into it the perfection of all virtues,

---

[1] "Scienter nescius, et sapienter indoctus." (S. Greg., "Dialog.," L ii., C 1.)

[2] 2 Cor. iv. 11.

and turning them into love and liking. It draweth the soul from vain beholding to contemplation of the secrets of God, from sensuality to spirituality, and from earthly feeling to heavenly savour."[1]

But the price of this perfect love is undoubtedly the sacrifice of self; as S. Augustine says: "The price of Charity is yourself".[2] "We must die that God may live in us," says S. Francis of Sales.[3] Is not this thought the keynote of the "Imitation," which the author sounds again and again? "My son, thou must give all for all, and be nothing of thine own." "Leave thyself and thou shalt find Me."[4] What a depth of meaning is contained in these sentences which we read and re-read so familiarly! Do we ever think of striving to make them realities in our own souls? For what is involved in giving "all for all"? Let us learn from the enlightened Thauler. "If a man wish," says he, "to be perfectly one with God, his interior powers must be brought, as it were, to silence and death; the will renouncing its desires, the intellect its knowledge, and the memory and other powers their various objects. Such a death, extinguishing man's natural light, is hard indeed. But life here is found more abundantly in death, and 'light shineth in darkness'."[5]

---

[1] Hilton, "Scale of Perf.," P 3, C 4.

[2] "Pretium Caritatis, tu." (S. Aug., Serm. 34 de vers. Ps. cxlix., C 4.)

[3] S. Fran. of Sales, "Spir. Conferences," Conf. 20, "Intention in ent. Relig.".

[4] "Imit.," B iii., C 27 and 37.

[5] Thauler, Serm. 2 in feriis Pasch. Thauler here speaks what may be called his one great thought, viz., that the natural man

Let us remember that neither the senses, nor the imagination, nor the memory, nor the intellect, can reach to God. Rather they lead us from Him, apart from the governance of His love. Love alone attains to God. Therefore live in love, and die to all the rest.[1] " To give all for love is a most sweet

must stay his natural activity to enable the soul to be actuated in its faculties by a Divine life, informed by the Spirit of God. This central point of mystical science is dwelt on by S. John of the Cross, Blosius, Harphius, and others; and before them by S. Augustine, S. Gregory, S. Bernard, S. Thomas, &c. It is but a drawing out of the general principle of self-denial given us by our Divine Lord in the Gospel. The Canticle expresses it in the words: " I sleep; and my heart watches " (Cant. v. 2), *i.e.* my natural powers yield their activity, but my love is engaged with God. This applies—(1) to the time of internal prayer; (2) to the soul's mode of action out of prayer.

In prayer, the soul desiring nought but union with the Beloved, willingly withdraws its faculties from creatures and their images. As S. Gregory says, " Contemplative souls turn inwards to themselves; nor do they draw with them the shadows of corporal things, but rising to the Divine light, they shut their eyes to the images of earth ". (S. Greg., " Moral.," L vi., C 17.) In this prayer, however, love is left in activity, as being the bond of the Divine union, exercising itself both actively (in aspirations to God), and passively (in communications from Him). Out of the time of prayer, perfect souls may still be said to renounce their natural operations, in this sense, that in their various actions they move from the Divine principle, viz., God's love, and are " led by the Spirit of God " (Rom. viii. 14), the natural faculties still moving freely under the Divine Spirit. To move in a natural way, independently of the Divine love, would be regarded by them as an infidelity to love, and a " returning to what they had left ". (" Imit.," B iii., C 37.) Souls, however, still unpurified, yet on the way to perfection, are but partially under the influence of Charity. Their natural powers, therefore, often assert themselves, and mingle their operations with those of the Divine Spirit. Hence in time of prayer they labour to develop the habit of love, and to renounce their natural activity, in view of attaining ultimately to contemplation and union.

[1] " Die," *i.e.*, renounce natural operations, unless they proceed from the higher love. Hence S. Augustine, " Moriar, ne moriar " (" Confess.," Lib. i., C 5), and S. Paul, " I die daily " (1 Cor. xv. 31).

bargain."[1] It is not a dead sacrifice, but a happy
exchange. It is losing a little, to gain much. We
leave the regions of darkness and misery for the
realms of light and joy.[2] The Divine Spirit
gradually supplants the natural. As darkness
yields, the light increases. The old life weakens,
and the new one gathers strength. "If any be in
Christ a new creature, the old things are passed
away, behold all things are made new."[3] As the
natural man is subdued, he is more easily controlled;
and as the spiritual man strengthens, he acquires a
readier command over the various powers and
senses. "Dominus mortificat, et vivificat."[4] The
Spirit of God, living in the soul, mortifies and
vivifies it ; slaying its fleshly loves by mortification,
then animating it with the higher love of Divine
Charity. The continued purgation under the Spirit
of God brings a constant access of light and love.
The weakness experienced during the period of
transition, when mind and heart were enfeebled by
the passing trial ; when the affections, unlinked from
natural ties, yet not wholly given to God, were so
apt to be caught up by creatures ; all this is being
now gradually expelled as mists before the rising
sun. "Arise, shine, for thy light, is come, and the
glory of the Lord is risen upon thee."[5] "O Love,
let me live in thee, and die to all created things.
O Love, Love, live, reign, and wholly possess my

---

[1] D. Gertrude More, "Confess.," 28.

[2] "De tenebris vos vocavit in admirabile lumen suum." (1 Pet.
ii. 9.)

[3] 2 Cor. v. 17.   [4] 1 Kings ii. 6.   [5] Isa. lx. 1.

soul! O when shall my soul, having transcended
itself and all created things, be firmly united to
Thee, the Beloved of my heart? And the more we
love, the more able we are to love, and the more
easy it is to love. And love making all pains,
difficulties, and afflictions sweet, what is there left
to suffer? Verily, it is strange that we, who have
dedicated our souls wholly to Thee, should love,
seek, or desire anything but Thee. Where, my
Lord, have Thy spouses in these days placed their
hearts? Where, I say, seeing that they seek and
desire so much to have the favour of creatures, and
to draw their hearts from Thee unto themselves?
Oh, who would seek anything but God, seeing that
He is not more willing to give us anything than
Himself? All we can give Him is nothing, unless
we entirely give Him ourselves. Yet, if we do this,
so much doth His Divine Majesty esteem this gift,
that for it He will give us Himself. All His gifts
and graces are a means to prepare us for this end,
if we use them rightly and according to the just
will of God. O Lord, if we cannot serve Thee in
great matters, let us have no hearts but to love
Thee. Oh, how happy are those souls who love
nothing but Thee! Do we not deserve to live in
perplexity and misery, if we do not leave all other
things, to set our whole love upon Thee?"[1]

[1] Dame Gertrude More, "Confessions," 15, 16, 44, 51, &c.

CHAPTER II.

THE PRINCIPLE OF THE SPIRITUAL MAN.

"GOD is the life of the soul," says S. Augustine, "as the soul is the life of the body: and the body lives rightly according to the soul, when the soul lives according to God."[1] From which words we gather that as the soul is the moving principle of the natural man, so the Spirit of God is the moving principle of the spiritual man.

The soul of man is God's own domain; and therefore, our Lord says, "the kingdom of God is within you".[2] But the Divine Spirit, in governing the soul, moves it according to its nature, that is, by means of its love: *mediante habitu Caritatis.* S. Thomas enters carefully into the explanation of this, which is a point of much importance to those pursuing an interior life. He says that the Spirit of God so moves the soul as to allow it to be at the same time its own free mover under Him.

---

[1] "Sicut vita corporis anima, sic vita animæ Deus. Tunc autem recte vivit caro secundum animam, si anima vivit secundum Deum." (S. Aug., Enar. in Ps. lxx., Serm. 2, and Serm. 156 de verb. Apost.)

[2] S. Luke xvii. 21.

And in order hereto, a habit is created within it, from which the soul itself acts freely, easily, and sweetly ; the Divine Spirit at the same time using this habit, and moving the soul by means hereof. This created habit is Divine Charity, which is God's own virtue ; for "God is Charity".[1] In its very nature, this Charity is a bond of union and a principle of action :[2] so that both God and the soul by means of it live and act together[3] Thus the Spirit of God "reaches from end to end mightily, and ordereth all things sweetly".[4]

As, therefore, in the natural life, the soul moves the various powers which it holds in itself and in the body, by the active principle called the will, so in the life of grace the Spirit of God moves the soul to the various virtues of the spiritual man, by the active principle called Charity. As nature sees by the intelligence, and loves and moves by the will, so grace sees God by faith, and loves and serves Him by Charity. The soul moves the natural man to act by the power of will ; and God

[1] 1 John iv. 16.

[2] " Amor est virtus unitiva : " et " virtus est habitus operativus ".

[3] The words of S. Thomas on this are as follows: " Oportet quod si voluntas moveatur a Spiritu Sancto ad diligendum, etiam ipsa sit efficiens hunc actum. Unde Deus singulis rebus indidit formas, per quas inclinantur ad fines sibi præstitutas a Deo ; et secundum hoc ' disponit omnia suaviter '. Unde maxime necesse est quod ad actum Caritatis in nobis existat aliqua habitualis forma, superaddita potentiæ naturali, inclinans ipsam ad Caritatis actum, et faciens eam prompte et delectabiliter operari. Oportet ergo ponere Caritatem esse habitum creatum in anima, quæ quidem manat ab amore qui est Spiritus Sanctus." (S. Thom., 2 2, Q 23, Art. 2, and 1 Sent., D 27, Q 1, A 1.

[4] Wisd. viii. 1.

moves the spiritual man to act by the power of the love of Charity.[1]   The Divine Spirit, therefore, as the Increated Charity, lives and works within the soul, by means of His own created Charity ;[2] making thus the virtue of Charity the bond of our union with God, and the proximate principle of our spiritual life, action, and merit.[3]

This Divine principle, from being at first as a germ within us, energises, strengthens, and expands, by the nourishment and exercise it receives in Prayer, Mortification, and the works of life, until its virtue passes to the powers of the soul, and even the senses and members of the body,[4] leavening them all with its Divine influence, governing their movements, and ordering and regulating their operations; thus bringing to our nature its full measure of accidental perfection.[5]

[1] " Quid in nobis Spiritus operatur ? Profecto monet, docet, et movet.   Monet memoriam, docet rationem, movet voluntatem." (S. Bern., Serm. 1 die Pent.)

[2] " Unde Caritas non potest naturaliter nobis inesse, neque per vires naturales esse acquisita, sed per infusionem Spiritus Sancti, qui est Amor Patris et Filii, cujus participatio in nobis est ipsa Caritas creata." (S. Thom., 2 2, Q 24, Art. 2.)

[3] " Caritas est sicut principium proximum.   Et actus aliarum virtutum non sunt meritorii, nisi inquantum sunt informati Caritate. Caritas est principium omnium bonorum operum quæ in finem ultimum ordinari possunt." (S. Thom., 3 Sent., Dist. 30, Q 1, Art. 5 ad 1 & 2, & in C, & 1 2, C 65, Art. 3.)

[4] " Sicut virtus membra corporis ordinat ad actus exteriores debitos, ita ordinat appetitum sensitivum ad motus proprios.   Sic bona operatio hominis est cum passione, sicut et cum corporis ministerio." (S. Thom., 1 2, Q 59, A 5 in C, & ad 3.)

[5] " Quia Caritas habet pro objecto ultimum finem humanæ vitæ, scilicet beatitudinem æternam, ideo extendit se ad actus totius humanæ vitæ, per modum imperii.   Et Ille cujus scientiæ et potestati omnia subsunt, sua motione ab omni stultitia, et ignorantia, et

It must be remembered, however, that while
Charity is the active principle of grace, Cupidity or
self-love is a corresponding power in nature,[1]
making an antagonistic principle with us; so that,
if Charity is to develop from a weak habit into a
strong ruling power and presiding influence, it
must labour to dispossess the master-faculty, viz.,
the will, of its cupidity, in order itself to gain command of the soul.   This shows us how important
it is to begin in early years the formation of our
spiritual habits.   Habits of some sort *will* be forming; so that if Charity does not secure them,
Cupidity necessarily will.   We know that the
repetition of acts makes a habit.   But our will
moves us to act.   And love moves the will.   Now,
the two ruling loves are Charity and Cupidity;
Divine love and self-love.   One belongs to Grace,
the other to Nature.   Charity is the moving principle of the spiritual man, and Cupidity that of
the natural man.   Charity loves God above all,
and everything else in reference to Him, and
according to Him.   Cupidity loves itself and
creatures, without reference to God, and according
to itself.   One is love rightly ordered; the other,
love wrongly ordered.[2]   And as "the flesh lusteth

hebetudine, et duritia, et timore, et cæteris hujusmodi, nos tutos
reddit.   Et dona Spiritus Sancti faciunt nos bene sequentes instinctum Ipsius."   (S. Thom., 2 2, Q 23, Art. 4 ad 2, & 1 2,
Q 68, Art. 2 ad 3.)

[1] "Cupiditas est amor pravus, cum propter se amatur creatura."
(S. Aug., Enar. in Ps. ix. 15, and "de Trinit.," L ix., C 8.)

[2] "Caritas est amor rectus.   Cupiditas amor pravus."   (S.
Aug.; Enar. in Ps. ix. 15.)

against the spirit, and the spirit against the flesh,"[1] so Charity wars against Cupidity, and Cupidity against Charity ; so that the strength of one is the weakness of the other : " nutrimentum Caritatis est imminutio Cupiditatis ".[2]

When, then, we resign the natural life, and offer ourselves to God, to be possessed and ruled by His Spirit, Charity, as the Divine virtue, takes her seat as the queen of the soul,[3] and assumes the command of the will, and through the will, of the other powers.[4] Then by ordering the various operations, she gets the formation of habits into her own hands, and is thus able to unform the natural and form the spiritual man. The old man, however, does not die so easily, and the twofold life and love remain long in conflict within us, each being an active principle to the soul. " Caritas radix bonorum, et Cupiditas radix malorum."[5]

Seeing, therefore, that the repetition of acts forms the habit, and that, when the habit is formed, we act with readiness, ease, and pleasure, we must see how vastly important it is to abstain consistently from acts proceeding from the principle of Cupidity ; this being the root of evil in the soul ;

---

[1] Gal. v. 17.

[2] S. Aug., " de divers Quæst. oct. trib.," Q 36.

[3] " Ponam in te thronum Meum."

[4] " Amor omnia sibi subjicit ; omnia suis profectibus servire cogit. O fortis virtus, Caritas, quæ neminem spolians, omnia rapis ! Omnia facis tua, et nemini aufers sua." (Rich. a S. Vict., " de grad. Carit.," 1.)

[5] S. Aug., " de Gratia Christi," L i. 21.

and every such act serving as a nourishment thereto. On the other hand, we must see how it concerns us to act faithfully from the higher principle, viz., that of Charity, as being the source of our spiritual good, and God's own movement within us,[1] so making our actions a constant nourishment to our love. By this means the repetition of acts and the corresponding formation of habit is given to Charity, and thus the weight of our love is on the right side. "We take the weight of our love" (says S. Augustine) "from Cupidity to Charity, till the former is consumed, and the latter made perfect."[2]

Doubtless, in order thus to withdraw ourselves from the Cupidity of nature, and give the full force of our love to Charity, we shall have to make this work the one project of our life; in such a way, that of all we do, day by day, we may be able to say, "Caritas est hic," Charity is here; *i.e.*, God's

---

[1] "In ordine ad finem ultimum supernaturalem, non sufficit ipsa motio rationis, nisi desuper adsit instinctus et motio Spiritus Sancti; secundum illud, ' Qui Spiritu Dei aguntur, ii sunt filii Dei '. (Rom. viii. 14.) Et ideo ad illum finem consequendum, necessarium est homini habere donum Spiritus Sancti, per quem bene sequatur instinctum divinum." (S. Thom., 1 2, Q 68, Art. 2.) " By these terms " (says F. Baker) " are intended one and the same thing— Divine call, Divine tract, voice, admonition, motion, instinct ; by which the speakings and deeds of God in and upon a soul are expressed." (F. Baker, " Life of D. Gertrude More," in MS.) From which we see how the teaching of F. Baker and Gertrude More, on the " Divine call," agrees with that of S. Thomas above, who speaks of it as "instinctus et motio Spiritus Sancti," and " instinctum divinum ".   And all these terms correspond to " Caritas," as being the inward habit or principle by which God governs and moves the soul.

[2] " Jubemur itaque detrahere de pondere Cupiditatis, quod accedat ad pondus Caritatis, donec illud consumatur, hoc perficitur." (S. Aug., " Epist. ad Hilar.," 9.)

love is my principle of action, the Divine Spirit
moves me hereby; and however varied the works
of life may be, they are the many operations of the
one Charity, proceeding from the self-same Spirit,[1]
the principle of Cupidity being promptly suppressed as soon as it asserts itself. Much, indeed,
is implied here, which may be expressed in the
following manner: Caritas sola, dulce principium activum; reliqua omnia in silentio et servitio.
Charity alone, sweet moving principle. All the
rest in silence and service.[2] Here we see the
heart alive with Divine love, and the other
-powers in silence and subjection to it; silent in
prayer, subject in action.[3] These powers are the
intellect, the memory, imagination, senses. None
of them can reach to God. Love alone attains to
Him. Hence, "God will have us to transcend
reason by ardent love".[4] "O dear Charity, by
which we love God, we choose God, we advance to
God, we attain to God, we possess God."[5] In its

[1] "There are diversities of graces, but the same Spirit; and
there are diversities of operations, but the same God, who worketh
all in all." (1 Cor. xii. 4.)

[2] That is, moving "*sub influxu Caritatis*," as shown pp. 60 & 154.

[3] "Hæc est unitio per amorem. Iste amor transcendit omnem
intellectum et scientiam. Sola affectiva tunc vigilat; et silentium
omnibus aliis potentiis imponit." (S. Bonav., "in Hexæmer,"
Serm. 2.)

[4] "Imit.," B i., C 14. "O amor præceps, vehemens, flagrans,
impetuose, qui præter te aliud cogitare non sinis! fastidis cætera,
contemnis omnia præter te, te contentus." (S. Bern., Serm. 79
in Cant.)

[5] "O bona Caritas, per quam Deum diligimus, Deum eligimus,
ad Deum currimus, ad Deum pervenimus, Deum possidemus."
(Hugo a S. Vict., "de laude Carit.".)

very nature love is a bond of union, uniting the
lover with the Beloved ; to which end the other
powers would be powerless. The soul, therefore,
desiring, union with God, as the very end of its
existence, withdraws itself from the operations of
its lower powers,[1] and gives itself wholly to the
operations of Divine love.[2] In return, God gives
Himself to the soul, working in the powers thus
left free for Him. The intellect, in place of its
natural light, now receives the light of God. The
memory, in return for leaving its past forms and
images, now receives Divine impressions and re-
membrances. The imagination and senses, having
renounced their natural activity, share the pleasures of the soul in being all for God. Of these
powers we may now say, Totæ abstrahuntur, totæ
dedicantur. A servitio proprio totæ abstrahuntur. Servitio Caritatis totæ dedicantur ; i.e., They
are wholly taken, wholly given. Wholly taken

---

[1] " Tu vero sensus relinque, et intellectuales operationes, et
sensibilia omnia, et intelligibilia, ut ad unionem Ejus, qui supra
scientiam est, assurgas." (Denis Areop., " de Theol. Myst.," i.)

[2] " The soul has no need of using the discursory operations of
the understanding, which would be mere amusement and loss of
time. We do not require the help of reasoning to excite ourselves
to love an object, of which we have a clear and simple view. It
suffices that the will should receive the impression of the sweetness imparted by the Divine presence. The other powers, without
being actively exercised, have only to enjoy the repose produced
by the presence of God. Thus they cease to act. The will alone
is sweetly occupied." (S. Francis of Sales, " Love of God," B vi.,
C 8 and 9.) When, however, it is said that the " will only " is
active, this means active as the moving principle under Divine
love. The other powers may move by the Divine principle. But
as their movement is now subject to God, they are regarded rather
as recipients, the will being the active mover under God.

from serving themselves. Wholly given to the service of love.

What is all this but doing our best to keep the "greatest and first commandment" of loving God with our whole heart, and soul, and strength? For if we thus entirely love God, what room can there be for love apart from Him? As S. Augustine says, "What remains to you of your heart for loving yourself? What remains of your soul? What of your mind? "*Ex toto,*" *inquit.* He who made you requires "your all".[1] "He who is joined to the Lord is one spirit."[2] He renounces the natural spirit to attain to the Divine.[3] He

[1] "Quid remanet de corde tuo, unde diligas teipsum? quid de anima tua? quid de mente tua? Ex toto, inquit. Totum exigit te, Qui fecit te." (S. Aug., Serm. 34 de v. Ps. cxlix.)

[2] 1 Cor. vi. 17.

[3] The great advantages of renouncing the natural activity of the various powers as signified above, leaving the will active in Divine love, may be readily understood. These powers are often springs of evil to the soul, withdrawing us from God, and strongly inclining us to the perishable satisfactions of creatures. Look at the mischief wrought in our lives by the activity of the senses, the eyes, the hearing, the taste, and touch. How often have they led us away from God. Look at the wild movements of the imagination. See the amount of energy consumed by the efforts of the memory engaging itself with so many vain forms and images. In fine, the noble intellect, apart from the presiding influence of Charity, debases itself in a thousand ways, and becomes the instrument of ruin to countless souls. Seeing all this, therefore, let us lay the axe to the root. Resign the natural operations of these powers, and yield them to God; collecting our energies in the will, by a complete devotion, with the whole heart, soul, and strength, to Divine love. Then God takes the soul and all its powers as His own, and governs them according to Himself. Thus we escape our natural misery, and live in Divine security; and our powers are the subjects of Divine, instead of natural, operations. Hence flow the gifts and fruits of the Holy Ghost, and untold happiness to the soul. Moreover, the devil would try in vain to hurt a soul that is all Charity. On the senses, imagination,

"refraineth from all things,"[1] to give his attention and energy to the work in hand.

S. Augustine again teaches this when he says that our love is as the *hand* of the soul. If it wish to cleave to God, it must leave its hold of other things.[2] S. Thomas is of the same mind, when he tells us that the more we withhold our love from inferior things, the more perfectly we are able to direct it to the one thing.[3] And S. Francis of Sales explains it at length in the following passage. "When a soul is divided between many operations, it acts with less vigour and perfection ; because, being finite, its active virtue is also finite ; and being attentive to several things, it is less attentive to each of them. We cannot quietly consider a person's features, and at the same

memory, intellect, he may work. These, too, are the subjects of numberless perplexities, temptations, disturbances, scruples, obscurities. Let these powers therefore die to themselves, and live to God by love; and we escape both our own misery and the wiles of the devil. "How secure will the soul then be," says S. John of the Cross, "when all these operations and movements have ceased. It is then delivered from itself, and the world, and the devil, who, when the affections and operations of the soul have ceased, cannot assault it by any other way or means." (S. John of the Cross, "Obsc. Night of the Soul," B ii., C 14 and 16.)

[1] 1 Cor. ix. 25.

[2] "Intendite amorem hominis. Sic putate quasi manum animæ. Si aliquid tenet, tenere aliud non potest. Ut autem tenere possit quod datur, dimittat quod tenet. Non occupetur amor tuus, quo potes inhærere Deo." (S. Aug., Serm. 125 de verb. Joan.)

[3] "Manifestum est quod cor humanum tanto intensius in aliquid unum fertur, quanto magis a multis revocatur. Sic igitur tanto perfectius animus hominis ad Deum diligendum fertur, quanto magis ab affectu temporalium revocatur." (S. Thom., "Opusc. de perfect. vitæ Spir.," C 6.)

time listen attentively to the harmony of music. And if we are talking earnestly, we cannot attend to anything else. Hence, if the soul employ her forces in different operations of love, the action so ·divided is less vigorous and perfect. Since, then, love is an act of the will, we must collect its powers, and restrain them within the limits of spiritual operations, if we desire that it should be noble and active. By applying ourselves to the operations of the sensitive part of the soul, we deprive the spiritual operations, and consequently real love, of much strength."[1] We learn, then, from the teaching of the holy Doctors, that we are to aim at gathering up the whole love of our heart into Divine Charity, so as to be under the influence of one only principle,[2] the principle of the Spirit of God; the "Charity of God, poured forth in our hearts by the Holy Ghost ".[3] By this principle our nature is gradually purified, illuminated, and perfected ; the lower powers serving the higher, and the higher living and moving under the influence of the Divine Spirit. Thus is the soul brought under the Divine governance—under the *one* light, *one* love, *one* principle ;[4] the light, the love, the

---

[1] S. Fran. of Sales, "Love of God," B i., C 10.

[2] " The end of the contemplative life is to reduce all things to unity, rejecting multiplicity and diversity as much as may be. Wherefore if I desire to taste the sweetness of contemplation, I must avoid that multiplicity which is contrary to this unity." (De Ponte, " Med.," Vol. iii., P 3, C 2.)

[3] Rom. v. 5.

[4] " He to whom all things are one, who sees all things in one, who draws all things to one, may be steady in heart, and peaceably repose in God." (" Imit.," B i., C 3.)

principle of the Spirit of God, the natural light, love, and principle being in sweet subjection thereto.[1]

Let us keep to our principle consistently. "Tene eam, ne dimittas : quia ipsa est vita tua."[2] By constant exercise it gathers strength, diffusing its virtue through our powers, and finally gaining a calm and sweet possession of the soul. It becomes a settled habit, the habit of habits, disposed to its acts, readily, easily, and sweetly. Thus by oneness of inward life and principle, the soul gets rid of her former multiplicity, and attains to the holy simplicity that likens her to God, and so makes her fit to treat with Him, and be united with Him.

[1] " Sicut in vita corporali, corpus non movetur nisi per animam per quam vivit, ita in vita spirituali omnis motus noster debet esse a Spiritu Sancto." (S. Thom., in Pauli Epist. ad Gal. v.)

[2] Prov. iv. 13.

CHAPTER III.

THE INCREASE OF CHARITY.

"WHEN I was a child, I spoke as a child, I understood as a child, I thought as a child; but when I became a man, I put away the things of a child."[1]

Thus speaks the inspired Apostle in his memorable Chapter on Charity. And we learn from this comparison the need we are under of developing in the spiritual life, as we do in the natural, from the weakness of childhood to the strength and ability of full-grown manhood. In the early years of spiritual life, Charity is as a child, living indeed in the soul, but weak in its life, and consequently unequal to vigorous action.[2] The natural man lives too; moving, alas! more readily, and growing more rapidly than the spiritual man. The development of each life depends on the repetition of acts, forming corresponding habits, and to which side that repetition is given.[3] It is clear, for instance, in the natural life, that a constant

---

[1] 1 Cor. xiii. 11.   [2] " Operatio sequitur esse."

[3] " Hujus disciplinæ fit homo particeps non statim, sed successive, secundum modum suæ naturæ." (S. Thom., 2 2, Q 2, Art. 3.)

repetition of the acts of any particular art, such as
music or painting, will in course of time impress a
habit thereof within the soul, and so develop the
accomplished artist or musician ; so that what in
the beginning was difficult of execution and imperfect in result, has become by practice both easy
and perfect. It is the same in spiritual life. We
possess in early years the gift of Divine Charity,
by virtue of the state of Grace. But we are as
children and weak beginners. We are not as yet
practised in the Divine art. Application is needed,
and the repetition of spiritual acts. We must
awaken our interest in the great work, and give
ourselves mind and heart to it ; the more so, because if our thoughts and affections are not given
to these incomparable treasures of inward life, they
will infallibly turn to goods of a lower order, and
be captivated by the perishable gratifications of
creatures.[1] It behoves us then to be wise in time.
Why should we prefer the vain pleasures of sense
to the pure enjoyments of the spirit ? Why should
we bestow so much time and care on the lower
powers of our nature, and make so little account of
the highest resources of the soul ? "O ye children
of men, how long will you be dull of heart ?
Why do you love vanity, and seek after a lie?"[2]
"That which is of little or no profit takes up our
thoughts ; and that which is above all things

[1] " Quicunque avertitur a fine debito, necesse est quod aliquem
finem indebitum sibi præstituat : quia omne agens agit propter
finem." (S. Thom., 2 2, Q 45, A 1 ad 1.)
[2] Ps. iv. 3.

necessary is negligently passed over."[1] We "have eyes, and see not".[2] Is it not a dictate of right reason to choose the higher good rather than the lower? "O Lord God, who is like to Thee? Behold the nations are as the smallest grain of a balance! Behold the islands are as dust! and the inhabitants of the earth as locusts. I, the Lord, am the First and the Last. And to whom have you likened Me, and made Me equal, saith the Holy One? Lift thine eyes, and see who hath created these things."[3] "Never suffer any of the things My bounty has created for the use of man to hinder thee from loving Me; for to this end have I made creatures and given them to man, that he, knowing more fully through them the riches of My bounty, may love Me in return with a larger affection."[4]

What, then, is it to choose God? It is to give Him the deliberate preference of our hearts, and make His Divine Charity our sovereign love, ruling all other loves. We are not to divide our affections, but to devote them to God, and to have all the rest according to Him.[5] His love then governs the

---

[1] "Imit.," B iii., C 44.

[2] "Oculos habent, et non videbunt." (Ps. cxiii.)

[3] Isa. xl. 15, 22, and xli. 4.

[4] S. Cath. Sien., "Dial. on Consum. Perfection".

[5] This is important to observe in effective Charity—that is, in all our outer works, day by day, and hour by hour, proceeding from the Divine principle. Our actions are to be not only *for* God, but *by* Him, and *according to* Him, if we will attain perfection: *pro Deo, per Deum, secundum Deum.* What is this but saying that God is to be our beginning, continuation, and end? "I am Alpha and Omega, the beginning and the end." (Apoc. xxii. 13.)

will, and through the will the other powers of soul
and body ; and consequently the operations of the
entire man.   Thus, as Seneca says, our life is "all
of a piece," and " we carry a Divine mind through
all the accidents of life ".[1]

But if the principle of Charity is to move us
effectually, rising above the natural man, and carrying us through the works and trials of life, it is evident that it must emerge from the state of its first
weakness, and advance towards the strength needful
for its great enterprise.   In other words, Charity
from being as a tender child must gather power by
daily nourishment and exercise, until it attains to
the development of the " perfect man," so as to be
equal to the great undertakings that God will
prepare for it, and be able to exercise its acts,
hitherto difficult and imperfect, with the promptitude, ease, and sweetness that belong to the state
of perfection.

That our Charity is capable of increase is certain,
with the certainty of Faith.[2]   " This I pray, that
your Charity may more and more abound," says
S. Paul.[3]   And Holy Church prays, " Grant us, O
God, an increase of Faith, Hope, and Charity ".
The inner man must be renewed, as the Apostle

Our actions are *for* God, by the morning oblation, or the habitual
reference to Him.   They are *by* Him when we move from His
principle, which is Charity.   They are *according to* Him when we
do them according to the rules of perfect Charity to God and one
another.   How evident it becomes that we need the formation of
the habit of *affective* Charity, in order to secure its operations
effectively.   " *Operatio sequitur esse.*"

[1] Seneca, Epist. 21 and " de vita beata," C 16.
[2] Conc. Trid., Sess. 6, Can. 24.   [3] Philip. i. 9.

says, "day by day".[1] And, indeed, the Fathers and Doctors of the Church warn us that in the way of God there is no such thing as a standstill, but that if we advance not, we recede; according to the sentence in Job, "man never continueth in the same state".[2]

Cassian gives us the Abbot Theodore's instruction on this point. "It is necessary," says the Abbot, "to renew the inward man, to press forward to the things that are before us, otherwise we shall fall back. The mind cannot remain always in the same state. He who wishes to ascend a river must apply his oars, and by the vigour of his exertions cleave the current, and not allow his hands to loose their grasp, or his boat will glide backwards down the swift waters, or be dashed in pieces against the rocks. This, therefore, will be an evident proof of our falling away, if we imagine we have nothing more to acquire; no further steps to take; if we cease for a single day to progress towards a higher state of virtue. We acknowledge God alone as immutable. He is always perfect, to whom nothing can be added. As to ourselves, not to gain is to lose, and not to advance is to fall back."[3]

S. Augustine teaches the same, when he says, that "love is always either rising or falling".[4] "Always add," he continues, "always advance, stay not on the way, turn not back, turn not aside.

---

[1] 2 Cor. iv. 16.　[2] Job xiv. 2.　[3] Cassian, "Conf.," 6, C 14.
[4] "Omnis amor aut ascendit, aut descendit." (S. Aug., Enar. in Ps. cxxii.)

If you say 'enough,' you are lost."[1] S. Gregory uses the same example as Cassian, telling us that we must imitate those who strive against the current; that there is no remaining stationary; but that we fall to the lowest, if we strive not for the highest.[2]

S. Bernard expresses himself to the same effect. He tells us that the soul necessarily fails when she ceases to advance.[3] "The just man" (he says) "never counts himself to have apprehended. He never says 'enough,' but always hungers and thirsts after justice; ever striving to advance from good to better. For he has not pledged himself to the Divine service for a year, or a time, as a servant to his master, but he is bound to God for ever. 'Inclinavi Cor meum ad faciendas justificationes Tuas, in æternum.'"[4]

S. Teresa also says: "In a spiritual life, he who does not advance, recedes. I consider it impossible for love to stand still."[5] And does not the wise

[1] "Semper adde, semper ambula, semper profice; noli in via remanere; noli retro redire; noli deviare.   Si dixeris 'sufficit,' periisti." (S. Aug., Serm. 169 de verb. Ap. ad Phil.)

[2] "In hoc mundo, humana anima, quasi more navis est contra ictum fluminis conscendentis, uno in loco nequaquam stare permittitur; quia ad ima relabitur, nisi ad summa conetur." (S. Greg., "de Cura Past.," P 3, a. 35.)

[3] "Necesse est spiritum aut proficere semper, aut deficere." (S. Bern., Epist. 254.)

[4] "Nunquam justus arbitratur se comprehendisse. Nunquam dicit, 'satis est'; sed semper esurit, sititque justitiam; semper de bono in melius proficere, totis viribus conaretur.   Non enim ad annum, vel ad tempus, instar mercenarii, sed in æternum Divino se mancipat famulatui. 'Inclinavi Cor meum ad faciendas justificationes Tuas, in æternum.'" (S. Bern., Epist. 254.)

[5] S. Teresa, "Int. Castle," C ult.

man tell us that the souls of the just are in constant
progress towards perfection? "The path of the
just, as a shining light, goeth forward and increaseth
to perfect day."[1] And even the glorious Apostle,
he who was a vessel of election, and able to say,
" I live, not I, but Christ liveth in me,"[2] still declares
his persuasion that he had not yet reached perfection, but that he stretched forth and pressed
towards the mark. " Not as though I had already
attained, or were already perfect ; but I follow after,
if by any means I may apprehend. Forgetting the
things that are behind, and stretching forth myself
to those that are before, I press towards the mark."[3]

It is clear, then, that our Charity must go on
increasing. It never finds its term in this life. The
highest Saint must still move onwards. Our work
is not done till we reach perfection ; and our perfection is not complete till we gain our end ; and
our end is not attained till we attain to God. But
the increase of our Charity is the progress of the
soul to our perfection, to our end, and to God.
Because love alone is the bond of union. For " by
love we choose God, we advance to God, we attain
to God, we possess God ".[4] As Charity therefore
increases, the soul advances.[5] So that our proficiency lies not in much thinking, or much external

---

[1] Prov. iv. 18.   [2] Gal. ii. 20.   [3] Philip. iii. 12.

[4] " O bona Caritas, per quam Deum diligimus, Deum eligimus,
ad Deum currimus, ad Deum pervenimus, Deum possidemus."
(Hugo a S. Vict., " de laude Carit.".)

[5] " Imus, non ambulando, sed amando." (S. Aug., Ep. 155
ad Mac.)

doing, but in much loving, as S. Teresa tells us.[1] And all for the same reason, which an ancient author well expresses, when he says that "love *attains* to God, but thought or understanding, never".[2]

This progress of the soul to God is explained as follows by the Angelic Doctor: "We are called travellers or pilgrims, because we are on the way to God, who is our last end. We advance by approaching to God : and we approach to Him, not by the steps of the body, but by the love of the soul. Now Charity it is by which we thus approach to God, because by it the soul is united to Him. Therefore, Charity must increase. For if it increase not, our advance to God would cease. Charity therefore in this life may always more and more increase ; and as it increases, the capacity for receiving it expands within us. So that no limit to its increase in the soul may be placed here below."[3]

The increase of Charity may, perhaps, be understood in some measure, by reverting to the example

[1] "The proficiency of the soul consists not in much thinking, but in much loving." (S. Teresa, "Founds.," C 5.)

[2] "Divine Cloud," C 6.

[3] "Ex hoc dicimur esse viatores, quod in Deum tendimus, qui est ultimus finis nostræ beatitudinis. In hac autem via, tanto magis procedimus, quanto magis Deo propinquamus ; cui non appropinquatur passibus corporis, sed affectibus mentis. Hanc autem propinquitatem facit Caritas, quia per ipsam mens Deo unitur. Et ideo de ratione Caritatis viæ est, ut possit augeri. Si enim non posset augeri, jam cessaret viæ processus. Ergo semper Caritas in via potest magis et magis augeri. Quia semper Caritate excrescente, superexcrescit habilitas ad ulterius augmentum. Unde relinquitur quod Caritatis augmento nullus terminus præfigatur in hac vita." (S. Thom., 2 2, Q 24, Art. 4, & Art. 7 in sed c. & corp.)

of the crystal before the light : the crystal representing the soul, and the light God.   God shines upon the soul by the light of His love.   This light, however, is hindered from fully reflecting itself, by the spots and shades of venial sins and imperfect habits, which the soul retains.   But as God communicates Himself, and Charity works within us, the spots and shades gradually diminish under the Divine influence, and so give Charity further space wherein to shine.   And as, in course of time, the dark misery of the soul yields to God's " consuming fire," [1] Charity gathers in its power, and extends its action.   In other words, it increases *iutensively* and *extensively,* [2] until, by complete self-renunciation, and the full communication which God then makes, all the dark stains and shades are expelled and absorbed by the Divine light and love ; [3] and the soul, as a spotless crystal, reflects the brightness of God's image, and is transformed in Divine beauty.   "We all, beholding the glory of the Lord, are transformed into the same image,

[1] "Our God is a consuming fire."   (Heb. xii. 29.)

[2] " Caritati non convenit quantitas dimensiva, sed solum quantitas virtualis, quæ attenditur secundum radicationem in subjecto. Et hoc intensive, ut magis diligatur : et extensive, ut plura diligantur.   Sic ergo Caritas augetur, secundum quod magis reducitur in actum illius, et magis insit ; et quod perfectius similitudo Spiritus Sancti participetur in anima."   (S. Thom., 2 2, Q 24, A 4 ad 1 & 3, & A 5 ad 3.)

[3] " Love is a fire, burning and shining.   When it burns in the will, it shines in the understanding.   And since the beauty of Him whom we love is infinite, the sight of Him kindles yet fiercer flames of love in the heart.   Then there springs still stronger desire of beholding Him.   And so there is no ending ; till the soul cleaves to her Beloved, and becomes one Spirit with Him for evet."   (Card. Bona, " Via Comp.," C 9.)

from glory to glory, as by the Spirit of the Lord."[1]

We know well that, in the natural life, the growth of the body and its strength depend upon the nourishment it takes. So also in spiritual life. If Charity is to grow and strengthen, it must receive its proper nutriment. We nourish the body by a repetition of acts, assimilating various substances to ourselves, being careful to avoid whatever would injure the constitution or impede the working of its functions. So Charity is nourished by a repetition of spiritual acts, apt in their nature, and by the power of assimilation, to intensify her virtue, and exercise and strengthen her power of action ; being vigilant, lest we take in anything that would injure the spiritual constitution, or interfere with the order and regularity of Charity's delicate functions.

From the preceding chapter we see that we must be constantly striving to make all that we do become a nourishment to our Charity, otherwise, the natural man quickly steps in, and finds in the self-same acts an aliment for cupidity. As, however, in the natural life some substances are, in their nature, more nutritious than others, so in the spiritual life some acts serve Charity as good nourishment, others as better, while others may be considered the best spiritual nourishment.

Denis, the Carthusian, points to this as "a primary means of progressing in Charity, viz. : the making all we do, our words, works, intentions,

---

[1] 2 Cor. iii. 18.

affections, and operations, referable to our progress in Divine love ". "Such continual strivings for the growth of Divine Charity" (says he) "obtain its increase within us."[1] "And as we renew our endeavours, God gives fresh succours; as our Lord says (S. Matt. xxv. 29), 'to everyone that hath, shall be given, and he shall abound'. Grace, therefore, gets grace; a greater one follows a lesser; progress serves to further progress; gain follows gain; and merits increase merits; the soul striving the more as it obtains more; and new acquisitions spurring it on to fresh endeavours."[2]

The commonest actions of life, done from the principle of Charity, serve to nourish the Divine life within us, as each act goes to strengthen the corresponding habit. But acts done from the same principle, and which involve self-sacrifice, are still better nourishment, according to S. Augustine's saying, that the "nourishment of Charity is the diminution of Cupidity,"[3] because the displacement

---

[1] "Primum ergo medium proficiendi in Caritate est assidue ac intente hoc ipsum considerare; et omnem conversationem, occupationem, cogitationem, locutionem, affectionem, intentionem, et operationem ad Caritatis referre profectum; nempe, ad sanctæ Caritatis incrementum ita in omnibus aspirare, et pro illo tam fideliter laborare, actualiterque illud sic incessanter adspicere, meretur præcipuum Divini amoris incrementum." (Denis Carthus., "de laude Vitæ Solit.," A 35.)

[2] "Quantum nos addiderimus ad conatum, tantum Deus apponet ad subsidium; sicut ait, 'habenti dabitur, et abundabit'. Gratia ergo de gratia nascitur; major de minori; profectus profectibus serviunt; et lucra lucris: et merita meritis lucra efficiunt. Et quanto plus quis acquirere cœperit, tanto plus conetur, ac delectetur acquirere: ut acquisitionis lucrum acquisitionis nutriat appetitum." (Denis Carthus., "de laude Vitæ Solit.," A 35).

[3] "Nutrimentum Caritatis est imminutio Cupidatis." (S. Aug., "de div. Quæst. Oct. tr.," Q 36.)

of self-love gives the more room to Divine love. Sometimes we may not only move from the principle of Charity, but our object may be a direct act of the virtue, and at the same time involving the sacrifice of the natural man. Who that desires to be rich in Charity would not embrace, and even seek for, these valued opportunities of strengthening the Divine habit within the soul? Let us not forget that our Lord tells us to be "rich towards God".[1]

If, however, we wish to provide to the full extent for Charity's increase within us, by securing to ourselves the full merit and perfection of our lives, not only must our actions be done *for* God, *by* the principle of His love, but they must be throughout *according to* Him:[2] which means that they must be well done,[3] in the spirit of one aspiring to perfec-

[1] S. Luke xii. 21.

[2] " Secundum Deum : " according to God ; which is according to all perfection. " That the man of God may be perfect, furnished to every good work " (2 Tim. iii. 17) ; " fashioned according to Him who is holy ". (1 Pet. i. 14.) To a soul undertaking in earnest a spiritual life, the words " secundum Deum " will be a constant reminder of its work. For the business lies in renouncing the natural life " according to man," and taking the new principle " according to God," making it work consistently in our ordinary actions, animating them with the soul of Divine love, in place of the old principle of self-love. The soul has to be therefore constantly vigilant, having an assurance that it is moving " according to God ". The texts of S. Paul, in the eighth chapter to the Romans, where he speaks of living " according to the spirit, not according to the flesh," correspond to this ; as also his words to the Ephesians, where he tells us to " put on the new man," " secundum Deum creatus ". (Eph. iv. 24.)

[3] " He hath done all things well." (S. Mark vii. 37.) " Si bonum sit quod fit, non autem bene fiat, non erit perfecte bohum : unde nec habitus qui est talis operis principium, habebit perfecte rationem virtutis. Virtus quædam perfecta dicitur ex hoc quod potest in opus perfecte bonum ; quod quidem est, dum non solum bonum est quod fit, sed etiam bene fit." (S. Thom., 1 2, Q 65, Art. 4.)

tion, that is, they must be according to the order of perfect Charity, to God, and to one another. No doubt such perfect operations are the result of a perfectly-formed habit of Charity within, according to the well-known adage, "operatio sequitur esse"; therefore, souls are not to expect to find such perfection ready-made, and waiting for them. The full-blown rose develops by slow degrees. We must abide God's time, and the laws of nature and grace ; striving, in the meantime, day by day, for the perfection of our actions ; working consistently at the development of the habit, by the use of our instrumental means to this end, and having all the rest in "preparation of heart".[1] The soul grows like the tree, imperceptibly. If it is only well planted and cultivated, the fruits will come in their due season, in all sweetness and abundance.

Vocal prayer, meditation, affective acts, aspirations, and contemplation, being communications, in various ways and degrees, with the source of Charity, and so bringing the soul under the direct influence of God's light and love, are foremost among the means of nourishing the Divine life. Thus the soul refreshes itself, and renews its strength day by day at the Fountain-head, by fresh accessions of Divine light and love then received. And, as in nature, causes act on matter which is *near* them, and tend to produce their like, while they cannot influence that which is distant, so God, who is of all causes the noblest and strongest,

---

[1] " Thy ear hath heard the preparation of their heart." (Ps. ix. 17.)

operates on man, making him like Himself, provided only that man draws near to Him, not with
the body, but with the thoughts and affections of
the soul. Self-examination and confession, wisely
used, are efficacious, instrumental means for ridding
ourselves of the impediments to Charity ; and, by
purifying and reviving the soul, enable it the better
to assimilate the nourishment it takes. But because
they are instruments that may sometimes easily *hurt
certain souls* in the hidden paths of Divine love, such
have to be guarded against any unwise use of them :
for a good instrument may not be well used, and so
prove injurious, instead of being helpful. It must
not be forgotten that the Sacrament of Penance is
a Sacrament of the " dead " : that is, made chiefly
for the benefit of those in mortal sin. Souls, therefore, living in grace, and walking in the ways of
love, and so having no will for deliberate sin, must
be careful how far they commit themselves to
repeated exercises of self-examination and confession of their miseries ; lest overmuch introspection
lead to trouble and entanglement of the conscience,
and thus undue fears, perplexities, and scruples be
bred, and quickly multiplied: which things become
serious impediments in the way of perfection.[1] Let

---

[1] F. Baker, in his " Treatise on Confession," says : " For want
of holding a good and discreet course in the matter of examen and
confession, divers souls are clean hindered in the way of perfection. The soul therefore ought to be wary how he put himself
into it, as also the confessor, how he urge the party unto it. And
unless it appear that it may be handled with profit, they should
forbear, and let it alone, holding on in other and far more profitable exercises of a contemplative life, which will of themselves
suffice to bring a soul to perfection. Believe me, venial sins of

the teaching of the Council of Trent be well remembered, viz.: that "venial sins, while they may be confessed, may also, without fault, remain unconfessed, and be expiated by many other remedies ".[1] And let the doctrine of S. Thomas be known, that Divine Charity itself suffices to purify the soul from venial sin.[2] It is of great importance to remember here that we are creatures of habit, and that our acts make our habits. Habits of fear or habits of love are gradually developed, by a repetition of their corresponding acts. Love, being the way to God, is the way of perfection ; and souls tending to perfection must be taught to "walk in love ".[3] Let them see, therefore, how far their examens and confessions are instrumental to their

frailty do nothing near so much harm a soul in the way of perfection, as doth inordinate fear and scrupulosity. I daresay that of forty well-minded souls in Religion, scarce is there one or two but are more hindered than advanced in the way to perfection by the use of confession of venials as nowadays practised. For divers souls are by it more and more established in fear, and consequently in self-love, this being the root and cause of fear ; and so they grow more and more in self-love, with less and less love towards God. Had I a careful and well-minded soul (and many such there be), I think it would suffice if she tell me whether she knew of any matter of confession and absolution since her last confession, and she answering 'No,' I should say: ' God be thanked '; troubling neither her nor myself any further in the business." (F. Baker, " Treatise on Confession ".)

[1] " Venialia, quanquam in confessione recte dicantur, taceri tamen citra culpam, multisque aliis remediis expiari possunt." (Conc. Trid., Sess. 14, C 5.)

[2] " Ad remissionem venialis peccati sufficit aliquis actus procedens ex gratia, sicut cum aliquis ferventer movetur in Deum. Caritas tollit per suum actum peccata venialia. Et potest esse tam fervens motus Caritatis, quod omnia peccata venialia consumat." (S. Thom., 3, Q 87, Art. 3 ; Q 79, Art. 4 ad 3 ; & 4 Sent., D 16, Q 2, A 2, S 2 ad 1.)

[3] Eph. v. 2.

love.   Do they find, by experience, that their
thoughts and affections are hereby the better raised
to God ? or are they not rather by these means
kept in their "mournful lurking-holes," and so
hindered from rising to the light of Divine contemplation ?   Instead of this, they should be taught to
transcend their faults and fears, by the higher
exercises of Divine love, which of their own virtue
suffice to cleanse the soul.[1]   "Thou must hate all
fleshly loves and fears, without ceasing," says
Walter Hilton : "for with the precious liquor of
God's love only may thy heart be filled, and with
none other."[2]

The most holy Eucharist is a participation of
Divine Charity itself ; and is given by God, in the
immensity of His love, for the direct purpose of
nourishing the life of Charity within the soul.
What is this gift of God's overwhelming con-
descension but the mystery of Incarnate Charity?
Here is the "Fons Caritatis," the Fountain of
Charity, in our midst ; the hidden, active, suffering,
glorified life, all together ; the model life of Divine
Charity, by contemplation, action, and sacrifice,
combining in perfect love for God and men.   In
holy Mass our Lord makes, day by day, His
immense "actus Caritatis": His act of Charity,

---

[1] F. Baker tells us that "two of the greatest impediments to
well-minded souls in these days are, first, a sticking to certain
customary exercises in Meditation, ever abiding therein, and not
looking after another kind of internal Prayer, more proper for the
soul.   The other is, the not using Confession in the manner it
should be used, with transcension of inordinate fears and scruples."
(F. Baker, "Treatise on Confession".)

[2] Hilton. "Scale of Perf.," P 1, C 17, and P 2, C 3.

by the oblation of Himself, for His own great ends, and the vast needs of souls. And in Holy Communion, He becomes the "nutrimentum Caritatis": the nourishment of our Charity, strengthening the life of His love within us, that we may live by Him,[1] and attain to the "perfect man, to the measure of the age of the fulness of Christ".[2]

Then all the modes of exercising Charity to our neighbour, whether by spiritual or corporal works of mercy, become so many direct means of increasing and developing the Divine virtue within us. And if these occasions involve, as they frequently do, mortification to the natural man, so much the better do they nourish the spiritual man. Self-sacrifice is the test of our love to others, as it is of love to God. "Be assured," says S. Teresa, "that the further you advance in the love of your neighbour, the more will you advance in the love of God. For the affection which His Majesty has for us is so great, that, as a return for the love we show our neighbour, He will cause the love we have for Himself to go on increasing."[3] Thus it is, as S. Gregory says, that "Charity reaches both to the highest and to the lowest. By its love to God it rises on high. By its love to men' it descends low. And while it descends downwards, it rises upwards; and by reaching to the lowest, it

---

[1] " He that eateth Me shall live by Me." (S. John vi. 58.)

[2] Eph. iv. 13.

[3] S. Teresa, "Int. Castle," M 5, C 3.

attains to the highest."[1]   Let us aim, therefore, at
making Charity at once the principle and the end
of all our actions;[2] so that thus our outer works
may constantly nourish our inner life, and the
spiritual man may develop, and not deteriorate in
the midst of external things.

When, indeed, a soul is wholly given to God, so
that His Divine love is henceforth substituted as a
ruling-principle, in place of its own self-love;
when this life of Charity has by the repetition of
its acts become a well-developed spiritual habit,
diffusing its virtue through the soul, and reaching
gradually to the operations of the entire man,
moving him to action promptly, easily, and sweetly,
then it is that the soul at length attains to the
habitual union of its powers with God.[3]   Then it is

[1] "Compage Caritatis, summis simul et infimis junctus, virtute
spiritus ad alta rapitur, et pietate in aliis æquanimiter infirmatur.
Et tunc ad alta mirabiliter surgit, cum ad ima proximorum se
misericorditer attrahit.   Et cum benigne descendit ad infima,
valenter recurrit ad summa."   (S. Greg., "de cura Past.," P 2,
C 5.)

[2] "Caritas comparatur ad omnes alias virtutes, et ut motor, et ut
finis, et ut forma."   (S. Thom., 3 Sent., D 27, Q 2, Art. 4 q 3.)

[3] Habitual union—called habitual in the sense of being permanent and abiding in the powers, as distinguished from actual or
transient union.   This habitual union is the result of the oft-
repeated acts which the soul elicited from its one consistent
principle of love.   "The most excellent union of the soul with
God" (says Lallemant), "and that to which all the exercises of
the active and the contemplative life tend, is an habitual union,
by which the principal powers of the soul remain continually united
to God at all times, in all places, without causing a person to be
less capable of acting externally."   (Lallemant, "Spir. Doctrine,"
P 7, C 4, A 9, § 3.)   "In the unitive way" (says Schram) "man
is wholly in union with God, as far as is possible in this life.   He
is united with God—1, in memory, by a constant remembrance of
Him; 2, in intellect, by continually thinking of Him; 3, in will,

ripe for exercising Charity in its highest degree, which consists in contemplative love disposed to action, and becoming active from the abundance and plenitude of contemplation. Then it is that the soul, as a true lover, leaves the Divine embrace to do the Divine Will.[1]

For "when the soul," says Richard of S. Victor, " is wholly imbued with Divine love, what remains but to propose to it the good, well-pleasing, and perfect will of God as its form to be attained of perfect virtue? Then it applies and accommodates itself easily and lovingly to the Divine pleasure. And as liquid metal runs into whatever channel it is directed, so the soul now readily and willingly inclines itself to whatever paths Divine Providence may mark out for it. And here Christ our Lord is proposed as its model, who, ' when He was in the form of God, emptied Himself, taking the form of a servant '. This is the pattern to which everyone aspiring to the highest degree of consummate Charity must be conformed. For whereas, before,

by always loving Him; 4, he is united to God in his other powers, by moving to their respective acts from love to God, because He wills, and as He wills." (Schram, " Theol. Myst.," P 2., prin.)

[1] S. Thomas teaches that it belongs to the perfection of love sometimes to leave the presence of the one loved, in order to attend to his interests. So that he who leaves his friend in order to serve him, will have a greater love than another who will not sacrifice the enjoyment of his presence. "So also" (says the Angelic Doctor) " it is in Charity. Some rise to such a height of Divine love as to be willing to sacrifice the enjoyment of contemplation, though it be their chief delight, in order to serve God in the salvation of their neighbour. This perfection is proper to priests and others, who give themselves to the service of their brethren." (S. Thom., "Quodl. de Carit.," A xi. ad 6.)

in contemplative love, the soul was, as it were, in the 'form of God,' now it begins to 'empty' itself, taking the 'form of a servant,' and is found again 'in habit as a man'."[1] "In the first degree of Charity, therefore," says Richard of S. Victor, "God enters into the soul. In the second, the soul is elevated to God. In the third, the soul wholly passes into God. In the fourth, the soul turns outward for the sake of God. The soul enters by meditation. It ascends by contemplation. It is led on in jubilation. It goes outward from compassion. The soul ascends to itself. It transcends itself. It is transformed in the brightness of God. It is conformed to the lowliness of Christ."[2]

From this sublime teaching, we see that our Lord Himself is the model of perfect Charity, and that as He, when He was in the form of God, emptied Himself in the abundance of His love, and took the form of a servant, by coming in our midst to serve our interests : so the soul, aiming at perfect love, first gives itself wholly to God, then, when He possesses its powers by the state of habitual union, thus raising it to the "form of God," He sends it back into activity with its new and Divine life and principle. Likened now to Christ, it "empties" itself of the enjoyment of contemplative repose, and takes the "form of a servant," by serving the interests of God in the work of

---

[1] Richard a S. Vict., "de quatuor grad. viol. Carit.".
[2] *Ibid.*

souls. Hereby its love appears in perfection. For while interiorly it enjoys the Divine habitual union, it overflows of its abundance into the souls of those around it, thus causing the Divine love to increase greatly both in itself and others ; and so again resembling Him of whom it is said, "of His fulness we have all received ".[1]

Let us advance, then, towards the habitual union of all our powers in God ; this being the end of all the exercises of the active and contemplative life.[2] "When, O Lord, shall all the powers of my soul be wholly united in singing Thy praises, and not be any more divided ? "[3] But habitual union is only attained by habitual love. And habitual love is gained by the repetition of its acts.

Let us learn from the wisdom of the world. Men carefully nourish their natural life and their natural love. Shall we not attend with equal care to the life of the soul, and let the highest and best of all loves, that of God Himself, receive its constant nourishment, in order that it may increase more and more, and at length attain the fulness of its life, and the perfection of its operations within us ?

Let us aim at making everything we do, and everything we suffer, a nourishment to Charity ; and let us seek .for opportunities of increasing,

---

[1] S. John i. 16.

[2] Finis totius vitæ contemplativæ et activæ, est unio cum Deo habitualis, per Caritatem perfecte in anima regentem, et plene in actibus fluentem.

[3] S. Teresa, "Life by herself," C 17.

strengthening, and developing the Divine virtue in our souls, with the same earnestness that men of the world strive to improve their position and increase their gains. If we do not secure this activity to Charity, the natural man will of necessity get it for himself. Our thoughts and affections must exercise themselves somewhere, must feed upon something. Let us give our activities to the higher life of Charity, and deny them to Cupidity. Then the habits of the soul form accordingly. Charity strengthens and Cupidity weakens, and thus the soul goes on to its perfection.

CHAPTER IV.

THE NOURISHMENT OF CHARITY BY PRAYER.

LET us endeavour to regard God as the sweet Fountain of Infinite Charity, and ourselves as the recipients into which the bright streams of His bountiful love are incessantly flowing. We desire to be filled with His life of Charity, and its diffusions of Divine light, love, strength, and sweetness. It is our one aim to attain to this "fulness of God": "ut impleamini in omnem plenitudinem Dei".[1]

How then is this gift of the Most High to spread its virtue, and strengthen within us, till it gains the full possession and command of our souls? In general, it may be said that prayer and mortification are the two indispensable means to be used in attaining to the end of perfect Charity, since our progress to perfection is by the *increase* of Divine love and the *decrease* of self-love. Now, it is by prayer that Charity increases, and by mortification that Cupidity decreases; by prayer that the spirit is lifted up, and by mortification that the flesh is put down. Hence, prayer and mortification are to

---

[1] Eph. iii. 19.

be Charity's inseparable attendants through life, as handmaids accompanying their Queen, and both have to grow continually in perfection to the end of our lives.

While we are yet imperfect, we have to seek our way onwards to the Fountain of Charity,[1] by the ordinary aids of vocal prayer and meditation, labouring, it may be, in the dark, but searching for the ways of light. As the soul becomes purer, by means of detachment and mortification, it will be drawn more towards affective prayer, because, as the habit of love grows, it must needs assert itself in view of advancing to the object of its love. Its acts, however, may be for some time forced and laboured, on account of the remnants of imperfect habits within, not as yet under the sway of Charity. But as the soul advances in disengagement from creatures and love of God, it proceeds with greater ease, because the higher habits strengthen with exercise. Then it passes onwards to spontaneous

[1] The example of the Fountain is much liked by holy writers, expressing, as it does, God as the ever-flowing and over-flowing source of all goodness. And as the streams of His light and love flow from Him into souls prepared to receive them, the flowings of the Fountain are taken to signify the gifts of infused contemplation. In this sense S. Teresa loved to consider it. "Whoever drinks," she says, "of the Fountain of living water shall not thirst; that is, shall not thirst for earthly things. If we drink of it only once, I am certain it leaves the soul pure, and cleansed from all her faults. And consider how our Lord invites all. I do not say, however, that it is in your power to arrive at contemplation, but that you should use all your exertions to attain to it. It is not your choice, but our Lord's. But if you do what lies in you, and dispose yourselves for contemplation, I believe He will not fail to give it you, if you have true humility and mortification." (S. Teresa, "Way of Perf.," C 17 and 19.) It is of us to cleanse the vessel; it is of God to fill it.

and loving aspirations, and these it elicits with readiness and delight, as being the proper acts of an acquired habit.

These loving aspirations, in conjunction with mortification, are named by Blosius as a sure means of bringing the soul to perfection. " Aspirations and fervent desires," he says, " joined with true mortification, are a sure, quick, and easy way of attaining to perfection, for they effectually pierce through and clear away every barrier between the soul and God."[1] And when mortification has done its work, setting the soul free from "fleshly loves and fears," the spirit is at once disposed to contemplation ; first, to that which is "active," wherein the soul, under the influence of Divine light, love, and movement, unites itself "actually and actively to God, by fervent and amorous, yet quiet elevations of the spirit ".[2] Afterwards, to that which is " passive " or infused, whereby God gives to the soul a certain " inflowing of Himself,"[3] His presence, light, love, and sweetness ; secretly teaching and inflaming it, while it remains lovingly intent on Him. Which passive contemplation is a pure gift of God's goodness, not to be acquired by any strength or efforts of our own, since it is the Divine Lover's own communication of Himself. But we may fully trust that if a soul be rightly disposed by mortification and prayer, and previously grounded in

[1] Blosius, "Instit. Spir.," C 5.
[2] F. Baker, "S. Sophia," T i., S 1, C 4.
[3] S. John of the Cross, "Obs. Night of the Soul," B ii., C 5.

humility, God will not fail to give it, since for this we have been made, viz., Divine knowledge and love ; and our Lord says, that, "if any man hear His voice, and open to Him the door, He will come in to him".[1]   "Provided," says S. John of the Cross, "that the soul be detached, and abide in poverty of spirit, it is impossible that God will not perform His own work, yea, more impossible than that the sun should not shine in a cloudless sky. As the rising sun shines into thy house, if thou dost but open thy windows, so God will shine in upon the emptied soul, and fill it with good things."[2]   Whether this contemplation be active or passive, it is here considered as "ordinary". Contemplation "extraordinary" is reserved to God's own good pleasure, nor is it to be aspired to as necessary in itself to the soul's perfection. Whereas, ordinary contemplation is the proper term of the way on which meditation sets out, since we seek God in order to find Him, and He begins His work in us that He may finish it.[3]

The gradual passage of the soul from meditation onwards, through affective acts and aspirations to contemplation, is described, as follows, by the venerable author of " Sancta Sophia ".   " The soul, aspiring to union with God, as yet absent, begins its inquiry by meditation.   Here the soul *labours* to

---

[1] Apoc. iii. 20.

[2] S. John of the Cross, " Living Flame of Love," S 3, line 3.

[3] " Deus incipit ut perficiat.   Hence, says Schram, " Ad leges ordinarias Divinæ providentiæ spectat contemplatio post meditationem, sicuti terminus post viam ; ne providentia minus provida censeri posset." (Schram, " Theol. Myst.," § 241.)

represent the Divine Object, with all the motives of admiration and love it can invent, *to the end* that the will, by pure love, may rest in God. When the affections so abound, and are sufficiently ripe, that discourse is not needful, or becomes of little efficacy; let the soul betake herself to the exercise of the will, in which, ordinarily, a very long time must be spent, before she can chase away distracting images, and before the heart be so replenished with the Divine Spirit, that, without election or deliberation, it will of itself, almost continually, break forth into aspirations and pure elevations of the superior will. As, however, the will forces itself, with some violence, to untwine and withdraw its adhesion from creatures, that it may be firmly fixed in her only good, at last, by long custom, the force by little and little diminishing, the *Object begins to appear in its own perfect light*, and the affections flow freely to it, but yet with a wonderful stillness. Then such souls are said to have arrived at contemplation, or mystic union." [1]

It is evident, therefore, that, in the earlier stages of spiritual life, we must take the ordinary means of searching our way to God, by aid of meditation. "Here," says S. Teresa, "souls are almost always occupied, by the operation of the understanding, in discourse of meditation, and they do well, because more is not given to them. Still, it would be good sometimes to employ themselves in making acts of love and praise to God, doing it as best they can :

[1] F. Baker, " S. Sophia," T iii., S 4, C 1, and T i., S 1, C 4.

for these acts powerfully excite the will.   And let
them take care when our Lord bestows such affections upon them, not to forsake them, in order to
finish their usual meditation.[1]   For, to advance, we
must remember that the business does not consist
in *thinking*, but in *loving* much. Do, therefore,
whatever may excite you most to love."[2]   To the
use of meditation must be joined, as already said, a
consistent exercise of mortification ; that is, a renunciation of "fleshly loves and fears,". this being
the practical outcome of meditation, and the
necessary means for ridding our souls of the impediments to contemplation.

We may say that to meditate is to *seek* God.
But to contemplate is to see, feel, and enjoy Him.
As S. Paul said to the Athenians : " He hath made
of one all mankind, that they should seek God, if
happily they may feel after Him, or find Him ".[3]
Meditation says, " I sought Him whom my soul
loveth, I sought, and found Him not ". Contemplation says, " I found Him whom my soul loveth ".[4]
It need hardly be said that we seek in order to find.
And yet how many there are who never get beyond
meditation, who do not even think of getting
beyond it ! as though the sight of God, the
possession and enjoyment of Him, were not the
very *end* at which we are aiming, and meditation
but a means by which to gain it. "Ever seek,

---

[1] " In affectibus est omnia virtus orandi." (Hugo a S. Vict.,
" de modo Orandi," C 7.)

[2] S. Teresa, " Int. Castle," M 4, C 1.

[3] Acts xvii. 26.   [4] Cant. iii. 1.

therefore, with great diligence in Prayer, to come to the spiritual feeling or sight of God."[1]

In undertaking the exercise of meditation in early years, it would be of much benefit to beginners to be instructed clearly in the need there is to fix the eye upon the one object to be aimed at and attained.[2] For want of this, many are apt to begin the study of spiritual things, by diffusing their thoughts amidst a multiplicity of subjects, instead of gathering their energies, and directing them to the main point, making their various considerations subservient to this. Hence, "their prayer is desultory, directed towards one point to-day, and another to-morrow. Time is spent, but nothing is done ".[3]

The children of the world are wiser than the children of light. One who wishes to become learned in science, begins by fixing in his mind the nature of the science he has to acquire. He has it clearly and constantly in view, and having determined to make it his object, he at once sets himself "in order to the end ".[4] He makes his use of other things subservient to this. To secure his purpose, he withdraws from distracting cares, training his mind to application and attention. The books he chooses, and the masters he seeks, are such as he knows will help him to his end. To this

[1] Hilton, " Scale of Perf.," P 1, C 12.

[2] " Causa orationis est desiderium Caritatis."(S. Thom., 2 2, Q 83, Art. 14.)

[3] F. Sweeney, " Life of F. Baker ".

[4] " In ordine ad finem."

set purpose, even the common requirements of daily life are referred: paper, pens, ink, books, food, as also his rest, exercise, and recreation. By diligence and perseverance, the end is approached and attained. He becomes master of his science, able to use and enjoy it for his own benefit, and that of others.

What we observe here is the clear manner in which the *end* was viewed from the first, and the way in which all else was made to serve it. In like manner, when we enter on a spiritual life, it concerns us before all things to place clearly before ourselves the object we have to attain, which is union with God by perfect Charity. As, then, we begin to search our way onwards by meditation, let us choose those thoughts, books, and subjects which may help to pave the way towards this most desirable end. Let the various considerations suggested to us be brought to bear upon our one project, thus serving their purpose as means to the end, and not merely engaging the mind with a series of fugitive impressions. "We meditate" (says S. Francis of Sales) "to acquire the love of God. And love attained leads us to contemplate."[1]

It will be easy to see how Divine Charity most readily enters into every consideration connected with Christian truth and virtue, fixing each in its proper place, and shedding light and love over all.[2]

[1] S. Fran. of Sales, "Love of God," B vi., C 3.

[2] "Caritas est intima vis et medulla virtutum. Hæc est quæ vitam ordinat, affectus inflammat et informat; excessus corrigit, mores componit, valens ad omnia, et omnibus prævalens." (Rich. a S. Vict., "de grad. Car.," 1.

The meditation, for instance, on our last end, at once touches upon Charity; since it is by means of this Divine virtue alone that our end is attained. For, as Hugh of S. Victor says, "It is by Charity that we love God, that we choose Him, that we approach to Him, that we attain to Him, that we possess Him ".[1]

The thought of death impresses us with the necessity of guarding our Charity and increasing it, so as to meet God as the one chosen Friend that we have loved and served on earth. Then it is that He appears as the Bridegroom of the soul. "Behold the Bridegroom cometh! go ye forth to meet Him,".[2] clad in the nuptial garment of Charity.[3] The work of our present life is to weave this nuptial robe. Let not the Bridegroom find it blemished and stained. Delay not the "spinning of the wool".[4] Work it in gold, and silver, and precious stones: that is, bring the habit to perfection by the working of the act, day by day, and hour by hour, so that, when our Lord comes, you may go forth adorned and ready-arrayed to meet Him. The judgment after death is decided by the Charity in the soul. The gold must be separated from the dross. The gold of Charity passes. The dross of Cupidity is condemned.

[1] " O bona Caritas, per quam Deum diligimus, Deum eligimus, ad Deum currimus, ad Deum pervenimus, Deum possidemus." (Hugo a S. Vict., " de laude Carit.".)

[2] " Ecce sponsus venit, exite obvium Ei." (S. Matt. xxv. 6.)

[3] " Recte Caritas nuptialis vestis vocatur. Sola quippe dilectione Dei actum est, ut Ejus unigenitus mentes sibi electorum hominem uniret." (S. Greg., Hom. 38 in Evang.)

[4] " Spir. Combat," C on " Sloth ".

Hell is because of the absence of Charity. Heaven is the realm of Charity, Perfect Charity is the condition of admittance there, and its rewards are measured by our several degrees of Charity.[1] The various vices have to be considered and en- countered as impediments to Charity. The different virtues to be known and practised, as the means of exercising, strengthening, and developing Charity. In considering our Lord's life on earth, we regard Him as the model of perfect Charity ; and as we ponder on His sacred words, and meditate on the different stages of His hidden, active, suffering, and glorified life, we see Divine Charity energising in all its perfection.[2] We regard God Himself as the Fountain of Eternal Charity, overflowing in love to His creatures, and inviting us to love Him in return.[3] Thus is brought about a happy " treaty of friendship" between God and the soul,[4] by which He loves us, and we love Him ; He gives Himself to us, and we give our- selves to Him ; He abides in us, and we abide in Him ;[5] He enjoys Himself in us, and we enjoy ourselves in Him ; He works in us, and we in Him.

[1] " Caritatis via disponit mansiones; et diversitas in merendo tota reducitur ad diversitatem Caritatis." (S. Thom., 4 Sent., D 49, Q 1, A 5, q 4.)

[2] S. Catherine of Siena, in one of her letters, written in ecstasy, says of a good religious soul: " If you speak to Christ, and say, ' Who is this soul ? ' He will answer, ' It is another Myself, made so by perfect love ' ". (" Letter " 129.)

[3] " With Thee there is the fountain of life." (Ps. xxxv. 10.)

[4] S. Teresa, " Life," C 8.

[5] " He that abideth in Charity abideth in God, and God in Him." (1 John iv. 16.)

To this mutual love we remember that Charity is the only *way.* " O good Charity, thou art the way, and the highest of all ways. Thou art the way of God to men, and the way of men to God. Thou leadest men to God, and thou bringest God to men. Neither He nor we can pass to one another but by thee." [1]

We look on our Blessed Lady as a divinely-given model of perfect Charity in a pure creature, remembering that, on account of her close proximity to God, as His mother, she had a proportionate closeness in the union of perfect love. In her we see nothing to dim the brightness of Divine Charity. She *begins* with perfection. What, then, must have been the progress and consummation of her Charity? What the height of her contemplations? What the perfection of her operations? She is " the mother of fair love," [2] and the mother of all true lovers. And the whole work of our perfection is to be placed in her hands, that through her "Christ may be formed in us ".[3]

We regard the Holy Angels in their hierarchical order, as displaying the glories of Divine love in its various modes and degrees, from the active services of their Charity to men, to their highest flights of Cherubic and Seraphic contemplation. . And the holy Patriarchs, Prophets, Apostles, Martyrs, and

[1] " Via igitur es, O Caritas, et caput viarum rectarum : via hominis ad Deum, et via Dei ad homines. Tu Deum ad hominem deducis ; tu hominem ad Deum dirigis. Nec ille nec nos, nisi per te, ad alterutrum transire possumus." (Hugo a S. Vict., "de laude Caritatis ".)

[2] Ecclus. xxiv. 24.   [3] Gal. iv. 19.

Saints we consider as exhibiting the many aspects of one love, whether in their life on earth, active, suffering, contemplative, or in the corresponding degrees of their merit and glory in heaven, their glorious virtues springing from their inmost love,[1] so that each virtue is considered as a particular expression of Charity, according to S. Augustine's sentence, that "all our good works are the one work of Charity".[2]

In contemplating Purgatory, we consider the yet imperfect Charity of the holy souls submitting itself to the purifying process there prepared, until the dross of cupidity being cleared away, they emerge in perfect Charity, and thus pass on to heaven.   In the Church on earth, we see the Blessed Sacrament as the ever-flowing Fountain of Charity, and Holy Mass as the perpetual *act* of Divine Charity, and the different Sacraments as conveying its virtue to the soul, or increasing its power within us.

"Whatever is contained in Holy Scripture, or the writings of the Saints" (says Lewis of Granada) "is either Charity or belongs to it, since Charity is the end and perfection of all the commandments."[3] This, too, was S. Augustine's mind.   "Charity," says he, "comprehends the length and breadth of God's entire word. If, therefore, you cannot search all the sacred writings, and penetrate the secrets of

---

[1] " Caritas radix est, fons, materque cunctorum bonorum." (S. John Chrys., Hom. 2 in die Pentec.)

[2] " Omnia bona opera nostra unum opus est Caritatis." (S. Aug., Enar. in Ps. lxxxix.)

[3] Lewis de Granada, " de perfect. amoris Dei," C 1.

the Scriptures, hold to Charity, on which dependeth all. In what you understand, Charity is clearly seen. In what you understand not, Charity lies hid. So that by holding to Charity, you hold both to that which is seen, and that which is hidden in the Divine Word." [1]

In dealing with the souls of others, we recognise Charity as the Divine life within them, by which the Holy Spirit works their sanctification, and leads them on to perfection, sanctifying and supernaturalising the love of the soul, and through the love the whole man : according to S. Augustine's sentence, " As a man loves, so he lives ". [2]

The whole duty of fraternal Charity, in attending to the spiritual and temporal needs of our neighbour, we regard as one of the chief and most necessary means of nourishing the Divine life of love within our souls, and of giving us constant opportunities for exercising and developing its power within us. " Caritas est hic." Charity is here : that is, not only is Divine love our inward principle of action, but the outward work is itself a direct act of Charity, and often involving the sacrifice of self, thus enabling the soul to advance

---

[1] " Totam magnitudinem et latitudinem Divinorum eloquiorum secura possidet Caritas, qua Deum, proximumque diligimus. Si ergo non vacat omnes paginas sanctas perscrutari, omnia Scripturarum secreta penetrare, tene Caritatem, ubi pendent omnia : et in eo quod in Scripturis intelligis, Caritas patet : in eo quod non intelligis, Caritas latet. Ille itaque tenet et quod patet, et quod latet in Divinis sermonibus, qui Caritatem tenet." (S. Aug., Serm. 350 de laude Caritatis.)

[2] " Talis est quisque, qualis est dilectio ejus." (S. Aug., Tract. 2 in Ep. Joan.)

by a double and treble action. Each duty of daily life becomes an occasion whereby Charity may energise; and trials, temptations, and sufferings are turned to account, as proving and purifying the Divine virtue within us.

All these are mentioned to show us how, in time of meditation, as we consider the great truths, or the life of our Lord, our Lady, and the Saints, the graces of Holy Church, the duties and trials of life, the virtues and vices, &c., we may turn our considerations to the service of Divine Charity; thus making the exercise of Mental Prayer what it is meant to be, a means to the end, an instrument of perfection. As the Abbot Moses said to Cassian: " It becomes us to practise retirement and meditation *with reference to our Object*, which is Charity. What will it avail us to perform with punctuality these ordinary exercises, if the main purpose for which we perform them is eluded?"[1]

Vocal prayer in like manner must be made to serve our great purpose, that "what we say with our lips may accord with our hearts".[2] At first, however, while the soul is infirm and imperfect (as Hilton says), she is "blunt and gross for spiritual work, being dry and unsavoury in herself. But afterwards, when grace cometh and toucheth her, she is made sharp and subtle, ready and able to spiritual work. Then the soul prayeth not as it did before,

---

[1] Cassian, "Conf.," 1, C 7.

[2] " Ut hoc versetur in ccrde, quod profertur in ore." (S. Aug., "Regula".)

after the common way of men. For now the mind is not troubled nor hindered by outward things, but wholly gathered together into itself, and the soul is set in the spiritual presence of God ; and, therefore, every word is sounded savourly, sweetly, and delectably, with full accord of mouth and heart. For why ? The soul is turned into the fire of love, and, therefore, every word is like a spark rising from a fire, inflaming and enlightening the powers of the soul, that she listeth ever to pray and do nothing else. And the body is as an instrument and a trumpet of the soul, in which the soul bloweth sweet notes of spiritual prayers to God." [1]

How much ought this to show us the need of growing inwardly in the life and habit of love, so that our hearts may be well attuned to our words ! How sweetly then will the words of the *Pater noster* rise from our souls to our lips, and go up-wards to our loving Father in heaven. "Our Father" at once denotes the mutual love between the soul and God, and the Charity we ought to have for one another. "Hallowed be Thy name" speaks the lover's zeal, wishing that the Divine Greatness and Loveliness may be known and loved by His creatures. "Thy kingdom come" is the ardent desire for the reign of God in our own souls and those of others, by Charity's unimpeded sway. "Thy will be done" is the total subjection of the lover's will to that of the Beloved. And the remaining petitions are various expressions of

[1] Hilton, "Scale," P 3, C 12.

Charity, supplicating the Divine Lover for the many needs of the souls of men.

In using the Rosary, the Stations of the Cross, and other devotions, we may easily form the habit of regarding our Lord and our Blessed Lady as the models of perfect Charity, seeing in each mystery the Divine virtue in all its perfection, and so making these devotions serve their proper end, which is the nourishment of the spirit, and its advancement by the ways of Divine knowledge and love to God.

Frequently are we saying the invocation to the Holy Ghost; we ask Him to come. "Veni Sancte Spiritus." We ask Him to fill our hearts, "reple tuorum corda fidelium," and to kindle in them the fire of His love. " Tui amoris in eis ignem accende." What is this but the expression of our desire to live by the Divine Spirit, that He may fully engage us, and animate our hearts and acts by the principle of His love? Day by day we praise and entreat God in His own words! and how readily does a true lover understand the language of the Beloved! "Such a one" (says Hilton) "seeth the truth of Holy Scripture wonderfully showed and opened above industry and study. For God is the Fountain of Wisdom. And by pouring His wisdom into a clean soul, He maketh it wise: giving it a new ability, and a gracious habit to understand the words and sentences of Holy Writ, unsought and unconsidered. For the lover of God is His friend, and, therefore, to him He showeth His secrets, as to a true friend, that pleaseth Him by love. And such gracious knowings in Holy Writ are as sweet letters sent betwixt a loving soul and the Beloved." And the soul findeth the "heavenly" sense of Scripture, which "belongeth only to the working of love, and that is when all truth in Holy Writ is applied to love".[1]

Look at the Psalm of the daily office, the " Beati immaculati ". Does not every verse speak our one great word and work? Notice the words, "lex, mandatum, verbum, testimonia, via, justificationes, justitia". Each of these words may be well taken as a different expression, phase, or exercise of the self-same Charity;[2] "like a spark rising from a burning fire, heating all the powers of the soul and turning them into love, and enlightening them so comfortably that the soul delighteth to chant the praises of God with spiritual mirth".[3] Among all the laws and ways of God, Charity ever stands the first and chief. Then let the words "justice" and "justifications" be turned into love. Justice, viz., the justice of God, as being the exercise of His Eternal Truth and Love, arranging in the ways of His wisdom for the vast needs of His creatures in the wonderful and manifold dispositions of His Providence, reserving to Himself the glory, and giving us the benefit and merit of what we do. And in regard

---

[1] Hilton, "Scale of Perfection," P 3, C 13.

[2] " Lex Christi, quid congruentius intelligi quam Caritas potest ? per quam semper in mente leguntur præcepta vitæ, qualiter in actione teneantur." (S. Greg., " Moral.," L x., C 4.)

[3] Hilton, " Scale," P 3, C 12.

to *loving* souls especially, giving them Himself, as they give themselves to Him; giving them His light and love, as they give Him their mind and heart; giving them *all*, in return for *all.* Hence, S. Augustine said, that Charity itself is the "truest, fullest, and most perfect justice";[1] since it is the Charity of God and of the soul too that leads them to give themselves thus mutually, as it were, in just exchange one to the other. "Thou givest me Thyself whole and undivided, if I give myself to Thee whole and undivided. And when I shall be thus all Thine, Thou enjoyest Thyself in me, and I enjoy myself in Thee. And if I shall abide wholly in Thee, as it is impossible for Thee to perish, so it is impossible for me to perish."[2]

"Justifications" may be taken to signify the laws of love, which make the soul just and holy before God. And as we say the words, " Inclinavi cor meum ad faciendas justificationes Tuas in æternum," we feel that the chord within vibrates to the sound without. " I have inclined my heart to do Thy justifications for ever." That is, I have bent my heart, I have altogether given it " *to do*"—not only to know, to learn, to consider, but to *do*—for Thee, for the love of Thy love, Thy ustifications, the works of Thy law of love. And his, not for a month, a year, or a few times, now nd then, but " for ever". It is my life-long ork, the work I have chosen for the love of

[1] " Caritas est verissima, plenissima, perfectissimaque justitia."
S. Aug., " de Natura et Gratia," C 42.)
[2] " Fiery Soliloquy of the Soul," C 15.

Thee. And as Thou never changest, so my relation to Thee changes not. I give myself to do the works of Thy law of love for ever.

Again, the frequent use of the words "vivifica me," at once tell us of Charity as the *soul* of our actions, as though we said, "animate me," "move me," vivify and spur me on by the principle of Thy love, and let not the lower loves of nature enslave me. "There dare no flesh-fly rest upon the pot's brink boiling on the fire. Even so can no fleshly delight rest upon a clean soul that is all bilapped and warmed in the fire of love, and blowing up praises and prayers to God."[1]

How frequently again the word "cor" occurs. "In toto corde meo exquisivi Te." "Justus cor suum tradet," &c. The heart is taken for the seat of love. And thus, again and again we profess before God our desire to seek and possess Him with an undivided love. "Mountains" in Holy Scripture are well understood to signify the heights of perfection. "Levavi oculos meos in montes:" as though we set ourselves to consider the way before and above us, and felt a longing desire to make the ascent. And the words "city" and "Jerusalem" may be applied to the City of God within the soul, wherein the Divine Master and King reigns by perfect Charity; or to the heavenly Jerusalem, whither loving souls are tending, and which betokens in spiritual life the state of perfect contemplation.

[1] Hilton, "Scale," P 3, C 12.

14

As, then, our office proceeds, we nourish mind and heart with the thought and love of our one project, and, at the same time, find a sweet spirit and interest in our words. As this habit gradually forms, we shall soon find a hidden meaning in other verses of the inspired writers. For Charity is light to the soul, as well as fire. And "in Thy light we shall see light".[1] Thus, the soul "readily turns all words that are literally spoken into spiritual understanding; and that is no great wonder, for the same Spirit that made the Scriptures expoundeth them to a clean soul for its comfort, and that is the Holy Ghost".[2] The same practice easily extends itself to the expressions of the Church's antiphons and prayers. How often, for instance, are we saying the Collect, "Actiones nostras quæsumus Domine aspirando præveni," &c. Here we ask that all our operations may proceed from God, and be completed by Him. Now, it is by means of the habit of Charity that God works within us, inspiring and assisting us, and moving us to act with Him, and according to Him. And we are reminded to beware of the lower principles of self-love and creature-love, that are so ready to assert themselves independently of the one light, love, and movement of God.

Then the words of the " Pretiosa " in daily use, " Dirigere et sanctificare digneris Domine," &c., tell us at once how our souls and bodies are rightly directed and sanctified in the law of God and the

[1] " In lumine tuo videbimus lumen." (Ps. xxxv.)
[2] Hilton, " Scale of Perf.," P 3, C 13.

works of His commandments, by the influence and operations of Divine love. And again and again in the Collects of the Office, the histories of the Second Nocturn, and the Homilies of the Holy Fathers, our souls will be touched either by the sweet sound of "Caritas," or by the hidden meaning of the words used, which all point to the workings of love. Need it be said that by the same light of Charity we readily find the rich meaning that underlies the exquisite sentences of the book of the "Imitation"? According to the author's own testimony, "The more a man is united in himself, and interiorly simple, the more and higher things doth he understand without labour, because he receives the light of understanding from above. From one word are all things, and this one all things speak. Without this word no one understands or judges rightly."[1] And, indeed, the same may be said of the understanding of other spiritual books, "for" (says S. John Climacus) "Divine Charity is an ocean of illumination".[2] And "God hath given wisdom to them that love Him".[3] And in this manner, no doubt, but that vocal prayer and spiritual reading may both become in time contemplative and true acts of contemplation ; for the reason that the soul most readily finds God as soon as it sets itself to consider Him, and speak to Him. And God Himself waits not, but quickly "pours Himself" into a

---

[1] "Imit.," B i., C 3.
[2] S. John Clim., "Ladder of Perf.," D 30.   [3] Ecclus. i. 10.

loving soul.[1] "We will come to him, and make Our abode with him, and I will manifest Myself to him."[2] Its prayers and readings now become the "sweet flowings of love" upon the "sweet habit within," breaking down the barriers of "fleshly loves and fears," all for God's own great ends and the vast needs of souls. And the stream of living water makes glad the city of God within the soul. "Fluminis impetus lætificat civitatem Dei."[3]

Passing now to the prayer of aspirations, these, as proceeding from a formed habit of Charity, grounded on humility, and accompanied by mortification, bring the soul straight to the gate of contemplation.[4] "This prayer is always heard of God" (says Hilton). "It yieldeth grace to Him, and receiveth grace again. It maketh a soul familiar with Jesus, and with all the Angels in heaven. And although it be not *perfect* contemplation, nor the working of *love by itself*, yet it is in part contemplation, and the soul that hath this freedom and spiritual savour in praying hath the grace of contemplation in the manner as it is."[5]

---

[1] "Festinus ingerit Se." (Scala Claustr., C 5.)

[2] S. John xiv. 23.　　　[3] Ps. xlv. 5.

[4] "There may be sundry ways to contemplation, nevertheless there is but one *gate*. This is a rich nought, and a lightsome night. For except a soul be first smitten down by humility and withdrawn from earthly things, it is not able to bear the shinings of spiritual light, nor receive the precious liquor of perfect love. Therefore apply thy heart fully to the stirrings of grace, and use thyself to dwell in this darkness, and it shall soon be made restful to thee; and the true light of spiritual knowing shall spring up to thee, not all at once, but secretly, little by little." (Hilton, "Scale," P 2, C 8, 7, 5, 6.)

[5] Hilton, "Scale," P 3, C 12.

Nor do these aspirations leave a loving soul outside the gate, but quickly introduce it. Loving aspirations become active contemplation, for they lift both mind and heart to God, and God meets the loving soul. Now, it is that "we speak to God, and He speaks to us. We aspire to Him, and breathe in Him ; and He reciprocally inspires us, and breathes on us. And of what do we discourse? of what can love discourse, but of the Beloved? Where love reigns, the sound of exterior words is not necessary, the soul alone treats with God alone, speaks to God, and hears God speak. Eyes speak to eyes, and heart to heart, and none understand what passes, save the lovers who speak."[1] And as acts make habits, and habit becomes the spring of fresh action, we must see how effectual an aid the use of these aspirations will be in our endeavours to attain to the perfect habit of Divine Charity ; and this not only during our set times of recollection, but at frequent intervals during the day. As repeated drops of water make a hollow in the stone, so repeated acts of love gradually make the Divine impression in the soul. Hence it is that a loving soul, pursuing the ways of internal prayer, finds it "impossible to fix herself continually in meditation, or to rest in any degree of affective prayer, because the nature of such spiritual operations is to become more and more pure, abstracted, and universal ; and to carry the affections still higher and further into God, the activity of the understanding continually abating,

[1] S. Fran. of Sales, " Love of God," B vi., C i.

and the activity of the will continually increasing, and getting ground upon the understanding, till at last all its operations become so quieted and silenced, that they cease, or at least become imperceptible, and the whole exercise of prayer is reduced to operations of the will and affections :[1] which likewise grow by practice more and more natural, quiet, pure, silent, subtle, imperceptible, and profound, the Divine Spirit drawing the soul in her exercises ever more and more unto Himself".[2]

"Happy therefore are those who, after having applied to meditation, by proposing to themselves the different motives calculated to excite the love of God, substitute the simple view of the mind, in place of multiplied reasoning and reflections, and, reducing their thoughts to one which includes all others, establish themselves in unity of contemplation."[3] "For by discourse the soul seeks, and by affection she tends to God, that she may contemplate and repose within Him. And as rest is the end of motion, so contemplation is the end of all other exercises, internal and external."[4] "After persevering, therefore, in discursive prayer, and being long exercised in affections of the will to God, the soul will by little and little grow so well

---

[1] "Ut meditatio ad contemplationem disponere possit, potius *affectiva* quam intellectiva esse debet, et aspirationibus jaculatoriis inflammata ; et quasi semper diu, noctuque continuata. Hoc enim modo ignis Divini amoris cor per scintillas exardescere facit, ut per ignem excitetur incendium." (Schram, "Theol. Myst.," § 257.)

[2] F. Baker, "S. Sophia," T iii., S 2, C 5.

[3] S. Fran. of Sales, "Love of God," B vi., C 5.

[4] F. Baker, "S. Sophia," T iii., S 4, C 1.

disposed to Him, that she will have less need of prescribing to herself determined forms of acts or affections. On the contrary, Divine love will become so firmly established in the soul, so wholly and solely possessing it, that it will become, as it were, a new soul unto the soul, as constantly breathing forth fervorous acts of love, and as naturally, almost, as the lungs do send forth breath. And here begins the state of pure contemplation, the end of all the exercises of an internal life." [1]

"Contemplation is a perception of God and Divine things, simple, penetrating, and certain ; proceeding from love, and tending to love. It is the employment of pure and perfect Charity. Love is its principle, its exercise, and its term. Without contemplation we shall never render to God a perfect service. But with it we shall do more for ourselves and others in a brief time than we should otherwise do in several years." [2]

It is not to be doubted that God will draw our souls to contemplation as soon as He sees they are disposed thereto.[3] "O Lord God, Thou art not estranged from him, who does not estrange himself from Thee."[4] Thou sayest, "Seek, and you shall find ".[5] And again, "Draw nigh to God, and He will draw nigh to you ".[6]

[1] F. Baker, " S. Sophia," T iii., S 2, C 1.
[2] Lallemant, " Sp. Doctrine," P 7, C 4, A 4 and 5.
[3] " Divinam bonitatem decet, ut ubicunque dispositionem invenit, perfectionem adjiciat." (S. Thom., Suppl. Q 14, Art. 4.)
[4] S. John of the Cross, " Prayer of the Enamoured Soul," fin. op.
[5] S. Matt. vii. 7.   [6] S. James iv. 8.

That contemplation is a gift of God, we know, since " every good and perfect gift is from above, coming down from the Father of lights ".[1] But that God is ready to bestow it upon every soul in the right disposition to receive it, we cannot doubt. Will the Divine Lover withhold Himself from a loving soul ? Does He not rather say, Come ? " The spirit and the bride say, Come. And he that thirsteth, let Him come. And he that will, let him take the water of life freely." [2] And further, let us not forget that God has *made* our souls for union with Himself, by Divine knowledge and love. And does He not stand at the door of our hearts and knock, waiting to come in, till we hear His voice, and open to Him the gate ?[3] Is not the kingdom of God within us ?[4] And does He not promise to make His abode there, and manifest Himself to the soul that loves Him ?[5]

Doubtless the finding of God in contemplation will require the seeking Him with our whole heart. " In toto corde meo exquisivi Te." [6] " You shall find Me, saith the Lord, when you shall seek Me with all your heart." [7] And it is certain that this fulness of heart towards God will involve not only

---

[1] S. James i. 17.   [2] Apoc. xxii. 17.

[3] " Behold, I stand at the door and knock. If any man shall hear My voice, and open to Me the door, I will come in to him." (Apoc. iii. 20.)

[4] " The kingdom of God is within you." (S. Luke xvii. 21.)

[5] " If anyone love Me, My Father will love him, and We will come to him, and make Our abode with him ; and I will manifest Myself to him." (S. John xiv. 23, 21.)

[6] Ps. cxviii. 10.   [7] Jer. xxix. 13.

great strength and purity of love, but also the mortification of the natural man. Indeed, this mortification is the counterpart of true love. But granted these dispositions, viz., that the soul is established in humility and mortification, and elevated by fervent love and aspirations, and it is not to be doubted that the grace of contemplation will be given.[1] "Christ will come to thee, discovering to thee His consolation, if thou wilt prepare Him a fit dwelling within thee."[2] The soul will of its own nature go to God. A steel, tied by a thread, will not be drawn to the magnet; but let the thread be cut, and it flies to its object. So, God is our object. As long, however, as the soul is held by attachments, it is hindered from going to God. Remove the impediments, and God at once draws it to Himself.[3] If we are not drawn, it is because we are held. Let us only be free, and God will draw us. "What was the reason why some of the Saints were so perfect and contemplative? Because they made it their study wholly to mortify in themselves all earthly desires, and thus they were enabled with the whole interior of their heart to cleave to God.

---

[1] "Non contemplationis gratia summis datur, et minimis non datur. Sed sæpe hanc summi, sæpe minimi, sæpius remoti aliquando etiam conjugati percipiunt. Si ergo nullum est fidelium officium a quo possit gratia contemplationis excludi, quisquis cor intus habet, illustrari etiam lumine contemplationis potest." (S. Greg., Hom. 17 in Ezech.)

[2] "Imit.," B ii., C 1.

[3] S. Bernard names the four great impediments to contemplation as follows:—(1) "Sensus egens," desires of sense; (2) "Cura pungens," anxious cares; (3) "Culpa mordens," worrying faults; (4) "Irruentia phantasmata," distracting images. (S. Bern., Serm. 23 in Cant.)

If we were dead to ourselves, and no ways entangled in our interior, then we might be able to relish things Divine, and experience something of heavenly contemplation."[1] "Unless a man be at liberty from things created, he cannot freely attend to things Divine."[2] "Forsake all, and thou shalt find all."[3] Free yourself from impediments, by complete renunciation, and you shall find the Divine *all* in contemplation.   It is of us to cleanse the vessel : it is of God to fill it.

The contemplation we are here considering is that which is "ordinary," and is defined as "the elevation of the soul to God, by a simple and intensely-loving gaze".[4]   In it the soul may alternate between activity and passivity, according as it raises itself to God, or God works in it.   But the passive operation is perfect contemplation ; and the active the preparation and disposition thereto,[5] since God is here giving His own gift of Himself, and is therefore the principal worker, the soul passively co-operating with Him.[6]   Hence contemplation is called supernatural, infused, and passive. And "as he that hearkens and listens attentively, using nothing of his own discourse, receives purely and truly the doctrine which the Master teaches, so the soul in contemplation, with little labour and much delight, receives interiorly profound inspira-

---

[1] " Imit.," B i., C 11.   [2] *Ibid.*, B iii., C 31.   [3] *Ibid.*, B iii., C 32.

[4] " Elevatio mentis in Deum, per simplicem intuitum, ardentissime affectuosum." (Schram, " Theol. Myst.," § 238, S 3.)

[5] The active is *dispositive* to the passive.

[6] " In qua Deus præcipue est agens, et homo passive cooperans." (Scaramelli, " Theol. Myst.".)

tions, illustrations, and marvellous sentiments of God, with which He instructs, feeds, and inflames her in the affections of love, even to a receiving within her the Word Incarnate, which is God Himself, by the perfect union of Charity ".[1]   " Then God lovingly caresses the soul, stirring with such heavenly sweetness its knowledge and love, that it seems rather led and sweetly urged by Him than moving by itself; rather breaking forth into acts passively under Him, than producing them of its own accord."[2]   And "casting aside her own operations, she resigns herself entirely to those of God, abandoning to Him her being and its powers, to live and act only through Him.   This prayer passes in the profound depth of the soul, where God dwells as in a secret sanctuary, far removed from the tumult of creatures, in a sweet, calm solitude, hidden from the world through its own fault.   Few place themselves in a condition to enter there ; rather they lay themselves under a positive inability to do so.   Few have sufficient recollection and purity of heart to reach it, being poured out on external things, and entangled in the senses. Therefore it is that they render themselves unworthy of a favour which God communicates only to the few, who by their fidelity dispose themselves to receive it."[3]

" The blessed fruit of all our labours is perfect

---

[1] De Ponte, " Medit.," Vol. iii., P 3, C 2.

[2] Joan a Jesu, " Theol. Myst.," C 6.

[3] Rigoleu, " Ment. Prayer," C 3, § 1.

contemplation, the advices about which (in books) are not meant for the informing of those that are arrived thereat — for they have a Divine light shining brightly in their hearts, beyond all human instructions—but for the encouragement of those that tend towards so Divine a state that will abundantly recompense all the labours, pains, bitternesses, and contradictions that occur in the way. Let nothing hinder souls, therefore, from pursuing the ways of Prayer proper to contemplation, with all courage and perseverance, till they come to drink of this water of life." [1]

But "no one knoweth, save he that receiveth. Little study is needed, but much love. Seek it from grace, not from science ; from the Divine Lover, not a human teacher." [2]

When a soul first touches upon contemplation, it finds the presence of Him whom in meditation it had sought. So far, however, contemplation is only in *act* (per modum actus), enjoyed occasionally in times of recollection, and quickly interrupted by natural activity and impressions from without. The contemplative *habit* has yet to be formed, which will give to the soul the habitual enjoyment of the Divine presence, light, love, strength, and movement (per modum habitus). Then "it worketh all its works in God, and God works His works in it. Then can it see

---

[1] F. Baker, " S. Sophia," T iii., S 3, C 7.

[2] " Sed nemo novit, nisi qui accipit. Parum est dandum inquisitioni, multum unctioni. Interroga gratiam, non doctrinam; sponsum, non magistrum." (S. Bonav., " Itiner. Mentis," C ult.)

grievous things and not be terrified, because it possesséth nothing it can lose, and is certain that God cannot lose His own. In its look there is no confusion, narrowness, doubt, or fear ; for the soul seeth itself one spirit with God. This look is immense ; and so mighty, keen, and strong is it that no power and nothing strange can subsist before it : for vanity cannot stand before the face of Truth. And thus all things are broken through by one simple and naked gaze." [1]

Like all other habits, that of contemplation will be gained (in the ordinary course) by the repetition of its acts. For God works in man according to his nature.[2] The soul, therefore, in time of Prayer will raise itself to God by loving acts and aspirations. Frequently during the day, sitting or walking, it will turn to Him readily and easily, as to its own chosen Friend and Divine Lover, giving free scope to whatever the Holy Spirit may incline it. "Treat with Him," says S. Teresa, "as with your Father, your Brother, your Lord, your Spouse : sometimes in one way, sometimes in another. He will teach you what you must do to please Him, and will soon become very familiar with you." [3]

As the soul thus lifts itself to God by ardent desires and affections, seeing that *love* is the bond of union, it begins to resign the discursive operations of the intellect, as also to abate the activity of its

---

[1] " Fiery Soliloquy of the Soul," C 10, 11, 25.
[2] " Quidquid recipitur, per modum recipientis recipitur."
[3] S. Teresa, " Way of Perf.," C 28.

other powers, viz., memory, imagination, and senses,[1] whereby it joins an excellent mortification to its prayer. By this powerful union of prayer and mortification—the one lifting the spirit to God, the other suppressing the activity of the natural powers —the soul attains to that simple, intensely-loving gaze that brings it to the point of perfect contemplation.[2]

"Thus the soul shows its love, and calls its Beloved. But God (whose 'eyes are on the just, and His ears open to their prayers') waits not till they have finished their loving acts, but, breaking in upon them in the midst of their prayer, quickly pours Himself in, meeting the soul, anointing it with the sweetness of heavenly dew—wonderfully strengthening, vivifying, inebriating it ; and in this contemplation its carnal nature is so absorbed that it becomes, as it were, wholly spiritual.

"But the Beloved recedes. He withdraws Himself, suspending the sweetness of contemplation." (" He

---

[1] " Tu vero sensus relinque, et intellectuales operationes, et sensibilia omnia, et intelligibilia, ut ad unionem Ejus qui supra scientiam est, assurgas." (Denis Areop., " Theol. Myst.," i.)

[2] Perfect contemplation is attained when the soul, from being grounded in humility, mortified in its affections to and impressions of created things, and elevated to God by the prayer of loving acts and aspirations, finally stays the activity of its powers, and becomes a recipient of the Divine inflowing, or passive operation ; either by a simple and most loving sense of the presence of God, or by other communications of Divine light, love, and movement, that God may wish to make. This contemplation is called perfect in comparison to that which is active, wherein the soul acts, whereas here God acts. The action of God is perfect ; that of the soul imperfect. All this is still within the limits of ordinary contemplation, infused and supernatural, as not exceeding God's ordinary laws in the supernatural order. It may be called perfect ordinary contemplation.

suffers Himself to be *found* but not *detained*." [1])
"Nevertheless He remains within, for the governance of the soul. Fear not when He hides His face.
For you He comes—for you He goes. He comes
for your consolation; He goes for your admonition.
Lest, if the Beloved were always with you, you
might begin to despise your brethren, and to attribute His continued presence no longer to Grace,
but to Nature. Lest, therefore, you should mistake
your exile for your home, your Beloved comes and
goes, as though He said: 'Behold, you have tasted
a little; but if you wish to be filled, you must run
after Me, in the odour of My ointments'." [2]

From this choice passage we see how the active
contemplation is succeeded by the passive: that is,
how the soul invites and, as it were, constrains God,
by its loving aspirations; and how God waits not,
but "breaking in" upon it, quickly "pours Himself
in," embracing the soul, manifesting Himself, and
remaining with it, as the Beloved with His lover,
that it may see, taste, and enjoy His Divine sweetness.[3]

Here the soul is "patiens divina," receiving or

[1] Ex. S. Bern., in Cant.
[2] " Scala Claustr.," C 8, int. op. S. Bern.
[3] "Gustate et videte quoniam suavis est Dominus." (Ps. xxxiii.
8.) "Deus, cum viderit mentem hominis spiritualis Caritate
flammigeram, puritate ac virtute fulcitam, ad divina fortiter aspir-
antem, mox dignantissime, amorose, ac frequentissime ei occurrit,
succurrit, cooperatur, Seque ei communicat, manifestat, infundit,
eam ad Se elevat, intra Se rapit, amplectitur, deosculatur, atque Se
ei intuendum, gustandum, fruendum, offert ac exhibet, habetque
complacentiam magnum in ea, et tanquam amicam ac sponsam
apprehendit, et Sibi adstringit." (Denis Carthus., "de fonte
Lucis," Art. 16.)

suffering Divine things rather than doing them : being the recipient, as S. John of the Cross says, of "a certain inflowing of God, which cleanses it of its ignorances and imperfections—habitual, natural, and spiritual ; whereby God secretly teaches the soul, and instructs it in the perfection of love, without efforts on its own part beyond loving attention to God, listening to His voice, and admitting the light He sends.[1]

" In this state the soul must be lovingly intent on God, without eliciting other acts beyond those to which He inclines it. It must be, as it were, passive, simply and lovingly intent upon God, as a man who opens his eyes, with loving attention. For God is now dealing with the soul in the way of *bestowing*, and the soul must deal with Him by the way of *receiving*, so that knowledge may be joined to knowledge, and love to love. Consequently, if the soul will at this time make efforts of its own, and encourage another disposition than that of passive, loving attention, most submissive and calm, and if it does not abstain from its previous discursive acts, it will place a complete barrier against those graces which God is about to communicate to it in this loving knowledge."[2]

As, however, the soul is here united with God in the bonds of friendship, and the love of friendship is mutual love and mutual communication, so it is to be expected that, in the time of prayer, there

---

[1] S. John of the Cross, "Obsc. Night of the Soul," B ii., C 5.
[2] *Ibid.*, "Living Flame of Love," S 3, L iii.

would be a flow and re-flow of loving acts between the lover and the Beloved. "My Beloved to me and I to Him."[1] Hence the prayer of contemplation passes from the active stage to the passive, and again from the passive to the active, according to the mutual communications of God and the soul, and their operations respectively. How frequently and intimately God may manifest and communicate Himself will depend on the soul's fidelity and purity, and the good pleasure of the Divine Spirit who "breatheth where He will".[2] A pure soul reflects habitually the Divine presence. "I seek a pure heart; and there is the place of My rest."[3] In pure souls God lives, and speaks, and works, and enjoys, and manifests Himself. Here is His paradise on earth. For "where God is, there is heaven. And where the King is, there is the court," says S. Teresa.[4] We may well suppose that the Angels and Saints would feel delight in reflecting themselves on the brightness of such a soul.[5]

An observation of S. Teresa must be made here. She says: "It is good to utter, from time to time, some sweet word, like one blows a candle when it has gone out, in order to light it again. But if the candle be burning, our blowing serves only to extinguish it."[6] This is to tell us that in the time

---

[1] Cant. ii. 16.   [2] S. John iii. 8.   [3] "Imit.," iv. 12.
[4] S. Teresa, "Way of Perf.," C 28.
[5] "Solent Angeli adstare orantibus: et delectari in his quos vident levare puras manus in oratione." (S. Bern., Hom. 2 sup. "Missus est".)
[6] S. Teresa, "Way of Perf.," C 31.

15

of prayer, as well as of action, the contemplative habit must be nourished by sweet words of love to God, rekindling the Divine flame, by gentle blowings of the spirit, when it becomes weakened and obscured in the multiplicity of outward things. If, however, the light of God's countenance is shining upon us, let not the soul disturb herself by making needless acts and aspirations, lest by thus blowing the light which already burns be extinguished. "We should extinguish the spirit," says S. John of the Cross, "if, when God communicates the Divine Spirit to us passively, we should then actively exert the intellect. In its own strength the soul cannot influence itself supernaturally. It is God that so influences it, but with its own consent. This Spirit unites not with the powers of the soul in true intelligence and love, until the imperfect action of those powers shall have ceased. The difference, therefore, between the active and the passive operation, and the superiority of the latter, is the same as that between the search after an object and that object found ; between a work proceeding and the work performed." [1]

When, however, the Divine Lover withdraws, or seems to withhold, the sense of His presence, then let the soul betake itself to aspirations and acts, and if needs be, meditation, in view of rising again to active contemplation, and attaining once more, God so willing, to the Divine passive operation. Let it cry with the Psalmist, "Cast me not away

[1] S. John of the Cross, "Ascent of M. Carm.," B iii., C 12.

from Thy face, and take not away Thy Holy Spirit from me." "Show me, O Lord, Thy ways, and teach me Thy paths." "Faciem Tuam illumina super servum Tuum." "Deus meus, ne sileas a me." Then let it stir the fire of Divine love within its breast, by loving affections to God. Let it renew its renunciation of all things apart from Him, and offer itself unreservedly again to the Divine will. Grieving for its weaknesses and miseries, let it cast them forth into the sea of God's mercies and bring itself once more to a "rich nought,"[1] or poverty of spirit, by complete renunciation, that God may be its life, its principle, its light, its love, its all. Thus in some way it constrains the Divine Lover, who "waits not," but, "breaking in" upon the loving soul, quickly again "pours Himself in,"[2] becoming once more its light, love, principle, strength, and mover; enabling it to "walk in interior breadth and largeness, in which no littleness is found, but a free and deiform gaze,"[3] and establishing it more and more in the Divine habitual union.

This contemplation, which is ordinary, though infused and supernatural,[4] may be briefly divided into three stages or degrees, viz., Recollection, Quiet, and Union,[5] each of which may be ordinary,

---

[1] "Hilton, "Scale," P 2, C 8.

[2] " Festinus ingerit se." (" Scala Claustra," C 5.)

[3] " Fiery Soliloquy of the Soul," C 8.

[4] " Contemplatio ordinaria est infusa, quia non fit nisi ex viribus gratiæ, imo ex aliquo ex donis Spiritus Sancti infusis. Et dispositio ad eam ex parte recipientis etiam solum habetur ex viribus gratiæ. Nec illam aliquis mereatur nisi ad summum de congruo." (Schram, "Theol. Myst.," § 241, 2 in Schol.)

[5] S. Alphon., "Theol. Moral. Praxis Conf.," C 9, § 2.

or extraordinary, according as they are enjoyed in
a lower or higher degree, or are within or above
God's ordinary laws in the supernatural order :[1]
the degrees of the ordinary leading onwards to the
dispositions requisite for the extraordinary, if God
may wish to bestow it, but which, exceeding as it
does His ordinary laws, is utterly in His own hands
to give or withhold as He pleases.   Nor is extraordinary contemplation to be regarded as necessary
in itself to the soul's perfection, being a free operation of Divine power and love, in modes entirely its
own.

The prayer of Recollection is enjoyed when the
soul collects her powers together, enters into her
own interior, and there finds the presence of God.
" It is of the utmost importance," says S. Teresa,
" to bear this truth in mind, that God is within us ;

___

[1] The Recollection, Quiet, and Union here treated are considered as " ordinary" contemplation, in contradistinction to the
modes and degrees which are " extraordinary " : for, as Mystical
Doctors say : " Contemplatio *generalissime* dividitur in ordinariam
et extraordinariam ".   (Schram, " Theol. Myst.," § 540.)   From
which it may be inferred that the various species of contemplation
in Recollection, Quiet, and Union may be both ordinary and
extraordinary ; which, indeed, the nature of the case, and God's
ordinary laws in dealing with men, seem to require.   For as the
soul progresses to God by little and little, and God on His part
gradually draws it onwards, and manifests His presence, it is to
be expected that these Divine communications would be made
also gradually ; wherein the soul may be more or less " agens
divina " or " patiens divina " ; first attaining to ordinary *acts* of
contemplation by a sense of God's presence ; then growing in the
disposition of Recollection ; afterwards receiving a certain quiet of
the powers, while love is in full activity ; then approaching to
Divine union in all the powers, first actually, or " per modum
actus " ; then habitually, or " per modum habitus " ; the soul being
admitted to more the further she advances, as says S. Teresa,
" Int. Castle," M 6, C 8.

and that we ought to strive to be there with Him." [1]
"And although, in regard of Himself, God is
present everywhere, yet in regard of the communication of His perfections, He is present in man's
soul after a far more noble manner than in any
part of the world besides: inasmuch as He communicates to the spirit of man as much of His
perfections as the creature is capable of, namely,
the supernatural graces of His Holy Spirit." [2] "God
is everywhere, but not everywhere *to us.* There is
but one point in the universe where God communicates with us, and that is the centre of our own
soul. There He waits for us. There He meets us.
There He speaks to us. To find Him, therefore, we
must enter into our own interior. Thus, when the
Prophet called on the people to return to God, he
cried, ' Return, transgressors, to the heart'.[3] And
our Lord emphatically says, 'The kingdom of God
is within you'." [4]

"I in them, and thou in Me. Abide in Me, and
I in you." [5] "Remember, then," continues S. Teresa,
"that there is within you a palace of surpassing
splendour. For, truly, no building can be compared
in beauty and magnificence with a pure soul. In
the midst of this palace dwells the great King who
deigns to be your constant guest. And here He
sits upon a throne of priceless value, and this throne

[1] S. Teresa, "Way of Perf.," C 28.
[2] F. Baker, " S. Soph.," T i., S 3, C 4.
[3] Isaias xlvi. 8.
[4] Bishop Ullathorne, " Groundwork," L iii.
[5] S. John xvii. 23 ; xv. 4.

is your heart. But here is the point. We on our part must, with a full and hearty determination, make over to Him entirely this interior palace, so that He may deal with it as with His own property, turning out and putting in whatever He pleases. God does not give Himself entirely to us till we give ourselves entirely to Him. Without this He never works those effects in the soul, which He does when she is entirely His, without any reserve or obstacle. For He is a special Friend to order and propriety ; so that if we fill this palace with rabble, and, instead of ornament, disfigure it with trifles, how is it possible that our Lord can dwell there with all His court? It is as much as we can expect if He stays there ever so short a time, in the midst of such confusion." [1]

From this it appears that in the prayer of Recollection the soul shuts the gate to external things, and retires into her own interior. Here she finds the presence of God [2] as in His own proper mansion. [3] There He lives, enjoying Himself in the soul, and the soul enjoying itself in Him. There He works as a Master-artist, writing His law of love in the midst of the heart ; [4] inscribing His own Divine characters on the soul ; taking out and putting in

---

[1] S. Teresa, " Way of Perf.," C 28.

[2] " The presence of God is infinitely more advantageous to the soul than all spiritual books collectively." (Rigoleu, " Div. Union," C 7.)

[3] " Mansionem apud eum faciemus." (S. John xiv. 23.)

[4] " I will write My law in their heart." (Jerem. xxxi. 33.)

what He pleases ; speaking to it,[1] drawing,[2] teaching,[3] and gradually perfecting it. Can it be that we should go outside in search of strangers, leaving our Lord to stand alone within us?[4]   "What is it thy soul seeks in external things, who carries within herself so secretly the kingdom of heaven?"[5] Dear Lord God, and yet Thou sparest us!   Thou remainest within, loving, courteous Lord, close to us in our disordered chamber, waiting for us till we come to Thee ; hasting to have us with Thee, ready again to speak, to work within us, and fill us with good things! Ah! "what an abode ought that to be in which a King so powerful, so wise, so pure, so full of every perfection, delights Himself!"[6]

"We should try, therefore, to disengage ourselves as far as may be from external things, that we may occupy ourselves more easily with God in our own interior.   And even when engaged with external occupations, we should often turn our thoughts within, if it be only for a single moment.   The mere

---

[1] "I will hear what the Lord God shall speak within me." (Ps. lxxxiv. 8.)   "Sometimes the soul not only feels that God is present, but also hears His voice.   In these circumstances penetrating, piercing, and persuasive lights perform the office of words.   God sometimes speaks alone, and at other times the soul converses in her turn.   This conversation is carried on so sweetly and secretly, that no sound is heard to interrupt the soul's repose." (S. Fran. of Sales, "Love of God," vi. 11.)

[2] "No man can come to Me, except the Father, who hath sent Me, draw him." (S. John vi. 44.)

[3] "It is written, They shall all be taught of God." (S. John vi. 45.)

[4] "Ecce intus eras, et ego foris." (S. Aug., "Conf." L x., C 27.)

[5] Suso, "Etern. Wisd.," C 9.

[6] S. Teresa, "Int. Castle," C 1.

act of calling to mind what a Companion we have within us is of great importance. Let us be convinced that if we please, we need never be separated from His sweet company."[1]

S. Teresa tells us that, by means of this prayer of Recollection, the Divine Master forms and teaches the soul far more quickly than if she followed any other way; that He leads her hereby to the prayer of Quiet; and that those who practise it may rest assured that they are following an excellent way; and that at last they will be allowed to drink at the Fount of perfect contemplation.[2]

The soul, therefore, enjoying in this prayer the presence and sweet converse of the Beloved, and knowing that pure love is the bond of its union, seeks to be wholly given to the exercise of love; and in view of attaining to this, begins to impose silence on the other powers, viz.: intellect, memory, imagination, and senses; seeing these so apt in their activity to be downdrawing to the Spirit in the exercise of its love.[3] Now it is that the soul is touching on the prayer of Quiet. "So quiet are the faculties" (says S. Teresa) "that they will not stir, feeling that love alone is necessary, and that aught else disturbs them and becomes an obstacle to love. When the will perceives herself in this quiet, let her not heed the understanding, or thought, or imagination, any more than she would heed a fool.

---

[1] S. Teresa, "Way of Perf.," C 28.   [2] *Ibid.*

[3] "Tu vero sensus relinque, et intellectuales operationes, et sensibilia omnia, et intelligibilia; ut ad unionem Ejus qui supra scientiam est, assurgas." (Denis Areop., "Theol. Myst.," i.)

For if she seek to carry any one of these with her, she must of necessity be occupied and somewhat disquieted. This would be all labour and no gain, and we should lose what our Lord gives us without labour. For here, without any labour of the understanding, the will continues loving, as it were swallowing the milk which our Lord puts into her mouth, and enjoying its sweetness. Let her not, then, care to know *how* she enjoys or *what* she enjoys : for if she contend with the understanding, she will let the milk fall from her mouth, and so lose that divine nourishment."[1]   "The repose now enjoyed may be more or less profound. Sometimes it increases to so great a degree that all the powers of the soul, except the will, seem inactive and motionless. The soul does nothing but receive the impression of the happiness, which results from the presence of her Beloved. But the will's movement is sweet and easy. It does not disturb the soul's repose, but dilates the heart, giving the delectation of the Divine presence, which, in its turn, brings content to the soul and the calm of repose."[2]

"But, of ourselves, we must not allow the understanding to cease from its acts. It is God who suspends it, by putting before it that which astonishes and engages it ; so that, without making any reflections, it shall comprehend in a moment more than we could comprehend in many years, with all the efforts in the world."[3]

[1] S. Teresa, " Way of Perf.," C 31.
[2] S. Fran. of Sales, " Love of God," B vi., C 7 and 8.
[3] " S. Teresa, " Life by herself," C 12.

"Alas! my Love, Thou art far above all other loves! Earthly lovers, however greatly they may love, must needs bear to be distinct and separate from each other. But Thou, O unfathomable Goodness and Fulness of love, meltest away into Thy beloved's heart, and in virtue of Thy being all in all, pourest Thyself so utterly into the soul's essence, that no part of Thee, the loved one, remains outside, and is not lovingly made one with Thy beloved."[1]

As repetition of acts gradually forms a corresponding habit, so the soul from thus repeatedly enjoying the Divine presence in the prayer of Recollection, and strengthening both its love of God and mortification of self in the prayer of Quiet, gradually attains to the *habit* of contemplation and union, whereby God gains the full possession of His kingdom within us, and occupies all the powers of the soul as His own. This is the *end* of all the exercises of the contemplative and active life, the habitual union of all the powers of the soul with God.[2] Then it is that the various powers which in

[1] Suso, " Life by himself," C 54.

[2] Finis totius vitæ contemplativæ et activæ est unio cum Deo habitualis, per Caritatem perfecte in anima regentem, et plene in actibus fluentem. " Sic homo ad apicem perfectionis Christianæ in hac vita assequibilis in via unitiva ascendit; in qua totus cum Deo, inquantum in hac vita mortali possibile est unitur. Unit namque via unitiva hominis *memoriam* cum Deo, ut Illius semper memor sit. Unit ejus *intellectum* cum Deo, ut de Ipso semper cogitet. Unit ejus *voluntatem* cum Deo, ut Illum semper amet. Unit reliquas hominis potentias cum Deo, quatenus homo earum actus exercet ex amore Dei, et quia, et quomodo Deus vult. Hæc unio stabilis est, firma, continua, perpetua, quantum per gratiam Divinam in hac vita fieri potest." (Schram, " Theol. Myst.," § 162.)

the prayer of Quiet stayed their activity by the cessation of their acts, in order that the fire of God's love might draw all the soul's energies to itself, now being themselves perfused with its influence, return to their activity with a new and Divine principle ; and the soul, as S. Gregory says, " being kindled in contemplation, gives itself more perfectly to action ".[1] Thus the soul which had abandoned the active use of its powers, for the sake of receiving passively the inpourings of God's love, now that the Divine fire has spread its virtue through them, and engaged them all for God, recovers their use and returns to the duties of active life, with an inward Divine spirit, which renders them Christ-like and perfect.[2] " Here," says S. Teresa, " the active and contemplative life are united. Our Lord is then served by all the faculties : for the will is busy at her work, and continues in her contemplation, and the other two powers serve as Martha, so that she and Mary walk together. This is no act of ours, it is supernatural. But it is good to seek for more solitude in order to make room for our Lord, and let His Majesty work as in His own. In this prayer the soul does not receive the Divine nourishment by swallowing it down" (as in the prayer of Quiet), " but she finds it within herself, without perceiving how our Lord puts it there. Here there is a union

---

[1] " Ut per hoc quod contemplativa vita mentem accenderit, perfectius activa teneatur." (S. Greg., Hom. 14 in Ezech.)

[2] " A vita activa proceditur ad vitam contemplativam, secundum ordinem generationis. A vita autem contemplativa reditur ad vitam activam, per viam directionis, ut scilicet vita activa per contemplationem dirigatur." (S. Thom., 2 2, Q 182, Art. 4 ad 2.)

of all the three powers, and He that created them
delights them and employs them all."[1]

" In the state of union, God enters into possession
of the powers as their absolute Lord, guides and
governs them Himself divinely by His own spirit
and will : as it is written, 'He who is joined to the
Lord is one spirit'; the operations of the soul,
therefore, in this state, are the operations of the
Holy Ghost, and consequently Divine."[2] "O God,
Thou givest me Thyself to be mine, whole and undivided, if I give myself to Thee whole and
undivided.   And when I shall be thus all Thine,
Thou enjoyest Thyself in me, and I enjoy myself
in Thee.   Thus Thou art in me and I in Thee.
And when we love what is good in one another,
this is nothing else but the love of Thee; and if I
shall abide wholly and entirely in Thee, as it is
impossible for Thee to perish, so it is impossible
for me to perish. And in this union I have no need
to turn away from creatures, however ignoble they
may seem. But so I must stand in the midst of all
creatures, as to be inclined towards them without
sensuality, and to turn away from them without
irksomeness or pain."[3]   "And if only I am able to
attain to this, namely, to stand in the sight of our
Lord, having all things in common with Him within
a pure heart, what is there more that I can desire ?
' If thou shalt abide in Me' (saith God within me)

[1] S. Teresa, " Way of Perf.," C 31.
[2] S. John of the Cross, " Ascent of M. Carm.," B iii., C 1.
[3] " Fiery Soliloquy of the Soul," C 15.

'thou wilt be able to do without everything, and yet thou shalt want for nothing.'"[1]

"Let a man, therefore, found and set himself firmly in the one highest and Eternal Good, which no accidents can reach; walking continually before the face of God, and therein looking at all things according as the One Incommutable Good, in which he is founded, understandeth. And this Wisdom will be a companion to him on his journey, and at home, in every place, and at all times; a never-failing light in darkness, a pleasant friend to converse with, who will keep him gladsome company at times of silence and leisure; an inward unction, lightening every trouble. Guarded by the friendship of this companion, he will want no other, but will abound within in all things, because he possesseth that in which all things are. And in his poverty, i.e., because he is destitute of worldly things, and because all things are destitute of him, he will be as liberal and bounteous inwardly with that companion of his, as if he were lord of the whole world. This is the straight path of the elect of God, where the naked, formless, and incommutable truth keepeth itself in the highest part of the spirit, and showeth its ineffable riches. Nor do I look from below at accidents and circumstances, but from above do I look at all things. And the truth crieth out for me with a terrible voice to all strange things that are not at one with it, 'Come not here, for the place where I stand is

---

[1] "Fiery Soliloquy of the Soul," C 2.

holy ground'.   And it teacheth me ever to simplify
within me all things that are from without, and to
change them into interior unity." [1]

"Farewell then, all things else that disagree
with the one thing." [2]

[1] " Fiery Soliloquy of the Soul," C 23, 24.   [2] *Ibid.*, C 34.

CHAPTER V.

THE DEVELOPMENT OF CHARITY BY MORTIFICATION.

" ALWAYS bearing about in our body the mortification of Jesus, that the life also of Jesus may be
made manifest in our bodies."[1] The life of our
Lord upon earth was a life of perfect Charity, for
to His human soul was communicated the fulness
of Divine light and love. "In Him dwelleth the
fulness of the Godhead corporally."[2] But because
His soul received the fulness of Divine Charity, it
was necessary that it should be wholly subject to
the Divinity, as the recipient before the ever-
flowing fountain. This total subjection of our
Lord's human nature to the Divine may be called
the "mortification of Jesus". For although His
human faculties were the most perfect ever formed
by the hand of God, yet He did not proceed in
their operations "according to man," but ever
"according to God": as S. Augustine says, "When
a man truly lives, he lives not according to himself,
but according to God".[3] And in the life "accord-

---

[1] 2 Cor. iv. 10.　　　　　　　　[2] Col. ii. 9.

[3] "Cum homo vivit secundum veritatem, non vivit secundum
seipsum, sed secundum Deum." (S. Aug., "de Civ. Dei," L xiv.,
C 4.)

ing to God" resides the perfection of man ; God
Himself being the Fountain of all perfection, and
man the recipient thereof. Our Lord, therefore,
as the "perfect man," was in perfect subjection to
God. His intellect was the recipient of Divine
knowledge; His will of Divine love. His soul was
thus as clear crystal, reflecting the brightness of
the Divinity, the Divine Will being the ruling principle, and the Sacred Humanity the perfect and
willing instrument, having, indeed, its own life and
operations, yet living and operating in loving subjection to God. Our Lord Himself points to this,
when He says, "I do nothing of Myself".[1] " The
words that I speak to you, I speak not of Myself;
but the Father who abideth in Me, He doth the
works." [2] " I cannot of Myself do anything." [3]

Here is the strength of perfect Charity, sustained
by perfect mortification. Perfect Charity, because
the Divine love and will reign within our Lord's
human nature ; perfect mortification, because that
human nature has no selfish love, no inordinate
movement, but lives, loves, and acts in sweet subjection to the Divine Will. Here is the model life,
perfect Charity sustained by mortification. "All-
ways bearing about the mortification of Jesus, that
the life also of Jesus may be manifest in our mortal flesh."[4]

In pursuing spiritual life, it is quite requisite to
understand clearly the "rationale" of mortification ;
for truly holy writers are uncompromising in their

[1] S. John iv. 28.   [2] S. John xiv. 10.
[3] S. John v. 30.   [4] 2 Cor. iv. 10.

view of it. "It is certain that everything depends on the perfect abnegation of thyself," says S. Catherine of Siena.[1] The "Imitation" measures our advancement by our mortification : "The more thou dost violence to thyself, the greater progress wilt thou make".[2] "Without a constant study of mortification" (says Blosius) "a man cannot make progress, turn where he may."[3] "Nor is it so much by our own endeavours, as by the resignation, mortification, abnegation, and losing of ourselves that we shall reach perfection."[4] "We must die, that God may live in us," says S. Francis of Sales ; "it is impossible for us to attain to union with God by any other means than mortification."[5] Moreover, S. Paul makes no compromise between the old and the new man. We are simply to put off one, and put on the other.[6] And our Lord's injunction to all who would follow Him is that of general self-denial : "If any man will come after Me, let him deny himself".[7]

Let us remember, then, that the soul of man is the proper domain of God. "The kingdom of God is within you."[8] God's design is to dwell within us,[9] to fill our capacities, to govern us, to work within us. But since the first revolt of our nature from its allegiance to God, the domain of man's

---

[1] S. Cath. Sien., " Dial. on Consum. Perfection ".
[2] " Imit.," B i., C 25 fin.   [3] Blosius, " Instit. Spir.," C 2, § 5.
[4] Thauler, Serm. Dom. 5 p. Pasc.
[5] S. Fran. of Sales, " Conferences," Conf. 20, " Intention," &c.
[6] Eph. iv. 22.   [7] S. Matt. xvi. 24.   [8] S. Luke xvii. 12.
[9] " I will dwell in them, and walk among them." (2 Cor. vi. 16.)

16

soul has been invaded. The powers of evil have entered within us, and made our faculties their strongholds. The will, the intellect, the memory, the imagination and senses, have been drawn from the Divine subjection, and occupied by the opposing forces of the world, the flesh, and the devil. Life has gone on, and repeated acts have formed our habits. Had our acts been those of Divine knowledge and love, we might now be in a disposition to be occupied divinely. But if, by a repetition of contrary and imperfect acts, evil, human, selfish, imperfect habits have been formed, the soul is thereby occupied, and God's rights within it are so far supplanted. How, then, can God occupy His own, when it is thus estranged from Him? The opposing forces that have gathered within our powers must be driven back. The objects crowding in upon the faculties must be forbidden entrance. The soul must be released from all this foreign servitude, and left unencumbered and free.[1] Then let it turn with a single and full heart to God,[2] yielding its homage to Him, and beg Him to establish His reign within it, deposing the natural use of its powers, which have betrayed it into the hands of

[1] "Of what advantage are wings to an eagle when its foot is chained?" This shows how, if we are to rise to God by Prayer, we must be released from attachments by Mortification. "As long as anything holds me, I cannot freely fly to Thee." ("Imit.," B iii., C 31.) Thus Prayer and Mortification appear again as the two necessary instruments of perfection, both serving towards the union of perfect Charity: Mortification, by keeping down the flesh; Prayer, by lifting up the spirit.

[2] "Woe to them that are of a double heart." (Ecclus. ii, 14.)

its enemies; and taking henceforth the Divine will and love for its one, consistent moving-principle, by which the faculties, senses, and members will be divinely governed, and the whole man be brought into order under God. This is the very work of mortification. God sets His throne within the kingdom of the soul,[1] and rules the will by His own virtue of Charity. Under the will move the other powers, so that Charity, by governing the master-faculty, gains dominion over the rest.[2] Her aim is to be the one presiding power in the soul, that the kingdom of God within may be undivided. To attain to this she sees the necessity of reducing the natural man to subjection. For as long as we live, love, judge, and move by our own active, natural principle, our spirit is not Divine, but human. But this is a direct impediment to the reign of God within us, since "he who adheres to the Lord is one spirit".[3]

It is clear, therefore, that Charity must not only be a living principle of love to God, rising upwards to Him in the ways of prayer: it must become at the same time the principle of "holy hatred,"[4] by descending to the mortification of the natural man

---

[1] " Ponam in te thronum Meum."

[2] "Caritas est regula, rectificans voluntatem, qua rectificata tota anima recte vivit." (S. Bonav., "Centiloq.," P 3, S 40.)

[3] 1 Cor. vi. 17.

[4] "The soul, seeing that her own sensuality is the root of all sin, and the cause of her separation from her supreme end, conceives a certain ' holy hatred ' of her own inclinations, and a desire to kill the root of them, which is self-love." (S. Cath. Sien., " Hist.," A. T. Drane, C 4.)

in his "fleshly loves and fears," knowing, as S.
Augustine says, that if we hate rightly, we love.[1]
Charity is the bond of union between God and
man. It, therefore, has a "higher beholding" and
a "lower beholding". The higher beholding is of
God, in the way of prayer. The lower beholding
is of self, in the way of mortification. And there is
the "higher stirring" and the "lower stirring".
The higher is that of Divine love, spreading its
virtue in the soul, by ardent acts, developing the
habit. The lower is that of fleshly loves and fears,
working in the natural man ; and these are the
matter for mortification. The natural man must
die, that the spiritual man may live. "Verily,
until all fleshly loves and fears be cast out, a soul
can never feel the burning love of God, nor have
the homeliness of His gracious presence, nor a clear
sight of spiritual things. Thou must hate, therefore, all fleshly loves and fears in thy heart without
ceasing, for with the precious liquor of God's love
only may thy soul be filled, and with none other."[2]
In view of understanding in general the work of
mortification, we may refer to the Diagram, p. 42.
We see in Fig. I. Charity resident in the soul, but
hindered in her life and operations by the hold
which the natural man retains in all the ramifications of his Cupidity. Our plan must be to seize
upon the higher love of Charity, and by her power

---

[1] "Si bene oderis, tunc amasti." (S. Aug., Tract 51 in Ep.
Joan.)

[2] Hilton, "Scale of Perf.," P 3, C 1 ; P 1, C 17 ; P 2, C 3.

to renounce the lower self-moving principle of Cupidity, till all her miseries are dispersed, and the soul, as a pure crystal before the sun, reflects the brightness of the Divine light and love, as shown in Fig. 2; which is only saying, in other words, that we are to "put off" the old man and "put on" the new man—Charity and Cupidity being their respective moving-principles. It is only when mortification has done its full work, here or in Purgatory, that the soul will be able to reflect the purity of the Divine likeness, and thus be fitted for its eternal union with God. We see from this how effectually mortification brings the soul onwards to perfection, by ridding us of the opposing elements to perfect inward purity and Charity, as the grain of wheat rises not to life except it die first.[1]

Truly, in the ridding ourselves of these opposing elements lies the arduous work of mortification. And yet, without this, there is no possibility of getting to perfection. The work of our perfection is the work of transformation to the Divine likeness by perfect Charity.[2] But transformation implies the expulsion of all contrary qualities, as we see in the action of fire upon wood. "The difficulty is not in introducing a new form into the matter, but in disposing the matter to receive it. See how active the fire is in drying up the moisture of the wood. See the thick smoke it sends forth, and the time it takes to dispose it to burn. But as soon as the

---

[1] S. John xii. 24.
[2] "In eamdem imaginem transformamur." (2 Cor. iii. 18.)

wood has all the dispositions that are necessary, it presently takes fire, and is easily consumed. It is the same with us. All the difficulty consists in taking from our passions their strength and greenness ; in mortifying our appetites, in withdrawing ourselves from outward things. If we can but compass this, the rest will cost us nothing. Our soul will of itself move to God, and delight in conversing with Him. 'Similis simili gaudet.' But he who applies himself to mortification hereby spiritualises himself, rendering himself in some manner like to God ; and God reciprocally delights to converse and communicate with him. But when the heart is filled with passions, when we are still attached to creatures, pleasing ourselves in worldly conversation, loving our own ease and satisfaction, we are then so far from resembling God that we find it hard to converse with Him, taking no pleasure but in earthly things, because of the likeness we have unto them : Facti sunt abominabiles sicut ea quæ dilexerunt." [1]

To this let us add the following from Lewis of Granada : "All that is contrary or dissimilar to God is also opposed to His love. For as it is the nature of this love to unite the soul with God and transform it in Him, and as union presupposes a likeness between the things to be united, it follows that everything which hinders this likeness, hinders also union, and therefore love. Thus we see that fire does not unite with water, because they are

[1] Rodriguez, "Christian Perfection," Tr. on "Mortification," C 1.

contrary. Nor does water unite with oil, because, though not contrary to, it is unlike it. So, whoever desires Divine love must necessarily cast from his soul not only all mortal sins which are diametrically opposed to this love, but also all imperfections, and everything that is unlike to God ; that thus the soul may be united to Him and like to Him."[1] Hence the same author tells us that one unmortified inclination is enough to hinder our perfection :[2] which is indeed self-evident, since it is plain that imperfection is incompatible with perfection. "Whoever, then," says he, "aspires to perfection, let him make this rule to himself, that he have neither eyes, nor ears, nor tongue, except to God alone and His service, endeavouring to reject everything that does not help to this end."[3]

Here we see the indispensable necessity of becoming mortified men. Mortification rids us of the hindrances to God ; it removes from us all that is opposed and unlike to Him. When this is effected, the soul goes to God, as to its proper object ; as the steel freed from every fetter flies to the magnet. Nor can anything approach to one extreme, except in so far as it recedes from the other,[4] and when it reaches the point to which it tends, it is then completely withdrawn from the other. "If, therefore, a man tend to God, he cannot

---

[1] Lewis of Gran., " de perfect. amoris Dei," P 1, C 10.
[2] *Ibid.*, P 1, C 5.   [3] *Ibid.*, P 1, C 14.
[4] " In omni motu duo tantum sunt termini ; unus *a quo*, alter *ad quem*. Nec aliquid ad unum accedere potest, nisi prius recedat ab altero." (Lewis de Gran., " de perfect. amoris Dei," P 1, C 2.)

attain to Him except by leaving himself. Wood
cannot become fire except by losing its old form,
and yielding up everything contrary to the fiery
element. Nor can man, conceived in sin, and en-
compassed with flesh and blood, attain to a
transformation in Divine sanctity and purity,
except by relinquishing everything that hinders
his conformity hereto."

"But these impediments being removed by
mortification, the spirit forthwith springs into life
and vigour, disposed at once to go to God, and
God to come to it. For as a stone, unhindered,
falls downwards to its natural place, so the soul as
a spiritual substance, freed from earthly ties, rises
on high to spiritual things, as agreeing with its
nature. And the difficulty here is, not in the
rising to Divine love, which is an exercise of
incredible sweetness, but in removing from the soul
the impediments hereto." [1]

To what then shall we compare the soul that
chooses to live on in the indulgence of the natural
man, gratifying itself by a number of attachments
and desires, eager for the pleasures of sense, seeking
to satisfy itself with perishable love? It is like a
traveller on a long journey, whose eyes are clouded
with dust, so that he sees not the glorious sun above
him; whose feet are clogged with heavy earth; whose
hands are entangled in the meshes of a slimy net.
How deplorable is his condition! How sad and
weary his progress! Can he possibly reach his end

[1] Lewis de Gran., "de perfect. amoris Dei," C 2.

in this unhappy plight? And what is the cause of it all? He is simply fettered with impediments.[1] Let him but get rid of them, and he is a healthy man, able to run on his way rejoicing.

This is the figure of a soul trying to advance to God without mortification. What is it that clouds our spiritual vision, and hinders as by a curtain the eye of the soul from seeing with Divine light the things of God? The mind is shrouded with the veil of creatures around it, and darkened with their images;[2] "and although the object may be good, yet our affection for it is not so. For a sheet of gold before the eyes hinders the sight no less than a sheet of lead."[3] So that if the mind be entangled with a creature, even though in itself good, the sight of God is thereby intercepted. Mortification is needed, the mortification of the mind and memory, by which we free ourselves from a useless engagement with creatures, that thus the Divine light may shine unimpeded on our souls.[4]

---

[1] " Everything, according to the inclination thou hast to it, cleaveth to thee more or less." (" Imit.," B iii., C 27.)

[2] " Earthly images cannot but be downdrawing and obscuring to the soul, being so thick, gross, and heavy in comparison of the spirit to which they cleave. By this may be seen how great an evil the least incumbrance is, and how easily it is incurred; the great difficulty of the spiritual art lying in the riddance of the soul from such incumbrances, by its denudation and simplification." (F. Baker, Preface to " Div. Cloud".) Hence "contemplative souls," says S. Gregory, " turn inwards to themselves: not drawing with them the shadows of corporal things, but rising to the Divine light, they shut their eyes to images of earth." (S. Greg., " Moral.," L vi., C 17.)

[3] Lewis of Gran., " de perfect. amor. Dei," C 7.

[4] " Qui videt Deum, eo ipso moritur, ne amore teneatur." (S. Greg., " Moral.," L xviii., c. ult.)

What is it again that hinders us from advancing
speedily in the way of God, rejoicing in our course,
going from virtue to virtue? Our steps are clogged
by attachments to earth. We are drawn down and
held captive by the gratifications of sense. "And
how can a man direct the powers of his soul to the
wondrous things of God, who is full of the love of
earthly things; who has his intellect, will, memory,
affections, imagination, senses, and thoughts im-
mersed in and captivated by them? Where will
the love of God find in him a place vacant and
disengaged?"[1] The affections must be released
from the trammels that entangle them, then the
soul can advance to God ; but at present it is held,
and weighed down by the things of earth. "We
must give creatures their dismissal, if we wish
to attain to the sovereign good."[2] "Man cannot
become partaker of the Divine nature, unless he
transcend in mind and heart all created things,
and himself also."[3] Let Charity then proceed in
her work. She is the ruling power, and to her
belong the possession and governance of the soul.
Let her take, therefore, the soul's affections to
herself, and deny them to the natural màn. This
is mortification. It relieves the soul of the heavy
entanglements of creatures that encumber its path,
and enables it to go forward in liberty and joy.

[1] Lewis of Gran., " de perf. amor. Dei," C 4.
[2] Thauler, Serm. Dom. 5 p. Pasc.
[3] " Non potest homo Divinæ consors naturæ fieri, nisi seipsum
et omnia creata mente et affectu transcendat." (Card. Bona,
" Manuduc.," fin.)

What is it, in fine, that so hinders our powers of activity in the love and service of God? In things that please nature, we find plenty of scope for energy and interest. Why are not the energies of the soul devoted to spiritual things? The reason is clear. The poor soul is entangled with a multitude of desires,[1] and fond loves, and images of earth, that use up its energies, and waste its time, and tire its mind, and defile its heart, and weaken its spirit. How can it hope, as long as it is thus enslaved, to enjoy the "happy prerogative of a free mind," and the "grace of a delightful familiarity with God,"[2] that will enable it to serve Him readily, lovingly, and equally in all things? Let it extricate itself from the meshes of these earthly miseries that are entangling and enervating its powers. But how is it delivered from them? By the mortification which Charity imposes on it.[3] Charity claims the entire soul for God alone, and so rules the natural man into order. It, therefore, takes in hand the sword of mortification, and with it slays these "fleshly likings that keep a man far from the inward savour of the love of God, and from the clear sight of spiritual things".[4] Thus

[1] "What we most require for our spiritual growth is the silence of the desire before God; the language He most listens to is that of silent love." (S. John of the Cross, "Maxim" 285.)

[2] "Imit.," B iii., C 26 and 37.

[3] Caritas est principium mortificans.

[4] Hilton, "Scale of Perf.," P 3, C 8. The position of LOVE in the soul, and the way in which it "slays" all opposing elements, are principal points in Hilton's "Scale," and treated, as usual, in his masterly and captivating style. (*Vid.* "Scale of Perfection," P 3, C 7, &c.)

the bonds that held the soul captive are broken, and the spirit is free for the exercises and occupations of God's love. "Laqueus contritus est, et nos liberati sumus."[1]

When mortification has done its work, the soul attains to the happy state of disengagement and liberty of spirit, by which it. is detached from all irregular desire and love of creatures, and lives with God in a sweet unchanging disposition of Divine Charity. This "perfect divestment of ourselves," says Surin, "is the last disposition needed for entering the Divine solitude, whither grace draws us, and where, finding no bounds but God Himself, who has no limit, we shall enjoy immense liberty".[2]   With liberty comes alacrity of spirit, which makes the soul swift and joyful in the service of the Divine Lover, and to which S. Paul exhorts us when he says, "Rejoice in the Lord always".[3]   "Such souls," as St. Teresa says, "neither fear nor covet anything on earth. Afflictions do not disturb them, nor pleasures elate them ; in fine, nothing can rob them of their peace, since it depends on God alone ; and since nothing can deprive them of God, the fear of losing Him can alone disturb them.   Everything else in the world is in their eyes, as if it were not ; because it neither gives nor takes away their joy."[4]

In regard to the practice of mortification, a reference again to the diagram (p. 42) will help us

---

[1] Ps. cxxiii. 7.   [2] Surin, " Letter to M. Jean," V. ii., Letter 9.
[3] Philip. iv. 4.   [4] S. Teresa, " Found.," C 5.

in understanding what our general method should be.

Charity, be it remembered, is our moving-principle. But when we look into our souls (as in Fig. 1 of the diagram), we see there the rival love of Cupidity, which seeks also to be a moving-principle within us. All the appetites, passions, and other imperfect habits that are matter for mortification are seen to be the offspring of Cupidity or self-love, which, as S. Thomas tells us, is the root and cause of all our evils.[1] So that if Charity can but become the ruling power within us, and declare war against Cupidity, by destroying this main trunk, all the branches perish with it.

Divine love, therefore, becomes the mortifying principle to self-love, "slaying all sins in the soul, and reforming it in virtues ".[2] But the work is gradual. Again and again we are found lapsing on the ways of the natural man, and we have to own with the Apostle, "To will is present with me, but to accomplish I find not ".[3] Let us, however, put ourselves in the way to the "perfect work," [4] and undertake it fully in "preparation of heart". "Thy ear hath heard the preparation of their heart." [5]

As soon, then, as Charity perceives Cupidity

---

[1] "Inordinatus amor sui est causa omnis peccati. Propter hoc enim homo vel appetit bona, vel fugit mala, quia amat seipsum." (S. Thom., 1 2, Q 77, Art. 4 in c & ad 3.)

[2] Hilton, "Scale," P 3, C 6.   [3] Rom. vii. 18.

[4] "Patience hath a perfect work; that you may be perfect and entire, failing in nothing." (S. James i. 4.)   [5] Ps. ix. 17.

moving by any of the appetites and passions, for
its own selfish pleasure, it at once applies the
pruning-knife of mortification. "The time of
pruning has come."[1] "But believe me," says S.
Bernard, "what you prune will spring afresh.
What you banish will return. What you quench
will be rekindled. What you lull will rise again.
It is little, therefore, to have pruned once. We
must prune often ; nay, if possible, always. For if
you deceive not yourself, you will always find
something to prune. The time of pruning, then,
for us is always, as the need is also."[2] Thus are
we reminded by this great Father of our constant
need of mortification. And what is it all, but
giving the Divine Master the rightful place in His
own house, and putting the servants in due subjection to Him? "Lord, I have loved the beauty
of Thy house."[3] The soul of man is the house
of God. "The temple of God is holy, which
you are."[4] Let our Lord possess His own,
and "let all that is within me praise His holy
name,"[5] by a loving and ready service. Mortification is simply needed to effect this : to put the
servants, viz., our powers and senses, into loving
subjection to the Divine Master. "You call Me
Master and Lord ; and you say well, for so I am."[6]

[1] Cant. ii. 12.

[2] "Credite mihi: et putata repullulant: et effugata redeunt :
et reaccenduntur extincta: et sopita denuo excitantur. Parum est
ergo semel putasse. Sæpe putandum est; imo, si fieri possit,
semper : quia semper quod putari oporteat, si non dissimulas,
invenis. Nobis, Fratres, putationis semper est tempus, sicut
semper est opus." (S. Bern., Serm. 58 in Cant.)

[3] Ps. xxv. 8.   [4] 1 Cor. iii. 17.   [5] Ps. cii. 1.   [6] S. John xiii. 13.

Hence the same doctrine of mortification has been handed down to us from the early days of the Fathers of the desert. "It is to little purpose," said the Abbot Abraham, "for a Religious to have renounced all things at the commencement of his conversion, if he does not persevere in this disposition, and renounce them 'every day." [1] Thus of the Cenobites, the Abbot Piammon said: "They renew each day their first renunciation; not only of that which they possessed, but also of themselves". [2] We remember, too, how S. Augustine measures the development of Charity by the mortification of Cupidity. "The nourishment of Charity," says he, "is the diminution of Cupidity. Whoever, therefore, will strengthen his Charity, let him strive constantly to resist his Cupidity." [3] Because as the natural man dies by mortification, the spiritual man is enabled to live; according to S. Paul's words: "If you live according to the flesh, you shall die; but if by the spirit you mortify the deeds of the flesh, you shall live". [4] How well does S. Gregory teach us to join inner mortification to outward renunciation, in order to be able to attain to God. "It suffices not," he says, "to leave our possessions, unless we leave also ourselves. If a man leave not himself, he reaches not to God. Nor will it avail him to stretch beyond himself, if he slay not that which is

---

[1] Cassian, "Conf.," xxiv., C 2.   [2] *Ibid.*, xviii., C 7.
[3] "Nutrimentum Caritatis est imminutio Cupiditatis. Quisquis ergo eam nutrire vult, instet minuendis Cupiditatibus." (S. Aug., "de div. Quæst. oct. tr.," Q 36.)   [4] Rom. viii. 13.

within him.   Hence holy men strive to renounce
their desires, to leave the tumult of useless cares,
and the clamour of outward distractions, by taking
in hand the sword of mortification.   And as they
put on the strength of God, they yield up their
own.   And as they advance to eternal things, they
bid adieu to things temporal.   But then it is that we
attain to God, when we wholly die to ourselves."[1]

Hence we are admonished by the same holy
Father to beware lest, having renounced the world
externally, we become negligent in the work of
our perfection, and this for want of mortification.
" Holy men, in that they have forsaken worldly
things, and so progressed to a certain degree, fight
strongly every day against themselves, lest the
spirit should slacken through negligence, and under
plea of discretion, by indulging itself, fall short of
its due perfection."[2]

The necessity of working at our inward reformation by means of mortification has also been pointed
out in impressive words by the early Fathers of the

---

[1] " Nec sufficit nostra relinquere, nisi relinquamus et nos.   Quia
nisi quis a semetipso deficiat, ad Eum qui super ipsum est, non
appropinquat.   Nec valet apprehendere quod ultra ipsum est, si
nesciret mactare quod intra est.   Unde sancti viri ab importunitate
desideriorum temporalium, a tumultu inutilum curarum, a clamore
perturbationum, semetipsos sacri verbi gladio, mortificare non
desinunt.   Sic quo magis in Dei fortitudine convalescunt, eo a
propria virtute deficiunt; tunc vero in Deo plene proficimus, cum
a nobis ipsis funditus defecerimus." (S. Greg., Hom. 32 in Evang.,
& " Moral.," Lib. v., C 5, & Lib. xxii., C 14, &c.)

[2] " Sancti viri, in eo quod actiones hujus sæculi deserentes,
superant, robusto conflictu quotidie contra seipsos pugnant, ne
mens per negligentiam torpeat; et ne sub discretionis specie,
sibimet parcendo, a perfectione languescat." (S. Greg., " Moral.,"
L v., C 22.)

desert. " Some Religious, in their first fervour,"
said the Abbot Piammon, " seem desirous of becoming perfect in community life ; but when their first
ardour has cooled down, they strive no longer to
correct their vicious inclinations, which thus fester
more deeply, and become more dangerous, from
their concealment in the recesses of the heart. It
is certain, however, that virtue is not acquired by
dissembling vice, but by its suppression."[1]

The Abbot Daniel, on the same subject, says :
" When we have put off the carnal man, and separated ourselves from the conversation of the world,
let us be earnest in clothing ourselves with the
spiritual man ; lest, deceiving ourselves under the
appearance of having renounced the world externally, and thereby attained to some degree of
virtue, we grow remiss in the subjugation of our
passions, and through this supineness never reach
the perfection of our state ".[2] Nor let it be forgotten that the principle of mortification must be
maintained consistently and perseveringly through
life, no matter how far advanced the soul may be.
And for this reason, that mortification is the
counterpart of Charity. The spiritual man lives by
the death of the natural man ; and Charity lives
by mortification. " We who live are always delivered unto death."[3] But " he that will lose his
life shall find it ".[4] Hence Blosius tells us that in
mortification is hidden our true and sweetest life ;

[1] Cassian, Conf. 17, " Three different kinds of Religious," C 8.
[2] *Ibid.*, 4, " Warfare of the Flesh," C 19.
[3] 2 Cor. iv. 11.   [4] S. Matt. xvi. 25.

17

and as the grain of wheat lives by dying first, so he who dies to himself lives a new life in God.[1] The "Imitation" repeatedly teaches the same. "The more a man dies to himself, the more he begins to live to God."[2] "Son, leave thyself, and thou thalt find Me."[3] "Forsake all, and thou shalt find all."[4] Of S. Catherine of Siena it is recorded that "she would not tolerate the idea that there is any state of the soul, however exalted, in which the warfare with our own passions can ever be relaxed," and regarded it as a deadly delusion to suppose that this is only a practice for beginners. Hence, in her Dialogue, after describing various sublime stages of the spiritual life, she concludes with the emphatic warning that "there is no condition of the soul in which it ceases to be necessary for a man to put his own self-love to death".[5]

But alas! for our poor nature ; must it be said we have conquered great things, and are enslaved by little ones? And in the work of perfection, be it remembered, small things are of great consequence. A small chink in a vessel, if neglected, will cause the loss of all the liquor it may hold. And one small opening in a strongly-armed city will give an entrance to the enemy.[6] So if the imperfections of

[1] "In vera atque integra mortificatione, vera et jucundissima vita latet. Qui enim semper moritur in seipso, semper in Deo nova vita vivere incipit. Neque granum frumenti in herbam exurgit, nisi prius moriatur." (Blosius, "Instit. Spir.," C 2, § 5.)

[2] "Imit.," B ii., C 12.   [3] *Ibid.*, B iii., C 37.

[4] *Ibid.*, B iii., C 32.

[5] S. Cath. Sien., "Hist.," by A. T. Drane, P 1, C 4.

[6] "Tota civitas inimicis per neglectum loci unius aperitur." (S. Greg., Hom. 7 in Ezech.)

the soul are not remedied, the good things of the spirit are quickly lost, and the enemy gains an easy entrance.[1] "What folly is this," says S. Bernard, "that we who have forsaken great things, should now cling, at such risk, to small ones!"[2] Yet so it is. Religious who have left large possessions, kind friends, and so many of the pleasures and commodities of life, form strong attachments to small things ; to a place, for instance, or a certain work, in which they get so enwrapped that they are simply in bondage thereto ; or they engage in petty friendships[3] and idle gratifications, or cling to a particular room, or to a book, a lamp, a knife, a picture. "It is sometimes," says the "Imitation," "a little thing that hinders grace, or hides it from thee, if that may be called little, and not rather great, which hindereth so great a good."[4] How sad it is to find those who have commenced with such

[1] We are not to conclude from this that venial sins cause a *direct* diminution of Charity, in the sense of diminishing the degree of Charity attained, as a habit. Indirectly, however, venial sins and imperfect habits may be said to diminish Charity, by estranging the soul from God, and so depriving it of many lights and aids that would cause the increase of its Charity ; and also by inducing a cessation of acts, the habit of Charity is impeded in its growth or weakened in its power, and thus in some sense diminished. [2] S. Bern., Epist. 385.

[3] It need hardly be said that the friendships here contemplated are those which are " according to man," resting on imperfect creature and self-love ; not those " according to God," which are based on Divine Charity, whereby God is seen, and loved, and served, in the souls of others. How precious is the Charity that unites souls together in God! becoming the bond of mutual love and communication by which the fire of Divine love is more and more diffused, and the kingdom of God more firmly established in the hearts of men. " Ecce quam bonum et quam jucundum habitare fratres in unum." (Ps. cxxxii. 1.) [4] " Imit.," B iv., C 15.

great sacrifices, so far deteriorating in their course
as to transfer the affection of their hearts from
Divine things to trifles ; to see the tendency passing
into a disposition spreading and settling within
them, and by the repetition of act developing into
habit! Are not these the cracks and chinks
through which the precious liquor of God's love is
lost; the holes through which the enemy effects his
entrance ? " There have been many persons," says
S. John of the Cross, " who had made great progress
in detachment, and yet because they gave way
under the pretence of some good, as of society and
friendship, to petty attachments, have thereby lost
the spirit and sweetness of God, holy solitude,
and joy, and have injured the integrity of their
spiritual exercises, so as to be unable to stop before
all was gone."[1]

It may be asked, in view of remedying these
complications, where the weak point really lies.
Can the precise cause of them be shown ? and may
the cure be clearly known ? Among many Masters
let the enlightened Walter Hilton be our guide
here. His teaching goes to the root of the matter.
And here it is the root that needs the remedy. He
says : " Thou hast forsaken riches, and the having
much of this world, and art shut up in a cell. But
hast thou cleanly forsaken the *love* of all this? I
fear, not yet. For it is less mastery to forsake
worldly goods than to forsake the *love* of them.
Perhaps thou hast not forsaken thy covetousness,

[1] S. John of the Cross, " Ascent of M. Carm.," B i., C 11.

but hast only changed it from *great* things unto *small*—from a pound unto a penny, from a silver dish to a halfpenny one. These examples are childish, nevertheless they signify much. Thou art no good merchant. If thou believe not what I say, put thyself upon the trial. If thou have *love*, and *delight* in the having and holding anything thou hast, how mean soever it be, with the which love thou feedest thy heart ; or if thou have a desire and yearning to have something thou hast not, with the which desire thy heart is disquieted through thinking of the thing—this is a sign that covetousness is in thy image. And if thou wilt put thyself further to the trial, look if anything that thou hast be taken away from thee, or borrowed ; and for this thou art disquieted, angered, and troubled in thine heart ; both for the loss of that thing, which thou wouldst have again, and canst not ; and also art stirred against him that hath it, to strive with, and chide him that may restore it, and will not : this is a token that thou lovest worldly goods. For thus do worldly men when their goods are taken from them ; they are heavy, sorry, and angry ; chiding and striving with those that have them, both by word and deed. But thou dost all this in thine heart privily, where God seeth ; and therein thou art in more default than a worldly man, for thou hast forsaken in appearance the love of worldly things, but a worldly man hath not so ; and therefore he is excused when he strive for his goods by lawful means.

"But thou sayest that it behoveth thee to have

thy necessaries as well as a worldly man. I grant
it.   But thou shouldst not *love* it, for itself ; nor
have liking in the holding, nor in the keeping ; nor
feel sorrow and heaviness in the losing or the
withdrawing of it.   For, as S. Gregory saith : ' As
much sorrow as thou hadst in the losing of a thing,
so much love hadst thou in the keeping of it ' ; and
therefore if thy heart were whole, and thou hadst
truly a desire of spiritual things, thou wouldst set
at nought the love and liking of any earthly thing,
and it would not cleave to thee.   To love or to
have more than thou reasonably needest is a great
fault.   Also, to fix thy *love* upon the thing thou
needest, for the thing itself, is a fault also, but not
so great.   But to have and to use that thing that
thou needest, without *love* of it, as nature and need
require, is no fault.   Truly in this point I fear that
many who have taken upon them the state and
likeness of poverty are much hindered in their
pursuit of the love of God.   I accuse no man, nor
reprove any state ; for in each state there be some
good, and some otherwise.   But one thing I say to
every man or woman that hath taken the state of
voluntary poverty : as long as his *love* is bound, and
fastened, and glued with the love of any earthly
thing which he hath, or would have, he cannot have
or feel savourly the clean love and the clear sight
of spiritual things.   For, as S. Austin saith, ' Lord,
he loveth Thee too little who loveth anything with
Thee which he loveth not for Thee '.   For the more
love and covetousness of any earthly thing is with
thee, the less is the love of God in thy heart.   For

though it be that this love of earthly things putteth thee not out of Charity, yet verily it hindereth thee from the fervour of Charity, and also from that special reward which thou wouldst have in the bliss of heaven for perfect poverty ; and that is a great loss, if thou couldst see it."[1] " Thou must hate, therefore, all fleshly loves in thy heart without ceasing ; for with the precious liquor of God's love only may thy soul be filled, and with none other."[2]

What exquisite spiritual doctrine is this ! How telling, how practical, for souls aspiring to the perfect love of God, as the one governing love of the soul. This love does not extinguish other loves, but governs them ; that is, it does not extinguish loves which are subordinate to the love of God, proceeding from it, ordained to it, and according to it. But if any love be not thus subordinate, the love of God would extinguish it. Thus S. Paul tells us that "the wisdom of the flesh is not subject to the law of God, neither can it be ".[3] The law here may well stand for the law of love. So that we have one governing love, and other loves governed.

The cause, then, of so much spiritual infirmity is shown to be the disordered *love* of the soul.[4] We leave *things*, but not the *love* of things ; and "as long as a man's love is bound and glued with the love of any earthly thing, he cannot have or feel

---

[1] Hilton, " Scale of Perf.," P 3, C 7 on " Covetousness ".

[2] *Ibid.*, P 1, C 17, and P 2, C 3.   [3] Rom. viii. 7.

[4] " Inordinatus amor sui est causa omnis peccati. Propter hoc enim homo vel appetit bona, vel fugit mala, quia amat seipsum." (S. Thom., 1 2, Q 77, Art. 4 in c & ad 3.)

savourly the clean love and the clear sight of spiritual things ".[1] The whole work is one of love. The soul is encumbered with earthly and fleshly love, and has simply to be relieved by mortification. This being effected, the higher love of God at once flows in. It is of us to cleanse the vessel ; it is of God to fill it. Thus the soul gains its perfection by the perfection of its love.

And lest we should be deterred from undertaking in earnest such measures of unreserved self-denial, let us take heart from the teaching of spiritual masters, who tell us to make Charity itself our moving and sustaining power in the work of mortification ; since it is only the force of this love that enables us to deny so utterly the desires of the natural man. We want a strong principle, a spring of spiritual action, by which to do our work. What is stronger than love? " Love is as strong as death."[2] It "never falls away ".[3] It "carries a burden without being burdened, and makes all that is bitter sweet and savoury. Nothing is stronger, nothing higher, nothing sweeter, than love."[4]

Let us listen, then, to the Saints. " When once our Lord *impresses His love* in our hearts," says S. Teresa, " all things will be easy to us, and we shall work very readily."[5] But " to overcome our desires, and deny ourselves in all things " (says S. John of the Cross) " we require *another and nobler love*, that

---

[1] Hilton, P 3, C 7.   [2] Cant. viii. 6.   [3] I Cor. xiii. 8.
[4] " Imit.," B iii., C 5.   [5] S. Teresa, " Life," C 22.

of God, so that, having all our joy in Him, and deriving from Him all our strength, we may gain such resolution and courage as shall enable us easily to abandon all besides. For our carnal nature is influenced by such vehement desires, and so attracted by sensible objects, that if our spiritual nature were not on fire with other anxieties—those of *Divine love*—we should never overcome our natural satisfactions, nor have the courage to remain in the darkness of every desire."[1] And here we may remember how, when this Saint represents the soul as going forth to perfect mortification, signified by an "obscure night," he at once allows the sustaining counterpart of Charity, by saying that it goes forth "with anxious love inflamed ".[2] Once more : Lewis of Granada has the following impressive passage : "Among the various means we have of overcoming ourselves, the chief of all is Divine Charity itself. For the love of God, being directly opposed to self-love, wages the strongest war against it, and quickly drives it from the soul. And as the rising sun dispels the darkness of night, so that the more the light increases the more the darkness disperses, so, as the love of God engages us, self-love gradually disappears. Thus Charity itself is our chief means for ridding the soul of every contrary love. And with the love of God, God Himself enters the soul, and abides therein ; and with Him come so many sweet and

---

[1] S. John of the Cross, " Ascent of M. Carm.," B i., C 14.
[2] *Ibid.*, C 1.

holy consolations, that he who has once experienced
them is easily induced to renounce all other goods,
in order to enjoy this one alone. For as a poor
man would readily renounce his cottage in order
to gain riches and dignity, so a Christian soul
willingly rejects the love of passing things to
secure the higher and better love of things Divine.
Hence S. Augustine says that only one drop of
water from the river of paradise suffices to quench
our thirst for all things here below."[1]

Let us be encouraged, then, to pursue the work
of mortification, as being the *proximate means* of
attaining to the union of perfect Charity. "For as
in physics, when one body is expelled from a space,
another at once enters to fill the vacuum, so the
soul from which all self-love is expelled is immediately filled by God."[2] As soon as the soul is
emptied and cleansed by mortification, it is at once
engaged by God's Divine light and love : " ne detur
vacuum ". This shows us how mortification is the
immediate disposition for union with God. Prayer,
meditation, poverty, silence, recollection, regular
life, &c., are *remote* means of attaining to God,
inasmuch as they aid us powerfully by the light
and strength which they impart in coming to the
determination of renouncing ourselves in order to
be united with Him. But mortification *effects* this
renunciation. It empties the capacities, purifying
the mind and releasing the affections, so making

[1] Lewis of Gran., " de perf. amor. Dei," C 5.
[2] Card. Bona, " Princ. Christian Vitæ," P 2, § 2.

the necessary room for God to diffuse within us the light and fire of His Charity ; thus transforming the natural man into a spiritual man ; and this, as S. Augustine says, by the *transfer of our love* from created things to things Divine ; withdrawing our Cupidity from the former, and cleaving by Charity to the latter.[1]

Let not mortification, then, be regarded as a dead sacrifice, but as a happy exchange. We give up the old man in exchange for the new man. We leave the human spirit to find the Divine. We mortify the natural man to give life to the spiritual man. We weaken nature to strengthen grace. We renounce Cupidity to gain Charity. We deny self-love to enjoy Divine love. We lose our own will to find the will of God. Happy exchange! that frees us from all our evil, and brings us all our good !

As a conclusion, let the enlightened teaching of F. Baker be impressed upon us : " Both these duties of Prayer and Mortification are so absolutely necessary that they must neither of them ever cease, but continually increase in perfection and virtue to the end of our lives. For regarding Mortification, though self-love and pride may be subdued, yet as long as we are in bodies of flesh and blood, they will never be totally rooted out of us ; but even the most perfect souls will find in themselves matter

---

[1] " Qui de die in diem proficiendo renovatur, transfert amorem a temporalibus ad æterna, a visibilibus ad intelligibilia, a carnalibus ad spiritalia : atque ab istis Cupiditatem frænare, atque minuere : illisque se Caritate alligare, diligenter insistit." (S. Aug., ''de Trinit.," L xiv., C 17.)

for further mortification. And in regard to Prayer, our union with God thereby can never be so constant but that it will be interrupted ; so that the soul will fall from her height back some degrees into nature again. Nor is there any degree of it so perfect, pure, and spiritual but that it may, and by exercise will, become yet more and more pure, without limit. The diligent exercise of each of these doth much advance the practice of the other. For as mortification is a good disposition to prayer, yea, so necessary that a sensual, immortified soul cannot raise herself up to look to God with any cordial desire to please Him, much less be united to Him ; so by prayer the soul obtains light to discover the inordinate affections in her that are to be mortified, and strength of grace actually and effectually to subdue them. But prayer is a nobler exercise than mortification ; because in Prayer of Contemplation consists the essential happiness both of this life and that which is to come. So that mortification is to prayer as a means to an end ; since a soul mortifies her inordinations, to the end that she may be disposed to union with God. And secondly, because prayer is withal in itself the most excellent and effectual mortification ; for in it and by it the most secret risings of inordinate passions are contradicted. Yea, the mind and superior will are wholly abstracted and elevated above nature ; so that for the time all passions are quieted, and all creatures, especially ourselves, transcended and forgotten."[1]

[1] F. Baker, " S. Sophia," T ii., S 1, C 1.

CHAPTER VI.

THE RIGHT-ORDERING OF CHARITY BY
DISCRETION.

DIVINE Charity is at the same time "one and manifold," according to the words of Wisdom :[1] one in principle, manifold in operation. And every soul that progresses in the ways of the Spirit must needs be tending more and more to this oneness within, although its workings without may be, as S. Teresa says, "in a thousand different ways".[2] The reason is that Charity is union with God, who is One and most simple in nature, yet so vast and varied in His works. So, as the soul advances to God, it approaches more and more to His likeness, by rising to the oneness and simplicity of Divine life ; and its principle of love, gathering strength by concentration, is more and more fitted for its manifold operations; as Wisdom again says, "Being one, she can do all things ".[3]

[1] Wisd. vii. 22 : Let it be remembered that the love of God is the highest wisdom ; according to the inspired word, "The love of God is honourable wisdom " (Ecclus. i. 14) ; and S. Augustine, "Summa sapientia est Caritas Dei". (Epist. 140 ad Honor., C 18.)

[2] "It is the property of love to be always working in a thousand different ways." (S. Teresa, "Int. Castle," M 6, C 9.)

[3] Wisd. vii. 27.

While Charity, therefore, keeps the soul consistently to its one governing love, as the bond of Divine union and the spring of supernatural action, thus making it inflexible in principle, it allows great liberty of spirit and flexibility in matters of detail; according to S. Augustine's sentence, "Love, and do what you will";[1] as though he said, Keep true to your higher principle, and then move freely; "for 'where the spirit of the Lord is, there is liberty';[2] love itself will keep you right; if not, it is no love." Thus a soul becomes strong, stable, and equable from its interior oneness and simplicity; as the "Imitation" says: "He to whom all things are one, who sees all things in one, who draws all things to one, may be steady in heart, and peaceably repose in God".[3] At the same time it is large-minded and large-hearted in regard to the many details surrounding it, because it views these but as means leading to its end of perfect love;[4] and as they serve it more or less to this purpose, so it holds itself free to use or leave them, since "the lover is free, he is not held," and "love will be at liberty, lest its interior sight be hindered".[5] So the loving soul "stands in the midst of creatures as to be inclined towards them without sensuality, and turn away from them without irksomeness or pain".[6]

Owing, then, to so great a freedom of choice in

[1] " Dilige, et fac quod vis." (S. Aug., Tract 7 in Joan. Ep., 8.)
[2] 2 Cor. iii. 17.   [3] " Imit.," B i., C 3.
[4] " Ea quæ sunt ad finem." (S. Thom., 1 2, Q 8, Art. 2 & 3.)
[5] " Imit.," B iii., C 5.   [6] " Fiery Soliloquy of the Soul," C 15.

the use of means to the end, it becomes clear that the very Charity, which is our ruling and moving principle in all, should be *rightly ordered;* as the lover in the Canticle says, "He set in order Charity in me ".[1] For see the comprehensiveness of Charity. It comprises love to God, love to others, love to ourselves. It embraces the contemplative life, the active life, the suffering life ; these being the different operations of the one Charity. It takes in all the works of life, interior and exterior ; and these must be adapted to surroundings, individuals, and circumstances, and all used in order to our end.[2]

Now, will it not be difficult to see, to choose, and to move rightly in the midst of such diversity ? How liable we are to take mistaken views, to form false judgments, to draw wrong conclusions ! How many things are good in themselves, yet not good in particular circumstances ! When we turn to God in silence and prayer, the vast needs of souls seem to cry to us for help. Yet we are not to "cast our pearls before swine," nor become the victims of intemperate zeal. Nevertheless, while we avoid the labour involved in attendance on others, we seem to be shrinking from the "love of God by the sacrifice of self". And when we give ourselves to the service of our neighbour, do we not get over-involved in natural activity, and begin to lose our taste for Divine things? Then in a

[1] "Ordinavit in me Caritatem." (Cant. ii. 4.)
[2] "In ordine ad finem."

variety of ways we may be under the influence of different spirits, and to what extent it is very difficult to say.   There is the Divine Spirit, the human spirit, the diabolical spirit.   And we are told, " Believe not every spirit ; but try the spirits, whether they be of God ".[1]   " For whosoever are led by the Spirit of God, they are the sons of God." [2]

It is true that by adopting Charity as our moving-principle we thereby bring ourselves under the influence of the Holy Spirit, for " the Charity of God is poured forth in our hearts by the Holy Ghost ".[3]   But Charity is so manifold ; and amidst the continual diversity of its operations, what assurance have we that the work of our choice and the mode of our action are according to what God wills and moves us to, under the particular circumstances in which we find ourselves ?

All this tells us how much our love itself needs enlightening, directing, ordering, and rightly applying.   Till this be done Charity is not perfect.   Its habit, indeed, may be firmly established within us ; but it does not follow that our acts will be necessarily in accordance therewith.   As long as the natural man is alive and unreformed by the principle of the higher love, so long will our lower activities be apt to assert themselves, mingle their imperfect operations with those of Divine love, and so obscure the light of the Holy Spirit within our souls.   Thus we cannot see our way clearly ; nor can we tell what God would have us do.   Soon our

---

[1] 1 John iv. 1.   [2] Rom. viii. 14.   [3] Rom. v. 5.

steps falter, and we deviate from the right order to the end.[1] "Woe to you that put darkness for light, and light for darkness."[2] "Every plant which My Heavenly Father hath not planted shall be rooted up."[3]

Here we are brought to acknowledge the necessity of light as well as love ; in other words, of an enlightened Charity.[4] Undoubtedly light comes with love, and belongs to it ; according to the words of Ecclesiasticus, "Love Him, and your hearts shall be enlightened";[5] and as S. Paul says, "Being rooted and founded in Charity, you may be able to comprehend".[6] "Love is a fire, burning and shining. When it burns in the will it shines in the understanding."[7] Charity uniting the Spirit with God, thereby unites it with the Fount of light. Created Charity is in contact with the Increated Charity ;[8] and where the Spirit of God is, there are His gifts, Wisdom, Understanding, Knowledge, and Counsel ; the gifts of Divine Light, flowing from the heart into the mind.[9] Thus while Charity is the form, the animating spirit, and motive-cause

---

[1] "Ratio peccati consistit in deviatione ab ordine ad finem." (S. Thom., 1 2, Q 21, Art. 1 ad 3.)

[2] Isaias v. 20.   [3] S. Matt. xv. 13.

[4] "Illuminatos oculos cordis vestri." (Eph. i. 18.)

[5] Ecclus. ii. 10.   [6] Eph. iii. 17.

[7] Card. Bona, "Via Compend.," C 9.

[8] "Oportet ponere Caritatem esse habitum creatum in anima, quæ quidem manat ab amore qui est Spiritus Sanctus." (S. Thom., 1 Sent., Dist. 27, Q 1, Art. 1.)

[9] i.e., The gifts are in the mind, as the result of Charity in the heart. Hence, says S. Thomas, "Dona Spiritus Sancti connectuntur sibi invicem in Caritate". (1 2, Q 68, Art. 5.)

18

of the virtues and their various operations, Divine discretion directs and regulates Charity itself.[1] This discretion is love's own light in the mind,[2] and is therefore Charity rightly ordered,[3] and moving under the impulse of the Holy Spirit and His gifts.[4] Its definition may be given as the discernment of the mind in regard to the operations of the will, or, as philosophy would say, "the right view of things to be done".[5] Practically, however, discretion is not only a right viewing, but a right *doing* also.[6] In spiritual life, therefore, discretion is taken for the light of the Spirit of God in the mind, resulting from the love of God in the heart, showing the soul the right thing to be done, and moving its will to do it. Thus discretion presupposes the habit of Charity in the soul; and as the love of

---

[1] "Caritas informat omnes virtutes, sapientia vero dirigit." (S. Thom., in Pauli Epist. ad Coloss., C 3, Lect. 3.)

[2] "Ubi amor, ibi oculus." "Quia homo habens intellectum illustratum, et affectum ordinatum, per Spiritum Sanctum de singulis quæ pertinent ad salutem, rectum judicium habet. Ille autem qui non est spiritualis, habet intellectum obscuratum, et affectum inordinatum circa spiritualia bona. Et ideo ab homine non spirituali spiritualis homo judicari non potest, sicut nec vigilans a dormiente: unde dicitur i. Eth." "Unusquisque bene judicat quæ cognoscit." (S. Thom., in Pauli Epist. ad Cor. i., Cap. 2, Lec. 3.)

[3] "Discretio est ordinatio Caritatis. Discretio quippe omni virtuti ordinem ponit. Est ergo discretio non tam virtus quam quædam moderatrix et auriga virtutum, ordinatrixque affectuum, et morum doctrix." (S. Bern., Serm. 49 in Cant.)

[4] "Dona Spiritus Sancti faciunt nos bene sequentes instinctum Ipsius." (S. Thom., 1 2, Q 68, A 2 ad 3.)

[5] "Recta ratio agibilium."

[6] "Laus prudentiæ non consistit in sola consideratione, sed in applicatione ad opus, quod est finis practicæ rationis. Et ideo si in hoc defectus accidat maxime est contrarium prudentiæ." (S. Thom., 2 2, Q 47, Art. 1 ad 3.)

Charity burns, the light of discretion shines, and discretion becomes Charity enlightened, ordered, and applied to action ; or, it is the discernment and following of the Divine impulse, instinct, or call vouchsafed to the loving soul by the Divine Lover,[1] enabling it to walk "according to God," not "according to man";[2] and to follow the promptings of the Divine instead of the human spirit.[3]

No wonder, then, that the ancient Fathers made so much of Discretion; for viewed in this light it is nothing more or less than perfect Charity, or Charity perfected, which is our "all". Cassian tells us how the solitaries of the Thebaid conferred together, during the greater part of one night, upon the question of the direct way to perfection. "Each one gave his opinion according to his ability and judgment. Some thought it lay in fasting and watching, because by these exercises the Religious obtains greater purity of soul and body, by which he is more intimately united in friendship with God. Others placed it in the privation of earthly things, for then the soul would be stripped of whatever might be a hindrance to perfect union with the Creator. Another placed it in the faithful performance of the offices of Charity,

---

[1] " Nunquam Tua gubernatione destituis, quos in soliditate Tuæ dilectionis instituis." (Orat. Dom. inf. Oct. Corp. Christi.)

[2] " Qui ambulant non secundem carnem, sed secundum spiritum." (Rom. viii. 4.)

[3] " In ordine ad finem ultimum supernaturalem, ad quem ratio movet, secundum quod est informata per virtutes theologicas, non sufficit ipsa motio rationis, nisi desuper adsit instinctus et motio Spiritus Sancti ; secundum illud, ' Qui Spiritu aguntur, ii sunt filii Dei '." (S. Thom., 1 2, Q 68, Art. 2.)

to which our Lord in the Gospel has specially pro-
mised the kingdom of heaven.   When the greater
part of the night had passed away, S. Antony took
up the conversation, and said, 'All you have mentioned is indeed useful and even necessary for those
who desire union with God ; but to judge from
experience, the unhappy falls of many will not
permit me to attribute to the virtues you have
named the great safeguard for which we are en-
quiring.   Many have buried themselves in the
caves of the desert, been most assiduous in fasting,
disposed of all they possessed, and discharged
with the utmost fidelity all the duties of fraternal
Charity, and yet have fallen into illusions, and dis-
graced by a miserable death their former holy and
praiseworthy life.   If, therefore, that which was the
cause of their ruin be pointed out to us, we shall
discover the virtue which will conduct us to God.
Though they were rich in many virtues, they wanted
Discretion to guide them to their proper end.
They had not this mistress of virtues, which
teaches the soul to walk at all times in the way of
prudence, without deviating to the right hand by
immoderate zeal, or to the left by tepidity of spirit.
He who has not this discretion is not guided by
judgment and knowledge.   The eye of his mind,
as well as of his actions, will be involved in
obscurity, and he will grope on in the darkness of a
vexed and troubled spirit.'[1]   'Discretion,' said the
Abbot Moses, 'is the guide of life.   It is justly

---

[1] Cassian, "Conf.," ii., C 2.

termed the counsellor, without whose advice we should do nothing. Discretion contains that wisdom, understanding, and knowledge upon which our inward house is to be built, and into which our spiritual treasures are to be gathered. Hence we may conclude that no virtue can exist, or be brought to perfection, without the aid of Discretion.' Justly, therefore, was it decided by S. Antony that it was discretion which conducts the soul with unerring step to God, which guards and supports all the other virtues, and enables us to mount the topmost round in the ladder of perfection. For Discretion is the mother, the guardian, and the mistress of all virtues." [1]

Taking, then, Discretion for enlightened and rightly-ordered Charity, we may say that its first work is to "separate the precious from the vile ".[2] Bearing in mind that we have the twofold principle within us, viz., the self-love of the natural man and the Divine love of the spiritual man ; knowing the inclination of Nature to her own independent activity, and remembering how repetitions of act on either side develop the corresponding habits, it is the office of Discretion to " try the spirits whether they be of God ".[3] In this discernment it is to be remembered that Charity has regard to *God*, to *others*, and to *ourselves;* to God, for His own sake ; to others and to ourselves in reference to Him, and according to Him. And so manifold are Charity's operations in either of these ways, that

---

[1] Cassian, "Conf.,' ii., C 4.   [2] Jerem. xv. 19.   [3] 1 John iv. 1.

we need nothing more nor less than the light of
God within us to enable us to detect, in the midst
of such diversity, the one thing successively, day
by day, and hour by hour, that God wills and
moves us to.   Such is a spiritual life, and a true
Christian life, as S. Paul himself teaches when he
says, "If we live in the Spirit, let us walk in the
Spirit".[1]   And according to S. Thomas, "If we
live in the Spirit," we ought "in all things to be
led by Him.   For as in the natural life the body is
not moved but by the soul, so in spiritual life all our
movements should proceed from the Spirit of God."[2]

This light of God within the soul, which is
spiritual discretion and the instinct of the Holy
Spirit,[3] is communicated little by little in proportion as the soul is disposed to receive it, by being
grounded in humility, subdued to God by mortification, and brought near to Him by prayer.   By
such means it reaches what Walter Hilton calls a
"rich nought"; that is, by renunciation of all
things, it finds its "all" in God.[4]   By resigning the
lesser light it finds the greater light.[5]   "For except

[1] Gal. v. 25.

[2] "Si Spiritu vivimus, Spiritu et ambulemus. Si ergo Spiritu
vivimus, debemus in omnibus ab Ipso agi. Sicut enim in vita corporali, corpus non movetur nisi per animam per quam vivit, ita in
vita spirituali, omnis motus noster debet esse a Spiritu Sancto."
(S. Thom., in Pauli Epist. ad Galat. v. 25.)

[3] "Per virtutes theologicas et morales, non ita perficitur homo
in ordine ad ultimum finem, quin semper indigeat moveri quodam
superiori instinctu Spiritus Sancti."   (S. Thom., 1 2, Q 68, Art. 2
ad 1.)

[4] "Forsake all, and thou shalt find all."   ("Imit.," B iii., C 32.)

[5] "Quando lux increata exoritur, lux creata evanescit." (Blosius, "Instit. Spir.," C 12, § 4.)

a soul be first smitten down by humility and with-drawn from earthly things, it is not able to bear the shinings of spiritual light, nor receive the precious liquor of perfect love."[1] " Happy they who receive My light, who walk by the guidance of My light, and desire no other light but Mine. For they have the true light, the light which will never fade, which for them will never suffer an eclipse, but will con-tinue to enlighten them so long as they do not close their eyes to it."[2]

When Discretion has brought the soul under the habitual influence of the Spirit of God, governing through Charity, it belongs to her further, amidst the great variety of Charity's operations, to show the precise thing that has to be done in the particular circumstances in which we find ourselves, being aided herein supernaturally by the gift of counsel;[3] and not only is it her work to show the right thing, but to lead us actually to do it. For to fail in the *doing*, says the Angelic Doctor, is above all con-trary to Discretion ; because "as the end is the main point, so a failure in the end is the worst defect of all ".[4]

[1] Hilton, " Scale of Perfection," P 2, C 5 and 7.

[2] Words spoken to Maria Lataste. ("Letters and Writings," B ii. 3.)

[3] "Prudentia, quæ importat rationis rectitudinem, maxime perficitur et juvatur, secundum quod regulatur et movetur a Spiritu Sancto; quod pertinet ad donum consilii." (S. Thom., 2 2, Q 52, Art. 2.)

[4] " Laus prudentiæ non cofisistit in sola consideratione, sed in applicatione ad opus, quod est finis practicæ rationis. Et ideo si in hoc defectus accidat, maxime est contrarium prudentiæ : quia sicut finis est potissimus in unoquoque, ita et defectus circa finem est pessimus." (S. Thom., 2 2, Q 47, Art. 1 ad 3.)

When S. Paul says that "whosoever are led by
the Spirit of God, they are the sons of God,"[1] we
are at once brought to acknowledge that if we be
true children of God, we shall be led by His Spirit,
not by our own, since "we have received not the
spirit of this world, but the Spirit that is of God,
that we may know the things that are given us
from God; which things also we speak, comparing
spiritual things with spiritual. But the sensual
man peceiveth not these things, that are of the
Spirit of God; for it is foolishness to him, and he
cannot understand. For what man knoweth the
things of a man but the spirit of a man that is in
him? So the things that are of God no man
knoweth but the Spirit of God."[2]

How clearly does the inspired Apostle here teach
us to distinguish between the two principles, that
of the human spirit and that of the Divine Spirit.
When, then, a soul gives itself to God, to be "all"
for Him, what is the work of its life but to be simply
in sweet, loving, free subjection to the Spirit of God,
instead of living according to its own natural, self-
moving principle?[3] and when it renounces its little
"all," it finds the Divine all; and when it resigns
the use of its merely natural light, it finds the

---

[1] Rom. viii. 14.   [2] 1 Cor. ii. 11-14.

[3] "Rationi humanæ non sunt omnia cognita, neque omnia
possibilia. Unde non potest quantum ad omnia repellere stul-
titiam, hebetudinem, timorem, ignorantiam, et alia hujusmodi. Sed
Ille cujus scientiæ et potestati omnia subsunt, sua motione ab
omni stultitia, et ignorantia, et hebetudine, et duritia, et timore,
et cæteris hujusmodi, nos tutos reddit. Et ideo, dona Spiritus
Sancti, quæ faciunt nos bene sequentes instinctum Ipsius, dicuntur
contra hujusmodi defectus dari." (S. Thom., 1 2, Q 68, Art. 2 ad 3.)

higher light of God,[1] and says with S. Francis, "My God and my all". " Send forth Thy light and Thy truth ; they have led me, and brought me to Thy holy hill, and into Thy tabernacles."[2] The desire, therefore, of such a soul is to be led in all things, day by day, hour by hour, by God's own light and truth; according to the prophecy of Isaias, " All thy children shall be taught of the Lord ".[3] " Then shall thy light break forth as the morning; and thy health shall speedily arise, and the glory of the Lord shall gather thee up. Then shalt thou call, and the Lord shall hear ; thou shalt cry, and He shall say, Here I am. Then shall thy light rise up in darkness, and thy darkness shall be as the noonday. And the Lord will give thee rest continually, and will fill thy soul with brightness; and thou shalt be like a watered garden, and like a fountain of water, whose waters shall not fail."[4] Happy the soul that God thus takes into His own hands, and to whom He says, " I will give thee understanding, and I will instruct thee in the way in which thou shalt go ; I will fix My eyes upon thee ".[5] Yet she is not without anxieties, lest she should mistake the natural impulse for the Divine. Hence she cries with the Psalmist, " Make the way known to me wherein I

---

[1] " His qui moventur per instinctum divinum non expedit consiliari secundum rationem humanam : quia moventur a meliori principio." (S. Thom., 1 2, Q 68, Art. 1.)

[2] Ps. xlii. 3.

[3] Isaias liv. 13 : " Erunt omnes docibiles Dei "; S. John vi. 45.

[4] Isaias lviii. 8-11.   [5] Ps. xxxi. 8.

should walk ; for I have lifted up my soul to Thee.
Teach me to do Thy will, for Thou art my God.
Thy good Spirit shall lead me into the right land."[1]

In order to discern with certainty the movement
of the Divine Spirit, a number of correlative principles throw their light upon the mind. Thus
whatever is according to the Faith of the Church
is from the Spirit of God. Whatever opposes faith
is from the human or diabolical spirit. Hence in
matters of faith all the children of the Church are
in agreement together, because all are governed by
one and the same Spirit, the Spirit of God ; and
the first movement against faith is renounced as
the offspring of the human spirit insubordinate to
the Divine. Then for the governance of souls
there is the science of the Church in dogmatic,
moral, ascetic, and mystical theology. This, again,
is a reflection from the light of the Spirit of God ;
and a departure or withdrawal therefrom is at once
evidence of the private and human spirit. Let all
who deflect from the right way, either by tepidity
on the one hand, or by scrupulosity on the other,
learn in time to renounce their own human spirit,
which misleads them into such dangerous paths,
wherein they take "darkness for light, and light
for darkness";[2] and let the word of the Master be
sufficient for them ;—"Magister dicit". The science
of the Church is the word of the Master ; and the
word of the Master must stand : it must not only

---

[1] Ps. cxlii. 8, 10.

[2] "Woe to you that put darkness for light, and light for darkness." (Isaias v. 20.)

be heard—but *done.* "Why call you Me Lord, and do not the things that I say?"[1] "If you know these things, you shall be blessed if you *do* them."[2] Whatever, again, is in accordance with the duties of the state of life and office in which Divine Providence has placed us gives us a certain token of the presence of the good Spirit, because the calling to a particular state or office implies a call to the duties appertaining thereto;[3] so that, by giving ourselves to the works proper to our calling in life, we thereby gain an assurance of finding the movement of the Spirit of God. Here, however, as in all else, it must not be forgotten that the human spirit is still alive within us,[4] and while walking in the path of duty we have still to beware of the natural man, so quick at making claims and playing tricks; for the instant we deflect from the right order to the end,[5] we lose the influence of the Divine, and fall under that of the human spirit. "Show me Thy ways, O Lord, and teach me Thy paths."[6]

Further, the living voice of Superiors, as representing the authority of God, ensures to subjects in their obedience the influence of the Spirit of God; and this both in general and particular cases. "Let

---

[1] S. Luke vi. 4.   [2] S. John xiii. 17.

[3] "Quilibet tenetur servare spectantia ad statum suum."

[4] "Alas! the old man is still alive within me." ("Imit.," B iii., C 34.)

[5] "Ratio peccati consistit in deviatione ab ordine ad finem." (S. Thom., 1 2, Q 21, Art. 1 ad 3.)

[6] Ps. xxiv. 4.

every soul be subject to higher powers ; for there is no power but from God, and those that are are ordained of God. Therefore he that resisteth the power resisteth the ordinance of God. And they that resist purchase to themselves damnation."[1] It may be that sometimes in commanding, a Superior is not moved by the Spirit of God, but by his own imperfect human spirit. If so, he is accountable to God for departing from the right order to the end. But the Spirit of God still moves the subject to obey, except in cases of manifest sin. And we have the word of the Prophet Samuel, that " it is as the crime of idolatry to refuse to obey ".[2] Thus we see that subjects find their discretion in obedience, because in it they discern the movement of the Divine Spirit.[3] Let it be added that as the Superior represents the authority of God, he has also to represent the mind and very presence of God, and so govern both himself and others according to God ;[4] so that if the Divine Spirit moves the subject to obey, it may also move Superiors to command, both in the work enjoined, and in the manner of enjoining it.[5] How easy would it then be to govern, and how sweet to obey ! But the

---

[1] Rom. xiii. 1.   [2] 1 Kings xv. 23.

[3] " Ipsum quem pro Deo habemus, tanquam Deum in his quæ aperte non sunt contra Deum, audire debemus." (S. Bern., "de Præc. et Dispens.," C 9.)

[4] " Pascendas utique oves, non premendas suscepisti." (S. Bern., "de Consid.," Lib. ii., C 6.)

[5] " Ne sint cultores alieni, vastatores sui." (S. Greg., Hom. 21 in Ezech.)

impediment to all is the strong human spirit, not yet in subjection to the Divine. " Show me, O Lord, Thy ways, and teach me Thy paths."

Coming now to the ordinary works and trials of daily life, what is it that the loving soul desires but to be under the habitual influence of the Spirit of God ? But what is the precise thing, here and now, in these present circumstances, that God would have me do to serve and please Him, and this both in regard to the substance of my act and the mode of doing it ? Discretion it is, aided by the gift of Counsel, that discerns this very thing, and leads the soul to do it.[1] Hereby, in proportion to her docility and fidelity to the Spirit of God, the lover is able to recognise the Divine light, love, and movement, as though by the instinct of love. " I will hear what the Lord God shall speak within me."[2] " Speak, Lord, for Thy servant heareth."[3] And she prepares to move according to her Divine light and impulse. For " the Holy Spirit," says S. Thomas, " dwelling in the soul, teaches it what to do, by illuminating the mind and inclining the heart to the right thing ".[4] " But the sensual man perceiveth not these things that are of the Spirit of God ; for it is foolishness to him, and he cannot understand. For what man knoweth the things of

---

[1] " Donum consilii respondet prudentiæ, sicut ipsum adjuvans et perficiens." (S. Thom., 2 2, Q 52, Art. 2.)

[2] Ps. lxxxiv. 8.   [3] 1 Kings iii. 10.

[4] " Spiritus Sanctus mentem inhabitans, docet quid oporteat fieri, intellectum illuminando de agendis ; et etiam affectum inclinat ad recte agendum." (S. Thom. in Pauli Epist. ad Rom., C 8, Lec. 1.)

a man but the spirit of a man that is in him? So the things that are of God no man knoweth but the Spirit of God."[1]

But "who hath known the mind of the Lord, or who hath been His counsellor?"[2] " The Spirit breatheth where He will."[3] God moves different souls differently, and the same soul differently at different times; so that the rule of one is not necessarily the rule of another. To Jeremias it is said, " Thou shalt go to all I send thee ";[4] whereas Isaias is moved to ask, " Here am I, send me ".[5] Moreover, our Lord teaches us not to forestal the Spirit of God, but to wait our appointed time; when He says of Himself, " My hour is not yet come ".[6]

No wonder, then, that the Church bids us so repeatedly call upon the Divine Spirit to "come"; as though to remind us of the insufficiency of man's natural light and love apart from Him :

"Veni Sancte Spiritus   Veni Pater pauperum Consolator optime
   Et emitte cœlitus   Veni dator munerum Dulcis hospes animæ
   Lucis Tuæ radium.   Veni lumen Cordium. Dulce refrigerium."

By what signs, then, may we be able to discern the movement of the Spirit of God in regard to the one thing that God would have us do in the circumstances in which we find ourselves? This is the question that the loving soul ever desires to be satisfied upon; for which it entreats again and

[1] 1 Cor. ii. 14, 11.   [2] Rom. xi. 34.   [3] S. John iii. 8.
[4] Jerem. i. 7.   [5] Isaias vi. 8.   [6] S. John ii. 4.

again, day by day, the light of the Holy Ghost; and cries often with the Psalmist, " Show me Thy ways, O Lord, and teach me Thy paths ". Doubtless God does Himself take the guidance of loving souls in proportion as they · yield themselves to Him. " I am the Lord thy God, that teach thee profitable things, that govern thee in the way thou walkest."[1] And as love increases, light increases; because love gives God place within us; and " God is light; and in Him there is no darkness ".[2] " Love Him, and your hearts shall be enlightened."[3] Moreover, our Lord says of the loving soul, " I will manifest Myself to him ".[4] Yet as long as the natural man lives, he will be found mixing and mingling his imperfect operations with those of the Divine Spirit, and so getting again and again in his own light; so that the soul often finds itself in anxiety as to whether its movement come from God, or from the natural activity of its own human spirit, or even from the instigation of an evil spirit.

Now, Discretion it is that discerns between these spirits, and puts the soul at once under the Divine influence. By means of certain signs she gets an assurance that her movement is according to God. But it is only little by little the light comes, in proportion to the growth of love. " These lights," says Lallemant, " come to us by degrees, according to our interior disposition, and depart also in the

---

[1] Isaias xlviii. 17. [2] 1 John i. 5.
[3] Ecclus. ii. 10. [4] S. John xiv. 21.

same manner, leaving us in darkness ; so that we have an alternation of day and night. We ought to aspire after a perpetual day ; nor will it fail to shine in our soul when, having thoroughly purified it, we shall continually follow the guidance of the Holy Spirit."[1]

S. Bernard gives the following as a general rule. In *affective* Charity we have to prefer higher things to lower ; in *effective* Charity lower to higher : according to the word of the Master in the Gospel, " Incipiens a novissimis ".[2] It is evident that in the inmost affection of the heart (which is affective Charity) we must give God Himself the preference to all, because He is the highest of all. Then we have to prefer heavenly things to earthly things ; more perfect souls to less perfect ; and spiritual things to natural. But when we come to effective Charity, this order, says S. Bernard, is often, or even always reversed.[3] We are engaged with God in prayer, but we leave His presence to serve the needs of our neighbour. The peace of earth is considered before the glory of heaven. The solemnities of the Divine Office yield to the pressure of earthly business. And the more needy among our brethren call for our first attention. And "such as are the less honourable members,"

[1] Lallemant, " Spir. Doctrine," P 4, C 2, A 1, § 8.

[2] S. Matt. xx. 8.   There will no doubt be frequent exceptions *in praxi* to this rule of effective Charity, since " the Spirit breatheth where He will, and thou hearest His voice, but knowest not whence He cometh, and whither He goeth ; so is everyone that is born of the Spirit ". (S. John iii. 8.)

[3] S. Bern., Serm. 50 in Cantic.

says the Apostle, "about these we put more abundant honour".[1] Thus effective Charity does not consider the value of things, but the needs of men.[2] While, however, Charity effective descends to the lowest, Charity affective ascends to the highest, as S. Gregory says;[3] so that the soul is no loser; for "Charity does not cause the loss of Charity".[4]

In regard to the actions or omissions of daily life on all occasions of doing or suffering, whether for God or a creature, there are these conditions, says Father Baker:

1. "Either there is an exterior law commanding the thing or forbidding it, which is in all such occurrences to be esteemed an undoubted call of God. The exterior law is therefore to be faithfully kept, in the doing or forbearing of the thing occurring. The interior call is to be as faithfully kept, by doing or omitting the thing with the movement of the spirit of grace" (which is the spirit of love and of God).

2. "In actions which no law, human or Divine, commands or forbids, if they are extraordinary, they are not to be practised without the sanction of

---

[1] 1 Cor. xii. 23.

[2] "Nec pretia consideret rerum, sed hominum necessitates." (S. Bern., Serm. 50 in Cantic.)

[3] "Tunc ad alta Caritas mirabiliter surgit, cum ad ima proximorum se misericorditer attrahit. Et cum benigne descendit ad infima, valenter recurrit ad summa." (S. Greg., "de cura Past.," P 2, C 5.)

[4] Ven. P. Liebermann, "Life".

exterior authority.   The interior call is, however,
to be noted with esteem.   In actions implying no
inconvenience or notable singularity, the inward
call is a sufficient guide, and ought to be carefully
observed and obeyed, lest the soul, receiving God's
graces in vain, be deservedly deprived of them."[1]

" Show me, O Lord, Thy ways, and teach me
Thy paths.   Lead me in Thy truth, and teach me ;
for Thou art my God, and on Thee have I waited
all the day long."[2]

[1] F. Baker, Appendix to " S. Sophia ".
[2] Ps. xxiv. 4.

CHAPTER VII.

CHARITY IN ACTION.

INASMUCH as Divine Charity, by the combined aid of prayer and mortification, generates the contemplative habit,[1] it thereby disposes us to undertake successfully the labours of the active life. The contemplative element is to the active as the spirit to the body; that is, it gives a *Divine* spirit to the works of life.[2] For by means of contemplation the soul enjoys the habitual presence, light, love, strength, and movement of God; and is therefore fit to work the works of God. Whereas without the contemplative spirit, we bring the human element into Divine things, and thus the work of God, of the Church, and of souls, suffers.

We know that in the vast work of the Church for the souls of men, God is the first and principal Mover, working in us by His Holy Spirit our own sanctification and perfection; and through us by the same Spirit working in the souls of others. "There are diversities of graces, but the same

[1] "Contemplativa vita est Caritatem Dei et proximi tota mente retinere." (S. Greg., Hom. 14 in Ezech.)

[2] "Vita contemplativa activam vitam movet et dirigit." (S. Thom., 2 2, Q 182, Art. 4.)

spirit ; and there are diversities of operations, but the same God who worketh all in all." [1] We are but secondary causes. Our movement therefore must come from the First Cause. As the instrument that works must be in close contact with the hand that wields it, so if we are to work in God's hands for the souls of men, we must be in close union with Him, subject to His guidance and attentive to His will, thus labouring in His Spirit, and not in our own.

If then we hope for great results in our outer works, let us look to our inner spirit, since this is the source of our strength. "Spiritus est qui vivificat." [2] As in the natural life the soul is the moving-principle to the body, prompting and regulating the action of the members, so in the work of the Church the Spirit of God is the animating and governing principle, on whom the various members depend for their supernatural life and movement. This shows the need we are under not only of maintaining our union with the Divine Spirit, but, as far as may be, gaining a closer alliance therewith, so as to participate more fully of Its virtue, and thus increase the force and value of our external operations. The more we have of this Divine Spirit, the more of heavenly virtue resides within us, and passes into our actions, the fitter instruments we become in the hands of God, and the better able to work for the souls of others : because we offer then less impediment to Him "who

[1] 1 Cor. xii. 4.   [2] S. John vi. 64.

worketh all in all ".[1] Moreover, as in the body
the heart has a continual movement, but the arms
move only at intervals, so we ought to give ourselves always, and under all circumstances, to the
life of inward love, and only at appointed times
to outer works. And as the heart vivifies the arm
by the vital spirit it supplies, so the love of God
should animate our exterior occupations, by the
light, affection, and fervour which it communicates
to them. "Put me as a seal upon thy heart, as
a seal upon thy arm."[2] The heart signifies the
life of inward love, and the arm the works of active
life. Both lives, contemplative and active, may
be united in one person, as the heart and the arm :
and both are to be signed with the seal of the
Divine Lover, which is Charity : affective in contemplation, effective in action.

Does not our Lord' Himself teach us this, when
He says, "Abide in Me, and I in you. As the
branch cannot bear fruit of itself, unless it abide
in the vine, so neither can you, unless you abide
in Me"?[3] What words could declare more forcibly
our need of a deep interior spirit ? for our Lord
does not here say, "Come to Me," but "Abide in
Me," as a branch in the vine. Let My life and
My virtue be in you, and let the fruits of your
life be those of My Spirit. Let our first care
therefore be to maintain the strength of our inward spirit, by the union of love with God. Then
to give ourselves to external works as God may

[1] 1 Cor. xii. 6.   [2] Cant. viii. 6.   [3] S. John xv. 4.

move us: "Be ye steadfast and immovable:
always abounding in the work of the Lord ".[1]
Stability of soul first, with mind and heart established in Divine Truth and Charity. After this,
"abounding in the work of the Lord": by moving
from the inward habit to outward acts of Charity:
the principle of Divine love remaining unalterably
the same: whether in its workings within, or its
workings without: as the movements of both heart
and arm are governed by the same spirit.

Those are to be pitied who are applied, or who
apply themselves, to much external work, without a
sufficient previous formation of the inward life of
love, which unites the spirit with God. To Religious and Priests, who have to work the works
of God, this more especially applies. The true
happiness and sweetness of their state are not to
be found in external things. To "abide in love,"[2]
and "walk in love,"[3] this it is that ensures the
virtue from on high, which they need to serve
God and their neighbour worthily. How many
Religious persons, so laudably engaged externally,
are conscious to themselves of a *something* that
is wanting in their lives! The want is deep within
themselves, viz., union of the spirit with God, by
the contact of love. Love would be a new life
to them; and that is what they need—love as a
formed habit, disposed to its acts.

We are not therefore to depend for our happiness and strength of spirit upon "external things";

---

[1] 1 Cor. xv. 58.   [2] S. John xv. 9.   [3] Eph. v. 2.

on the contrary, we must be ever independent of them :[1] God alone being ever all-sufficient to the soul : His Eternal Truth amply satisfying the mind : His holy love and will bringing constant joy, peace, and contentment to the heart.

Let us then never depend upon particular places, persons, offices, or works for inward happiness of soul. Our inner life must rest on God alone; so that when all externals fail, we may be "steadfast and immovable" within. "We must place all our fortitude," said the Abbot Piammon, "in the strength of our interior man : not in the retirement of our cell, the society of holy souls, or in any external help whatever. For if He who has said, 'The kingdom of God is within you,' does not strengthen our souls by His Divine power, we shall in vain hope to avoid the snares of our enemies, even though we retire to a desert."[2]

What abundant opportunities are afforded in the exercises of a life "hidden with Christ in God"![3] and how sad it is not to develop these deep resources of the spirit ! Yet Religious persons are to be found to whom silence and solitude are insupportable. They cannot satisfy themselves without the excitement of external things : as though the first and principal tendency of the soul should not be ever to God alone; as though His ineffable riches and delights were not infinitely more satisfying than

---

[1] "Ut cor in silentio et libertate custodias." (Blosius, "Spec. Monach.," C 7).

[2] Cassian, "Conf.," xviii., "Three diff. kinds of Relig.," C 16.

[3] Col. iii. 3.

all created things together; as though the "grace
of a delightful familiarity" with Him [1] were not
above all things to be prized by our souls. Besides,
it is this loving attention to internal things that disposes us so well for things external. For as the
"Imitation" says, "No man is secure in appearing
abroad, but he who would willingly lie hid at
home".[2] And by the interior life, as Lallemant
says, "not only do we converse with God, but God
works with us, and manifests Himself to us; so
that, knowing His perfections and virtues—and
being, as it were, imbued therewith—we proceed to
exercise them in regard to our neighbour".[3]
Whereas, "if in our employments we practise the
exterior of virtue without the interior, we are
miserable, bearing the weight of exterior labour,
but never tasting interior unction and sweetness.
And this makes us fall into notable faults. Whereas, by means of recollection and prayer, we should
effect more in our ministrations with less difficulty,
weariness, and danger, and with more perfection to
ourselves, more advantage to our neighbour, and
more glory to God." [4]

We learn from this that the active element in our
life is not to drown the contemplative element, but
to proceed from it.[5] It is from the "abundance of

---

[1] "Imit.," B iii., C 37.   [2] *Ibid.,* B i., C 20.

[3] Lallemant, "Spir. Doctrine," P 6, S 3, C 7.

[4] *Ibid.,* P 5, C 2, A 3, § 4.

[5] "Cum aliquis a contemplativa vita ad activam vocatur, non
hoc fit per modum subtractionis, sed per modum additionis."
(S. Thom., 2 2, Q 182, A 1 ad 3.)

contemplation "[1] that our zeal in outer works is to bound forth, and not from natural activity. Then our profession reckons as higher than that of a purely contemplative life, whereas activity alone is considered lower than contemplation. For "as it is a better thing to *give* light than only to *have* light, so it is better to impart to others the fruits of contemplation than merely ourselves to contemplate ".[2] Contemplation and action, therefore, combined—that is, contemplative love disposed to active, and active love proceeding from contemplative—make the highest of lives. For it is the life of God Himself, Eternal and Incarnate. A contemplative life reckons next, as engaging itself with the highest of objects, viz., the knowledge and love of God. Thirdly, the active life, as giving itself to things external.[3]

[1] " Ex abundantia et plenitudine contemplationis." (S. Thom., 2 2, Q 188, Art. 6, and Constit. Ord. Præd. Prol.)

[2] " Dicendum quod opus vitæ activæ est duplex. Unum quidem quod ex plenitudine contemplationis derivatur, sicut doctrina et prædicatio; et hoc præfertur simplici contemplationi. Sicut enim majus est illuminare, quam lucere solum, ita majus est contemplata aliis tradere, quam solum contemplari." (S. Thom., 2 2, Q 182, A. 2.)

[3] " Aliud autem opus est activæ vitæ quod totaliter consistit in occupatione exteriori. Sic ergo summum gradum in Religionibus tenent quæ ordinantur ad docendum et prædicandum. Secundum gradum tenent illæ quæ ordinantur ad contemplationem. Tertius est earum quæ occupantur circa exteriores actiones." (S. Thom., 2 2, Q 182, Art. 2.)

When it is said that the mixed life is higher than the purely contemplative, and the contemplative than the active, this is understood as signifying higher in itself,—in the abstract, and objectively. If it be asked which life is the more meritorious of heavenly rewards, here the question stands subjectively. He merits the more, whether in contemplation or action indifferently,

In the close, inward adherence to Divine Charity
—the acting by its exclusive principle, and the
aiming in our outer works to bring it to its perfection as a habit of the soul—we find the contemplative element feeding itself by the active, and the
active element furthered by the contemplative.[1]
Thus the two lives act and react on one another,
and move in happy concert together as they should;
for they are near relatives, as Martha and Mary are
sisters, and love to remain together, serving our
Lord. Moreover, that this was the spirit of the
early Church we see from the apostolic rule of the
twelve, to divide their time between continual
prayer, and labour for souls: "We will give ourselves continually to prayer and the ministry of the
word ".[2]

Doubtless, the want of this contemplative spirit
will explain much of the imperfection that abounds
in our outer works; that is to be seen among
Religious communities, and even in the sacred
duties of the Priesthood. For, as the " Imitation "
says, " if our interior affection is corrupted, it must
needs be that our action be corrupted also ".[3] The
human spirit quickly steps in where the Divine
spirit is absent, and its activity soon grows into a

who works with a higher degree of Charity; since Charity is the
root and principle of merit, as being the Divine life within the soul,
operating affectively in contemplation, and effectively in action.

[1] " Sicut bonus ordo vivendi est, ut ab activa vita in contemplativam tendatur, ita plerumque utiliter a contemplativa animus ad
activam reflectitur, ut per hoc quod contemplativa mentem accenderit, perfectius activa teneatur." (S. Greg., Hom. 14 in Ezech.)

[2] Acts vi. 4.   [3] " Imit.," B iii., C 31.

habit, tending in its very nature to quench the contemplative spirit; as, on the other hand, if we are to attain to the habit of contemplation, we must needs suppress this activity of the natural man. "From a pure heart proceed the fruits of a good life." [1] If, therefore, we desire the best results in our outward labours, let us nourish the strength of our inward spirit; then, "being kindled in contemplation" (as says S. Gregory), "we may proceed the more perfectly to action ".[2]

When, therefore, the soul is thus inwardly established, it is fit to go forth to the labours of the active life. It is in union with the Source of light, and love, and strength, and grace; and "God delights to display His omnipotence in our weakness".[3] This is the soul's security in the midst of outward things.[4] Hence we see how Moses, that he might discern the ways of God in governing the people, ascended the mountain, as S. Gregory observes, and there, in the Divine presence, away from external tumult, he received the light and strength needed for his great work. "So also," continues the same Father, "holy men, when obliged to give themselves to the external works of the ministry, ever take refuge in the secret chamber of the heart, and there rise upwards to the heights of inmost thought. There it is, on the mountain of

---

[1] " Imit.," B iii., C 31.

[2] " Per hoc quod contemplativa vita mentem accenderit, perfectius activa teneatur." (S. Greg., Hom. 14 in Ezech.)

[3] S. Fran. of Sales, Int. to " Devout Life," P 3, C 5.

[4] " Mens humana, ex hoc ipso quod dirigitur a Spiritu Sancto, fit potens dirigere se et alios." (S. Thom., 2 2, Q 52, Art. 2 ad 3.)

contemplation, that, leaving the tumult of external things, they rise to secret intercourse with God, and learn His will in their dealings with the souls of men. And when the labours of the day are over they return to the bosom of contemplation, to renew the spirit, and kindle afresh the flame of inward love. For the soul soon slackens amidst external things, though in themselves good, unless it constantly returns to the source of its strength."[1]

The Saint then represents God as sending forth His preachers, thus refreshed with contemplation, and again recalling them to inward converse with Himself: "After the grace of contemplation, I again prepare My servants for the works of active life, and yet again recall them from their labours to the heights of inner contemplation. Thus I send them forth to labour, then call them home to live familiarly with Myself."[2]   S. Thomas tells us

[1] " Moyses, ut legis præcepta percipiat, in montem ducitur; atque ut interna penetrat, ab externis tumultibus occultatur.   Unde et Sancti viri qui exterioribus ministeriis deservire officii necessitate coguntur, studiose semper ad cordis secreta refugiunt, ibique cogitationis intime cacumen ascendunt.   Et legem quasi in monte percipiunt, dum postpositis tumultibus actionum temporalium, in contemplationis vertice supernæ voluntatis sententiam perscrutantur.   Et post opera exteriora quæ peragunt, semper ad sinum contemplationis recurrunt; ut illic ardoris sui flammam reficiant, et quasi ex tactu supernæ claritatis ignescant.   Citius enim inter ipsa licet bona, exteriora opera, frigescerent, nisi intentione solicita ad contemplationis ignem incessanter redirent." (S. Greg., "Moral.," Lib. xxiii., C 12, & Lib. xxx., C 2.)

[2] " Prædicatores Meos, cum voluero, post contemplationis gratiam, ad activæ vitæ ministerium compono ; quos tamen semper a bonis exterioribus ad internum culmen contemplationis revoco; ut modo jussi ad exercenda opera exeant, modo revocati ad speculationis studium apud Me familiarius vivant." (S. Greg., "Moral.," Lib. xxiii., C 12, & Lib. xxx., C 2.)

that Religious who thus join the contemplative and
active element together are under a more particular
need of attending carefully to spiritual things, and
leaving those external to their profession.[1] The
reason of which is, that activity in its nature tends
to neutralise the simplicity of contemplation and to
revive the multiplicities which contemplation had
dismissed. Whereas those who are withdrawn
from the distractions of activity, and so able to give
their thoughts and affections wholly to Divine
things, have not the like occasions against which
to defend themselves. Let the solitude of our cell,
therefore, be the preparation for our work. "Cella
continuata dulcescit."[2] Did not our Lord Himself
remain hidden for thirty years before beginning
His ministry among men? and did He not then
enter a solitude of forty days in the desert? and in
the midst of His labours did He not "rise very
early, and go into a desert place, and there pray"?[3]
then, into a mountain, passing "the whole night in
the prayer of God"?[4] Not for Himself surely did
our Lord give Himself to solitude and prayer, but
for us. What must not *we* do in preparation for the

[1] "Manifestum est quod majorem sollicitudinem spiritualium
requirit Religio quæ est instituta ad contemplandum et contemplata aliis tradendum, per doctrinam et prædicationem, quam illa
quæ est instituta ad contemplandum tantum. Quanto autem
sollicitudo spiritualium major requiritur, tanto magis impedit
sollicitudo temporalium. Unde illis competit vitam habere
maxime ab exterioribus sollicitudinibus expeditam." (S. Thom.,
2 2, Q 188, Art. 7.)

[2] "Imit.," B i., C 20.

[3] S. Mark i. 35.   [4] S. Luke vi. 12.

active life, when the All-Holy hides Himself from men, and retires to the desert in silence and prayer?

" It behoveth us first to be pure, wise, and enlightened ourselves : then may we hope to instruct, enlighten, and purify others. First let us ourselves approach to God : then we may succeed in leading others to Him." [1]

What light, love, and strength we need, if we are to enlighten, inflame, and strengthen others! And here it is, in the inward life, that we find our light, that we give and receive our love : here virtues are formed and strengthened : here we receive from God the movement to outward things. How close then should be our union with the Source of light, and love, and strength.

All this is to tell us how vastly important it is to live for God, before we begin to live for others ; how we must first order ourselves within, before spending ourselves on things without ; and how the soul must be well established in God, enjoying the "grace of a delightful familiarity" with Him,[2] in order to be able in the midst of external works to turn readily to the source of light and strength, and learn the Divine Will in the manifold needs of men.

"Our Gospel" is to be "not only in word, but in power, in the Holy Ghost, and in much fulness." [3]

---

[1] " Mundari prius oportet, et sic alios mundare. Sapientem prius fieri, et sic alios facere sapientes. Lumen fieri, et sic alios illuminare. Ad Deum accedere, et sic alios ad Deum adducere." (S. Greg. Nazian.)

[2] " Imit.," B iii., C 37.   [3] 1 Thess. i. 5.

"Hence," says S. Gregory, "let a preacher speak more by his acts than by his lips, that he may show the way by his works rather than his words:"[1] after the example of our Lord, who "began to do, and to teach":[2] first "to do," then "to teach". Sad would it be were we among those of whom S. Gregory says, "They contradict by their works what they say by their words".[3] "They send forth a sound, but they give not the spirit;"[4] and "what is born by word, is killed by example".[5]

The position of a true labourer for souls should be, as S. Thomas says, "midway between God and the people : receiving from God in contemplation, and giving to the people by action". Hence, says the Angelic Doctor, "priests should be perfect, both in the active and the contemplative life".[6] As they are constantly giving to others, so they should be constantly receiving from God. Then will they communicate of their abundance, not of

---

[1] "Hinc prædicator plus actibus, quam vocibus insonant : ut potius agendo quam loquendo, quo gradiatur ostendat." (S. Greg., "de cura Past.," P 3, C 6.)

[2] Acts i. 1.

[3] "Quod verbis prædicant, moribus impugnant." (S. Greg., "de cura Past.," P 1, C 2.)

[4] "Imit.," B iii., C 2.

[5] "Qui per verbum nascitur, per exemplum necatur." (S. Greg., "Moral.," L xxi., C 8.)

[6] "Prælatorum et prædicatorum est in utraque vita (contemplativa et activa) perfectos esse : utpote qui medii sunt inter Deum et plebem; a Deo recipientes per contemplationem, et populo tradentes per actionem." (S. Thom., 3 Sent., Dist. 35, A 3, q 3.)

their poverty,[1] imitating Him "of whose fulness we have all received ".[2] We are not to be drawn *from* God by the people, but we are to draw them *to Him*. Now a true inner life, a life wherein the Divine Spirit presides by Charity, and brings the soul into loving relation with God, is the best guarantee for working zealously among the souls of men ; not only because God is able to use so well such a one as an instrument in His hands, well fitted for action by its close union with Him,[3] but because Charity in its nature is an operative habit :[4] "Operatur magna," as S. Gregory says :[5] it works great things. For "where there is Charity, there is a great impetus," says S. Ambrose.[6] "This Queen of virtues, like the princes of the earth, takes pleasure in performing great exploits, to extend her dominion, and increase the glory of her empire."[7] "Hence," continues S. Gregory, "love is never idle ; for if it works not it is no love."[8] "The lover flies, runs, rejoices. He is free, and is not held. Love maketh light of what

[1] "De plenitudine, non de penuria largientes." (S. Bern., Serm. 18 in Cant.)

[2] S. John i. 16.

[3] "Sanctificatum et utile Domino, ad omne opus bonum paratum." (2 Tim. ii. 21.)

[4] "Virtus est habitus operativus." (S. Thom. 1 2, Q. 55, Art. 2.)

[5] S. Greg., Hom. 30 in Evang.

[6] "Ubi Caritas, ibi impetus magnus." (S. Amb., "de Isaac et anim.," C 4).

[7] S. Fran. of Sales, "Love of God," B vii., C 12.

[8] "Nunquam est amor Dei otiosus. Operatur enim magna, si est. Si autem operari renuit, amor non est." (S. Greg., Hom. 30 in Evang.)

is burdensome, and equally bears all that is unequal. It spurs us on to do great things, and makes
all that is bitter sweet and savoury."[1]

And as material fire is nourished by communicating itself to the objects around it, so the fire
of Divine Charity feeds its life, and extends its
power, by spreading itself among the souls of men.
Thus the active element nourishes the contemplative, and the contemplative guides the active;
and Charity is the life of both : affective in contemplation, effective in action. As the two eyes
are to the body, so are contemplation and action
to Charity.[2] She needs them both. One looks to
God, the other to our neighbour : both operations
of the one Charity. "We are not to leave God,"
says S. Gregory, "by attending to our neighbour,
nor to neglect our neighbour by attending to God,
because Charity even then rises on high, when it
descends low; and as it descends to the lowest,
it ascends to the highest"[3]—words of deep consolation to all those who aim at perfect love, and
at the same time are called to labour for the souls
of others, and who would so often fain attend

---

[1] "Imit.," B iii., C 5.

[2] " Duæ quippe vitæ, activa videlicet et contemplativa, quasi
duo oculi habentur in facie." (S. Greg., " Moral.," Lib. vi., C 17.)

[3] " Caritas 'bis tincta' esse debet, ut tingatur per amorem Dei,
et amorem proximi; quatenus nec ex compassione proximi, contemplationem Dei relinquat, nec plusquam debet inhærens contemplationem Dei, compassionem abjiciat proximi. Quia tunc ad
alta Caritas mirabiliter surgit, cum ad ima proximorum se misericorditer attrahit: et cum benigne descendit ad infima, valenter
recurrit ad summa." (S. Greg., Hom. 38 in Ev., & "de cura
Past.," P 2, C 5.)

20

quietly to God, when duty sends them forth to the distractions of activity.

When the right time comes therefore—that is, when duty calls, or obedience demands us, or the needs of others require it—we must be ready to leave the enjoyments of contemplation, and betake ourselves to the works of the active life.[1]   And we are to understand that by so doing, the life of love and the service of the Divine Lover are both consulted, as they should be, in the best way.   Charity does not cause the loss of Charity.   Our progress is simply in love, and in nothing else.[2]   And our perfection is in perfect love.   And perfect love is in the habit of Charity, disposed to its acts.   It is not therefore by *thinking* that we advance, but by *loving*.   If, then, Divine Love moves us to leave contemplation, and betake ourselves to action, there is our proficiency to be found, and nowhere else.

S. Teresa's teaching is much to the point here. "The true proficiency of the soul," says she, "consists not in much *thinking*, but in much *loving*.   I admit, indeed, that it is a favour of our Lord to be able to keep our thoughts fixed on Him and to meditate on His works, and that it is good to endeavour to do it.   But this is to be understood only when nothing comes to interfere with obedience, and the welfare of our neighbour, to which Charity binds us.   For in such points we must find

---

[1] "Consideremus invicem in provocationem Caritatis." (Heb. x. 24.)

[2] "Imus, non ambulando, sed amando." (S. Aug., Epist. 155 ad Maced.)

time to leave that which we desire so much to give to God—viz., being alone, meditating on Him, and rejoicing in the caresses He bestows upon us. To leave these delights for either of the two objects mentioned is to please Him, and do what He Himself has said, 'As long as you did it to one of these My least brethren, you did it to Me'. It would be a strange thing, if, when God should tell us to *do* something which regarded Him, we should' *not* do it, but stand gazing upon Him, because we thus pleased ourselves the most. This would indeed be a curious advancement in the love of God! Our love must appear, not in corners, but in the midst of occasions. And believe me, that although there may be more imperfections, and even some slight faults, yet our gain is beyond all comparison greater." [1]

Thus we are to give ourselves to action as readily as to contemplation, and to contemplation as readily as to action. They are as closely allied as Martha and Mary, and the Divine Lover is served by both together, because both are Charity : the one affective, the other effective : the one contemplative Charity, the other active Charity : two operations of the one love. And the mode of our employment is but an accident. We may, indeed, and should, " prefer the attendance on God before all external things " ; [2] but when God calls us to action, we are in reality attending to Him, loving

---

[1] S. Teresa, " Foundations," C 5.
[2] " Imit.," B iii., C 53.

Him, serving Him, and doing His will.   How
then could we think of "gazing upon Him" to
please ourselves?   We must simply say, *Caritas
est hic*, and go into our work with heart and
soul.

And here let us listen again to the Angelic
Doctor.   He tells us that "it belongs to the perfection of friendship sometimes to leave the presence
of our friend, in order to engage ourselves in his
service.   Accordingly, he has the greater love who
sacrifices the enjoyment of his friend to serve his
interests, rather than another who will not leave the
presence he enjoys.   But if he were willingly and
easily to leave his friend, and find a greater pleasure
elsewhere, his love then would be of little worth.
So also it is in Charity.   God is to be loved above
all.   But there are some who willingly, or without
much difficulty, leave the contemplation of Divine
things, and turn instead to creatures.   Such as
these show but little Charity.   Others there are so
delighted with contemplation as to be unwilling to
leave it, even to serve the Divine interests in the
work of souls.   But others rise to such a height of
Charity that, although the contemplation of God be
their greatest delight, they are ready to forego its
enjoyment for the Divine service in the salvation of
souls.   Such a one was S. Paul, who was willing to
be anathema (*i.e.*, separate) from Christ for his
brethren.   And this is the perfection proper to
priests and others, who give themselves to the service of their neighbour.   And they are signified by
the Angels on Jacob's ladder, ascending by contem-

plation and descending by action, in the care they have of the salvation of their brethren." [1]

From this angelic doctrine we see that the tendency of the loving soul is ever to enjoy the presence of the Beloved, and yet that its very love carries it forth into activity, and proves itself purer by the separation. This accords with the sublime teaching of Richard of S. Victor, who reminds us how our Lord, "being in the form of God, emptied Himself, taking the form of a servant". So every soul aiming at perfection must endeavour in imitation of the Divine Model to attain to the "form of God" by the union of contemplative love. When this union has become habitual, so that God occupies the powers as His own, He sends back the soul into activity with its new and Divine life.

---

[1] "Ad perfectionem amicitiæ pertinet ut aliquis propter amicum interdum abstineat etiam a delectatione quam in ejus presentia habet, ut in ejus servitiis occupetur. Secundum hanc amicitiam plus amat qui se absentat propter amicum, quam qui a præsentia amici discedere non vult. Sed si quis libenter vel faciliter a præsentia amici divellitur, et in aliis magis delectatur, vel nihil vel parum comprobatur amicum diligere. Sic etiam in Caritate. Deus maxime propter seipsum est diligendus. Sunt autem quidam qui libenter, vel sine magna molestia separantur a vacatione Divinæ contemplationis, ut terrenis negotiis implicentur; et in his vel nihil vel modicum Caritatis apparet. Quidam vero intantum delectantur in Divina contemplatione quod eam deserere nolunt, etiam ut divinis obsequiis mancipentur in salutem proximorum. Quidam vero ad tantum culmen Caritatis ascendunt, quod etiam Divinam contemplationem, licet in ea maxime delectentur, prætermittunt, ut Deo serviant in salute proximorum. Hæc perfectio in Paulo apparet, qui dicebat." (Rom. ix.) "Optabam anathema esse (*i.e.*, separatus) a Christo pro fratribus meis." Et hæc perfectio proprie est prælatorum et prædicatorum, et quorumcumque aliorum, qui procurandæ saluti aliorum insistant. Unde significantur per Angelos in scala Jacob, ascendentes quidem per contemplationem: descendentes vero per sollicitudinem quam de salute proximorum gerunt." (S. Thom., Quodl. "de Carit.," Art. 11 ad 6.)

Likened now to Christ, it "empties" itself of the enjoyment of contemplative repose, and takes the "form of a servant," by serving the interests of God in the work of souls. Hereby its love appears in perfection. For while interiorly it enjoys the Divine habitual union, it overflows of its abundance into the souls of those around it, and thus causes the Divine love to increase greatly, both in itself and others.[1] Let Charity then be active, in order to attain the full measure of its perfection.

A true lover is wholly devoted to the Beloved, and is, therefore, able to leave the Divine embrace to do the Divine Will; "Caritas est hic," and that suffices. If Charity is here, in this action, God is here, and the work of my perfection is here; which tells us that the Divine presence and love and our own perfection are to be found in our ordinary actions; *i.e.*, our external acts are to be vivified by the Divine principle, and the diffusion of Charity within draws the Divine Lover to the soul. Let God, therefore, call us to what external work He wills. He holds us "full securely" within.[2] And Charity, to be perfect, must proceed from habit to act—which is to say, that it must be affective and effective. Affective within, effective without.

Oh, with what alacrity does a loving soul apply itself to the interests of the Beloved! It is enough for it to know that the Divine Will awaits for its co-operation in these outer works, to move it

---

[1] Richard à S. Vict., "de quatuor grad. viol. Caritatis".
[2] From M. Juliana of Norwich.

promptly to bestir itself amidst the distraction that surrounds it. It knows that its perfection is in its love, and its love is in the Divine Will, and the Divine Will is in these very works. It says, therefore, with S. Augustine, " Domine, amore amoris tui facio istuḍ ".[1] Lord, for the love of Thy love I do this. To be unwilling to go forth into activity would show that it still held to a lurking love and will of its own, and was not walking in holy liberty with God. For "the lover is free ; he is not held ".[2] He is not in bondage to anyone or anything, but walks with the Beloved in Divine solitude and liberty. The mode of his employment is accidental. The inner reality is ever the same. The Divine presence, and love, and will, and movement are found in all.

" Who can say to what degree such a soul forgets her own repose ? Walking continually with God, how can she remember herself ? Her sole thought is to please Him, and to find means whereby to show Him her love."[3] And here is the Divine love identified with these very works ! Well, therefore, does S. Augustine say that " labour is not burdensome to those who love, but rather sweet : as we see in hunters, fishers, and men of business. For in what is loved, either there is no labour, or the labour itself is loved."[4] The labour is loved, be-

---

[1] S. Aug., "Confess.," Lib. ii., C 1.

[2] " Imit.," B iii., C 5. [3] S. Teresa, " Int. Castle," C ult.

[4] " Nullo modo sunt onerosi labores amantium ; sed potius ipsis delectant ; sicut venantium, piscantium, negotiantium ; nam in eo quod amatur, aut non laboratur, aut et labor amatur." (S. Aug., " de bono Viduit ".)

cause Divine love is in it, and serves the soul as its aliment. Thus the soul loves in its labour, and its labour feeds its love. And "all things," says S. Bernard, "whether done or suffered, are turned to its advantage".[1] As S. Paul had already said, "We know that to them that love God all things work together unto good".[2] Even "bitter and grievous things," says S. Augustine, "become light and easy by love".[3] Whatever has to be done, whatever to be endured, the desire to love and please God thereby is a strong, sustaining power within us, bringing joy to the soul; as S. Teresa says, "We make it our joy to please God".[4] This is how love works. It rises over all,[5] and sweetens both labours and pains. The thought of pleasing God brings sweetness to our pain, and turns labour into love.

It cannot be denied, however, that in the midst of outward labours the loving soul has an habitual tendency to the contemplative element. How could it be otherwise? Is not the lover's first love always for the Beloved? Has she not left "all things" to follow Him? And "where thy treasure is, there is thy heart also".[6] And where the heart's love is,

[1] "Amans, quæcunque, undecunque, sive quæ facit, sive quæ ei fiunt, omnia ad suum commodum revocat et retorquet." (S. Bern., Serm. 4 de Divers.)

[2] Rom. viii. 28.

[3] "Omnia sæva et immania prorsus facilia, et prope nulla, efficit amor." (S. Aug., Serm. 70 de verb. Evan.)

[4] S. Teresa, "Exclam.," C 2.

[5] "Omnia vincit amor." (Virgil, Buc. p. fin.)

[6] S. Matt. vi. 21.

there the thoughts most easily go.[1] Besides, in a
true lover active love is but the overflow of contemplative love.   Hence it comes to pass that the soul
frequently fluctuates between its love for contemplation and its zeal for action : desiring, above all,
the presence of the Beloved, yet fearing lest its love
of Divine solitude should cause it to neglect the
vast interests of God in the souls of others.   Thus
it is often straitened between the two : knowing the
value of solitary love on the one hand, and of
sacrifice on the other ; preferring "the attendance
on God before all external things,"[2] yet desirous of
"zeal according to knowledge".[3]

S. Bernard, doubtless from his own experience,
describes the anxious love and loving anxiety of
the soul thus apparently drawn at the same time in
opposite directions.   "The voice of love," he says,
"sweetly urges the soul to attend to the things of
God.   The lover hearkens, and hastens to the work
of souls.   For such is true contemplation, that it
not only kindles Divine fire within the spirit, but

---

[1] "There is my thought, where is that which I love.   If I love
heaven, I willingly think of heavenly things.   If I love the Spirit,
I delight to think of spiritual things." ("Imit.," iii. 48.)

[2] "Imit.," B iii., C 53.

[3] Rom. x. 2.   We may here distinguish between "inspirations;"
which are from the good Spirit, and "instigations," which come
from the human or evil spirit.   Let not apparent inspirations,
even "on the title of Divine love" (says Schram), "be easily admitted as Divine, unless they are in agreement with our state of
life, our bodily powers, the edification of others, and our own due
dispositions.   This chiefly regards *external* works of virtue ; for in
regard to interior love, God inspires us more and more ; whereas
in externals there must be due measure, more especially as God
may often move us to such things *affectively*, not *effectively*."
(Schram, "Theol. Myst.," § 1542 Cor.)

urges the soul with ardent zeal to gain others also to the love of God. Thus contemplation yields lovingly to action, and, in proportion to its gains, returns with ardour to its repose. Again it enjoys the sweets of inward life; then reverts with fresh alacrity to a further conquest of souls."

" But amidst these changes the soul oftentimes stands in anxieties, fearing lest its affections draw it over-much either to the side of contemplation or action, by which it might deflect ever so little from the Divine Will. Peradventure holy Job suffered in this wise, when he said, ' If I lie down to sleep, I shall say: When shall I rise? and again I look for the evening '.[1] That is, when I rest I fear to neglect work; and when I work I fear to disturb my rest. See how a holy soul is straitened between the fruits of labour and the rest of contemplation."[2]

But a moment's reflection suffices to fire a true lover of God with ardent zeal, and disposes him to sacrifice joyfully his contemplative repose to the needs of his brethren, such as S. Bernard himself expresses in the following:

"Strange thing! we endure the losses of Christ more patiently than we endure our own! Upon our own daily expenses we bestow a daily scrutiny! but we consider not the continual losses in our Lord's flock. An ass falls down, and some one is found to raise it! A soul falls, and no one is found to attend to it."[3]

---

[1] Job vii. 4.   .[2] S. Bern., Serm. 57 in Cant.
[3] S. Bern., " de Consid.," Lib. iv., C 6.

" How can that man flatter himself that he loves God, when he sees God's image in the mire, yet heeds it not, and passes on? Why does he not pour forth his soul in prayer for poor sinners? Why does he not preach, hear confessions, and instruct his neighbour, in order to gather up his Lord's precious blood, by converting souls to Him ? " [1]

" Thou art saved by God ; do thou, then, save others. Thou art thyself snatched by Christ from death ; do thou, therefore, snatch others from the dangers that lead to death. This is the office confided to thee by God : an office that excels all the works of the most virtuous of men—to be the companion and fellow-labourer of Jesus Christ ; and by thy zeal, thy cares, thy ardour, thy love, and thy prayers, to seek the lost sheep, lead it to penance, and present it before God, as a pure sacrifice. No gift is more agreeable to Him than to lead a saved soul before His throne." [2]

" I envied those greatly," said S. Teresa, "who, for the love of God, were able to spend themselves in working for souls. Thus when we read how the Saints converted souls, this thought excites within me more devotion, more tenderness, and envy than all the tortures endured by the Martyrs ; and by this feeling with which our Lord has inspired me, I see that He values one soul which we gain through His mercy by our prayers more than all the other services we can render Him." [3]

---

[1] S. Bonav., " Pharetra ".
[2] S. John Clim., "Epist. ad Ab. Raithu".
[3] S. Teresa, " Foundat.," C I.

Hence S. Bernard, overflowing in love to his brethren, pours out his soul in sacrifice before them. "Charity," he saith, "which seeketh not her own, easily persuades me to sacrifice things which my soul desires, to your requirements. To pray, to read, to write, to meditate, and other spiritual gains, these things for your sake I count as loss."[1]

"But if you will overflow in love to others," continues he, "see that you are first filled yourself."[2]

And here we return again to the principle, so simple, yet so potent in its influence, when once it has well engaged the mind, viz., that our acts proceed from our habits. "Unumquodque, quale est, talia operatur."[3] As each one is, so are his operations. "Operatio sequitur esse." The operations follow the nature. As, therefore, the soul *is*, so it acts. If, then, we wish to secure these manifold works of active love to others, it plainly concerns us to maintain, nourish, strengthen, and develop the Divine principle from which they all proceed. Therefore, "redite ad cor". Return to "the heart".[4] Bring yourselves under the influence of the one governing love, with its Divine light and movement. Then comes the Divine Lover to the

---

[1] "Caritas, quæ non quærit quæ sua sunt, id mihi facile persuasit, nil scilicet desiderabilium meorum vestris præferre utilitatibus. Orare, legere, scribere, meditari, et si qua sunt alia spiritualis studii lucra, hæc arbitratus sum propter vos detrimenta." (S. Bern., Serm. 51 in Cant.)

[2] "Implere prius, et sic curato effundere. Caritas affluere consuevit, non effluere." (S. Bern., Serm. 18 in Cant.)

[3] S. Thom., 1 2, Q 55, Art. 2 ad 1.

[4] Isaias xlvi. 8.

loving soul, making His abode therein, and manifesting Himself.[1]   And from the habit of contemplative love, uniting the lover and the Beloved,
the soul is able of its fulness to overflow in active
love to those around it.

[1] " We will come to him, and make Our abode with him, and I
will manifest Myself to him."   (S. John xiv. 23, 21.)

CHAPTER VIII.

CHARITY IN SUFFERING.

IN the life of eternity God will reign within us for ever and ever. The souls of the Blessed will be His everlasting kingdom. Divine knowledge will possess the intellect, and Divine love govern the will. As to the body, when glorified, says S. Thomas, " it will be altogether subject to the glorified soul : fitted and free to obey the spirit in all its acts and movements ".[1] Thus God will be " all in all," [2] and we shall be participators in His Divine life and happiness.[3] But, in order to attain to this, "all things must be subdued to Him ".[4] We are not to live *with God*, but He is to live *in us.* Otherwise, as S. Bernard says, "how would God be all in all, if there remained in man anything of himself?"[5] " He who is joined to the Lord is one spirit."[6] All our thoughts, desires, affections,

[1] " Corpus gloriosum erit omnino subjectum animæ glorificatæ, ut sit expeditum et habile ad obediendum spiritui in omnibus motibus et actionibus animæ." (S. Thom., 4 Sent., D 44, Q 2, A 3.)

[2] 1 Cor. xv. 28.

[3] " Divinæ consortes naturæ." (2 Pet. i. 4.)

[4] 1 Cor. xv. 28.

[5] " Alioquin quomodo omnia in omnibus erit Deus, si in homine de homine quicquam supererit." (S. Bern., " de dilig. Deo," C 10.)

[6] 1 Cor. vi. 17.

and operations must, therefore, be brought into full conformity with Him, in order that He may possess and govern our entire being : "that the soul" (continues S. Bernard), "filled with Divine love, forgetful of itself, may pass wholly into God, adhering to Him, becoming one spirit with Him, and saying, 'My flesh and my heart hath fainted, O God of my heart, and my portion for ever'. O pure and holy love, to be brought to this is to be deified! As iron put into the fire loses its old form and becomes as fire, and as the air illumined with the sun is transformed into brightness, so as to appear rather the light itself than that which is enlightened—so then in the Saints all human love must melt away, and be transfused ineffably in God. Otherwise, how would God be 'all in all,' if anything remained in man of himself? His substance will indeed remain, but in another form, another glory, another power."[1]

" But now we see not as yet all things subject to Him."[2] God, therefore, appoints the sufferings of this life, as the means for subduing our souls to Himself. "The Lord your God trieth you, that it may appear whether you love Him with all your heart and soul or no."[3] How much, alas! within us has yet to be subdued, before we can say with the Psalmist, "Ad nihilum redactus sum".[4] What shall we say of our life as it is at present? Is it not rather human than Divine? Could it with any truth be said of us that "we walk not according to the

[1] S. Bern., "de dilig. Deo," C 10.
[2] Heb. ii. 8.   [3] Deut. xiii. 3.   [4] Ps. lxxii. 22.

flesh, but according to the spirit "?[1]   And observe
the sign which tells by which we walk : " They that
are according to the flesh *mind the things* that are
of the flesh, but they that are according to the spirit
mind the things that are of the spirit ".[2]   What are
the things that we chiefly mind ?   Are they those
of the natural or of the spiritual man ?   Whither
do our thoughts run ?   Are they withdrawn from
external things, and readily given to things Divine?
or are they not captivated by the things of sense,
and with difficulty fixed on God ? .Where do our
affections lie ?   Are they from the inmost heart
given to God, so that our deliberate preference is
always for Him ?   or are they not often divided on
perishable love ?   Are we striving in any true sense
to love God with our whole heart, and soul, and
strength ?   What are our chief attractions ?   Are
they not to things that gratify the natural man—
the pleasures of sight and sound, a desire for ease,
an inclination to rove about, an appetite for news
and idle talk and selfish gratification ?   " These
fleshly things," says Walter Hilton, " make a man
far from the inward savour of the love of God and
the clear sight of spiritual things." [3]   Have we anything like the same relish for things of the spirit—
mental prayer, silence, sacred study, and works of
zeal and self-sacrifice for the benefit of others ?
Are we not rather inclined to indulge our natural
desires and attachments, instead of " cutting them

[1] Rom. viii. 4.   [2] Rom. viii. 5.
[3] Hilton, " Scale of Perf.," P 3, C 8, S 1.

up by the root out of our heart,"[1] so making room
for the higher and better things?

All this will show us how far we are as yet from
being fully subject to God, and how much there is
within us that is opposed and unlike to Him.
These are the dark miseries of our nature, of which
it may be said, " animam Deo improportionabilem
reddunt ".[2] They make the soul unfit for God, out
of proportion to Him, unlike to Him, and consequently unable to unite with Him. " It cannot
be," says Blosius, "that the soul should attain to
intimate union with God, unless it become wholly
pure and simple and like to Him."[3] " He is one,
and most simple ; therefore, the soul, to unite with
Him, must be one and most simple also."[4]

What, then, must be done? "We must die, that
God may live in us," says S. Francis of Sales.[5] " A
man ought to die daily in his affections, that he
may live to God alone, and become wholly spiritual.
The more spiritual he is, the more he is like to
God, who is a pure spirit, and the more disposed
to be united, and become one with Him."[6] " As

---

[1] "Imit.," B iii., C 27.

[2] S. Thom., Opusc. "de dilectione Dei," C 25.

[3] "Fieri nequit ut anima ad intimam cum Deo unionem per-
tingat, nisi tota munda et simplex effecta, similitudinem Dei
habeat." (Blosius, "Instit. Spir.," C 12, § 3.)

[4] "Deus unus et simplicissimus est. Non poterit anima unioni
apta esse, nisi una et simplicissima efficiatur." (Card. Bona,
"Manud.," fin.)

[5] S. Fran. of Sales, " Conf.," xx.

[6] "Debet homo quotidie mori in omnibus suis affectibus, ut
tandem soli Deo vivat, fiatque totus spiritualis. Et quanto spiri-
tualior, tanto Deo similior, magisque dispositus ut uniatur, fitque
unum cum Eo." (Lewis de Gran., "de perfec. amor. Dei," C 5.)

fire and water can never subsist together, both preserving their proper qualities, so he in whom God
lives must utterly die to all things." [1] " If Christ
be in you, the body indeed is dead, but the spirit
liveth." [2]

We have already seen that by means of active
mortification we are enabled to " die daily " [3] to a
number of vicious and imperfect inclinations, and
so gradually dispose ourselves to the Divine likeness and union. God, however, wishes to fashion
us " according to the operation whereby He is able
to subdue all things to Himself ". [4] He, therefore,
takes us into His own hands, and leads us through
the ways of passive mortification : that is, He prepares a variety of sufferings for us—temptations,
trials, loss of friends, humiliations, scruples, pain
physical and mental, changes of place and work,
failures of good endeavour, the breaking up of plans,
the loss of favour and regard, office, position, or
confidence, the loss of health and strength, decline
of energy, sickness, weariness, and finally agony
and death. Such is God's plan in dealing with our
souls. And what does it all signify ? It tells us
that we have within our nature certain elements
opposed to the purity of God's Spirit ; that God
wishes to bring us into eternal union with Himself,
which is a glory far outweighing all the sufferings
which lead to it ; [5] that this union cannot possibly

---

[1] Thauler, Serm. 2 in fer. Pasc.

[2] Rom. viii. 10.   [3] 1 Cor. xv. 31.   [4] Philip. iii. 21.

[5] " The sufferings of this life are not worthy to be compared
with the glory to come, that shall be revealed in us." (Rom. viii.)

be effected as long as we retain any contrary or
dissimilar elements within us ; that the sufferings
of this life are the means of subduing these imperfections of our nature to God ; and that, therefore,
He uses them as the instruments of His love upon
our souls, to cleanse and scour the spirit of its
fleshly loves, release it from the entanglements of
earth, and bring it to that state of nudity and void
which enables Him to transform the soul into His
own image,[1] filling it with His Divine light and
love, and making it a participator in His own life
and happiness. This is the love of God, by the
sacrifice of self. "Amor Dei, ad contemptum sui,"[2]
the losing our life in order to find it.[3] God subjects
us to Himself by suffering, and when the soul is
subdued to Him He gives it a new and Divine life,
so that suffering is for subjection to God, and subjection for Divine transformation : as S. Gregory
says, " God afflicts us outwardly that we may live
inwardly, and He strikes in order to heal ".[4] As
He said to the people of old, " I will kill, and I will
make to live; I will strike, and I will heal ".[5] "How
many and grievous troubles hast Thou shown me ;
and, turning, Thou hast brought me to life ! "[6]

[1] " In eandem imaginem transformamur." (2 Cor. iii. 18.)

[2] S. Aug., "de Civ. Dei," Lib. xiv., C 28.

[3] " He that shall lose his life shall find it." (S. Matt. xvi. 25.)

[4] " Deus electos suos affligit exterius, ut interius vivant. Unde
per Moysen loquitur, dicens, ' Occidam, et vivere faciam, per-
cutiam, et sanabo '. Occidet enim ut vivificet. Percutit ut sanet :
quia idcirco foris verbera admovet, ut intus vulnera delictorum
curet." (S. Greg., " Moral.," Lib. vi., C 14.)

[5] Deut. xxxii. 39.

[6] " Quantas ostendisti mihi tribulationes multas et malas : et
conversus vivificasti me." (Ps. lxx. 20.)

How the sufferings of earth aid us in attaining
to this transformation of our nature, it is not hard
to see.   The question is simply one of supplanting
human dispositions by those that are Divine, or
of bringing. a new form into old matter; "the
difficulty is not in introducing a new form into
the matter, but in disposing the matter to receive
it ".[1]   Self-love must yield to Divine love: self-
will to the will of God.   What can effect this better
than mortification and suffering, which are against
the love and will of the natural man?   By enduring
them patiently day by day, we are enabled to make
a repetition of acts, by which the natural love and
will are brought down, and the Divine love and
will embraced in their stead.   The repetition
gradually induces the habit, and in time we gladly
lose our own will, and wish only for that of God.
Thus God first subdues the soul by suffering, then
gives it His Divine life, light, love, principle, and
strength ; having its powers in sweet submission
to Him, making them recipients of His blessedness, and using them for His own interests
among the souls of men.

How impressively has S. Catherine of Siena
written of this : " The servant is not greater than
his master.   He suffers in love: and there his
self-will dies.   When once the will is dead, all
suffering disappears : for it is our self-will alone
that makes our tribulations painful.   When that
is dead, and we are clothed with God's will, suffering is a pleasure, and sensual pleasure becomes

[1] Rodriguez, " Christian Perf,," Tr. on " Mortification," C 1.

a pain. This is the way the Saints travelled. They knew that the eternal kingdom was not to be bought with pleasure. But when our will is one with God's will, then indeed we enjoy the foretaste of eternal life." [1]

"In a divested spirit," says Thaulerus, "God and His peace are always found, in adversity and prosperity. How could pain and trouble afflict him who sees, finds, and enjoys God in these very things, heedless of himself? Such as these enjoy heaven both here and hereafter. Whatever is done to them, or not done; whatever God Himself may, or may not do, all turns to their good." [2] "From death proceeds the life that dieth not. Nor is there any truer life in us than that which is born of death. If water is to become hot, it must die, so to say, to cold. If wood is to become fire, it dies to its former state. So if we are to be transformed, and to receive a new life, it must be by losing our old nature, and dying to ourselves. Hence our Lord says, 'He that shall lose his life shall find it'. [3] 'Nor is it so much by our own endeavours, as by the mortification, resignation, abnegation, and losing of ourselves, that we attain to perfection. If therefore you will be what you are not, you must deny yourself, lose yourself, and die to what you are." [4]

But if we look into our souls, we shall see how tightly we hold to, or are held by, our natural

[1] S. Cath. Sien., " Letters," 55.
[2] Thauler, in 2nd inst. D. Eckard.
[3] *Ibid.*, Serm. 2 in fer. Pasc.
[4] *Ibid.*, Serm. Dom. 5 p. Pasc.

desires and loves. Is not the memory filled with
images of earth? Can we turn our eyes and ears
from pleasant sights and sounds? Do we not
crave daily to gratify our fleshly likings? Do
we not seek for those who please and notice us?
Are we not eager for pleasure, and ready at a
moment for vain curiosity; news, and amusement?
Alas! how could we rid ourselves of these impediments to God, if the way of abnegation and
suffering were not provided for us? In mortifica-
tions which we prepare ourselves, our own will
may easily be found. But when God Himself
afflicts us with trials altogether against nature,
what room will there be for the natural man?
The whole endurance of these sufferings is in the
direction of the desired end. They are against self-
will, and they bring us God's will. They take
our thoughts from earth, and lift them upwards
to heaven. They turn us from the allurements
of creatures, and lead us to the contemplation of
God. And if the suffering be, as in many cases,
that of long bodily sickness, our various senses,
which we were so slow to mortify ourselves, are
now mortified for us. The eyes are closed in pain,
the taste for food gone, the ears troubled now
by sounds they loved before, the touch sensitive
to a straw. The energies of mind and body, so
long enslaved to earthly things, are now brought
into subjection to God. Is not all this a mercy?
Is it not desirable that we should be detached
from the things of sense, and attached to God
alone? that we should be brought into full sub-

mission to Him? that we should be divested of
the natural life, in order to receive that which is
Divine? "O God, Thou commandest that these
things should be endured, not that they should
be loved. For no one loves what he endures,
though he loves to endure it."[1]

Let us look to our *end*, and then judge of the
sufferings of this life in reference to it. Our end
is to be one with God—one in will and in
love, the pure recipients of His life and happiness.[2] But suffering it is that subdues the natural
man to God; and, therefore, it aids us directly
to our end : let it then be taken well, and rightly
used, viz., "in order to the end," of subduing the
soul to God. Then indeed it comes as a blessing
from the hand of the Divine Lover : for "whom the
Lord loveth, He chastiseth".[3] And so our Lord
places it among the beatitudes. The Apostles " rejoiced that they were accounted worthy to suffer";[4]
and S. Paul glories in the cross, in his "infirmities,
in reproaches, necessities, persecutions, distresses,
for Christ"; for "when I am weak, then I am
strong".[5] When I am weak according to man,
then I am strong according to God. And if we
were inclined to doubt the necessity of universal
mortification to the natural man before we can
attain to God, let us remember the Divine sentence, "Man shall not see Me, and live".[6] Whether

---

[1] S. Aug., "Confess.," L x., C 28.

[2] "I in them, and Thou in Me, that they may be made perfect
in one." (S. John xvii.)

[3] Heb. xii. 6. [4] Acts v. 41. [5] 2 Cor. xii. 9. [6] Exod. xxxiii. 20.

we hope in this life to attain to the union of perfect
Charity, or in the next life to the union of eternal
glory, in either case the natural man must die. He
must be wholly mortified, that God may live *in
him.* "No one seeing God," says S. Augustine,
"continues to live in the bodily senses. But
except he in some way die, either by leaving the
body altogether, or by an abstraction from his
fleshly senses, he is not raised to the vision of
God."[1] So that if, by means of active mortification
during this life, we have not attained to universal
detachment, God has the passive mortification of
death in store for us, which severs us of necessity
from all attachments here below, obliging us hereby
to yield up unreservedly the life of the flesh
and the pleasures of the senses, and to go forth
in nudity of spirit before Him: and all this by
way of suffering and sacrifice, that nature may
find no place, but God alone may reign. Then,
when mortification and suffering have done their
work, pain and trial will cease for ever. They
were the instruments prepared to fit our souls
for God. Now all is subject to Him; He will
reign within us for ever; and we shall be partakers of His own eternal life and happiness.

But let it be said that there is even now a
true and rightful way of sweetening our sufferings.

[1] " Nemo videns Deum vivit ista vita, qua mortaliter vivitur in
istis sensibus corporis. Sed nisi ab hac vita quisque quodammodo
moriatur, sive omnino exiens de corpore, sive alieanatus a carnalibus
sensibus, in illum non subvehitur visionem." (S. Aug., " Sup.
Genes. ad litt.," xii., C 27.)

S. Augustine felt it when he said,[1] "When I shall wholly cleave to Thee, labour and sorrow will cease ".[2] So did the author of the "Imitation," when he wrote, "Love makes all that is bitter sweet and savoury ".[3] And S. Teresa, when she said, "Crosses do not trouble souls in union with God ; for the presence of God which they carry with them soon makes them forget everything".[4] And Henry Suso, when writing his "Eternal Wisdom" he said that "those complain of the bitterness of the rind who have not found the sweetness of the kernel ".[5]

The sweetness of inward love is such that it rises above all things. "Many waters cannot quench Charity, neither can the floods drown it."[6] It "beareth all things, hopeth all things, endureth all things ".[7] "Love is as strong as death."[8] The desire of pleasing God by suffering for Him brings pleasure to our pain, and turns labour into love. And "love making all pains, difficulties, and afflictions sweet, what is there left to suffer?"[9] If the good pleasure of God is there, there is our joy. If the Divine will is there, there is our will also ; and the trial, as purifying our love, is welcome to the

---

[1] "Cum inhæsero tibi ex omni me, nusquam erit mihi dolor et labor ; et viva erit vita mea, tota plena Te." (S. Aug., "Confess.," L x., C 28.)

[2] S. Aug., "Conf.," L x., C 28.

[3] "Imit.," B iii., C 5.

[4] S. Teresa, "Int. Castle," M 7, C 3.

[5] Suso, "Eter. Wisd.," C 2.

[6] Cant. viii. 7.   [7] 1 Cor. xiii. 7.   [8] Cant. viii. 6.

[9] D. Gertrude More, "Confess.," 51.

soul. Any other desires would prove that our will was not one with God's will; and if so, this indeed ought to be suffering to us. Thus it is that the sweetness of God's presence, light, love, and movement so engages our spiritual nature, that the sufferings of sense become of no account, except as bringing to us the Divine will and love, which at once make them pleasing and desirable, since "we make it our joy to please God ".[1]

"This appears a most difficult thing," says S. Teresa, "not so much to do it, as to take pleasure in that which is directly opposed to our natural inclinations. But love, when perfect, is so powerful, that we forget our own pleasure, in order to please Him whom we love ; and however great our labours may be, when we know that thereby we please God, they become sweet to us."[2] For "nothing is sweeter than love : nothing stronger, nothing higher, nothing more pleasant, nothing fuller or better in heaven or earth."[3] "Who then shall separate us from the love of Christ? Shall tribulation, or distress, or famine, or nakedness, or danger, or persecution, or the sword? As it is writen, 'For Thy sake we are put to death all the day long ; we are accounted as sheep for the slaughter'. But in all these things we overcome, because of Him that hath loved us. For I am sure that neither death, nor life, nor angels, nor princi-

[1] S. Teresa, " Exclam.," C 2.
[2] *Ibid.*, " Foundat.," C 5.   [3] " Imit.," iii. 5.

palities, nor powers, nor things present, nor things to come, nor might, nor height, nor depth, nor any other creature, shall be able to separate us from the love of God, which is in Christ Jesus our Lord." [1]

[1] Rom. viii. 35.

CHAPTER IX.

THE DEGREES OF CHARITY.

CARITAS.

VIVIFICANS.—MOVENS.—IMPERANS.—PURGANS.
ZELANS.—REGENS.—IMPLENS.—DULCESCENS.
PERFICIENS.—ABSORBENS.—TRANSFORMANS.—DEIFICANS.

Note.—These degrees correspond to the three recognised ways in the spiritual life—purgative, illuminative, and unitive; although it is allowed that the three operations concur in each separate way. For Charity, even in its first degree, is the unitive principle, illuminating the soul to purify itself; and in its highest degrees the purifying and illuminating elements are still needed, owing to the weakness and deficiencies of the natural man.

By living in the state of Grace, we possess the first degree of Charity, "vivificans," because Grace vivifies the soul with a supernatural life, which elevates it to friendship, with God, and thereby animates the heart with Divine love. But Charity, in this first degree, may be compared to a child, beautiful in form and life, but far from its perfection, and weak in its powers and operations. Its formation and development from a feeble habit into a strong ruling power, governing and regulating the soul, until the whole man moves under its control, promptly, easily, and sweetly, is the whole work of a spiritual life, to which all our other exercises have to be made subservient, since "the end of the commandment is Charity".[1] "This is the supreme virtue," says Denis the Carthusian, "to the perfection of which all the precepts of God, the counsels of the Gospel, and the teachings of the Saints are ordained. For Charity is the life, the form, the mover, and the end of the other virtues; since by its means the soul is joined most closely with, and conformed to God, adheres to Him, and becomes one spirit with Him."[2]

We have, then, to take in hand this child of Charity, nourish it with holy thoughts and affections, guard it by recollection, train it by mortification, strengthen it by prayer, exercise it by the moral virtues, and dispose it by a constant repetition of acts to the fully developed habit of Charity, by which it attains to its measure of spiritual life and vigour, holding the different virtues in command,[3] and operating readily, easily, and sweetly. Then, as S. Paul says, it puts away the things of a child, and becomes a full-grown

[1] "Finis præcepti est Caritas." (1 Tim. i. 5.)

[2] "Caritas suprema est virtus, ad cujus perfectionem universa ordinantur præcepta Divina, Evangelica consilia, omnes item doctrinæ Sanctorum. Ipsa namque est cæterarum virtutum regina, motrix, forma, vita, et finis: quia per Caritatem maxime ac propinquissime conjungimur, conformamur, adhæremusque Deo, atque unum cum Deo efficimur, prout asserit Paulus: 'Qui adhæret Domino, unus Spiritus est.' (Denis Carthus., "Inflammatorium Div. Amor.," i., & "de profess. Monast.," A 1.)

[3] "Cum omnes aliæ virtutes ordinantur ad finem Caritatis, ipsa imperat actus omnium virtutum, et sic dicitur motor earum." (S. Thom., Quodl. "de Carit.," A 3.)

spiritual man—a "perfect man, according to the measure of the age of the fulness of Christ ".[1]

The great idea to grasp at the outset of spiritual life is that nature and grace are side by side within us, both active principles, but that grace is to preside and nature to serve. For it must be evident that nature without the guidance of grace will fail in Divine things, since the faculties need light, formation, and direction corresponding to their supernatural end.[2] These are communicated to them in the life of grace, by which the Spirit of God occupies the soul, working in the will by Charity, and through the will in the other powers by their corresponding virtues.[3] It must be owned, however, that although Charity lives within, the soul does not so easily move by its principle, being "drawn away and allured"[4] by the rival love of Cupidity. In the second degree, therefore, "movens," the resolution is taken of moving by Charity, and renouncing the antagonistic principle of Cupidity ; and, according as the soul acts with this resolution, the spiritual man grows and

---

[1] Eph. iv. 13.

[2] " Principia naturalia non sufficiunt ad ordinandum hominem in beatitudinem. Unde oportet quod superaddantur homini divinitus aliqua principia per quæ ita ordinetur ad beatitudinem supernaturalem ; sicut per principia naturalia ordinatur ad finem connaturalem." (S. Thom., 1 2, Q 62, Art. 1.)

[3] " Caritas est causa motiva omnium aliarum virtutum. Per modum imperii in omnibus nos dirigat quæ ad rectam vitam pertinent. Tamen requiruntur aliæ virtutes, quæ eliciendo actus, exequantur imperium Caritatis, ad hoc quod homo prompte, et sine impedimento operatur." (S. Thom., Quodl. "de Carit.," Art. 5 ad 1 & 9.)

[4] S. James i. 14.

strengthens, because the repetition of acts forms the habit of Charity, which brings the soul more and more under the influence of the Spirit of God. Again and again, however, nature is found to pre-vail against grace. We have the light to *see*, yet not the courage to *do*. Thus the mind and the will are out of harmony in their movements, and we experience what S. Bernard calls "a tiresome division and most bitter contradiction ".[1] But our very miseries have to be courageously turned to account. "God loves courageous souls," as S. Teresa said. Dejection and fear by occasion of our weakness, must be resisted and mortified,[2] and the soul must be renewed by fresh acts of love and oblation. This is most important to bear in mind, as the law of the formation of habit by the repeti-tion of act tells here with all its force—more especially in the young, whose habits are under-going or awaiting their formation ; and the results one way or the other on their future spiritual life, according as the repetition is given to the right side or the wrong, may be incalculable. Is the natural man at work, placing a series of acts, whether of over-indulgence or of undue fear or scrupulosity, that ought to be mortified? As the acts are repeated the habit gains ground. He is nourishing a worm that ought to be killed ; instead of which

[1] " Utinam hæc ut intellectum admonent, moveant et affectum ; ne sit intus amarissima contradictio, et divisio molestissima." (S. Bern., Serm. 5 in Ascens.)

[2] " Things which deject, perplex, entangle, or keep under the spirit are to be avoided by all lawful means in a contemplative course." (F. Baker, "Treat. on Confession ".)

it grows, and sucks the very sap from his soul. On the other hand, is the spiritual man acting from love? Each act tells in developing the habit of love. This habit of habits grows; and by means hereof the soul transcends its faults and fears, and runs along the high road of perfection, love continually rising, and faults and fears continually diminishing.[1]   All

[1] The "transcension" of faults and fears, as it is called, is an exercise of great utility to many souls, brought out with much force by F. Baker for the benefit of those who, having no will for grave sin, are yet conscious of many inordinations, miseries, and short-comings, withal wishing to progress in the way of perfection. Transcension is an easy and effectual method for the management of these frailties. Its exercise consists in *passing by* such imperfections and fears as so many impediments in our spiritual course, instead of stopping at them, and spending time needlessly in discussing and confessing them : finding their remedy indirectly, by cleaving to the principle of Divine love. In adopting this we may rest ourselves confidently on the distinct teaching of the Council of Trent regarding the confession of venial sins, viz., that while they may be confessed, they may also without fault remain unconfessed, and be expiated by other remedies. "Venialia, quanquam recte in confessione dicantur, taceri tamen citra culpam, multisque aliis remediis expiari possunt" (Conc. Trid., Sess. 14, C 5, "de Pœnitentia"), remembering how love itself is a purifying principle, and cleanses the soul from venial sin, as S. Thomas teaches: "Caritas tollit per suum actum peccata venialia." (S. Thom., 3, Q 97, Art. 4 ad 3.) S. Gregory teaches transcension by the example of a stag leaping over the obstacles of the way, and swiftly pursuing its course up the mountain height ;. and applying it to ourselves, quotes the words of the Psalmist, "Qui perfecit pedes meos tanquam cervorum". (Ps. xvii. 34.) So in ascending the mountain of perfection, it is most desirable to advance steadily, making Charity push her way onwards through the thick undergrowth of natural loves and fears, till she gain the regions of settled light and love. The conditions on which transcension may be habitually exercised are: 1, That the soul shall have utterly renounced mortal sin; 2, That it strive habitually against venial sin; 3, That it aim at making Charity its one moving principle; 4, That it tend to the perfection of Charity. These granted, let souls be encouraged to make use of the means of transcension. Love requires it; for love must reign, and she cannot abide any contrary element. Hence "perfect Charity casteth out fear". (1 John iv. 18.)

this is to show us the degree of "caritas movens," and to tell us how important it is to move rightly herein. As in starting on a journey, we· must at once set ourselves *in order to the end*, and then maintain our movement thereto consistently throughout ; so on the spiritual road we must start with the moving-principle of love, which alone attains to God,[1] and keep to it consistently through life—that is, if we wish to reach the end we have proposed, viz., our perfection by perfect Charity. The next degree is "imperans," or Charity commanding.[2] This supposes the soul as moving according to her resolution in the second degree by the principle of love ; yet the natural man, being still unmortified, hinders the sway of Charity within the soul. He has, therefore, to be brought to order ; and Charity must have the courage to take in hand the sword of mortification, and with it cut away the aliment on which nature feeds. Here again the law of repetition meets us, for there is no escaping it. If Charity rules and nature serves, so much for the repetition of good acts and their corresponding habits. But if the "old man" becomes master, beware of the formation of his habits !—"the last state of that man becomes worse than the first ".

S. Thomas points in weighty words to this law of our nature, according to which, if we neglect to

---

[1] " By love we may attain to God ; but by thought or understanding, never." (" Div. Cloud," C 6.)

[2] " Caritas imperat omnibus virtutibus, sicut voluntas omnibus potentiis." (S. Thom., 2 Sent., D 40, Q 1, A 5.)

act by the higher principle, our lower inclinations necessarily assert themselves, and, by thus hindering the acts of the higher habit, dispose it to decay and ruin. " It is evident," says he, " that the habit of virtue renders a man prompt in its operations. But if one *use not* the habit to govern the acts, of necessity other operations or passions of a lower kind, proceeding from the sensitive appetite or the influence of external things, assert themselves. Thus virtue is weakened or ruined by the cessation of its acts."[1] And this law, be it remembered, applies to the *mind* as well as to the *heart.* As when the sensitive appetite takes the leadership, to the detriment of our better will, we must at once use the habit of virtue to suppress or regulate its movement; so when imagination, inane fears, doubts, or scruples lead the mind adrift to the prejudice of right reason, judgment, and good sense,[2] we must at once recognise the disorder, and quickly use the higher intellectual habit to suppress, put in place, and duly govern these unruly movements of lower nature.

In reference to this, the Angelic Doctor continues : " So also it is with our intellectual habits, that make a man prompt in judging rightly things

---

[1] " Manifestum est quod habitus virtutis facit hominem promptum ad eligendum medium in operationibus. Cum autem aliquis non utitur habitu virtutis ad moderandas operationes, necesse est quod proveniant multa operationes vel passiones præter modum virtutis, ex inclinatione appetitus sensitivi, et aliorum quæ exterius movent. Unde corrumpitur virtus, vel diminuitur, per cessationem ab actu." (S. Thom., 1 2, Q 53, Art. 3.)

[2] " Do not become children in sense ; but in malice be children, and in sense be perfect." (1 Cor. xiv. 20.)

of imagination. If, therefore, one neglects to use the intellectual habit, strange imaginations rise up, sometimes leading the mind astray : so that, unless by a frequent use of the intellectual habit they be in some way cut down and suppressed, the mind is unfitted for judging rightly, or even wholly disposed to the contrary. Thus by the cessation of its acts the intellectual habit is weakened or even corrupted."[1]

Let us learn from these trenchant words of the Angel of the Schools to beware of the dark misery of our nature. If we cease to move by the higher habits of mind and heart, imagination and appetite are at once ready to assert themselves ; and Charity and right reason, by yielding their position and ceasing their acts, lose strength and weaken their hold, and tend to diminution and corruption.[2] Thus the soul gets disordered, and is so far removed from the Divine influence. How obscuring and down-drawing these unruly movements

[1] " Similiter etiam est ex parte habituum intellectualium, secundum quos est homo promptus ad recte judicandum de imaginatis. Cum igitur homo cessat ab usu intellectualis habitus, insurgunt imaginationes extraneæ, et quandoque ad contrarium ducentes, ita quod nisi per frequentem usum intellectualis habitus quodammodo succidantur vel comprimantur, redditur homo minus aptus ad recte judicandum, et quandoque totaliter disponitur ad contrarium. Sic per cessationem ab actu, diminuitur vel etiam corrumpitur intellectualis habitus." (S. Thom., 1 2, Q 53, Art. 3.)

[2] This does not imply that Charity may be *directly* diminished or corrupted, but that the overlying corruption of Cupidity increases, and mingles itself with the operations of Charity, thus indirectly impeding its increase and the virtue of its operations. These unruly elements are as so much lurking corruption in the soul. The odour of a soul habituated to them is as the odour of corruption. And to act from them is to stir, aggravate, and augment the corruption.

are to the spirit in its inner life with God and its progress to contemplative prayer, it is easy to understand. "Contemplation requires exceeding subtle, light, tender, and spiritual things, and a freedom from inordinate affections and passions, and from the images caused by them. Scrupulosity, pusillanimity, and dejection of spirit are, therefore, main impediments in the way of contemplation. By this may be seen how great an evil the least incumbrance is, and how easily it is incurred, the great difficulty of the spiritual art lying in the riddance of the soul from such encumbrances, by its denudation and simplification." [1]

Charity, being now our moving and commanding power, at once becomes a purifying principle to the soul ; and thus we reach the degree " purgans ". As a " consuming fire," [2] the Divine principle purifies the faculties from the dross of sin and imperfection in proportion as the soul yields herself to its influence, and gradually fashions the " new man according to God ".[3] As fire consumes wood, first expelling what is contrary to itself, then communicating warmth, heating the surface of the wood, and gradually pervading it until the whole is transformed into fire, so the fire of Charity enkindled in the soul by the Spirit of God purges away the contrary elements of sin, imperfect habits

---

[1] F. Baker, Preface to the " Div. Cloud," and Treat. on " Confession ".

[2] " Our God is a consuming fire." (Heb. xii. 29.)

[3] Eph. iv. 24.

and inordinations, then gradually enlightens and inflames the soul, occupying its inmost nature and transforming its human life into the life which is Divine. We see from this how much depends on the yielding up of our natural activity,[1] and getting as soon as possible under the influence of the higher principle of love. For then love does its work in the soul. It is itself the purifying principle. On the other hand, the relief from attention to our miseries is immense. We know what a fund of misery we have within us. But sad occupation would it be to be ever within ourselves, scrutinising our faults and perverse dispositions, and trying to remedy them by a direct combat with them. We know them, to renounce, forget, and transcend them. By cleaving to Divine love as our governing habit, and making it our one consistent principle of action, these opposing miseries of nature are indirectly, though effectually, overcome.[2] "Contemplative souls," says F. Baker, "do indirectly, yet efficaciously, mortify their passions by transcending them : scorning even to cast a glance upon creatures that would allure their affections from God, and which cannot be considered except in God without leaving some tincture and imperfection in the soul."[3]   "God roots out of the soul

---

[1] " Not only our sins and unmortified habits hinder God from working in us, but the activity of our own minds, and the impressions of the senses, which perpetually traverse and weaken the operations of God." (Rigoleu, " Way of Perf.," C 4.)

[2] " Si adhærebis superiori, conculcabis inferiora." (S. Aug., Enar. in Ps. xlv.)

[3] F. Baker, " S. Sophia," T ii., S 1, C 4.

its imperfect habits by the perfect habit," says S.
John of the Cross ; "its imperfections are quickly
lost in perfect love, as mould on metal is lost in
fire."[1] "During her recollection the soul finds
herself corrected by a certain presence which she
there finds of God.   For as a man looking towards
a wall not only sees the wall but also the things
that are between him and the wall, so the soul
regarding God sees the impediments that are
between Him and her.   These impediments are
not so much the actual sins or imperfections we
commit as the *affections* we have for them or their
causes.   These affections exist as perverse habitudes deeply grounded in the soul, but they come
to be corrected by elevating the soul out of nature
to an estate more of the spirit into God, better
than by calling them to mind in themselves.   This
rising out of nature into God is attained by
frequent elevations of the spirit in times of recollection.   Whereas the correcting only of actual sins
may leave the *affection* and *habit* much as they
were before.   It is the regard and presence of God,
and not of creatures or their images, that enlightens
the soul for the discovering of hidden inordinate
affections.   For He, being all light, enlightens the
soul to see these inordinations.   The contemplative
soul, therefore, in her recollections makes no
examen of her sins or inordinations ; but, seeing
God, she sees the impediments that are between
Him and her.   And such as lie lurking in her

[1] S. John of the Cross, " Sp. Canticle," S 26.

nature (and many such there be) God does not always discover them to the soul ; yet even in such ignorance the soul gets out of them by degrees. This she does by transcension of all natural desires and inclinations through the medium of recollection, quite as much too as if they had been visibly discovered in her sight. And so she comes to be amended in them before she discerns or knows them. Nor is there any reformation in the soul, or perfection, but by the said means of getting out of the habitation of nature and the inordinate desires of it, whether we discover them or discover them not." [1]

But until the higher habit of love is sufficiently formed within, it is to be expected that the soul will be again and again returning to the imperfect ways of nature. And "the more a person advances, the more readily will he perceive his faults ; and his purity will be as a mirror, which will hold up to him more and more his deficiencies. For the pure and enlightened eye always discovers spots." [2] In the midst of these trials we must learn to hold fast to the higher habit of love, and work in the strength of it consistently, so as by its power gradually to expel the "fleshly loves and fears," which as "perverse habitudes" cause the soul so often to lapse. And in view of constantly renewing the spirit after its falls, let the soul find means of quickly turning to the Divine Lover, sending

[1] F. Baker, "Life of Dame Gertrude More," C 9.
[2] Cassian, " Conf.," xxiii., C 7.

upwards its acts of love, oblation, contrition, self-renunciation, and resignation, casting its miseries into the sea of God's mercies, placing all once more in His hands, and taking Him again for its "one Good" and "only Love". For what can we love but the one Love and the one Good, "of whom, and by whom, and in whom are all things"?[1] "None is good but God alone,"[2] and we are the recipients of His goodness:

> Sweet Fountain of Eternal Goodness — Sweet flowings of Eternal Love!
> Sweet habit of habits, disposed to its acts—
> Caritas, affectiva, effectiva: sola, plena, ordinata:

which alone gives the Divine Lover full possession of His kingdom within us, and is the soul's perfecting principle, breaking down the barriers of fleshly loves and fears, all for God's own great ends and the vast needs of souls.

Thus the soul regains its inward calm, and finds once more the "homeliness of God's gracious presence". And then love strengthens, and returns to the work of purifying the spirit of its imperfect habits of thought and liking; lest from being neglected they "fester more deeply, and become more dangerous, from their concealment in the recesses of the heart".[3] But the valiant lover is ready for great exploits, and Jesus our King must gain the victories of His love. "Jesu, Victor Rex, miserere." As the soul thus yields up its natural activity, and

---

[1] Rom. xi. 36.   [2] S. Luke xviii. 19.
[3] Cassian, "Conf.," xvii., C 8.

gets more and more under the influence of the higher principle of love, love works its works more and more within it.   Everything moves according to its nature.[1]   From a loving soul therefore proceed loving acts.   "Operatio sequitur esse."   More and more does the soul now realise the truth that God is the "only Good," and must, therefore, be its "only Love"; recognising all the loveliness of heaven and earth, in nature and grace, in itself and others, as emanations of the Sovereign Good and Love ; and as it has given itself again and again to the "one Love," what can it do now but seek to draw, if it were possible, all other souls to the same loveliness of the Divine Lover, that thus its Charity may rise on high with two wings, the love of God and the love of our neighbour ?   It therefore brings itself in its "rich nought" before the greatness of the Divine Majesty, loving ardently the only Good, and rejoicing that God is its all. Then, desiring to see the Divine Fire kindled in the hearts of men, it makes an oblation to God of all our Lord's sacred merits, His life on earth, and in the Blessed Sacrament throughout the Church, with all the merits of our Blessed Lady, and the holy Angels and Saints, and holy souls in the Church suffering and militant, on behalf of the souls of men ; imploring God through these rich merits that He will draw them to Himself by the ways of His Divine knowledge and love.   It casts an eye over the world, and considers the souls that

---

[1] " Unumquodque agit secundum suam formam."

remain yet to be converted.   It remembers the
many who are sick unto death in body and soul.
It sees the "prisoners of the King" in the regions
of the Church suffering, and it desires to be in
God's hands for the benefit of all these souls;
remembering our Lord's command of loving others
as we love ourselves.   And as for itself it has a
full love of the Divine love, so for others also it
desires that the like love may be obtained.

But love not only desires great things for the
Beloved, but "spurs us on to do" them.[1]   Thus
the lover glows with active zeal.   As fire rests not
till it consumes all things within its reach, transforming them into itself; and as the more it finds
the more it feeds, so Charity purified and refined
seeks to spread itself, feeding on the variety of
good works that come within its reach; strengthening and extending itself, by animating the
soul in its operations and drawing other souls to
share in its delights.[2]   Thus it is that *affective*
Charity moves the soul to *effective* Charity, and
the habit produces acts.   This gives the Divine
virtue a greater perfection, because every virtue is
made perfect by its acts.[3]   " The Queen of virtues,
therefore, like the princes of the earth, takes
pleasure in performing great exploits to extend
her dominion and increase the glory of her empire."[4]

---

[1] " Love spurs us on to do great things." (" Imit.," B iii., C 5.)

[2] " Amor zelat.   Hic replet, fervit, ebullit.   Hic jam securus,
effundit exundans et erumpens."   (S. Bern., Serm. 18 in Cant.)

[3] " Unumquodque intantum perfectum est, inquantum est actu."
(S. Thom., 1 2, Q 3, A 2.)

[4] S. Fran. of Sales, " Love of God," B vii., C 12.

In the souls of men more especially Charity
desires to work. For here is the kingdom of God.[1]
Here is His rightful possession, His "homeliest
home,"[2] His heaven on earth.[3] And by Charity it
is that He lives, and reigns, and works within the
souls of men. Therefore the loving soul desires
to spread love within the souls of others, that God
may be able to come to His own, and make His
abode within them ; for thus our Lord makes His
abode depend upon the soul's love. "If anyone
love Me, My Father will love him, and We will
come to him, and make Our abode with him."[4]
And while love labours for others, it "lays up
treasures" for itself.[5] As S. Gregory says, "By
reaching to the lowest, it ascends to the
highest ".[6]

By such constant exercise the life of love
strengthens and expands within the soul. Divine
Charity is gradually leavening the powers of nature,
and bringing the faculties, senses, and members
under her control ; each power preserving its own
life and movement, but vivified, prompted, and
governed by Charity. The natural man, being
now brought into sweet alliance with the spiritual
man, no longer desires to move in his own imperfect

---

[1] " The kingdom of God is within you." (S. Luke xvii. 21.)

[2] " In us is His homeliest home, and His endless dwelling."
(M. Juliana of Norw., " Revel.," C 67.)

[3] " Cœlum est anima justi." (S. Greg., Hom. 38 in Evang.)

[4] S. John xiv. 23.

[5] " Lay up for yourselves treasures in heaven." (S. Matt. vi. 20.)

[6] " Caritas, cum benigne descendit ad infima, valenter recurrit
ad summa." (S. Greg., " de Cura Past.," P 2, C 5.)

and independent way, and the soul attains to the happy degree of " Caritas regens ".

When this is reached, Charity becomes *habitually* the one governing love of the soul ; all the powers and senses moving under her influence ; having been brought into this compliance by the practice of the earlier stages mentioned. Now it is that the soul (on account of the diffusion of the habit of Divine love) experiences within itself a sense of the presence of God : according to our Lord's promise to the loving soul, "We will come to him, and make Our abode with him ; and I will manifest Myself to him,"[1] which sense of the Divine presence is considered as the first degree of infused or supernatural contemplation.[2] For the habit of Charity, displacing the natural spirit, enables the Divine Spirit to reign in its stead. And as, when the clouds are dispelled, the sun forthwith appears in all its brightness, so when the dark miseries of nature have been eliminated, the Divine Spirit of God at once manifests His presence, and sheds His light and love within the soul.[3]

No wonder therefore that the soul in the enjoyment of this presence of God, and in the repose consequent upon the formed habit of Charity, should wish to withdraw from all particular con-

---

[1] S. John xiv. 21, 23.

[2] De Ponte, " Medit.," Vol. i., " Introd. on Ment. Prayer," C xi. 4; S. Teresa, " Life by herself," C 10 ; and Lallemant, " Spir. Doctr.," P 7, C 4, Art 2.

[3] " The presence of God is infinitely more advantageous to the soul than all spiritual books collectively." (Rigoleu, " Div. Union," C 7.)

siderations, and hold its faculties in silence before the Divine grandeur and loveliness, leaving the will in the full activity of love :[1] " Since," says S. Teresa, " God does not wish to have any disturbance either from the faculties or the senses. They have nothing to do here ; for God has discovered Himself to the soul, and all the favours He bestows now are without her doing anything on her part, except in resigning herself entirely to Him."[2] " Consequently," says S. John of the Cross, " if the soul will at this time make efforts of its own, and encourage another disposition than that of passive, loving attention, most submissive and calm, and if it does not abstain from its previous discursive acts, it will place a complete barrier against those graces which God is about to communicate to it, in this loving knowledge."[3]

All this regards the time of prayer, to which the loving soul constantly tends, preferring, as it does, " the attendance on God before all external things ".[4] Yet it is ever in readiness to serve the Divine interests, whether by action or suffering, moving in all things under the same principle,

---

[1] When it is said that the will is left in activity, the expression refers to the will being the active principle under Divine love. The other faculties, however, may move in concurrence with love, by the Divine principle. But as their movement is wholly subject to God, and sometimes almost imperceptible, on account of the soul's simplification by love, they are regarded now rather as recipients of Divine operation, the will being the active mover under God.

[2] S. Teresa, " Int. Castle," M 6, C 4, and M 7, C 3.

[3] S. John of the Cross, " Living Flame of Love," S 3, L iii.

[4] " Imit.," B iii., C 53.

finding in all things the same love, and the same habitual sense of God's presence. "A true lover ever keeps his heart on high. Whether he sit, or walk, or rest, or whatever he does, his heart is always true to God. Divine contemplation is sweet refreshment to him. The more he enjoys it, the happier he is ; for it is always sweet to think on what it is always sweet to love." [1]

Now it is that the soul, established in Divine love, attains to that happy freedom and alacrity of spirit which makes it swift in the service of God, and ready for action as well as contemplation, in imitation of God Himself,[2] and our Lord incarnate, and the holy Angels and Saints, who exercise so lovingly the works of the active life, without detriment to the inner spirit of contemplation. Thus it passes to the degree "implens," by which the faculties are emptied of the remnants of their former impressions and attachments, and filled with Divine fulness,[3] making the works of life full of the sweet spirit of Charity, and communicating it abundantly to the souls of others, in imitation again of Him "of whose fulness we have all received".[4]

Here let it be borne in mind, we must keep steadfastly true to the counterpart of mortification, for it is only by having the soul empty that God is able to fill it. It is of us to cleanse the vessel, it

---

[1] " Manuale," S. Aug., C 28.
[2] " Imitatores Dei estote." (Eph. v. 1.)
[3] " Ut impleamini in omnem plenitudinem Dei." (Eph. iii. 19.)
[4] S. John i. 16.

is of God to fill it. "The more thou dost empty thy heart of that which is thine own, the more abundantly will I fill it with that which is Mine." [1] This ridding the soul of the remnants of her former "perverse habitudes," and substituting in their place the one Divine habit of habits, will doubtless be done far more easily, effectually, and pleasantly, by constant recurrence to the exercise of "transcension," than by any other means ; that is, we are to pass by our miseries, brushing them away by the higher exercises of love, oblation, and self-renunciation, not searching into them, but "turning the spirit to God, scorning even to cast a glance upon creatures, that would allure us from God, and which cannot be considered except in Him, without leaving some tincture and imperfection in the soul". "Contemplative souls," says F. Baker, "do indirectly, yet far more efficaciously, mortify their passions by transcending them, that is, by elevating and uniting their spirit to God : by this means forgetting and drowning their sensual desires, yea, all created things, and chiefly themselves, in God." [2] "Let us transcend all things," says S. Gregory, "that we may attain to oneness of spirit within : no more occupied with the memory of our sins, but inflamed with the fire of love." [3]

Having now gained calm possession of the entire

---

[1] S. Cath. Sien., "Dial. on Consum. Perfection".

[2] F. Baker, "S. Sophia," T ii., S 1, C 4.

[3] "Transcendamus omnia, ut mente colligamur in unum ; non jam memoria vitiorum, sed amoris flamma succensi." (S. Greg., Hom. 22 in Ezech.)

nature, Charity strengthens and sweetens, thus attaining to the degree "dulcescens". Formerly it moved the faculties and senses with difficulty, on account of the unreformed ways of the natural man. Now it has gained an easy possession of the soul, and brought nature into sweet harmony with itself. Happy state! When the natural and the spiritual man walk in holy union together and can say with the Psalmist, "My heart and my flesh have rejoiced in the living God".[1] "Tu homo unanimis." ".Thou man of one mind didst take sweet food with me, and we walked together in the house of God."[2] The "man of one mind" is one in whom the natural and the spiritual have been brought into happy unison. The "sweet food" may well refer to all those acts which serve as the nutriment of Charity, and which the natural man has been taught to undertake readily and sweetly in conjunction with Charity. And hence both may say, "We walked together," since nature and grace have been brought into such pleasant agreement.

In this happy state the soul passes through troubling things without being troubled.[3] And things which were difficult before, on account of feeble and imperfect nature, are now, owing to the presiding power of Charity, undertaken with

---

[1] Ps. lxxxiii. 2.

[2] " Tu vero homo unanimis : qui dulces mecum capiebas cibos; in domo Dei ambulavimus cum consensu." (Ps. liv. 14.)

[3] "Turbatio in vita activa non contingit, postquam ad perfectionem venit; quia tunc delectabiliter et faciliter operatur, non perturbatus." (S. Thom., 3 Sent., D 35, Q 1, A 3, q 3 ad 2.)

readiness and joy. "Then," says S. Bernard, "will love be purified, and the will be renewed, or rather newly created. And things which formerly seemed difficult, nay, impossible, are now done most readily and sweetly. Send forth Thy Spirit, and they shall be created, and Thou shalt renew the face of the earth," that is, the earthly will is made heavenly. "Blessed are these souls who enjoy not only freedom from evil, but wonderful enlargement of heart." [1]

We cannot but own that the calmness and sweetness which the soul now enjoys, even in the midst of external works, and in which the body also participates, are the result of a well-developed *habit* of Charity ; that is, a habit of Charity readily disposed to its acts. This will appear the more in times of outward distraction, sudden calls, and emergencies, when we have at once to fall back on habits acquired : according to the saying of Philosophy, that "sudden movements are from habit".[2] How much it ought to convince us of the necessity of attaining to this most desired habit of habits![3] Let Charity become a fully-

---

[1] " Tunc purgabitur affectus, et voluntas renovabitur, vel potius nova creabitur ; et omnia quæ prius difficilia, imo impossibilia videbantur, cum multa dulcedine et aviditate percurrantur," &c. (S. Bern., Serm. 3 in Ascen.)

[2] " Repentina sunt ab habitu." (Arist.)

[3] S. Thomas gives three reasons why we need the *habit* of virtue—viz., in order that we may be able to act uniformly, readily, and sweetly. 1. That we may act uniformly ; for a person easily changes his mode of action, unless he be established in a settled disposition, called a habit. 2. That we may act readily ; for unless the soul, by means of an inward habit, be solidly built and

developed habit, in calm possession of the soul, governing all our other habits, and from its nature, as being perfect love, it sweetens the heart, and through the heart pervades the operations of the other powers and senses, and even bodily members. Thus we live in a happy equality, in the midst of the inequalities of life, "all things being broken through" by the one governing love, and love ordering all according to the interests of the Beloved.

When Charity has thus sweetened the spirit, and brought the operations of nature into harmony with itself, it advances to the degree "perficiens," by communicating to the acts and movements of our various powers and senses, interior and exterior, all the perfection they are capable of receiving, since "in the matter of love, the want of perfection is a notable fault".[1] It must not be forgotten that although Charity gives to the soul its essential perfection, yet the different faculties and powers moving under her command still require their own proper accidental perfection, by which they are enabled under Charity to move to their

fixed, it would have, before proceeding to act, to wait and enquire; as we see in one wishing to know without the habit of knowledge, or another desiring to act virtuously without the habit of virtue. Hence Philosophy tells us that sudden movements are from habit. 3. That we may act sweetly, which ensues as the effect of a formed habit; for habit being as a second nature, it causes our actions to flow naturally, and consequently delectably. Hence Philosophy reckons as a sign of habit, a pleasure in producing acts. (S. Thom., Quodl. "de Virtutibus," Q 1, A 1.)

[1] Sister Benigne, a holy lay sister of the Visitation. These words are given in her life, as communicated to her by the "Divine Love". ("Life," by M. de Leyni. P 3, C 5.)

respective operations promptly, easily, and sweetly. For want of being thus perfected, these subordinate powers serve Charity but imperfectly, and thus mar her progress and impede her work : just as an imperfect instrument hampers a perfect workman.[1] There is indeed much occupation here ; and well may S. Francis of Sales tell us that if we really desire to love God, we must make this love our one project, since all our exertions are not too great for the execution of such a design.[2] How often does Nature incline us to ease, idle indulgence, negligence, and listlessness ! How soon we lapse into inconstancy and instability ! and yet such things, as S. Jerome says, "holy love hath not".[3] We have need to be constantly vigilant of our Charity, lest it be said of us, " I find not thy works full before God".[4] Even in the holiest things, nature and cupidity find place, and mingle the dross of their imperfection with the gold of Charity. Let Charity therefore be the perfecting principle in the soul, by extending her rule, and diffusing her virtue through all the faculties and powers, communicating to them their separate accidental perfection, that thus the works of life may not only be referred to God as our end, but may proceed from

---

[1] " Operatio quæ a duabus potentiis procedit, non potest esse perfecta, nisi utraque potentia perficiatur per debitum habitum; sicut non sequitur actio perfecta alicujus agentis per instrumentum, si instrumentum non sit bene dispositum, quantumcunque principale agens sit perfectum." (S. Thom., 1 2, Q 58, Art. 3 ad 2.)

[2] S. Fran. of Sales, " Love of God," B xii., C 3.

[3] " Sanctus amor non habet." (S. Jerome, Epist. 2 ad Nepot.)

[4] Apoc. iii. 2.

Him as our principle,[1] and be directed according to Him.[2]

When Charity is perfect it becomes absorbing, transforming, and deifying. It would seem that these degrees are but rarely and scarcely attained in this life, except *inchoativè, imperfectè, et transitivè.* Nevertheless we are to *tend* towards an absorbing Charity, as bringing to our nature its highest perfection, leaving the Spirit of God to transform us as He wills into the resemblance of our Divine Model.

We must needs turn to the Saints to learn the ways of perfect love. "A soul that loves God perfectly," says S. Catherine of Siena, "ends by forgetting herself and all other creatures. In God she finds all that can delight the heart : all beauty, all sweetness, all quietness, and all peace. And so the bond of love between her and God drawing closer, she comes, as it were, to be wholly transformed in Him. And at length it comes to pass that she can love, delight, think, and remember no other thing than Him only."[3] "As the transformation of the soul in God makes it His," says S. John of the Cross, "He empties it of all that is alien to Himself. Thus it comes to pass that not in will only, but in act as well, the whole soul is entirely given to God without any reserve whatever, as God has freely given Himself unto it. The will

---

[1] " Ut cuncta nostra operatio a Te semper incipiat."

[2] " Ut qui sine Te esse non possumus, secundum Te vivere valeamus." (Orat., Dom. 8 post Pent.)

[3] S. Cath. Sien., " Hist.," by A. T. Drane, P 1, C 4.

of God and of the soul are both satisfied, each
given up to the other in mutual delight, so that
neither fails the other in the faith and constancy of
the betrothal. The soul is, as it were, absorbed in
God, and knows nothing else but His love and the
delights thereof. All its actions are love. All its
energies and strength are love. It gives up all it
has, like the merchant in the Gospel, for this
treasure of love hidden in God, and which is so
precious in His sight that the Beloved cares for
nothing else but love. The soul, therefore, seeing
this, occupies itself wholly with pure love for God.
The intellect is occupied in understanding what
tends to His service, in order that it may be
accomplished. The will, in loving all that is
pleasing to God, and in desiring Him in all things.
The memory, in recalling what ministers to Him,
and what may be more pleasing to Him. As to
the body, it is now ordered according to God in all
its interior and exterior senses, all the acts of which
are directed to God. ' Now I mind no flock.' I
do not now go after my likings and desires, for,
having fixed them all on God, I now neither feed
nor heed them. I have no other occupation than
to wait upon God. All my powers of soul and
body work in and by love. All I do is done in
love. All I suffer, I suffer in the sweetness of love.
Even the act of prayer and communion with God,
which was once carried on by reflections and other
methods, is now changed into love. So much so,
that the soul may always say, whether occupied
with temporal or spiritual things, ' My sole occupa-

tion is love'.   Happy life! and happy soul which
has attained to it!"[1]   That the ultimate end of
Charity is transformation in God we learn from
the inspired Word.   "We all, beholding the glory
of the Lord, are transformed into the same image,
as by the Spirit of the Lord."[2]   "As iron," says S.
Bernard, "cast into the fire, loses its own form and
becomes as fire itself; and as the air, bathed in the
light of the sun, is transfused with the sun's brightness, so as to appear light itself: so, in the souls of
the Blessed all human love will melt away, and be
transfused ineffably in God.   The substance of the
soul will indeed remain, but in another form,
another glory, another power.   To be brought to
this is to be deified."[3]

"God deifies those who are turned to Him," that
is, says S. Thomas, "by a participation of His
likeness; not by the property of nature."[4]   "By
the light of glory the creature becomes deiform.
For when a created intellect sees the Divine
essence, the Divine essence becomes the *forma intelligibilis* of the created intellect."[5]   "Ah, God! how
blessed is the man who strives after Thee alone!"[6]

---

[1] S. John of the Cross, "Spir. Canticle," S 27, 28.

[2] 2 Cor. iii. 18.

[3] "Sic affici, deificari est."   (S. Bern., "de dilig. Deo," C 10.)

[4] "Deificet Deus eos qui convertuntur ad Ipsum.   Deificet dico,
id est, deos facit per participationem similitudinis, non per
proprietatem naturæ."

[5] "Per lumen gloriæ fit creatura rationalis Deiformis.   Cum
enim aliquis intellectus creatus videt Deum per essentiam, ipsa
essentia Dei fit forma intelligibilis intellectus."   (S. Thom., Opusc.
"in Div. Nomin.," C 12, & 1 2, Q 112, Art. 1, & 1, Q 12, Art. 5.)

[6] B. Hen. Suso, "Life," Cap. ult.

CHAPTER X.

THE UNION OF ALL VIRTUES IN CHARITY.

"CARITAS RADIX EST, FONS, MATERQUE CUNCTORUM BONORUM."
S. Joan Chrys., Hom. 2 in die Pent.

How vastly are the truths of spiritual life treated by the Fathers and Doctors of the Church! "Vidi multos multa dicere," as S. Catherine of Siena says.

"I saw that many say many things, and speak differently of the virtues by which God is to be worthily served. And yet man's capacity is but small, his understanding dull, his memory weak. So that he cannot comprehend many things, or retain those he is able to perceive. And hence, although many set themselves to learn perfection, few are found to reach it."[1]

Truly, when the soul is still young and unformed in spirit—having withal many duties to attend to that divide its attention, yet aspiring to the best things—it is apt to turn with anxious heart to the Masters of spiritual life, and would fain know from them in one brief sentence the work it has to do for God. "Vidi multos multa dicere." 'Many authors say many things. Who will give me in one word the essence of perfection? I have not time to read long treatises with the care which they require; yet my mind wants a principle, a light within, by which to see my way, to judge, to order and regulate the works of life.

'Sometimes it seems that the Will of God will suffice for everything, and that conformity and abandonment hereto will carry me through all duties and difficulties. But grave authors speak of the restoration of the Divine image and resemblance in the soul as bringing to man the reformation and perfection of his nature.[2] Then there is

---

[1] S. Cath. Sien., "Dial. on Consum. Perfection".

[2] Albert Mag., "de adhær. Deo," C 3 ; Denis Carthus., "de laude Vitæ Solit.," A 1 ; Walter Hilton, "Scale of Perfection," B i., P 3, C 2 and 3, &c.

the principle of conformity to Christ our Lord, as the model of perfection. Again, S. Paul seems to make the work of spiritual life consist in putting off the " old man " and putting on the " new man," by mortifying the life of the flesh, and living according to the Spirit.[1] S. Augustine's view of Christian virtue is that *love is everything*, and the other virtues but different forms of the one love. Accordingly he defines virtue as being simply " the order of love ".[2] S. Thomas and S. Bonaventure place our perfection radically and essentially in Charity, as being the bond of Divine union and the principle of supernatural action.[3] Lallemant considers purity of heart and the guidance of the Holy Spirit as "the two poles of all spirituality by means of which souls attain to perfection,"[4] while Rodriguez places perfection in the ordinary actions of life.[5]

'Are all of these right together? or are there different plans of perfection? How much should I like to see, as on a target, the one point to aim at, and to gain !'

Thus might a young soul, high in its aspirations, ardent in its affections, hungering and thirsting for

[1] Eph. iv. 22.
[2] "Virtus est ordo amoris." (S. Aug., "de Civ. Dei," L xv., C 22.) See also S. Aug., "de morib. Eccles.," L i., C 15, and "de doctrina Christiana," L iii., C 10.
[3] S. Thom., 2 2, Q 184, Art. 3, and Quodl. "de Carit.," Art. 11 ad 5. S. Bonav., "Apol. paup.," R i., C 3, and "Centiloq.," P 3, S 40.
[4] Lallemant, "Spir. Doctrine," P 4, C 2.
[5] Rodriguez, "Christian Perf.," Vol. i., T ii., C 1.

spiritual life, say when it first turns itself in earnest
to higher things, and seeks with a kind of avidity
to satisfy its desires, by drawing from the rich and
varied stores deposited by the Saints and holy
writers in the treasury of the Church.

Without doubt there is a central point in spiritual life to be aimed at and to be gained, wherein
consists the essence of our perfection. And however much spiritual writers may develop their
principles, and draw out the manifold operations
of the Christian and religious virtues, unquestion-
ably they point to the same centre, and that
centre is undoubtedly the love of God, ór Divine
Charity.[1]   All the great principles tend to this,
or emanate from it.   Virtues either lead to Divine
love, or proceed from it.   Charity is the central
sun that attracts and quickens them.   " What
the root is to the tree, what the soul is to the
body, what the sun is to the world, all this is
Charity to the Christian heart," says Lewis of
Granada.[2]

For instance, it must needs be true that all our
perfection is found in the Divine Will.   For nothing
is good or desirable apart from the will of God ;
and the will of man must necessarily derive its
perfection from union therewith, since " none is
good but God alone,"[3] and we are the recipients of

---

[1] " Verbum Caritatis, verbum totius perfectionis : verbum con-
summans et abbrevians.   Consummans, cui nihil potest deesse.
Abbrevians, in quo pendet tota lex et prophetæ." (S. Aelred,
" Spec. Caritatis," L i., C 16.)

[2] Lewis de Gran., " de perf. amor. Dei," C 1.

[3] S. Luke xviii. 19.

His goodness. But the question at once occurs, Where is the Divine Will to be found? The answer is, In Charity. There can be no doubt of this. The will of God is either expressed in His commandments, or signified by His good pleasure. But in either way it is embraced and perfectly fulfilled by Charity alone. For certain it is that Charity itself is the greatest and first of all the commandments.: "Thou shalt love the Lord thy God with thy whole heart, and with thy whole soul, and with thy whole mind. This is the greatest and the first commandment."[1] Further, our Lord declares that the keeping of the commandments is the result of our love; so that by rightly loving Him we do the Divine Will, and we deflect from that Divine Will when we fail in our love. "If any man love Me, he will keep My word. He that loveth Me not, keepeth not My words."[2] Hence "all the law and the Prophets" depend upon the law of love;[3] that is, the teaching of the Prophets, and the details of the law, are ordained to the love of God and of our neighbour, which is Charity; or when perfectly possessed, they proceed from its principle, and become so many different operations of the one love. And the words of the Master are echoed by the disciple. S. Paul declares Charity to be the fulfilment of the law. "All the law is fulfilled in one word."[4] "Love is the fulfilling of the law;"[5] the reason of which is that love is the

---

[1] S. Matt. xxii. 37.   [2] S. John xiv. 23, 24.
[3] S. Matt. xxii. 40.   [4] Gal. v. 14.   [5] Rom. xiii. 10.

spring of our actions; and if it is only rightly-ordered love, it moves us to the observance of every law. Who is more obedient to the law than a loving soul? Its love it is that moves it to obey. So well did S. Augustine understand this, that he hesitates not to say, "Love, and do what you will,"[1] being persuaded that we shall not be moved to act wrongly while our love, which is the spring of action, is right. Moreover, "the end of the commandment is Charity";[2] which tells us that the various declarations of God's will all point to Divine Charity as their one object.

If we consider the will of God as signified by His good pleasure in the occurrences of daily life, what is it but Charity that brings us into prompt, easy, and sweet compliance with this Holy Will? Who seeks to please the Beloved more than a loving soul? It is the "true lover," as S. Teresa says, who "loves everywhere";[3] and it is this very love that leads it to seek the Divine Will, and to embrace it in whatever way it comes. For "love spurs us on to do great things, and makes all that is bitter sweet and savoury".[4] Let us listen again to the teaching of S. Catherine of Siena. Seeing that many teachers say many things, she humbly asks of God that she may receive some brief instruction in the way of perfection, that will embrace in few words the doctrine of the inspired

---

[1] "Dilige, et fac quod vis." (S. Aug., Tract 7 in Ep. Joan.)
[2] 1 Tim. i. 5.   [3] S. Teresa, "Foundat.," C 5.
[4] "Imit.," B iii., C 5.

books and holy writers, and so help her to serve God worthily, and thus attain to eternal happiness. The Divine Teacher then addresses her: "Know that the salvation and perfection of My servants stand in this one thing, that they do My will alone, ever striving to fulfil it in all things; that they attend to Me, and serve Me every moment of their lives. The more diligently they apply themselves to this, the nearer they approach perfection, since thus they are in union with Perfection Itself."[1]

She then ardently desires to do the Divine Will; but knows not clearly in what things it may be found, and therefore beseeches that she may be informed of this also; in answer to which it is said to her: "If thou seekest to know My will, that thou mayest perfectly fulfil it, behold in one word that which it is: that thou shouldst love Me to the utmost of thy power without ceasing; that thou shouldst love Me with all thy heart, and all thy soul, and all thy strength. On the fulfilment of this precept thy perfection depends; and therefore it is written that 'the end of the commandment is Charity,' and 'love is the fulfilling of the law'."[2]

Understanding from this that the Divine Will and her own perfection are to be found in the perfect love of God, she desires in the ardour of her soul to give herself to this perfect love. She is then instructed in the means of attaining to the perfection of Charity, by entire mortification, purity of heart, and total abandonment to God. En-

[1] S. Cath. Sien., "Dial. on Consum. Perfection". [2] *Ibid.*

lightened by this heavenly doctrine, she acknowledges that which is the practical point in spiritual science, namely, " By how much the more a man dies to himself, by so much the more he lives to God ".[1] This is the "game of love ".[2]

Let us turn now to the teaching of Albertus Magnus, Denis the Carthusian, and Walter Hilton, on the reformation of the soul according to the Divine image.[3] As God alone is perfection, since He alone is good, it is evident that man's perfection can be but relative ; that is, man attains to the perfection due to his nature, by his relation and resemblance to God. " The image of God," says Albertus Magnus, " is in the three powers of the soul—reason, memory, and will. As long as these are not wholly impressed with God, the soul is not deiform, as it was originally made. For God is the 'exemplar' (*forma*) of the soul, and it must be impressed with Him, as wax with the seal. But this is not fully done till the mind is illumined by Divine knowledge, the will wholly actuated by Divine love, and the memory absorbed in the possession of eternal happiness. And inasmuch as the perfection of our life in heaven is the consummate enjoyment of these things, it follows that their commencement here below is our perfection in this life."[4]

---

[1] S. Cath. Sien., " Dial. on Consum. Perfection ".

[2] Suso, "Etern. Wisd.," C 9.

[3] Albert. Mag., "de adhær. Deo," C 3 ; Denis Carth., "de laude Vitæ Solit.," A 1 ; Hilton, "Scale of Perf.," B i., P 3, C 2 and 3.

[4] Albert. Mag , " de adhær. Deo," C 3.

But since the fall of our nature the image of God in the soul has been overlaid with the "image of sin," "whereby," says Hilton, "man has fallen into a forgetting of God (in his memory), ignorance (in his mind), and love and liking of himself (in his will) ".[1] "Nevertheless we are restored again in hope by the Passion of our Lord. Seek, then, that which thou hast lost, that thou mayest find it; for God would be sought, and is desirous to be found. It behoveth thee to delve deep in thy heart, for therein God is hid. Nevertheless, thou art never the nearer Him till thou hast found Him. He is in thee, though He be lost from thee; but thou art not in Him till thou hast found Him. But this is His mercy, that He would suffer Himself to be lost only there where He may be found, so that thou needst not run to Rome or Jerusalem to seek Him there, but turn thy thoughts into thine own soul, where He is hid; as the Prophet said, 'Truly, Thou art a hidden God,' hid in thy soul, and seek Him there. If thou couldst find Him in thy soul, and thy soul in Him, I am sure for joy thereof thou wouldst part with the liking of all earthly things to have Him. Jesus sleepeth in thy heart spiritually, as He did some time bodily in the ship with His disciples; but they wakened Him, and He saved them. Do thou so. Stir him by prayer, and He will soon rise and help thee. Nevertheless, I believe thou sleepest oftener to Him than He to thee. For He calleth thee full oft with His sweet,

---

[1] Hilton, "Scale of Perf.," B i., P 3, C 2 and 3.

secret voice ; and stirreth thy heart full stilly, that thou shouldst leave the jangling of other vanities in thy soul, and hearken only to Him. 'Hear, O daughter, and consider, and forget thy people and thy father's house:' that is, forget the people of thy worldly thoughts, and the house of thy fleshly affections. See how our Lord calleth, and what hindereth thee that thou canst neither hear nor see Him. Therefore, put away those unquiet noises, and destroy the love of sin and vanity, and bring into thy heart the love of virtues and full Charity, and then thou shalt hear thy Lord speak to thee. As long as Jesus findeth not His image reformed in thee, He is strange, and the farther from thee. Therefore, frame and shape thyself to be arrayed in His likeness—that is, in Humility and Charity, which are His liveries; and then will He know thee, and familiarly come to thee and acquaint thee with His secrets, for thus He saith, 'If anyone love Me, My Father will love him, and We will come to him, and make Our abode with him, and I will manifest Myself to him'. If, therefore, thou wilt be like Him, have Humility and Charity." [1]

---

[1] Hilton, " Scale of Perf.," B i., P 3, C 3, § 2. The teaching of Denis the Carthusian upon this is as follows: " Quemadmodum rationalis creatura ad imaginem et similitudinem sui est condita Creatoris, sic sua reformatio, profectus, perfectio, finis, beatitudo, et gloria, in assimilatione actuali, conversione, reductione, adhæ-sione, et plena conjunctione cum suo productivo et salvativo con-sistit principio. Porro, assimilatio ista in actibus illis princi-paliter consistit, qui Deo intra se conveniunt, qui sunt operationes ad intra intellectus et voluntatis; videlicet plena divinæ veritatis cognitio, et perfecta divinæ bonitatis dilectio," &c. (Denis Car-thus., " de laude Vitæ Solit.," A 1.)

Is not this our work in hand—union with God in the interior kingdom of the soul by perfect Charity, grounded on humility? But Charity itself is the moving-power which effects the work. Because it loves God it brings the soul to the nought of humility to attain to Him, since the Divine greatness is reached only by the way of the soul's nothingness, as fulness can only occupy emptiness. Then when the groundwork of humility is laid, Charity progresses to God, by animating the works of life with the spirit of His love, and finally rises to Him by contemplation and union.

Hence, says Albertus Magnus, "there is no better, shorter, and safer way of attaining to these things, and everything else necessary to salvation, than LOVE, which contains the abundance of every good. For by love alone we are turned to God, united with God, transformed in God, made one Spirit with Him, beatified here by grace, and hereafter by glory. For love rests only in the Beloved: love, I say, which is Charity, is the way of God to men, and of men to God. God has no dwelling where there is no Charity. But if we have Charity we have God, because 'God is Charity'. Hence love admits no medium between itself and its object, which is God. Therefore, it never rests until it passes all things, and attains to Him, transforming the lover in the Beloved, so that one lives in the other. This love is the life of the soul, and its perfection; in which are the whole law and the Prophets. Hence the Apostle says, 'Love is the

fulfilling of the law,' and 'the end of the commandment is Charity'." [1]

If, again, we place perfection—as we must—in
conformity to Christ our Lord, as the model of
perfection, we are at once led to enquire by what
means we are to attain to this conformity. When
our Lord says, "Learn of Me," "He that followeth
Me walketh not in darkness," the question immediately arises, *How* are we to follow Christ?
The answer is, that our Lord's way is the way of
perfect love. He is the Divine Lover of God and
of men. For the love of God and of men He
became incarnate, lived on earth, taught the law of
love and the life of love, suffered in love, and died
for love; sent down the Spirit of His love upon
the Church, to be the ruling power of our lives and
actions, by "the Charity of God poured forth in
our hearts," [2] and left us the marvellous gift of
Himself to the end of the world, in the mystery of
love on the Altar, wherein He dwells as the Divine
Lover in the midst of those He loves—working
within us, nourishing and perfecting His life of love
in the souls of men. When, thèrefore, our Lord
says, "Follow Me," it is not with the steps of the
body, but with the love of the soul, that He desires
to be followed, as S. Ambrose tells us; [3] as S. Paul
had also said : "Be ye followers of God, and walk
in love, as most dear children ". [4]   Truly our Lord,

---

[1] Albert Mag., "de adhær. Deo.," C 12.   [2] Rom. v. 5.

[3] "Sequi jubet, non corporis gressu, sed mentis affectu." (S.
Amb., "in Lucam," C 5, v 27.)

[4] Eph. v. 2.

in His Sacred Humanity, is the perfect model of
perfect love: whether we consider Him in His
joyful, sorrowful, or glorious mysteries, perfect
Charity reigns throughout all. The faculties of
His human soul ever maintain themselves by the
power of the love that governs them, in subjection
to the Divinity; so that in all their operations the
love of God is their ruling principle. This indeed
is the life of Charity—for God's will and love
to govern the human will and love, His light to
illumine the intelligence, His remembrance to
fill the memory, and then for the operations of
the entire man to proceed under the influence
and guidance of the Divine Spirit: so that thus
the creature becomes the recipient of God's
life, light, love, and movement, and is made a
sharer in His blessedness, and a fit instrument in
His hands for the good of others. Happy the life
which is thus pervaded in all its parts by the Spirit
of God. " Whosoever are led by the Spirit of God,
they are the sons of God."[1] Thus it is by Charity
that we follow our Lord in the way of perfection.
" I in them, and Thou in Me, that they may be
made perfect in one."[2] " If you speak to Christ,"
says S. Catherine of Siena, writing of a good
Religious soul, " and say, Who is this soul? He
will answer, ' It is another Myself, made so by
perfect love'."[3]

Let us now consider the words of the inspired

---

[1] Rom. viii. 14. [2] S. John xvii. 23.
[3] S. Cath. Sien., " Letter " 129.

Apostle. S. Paul represents the spiritual life as a putting off the "old man" and a putting on the "new man," by mortifying the life of the flesh, and living according to the Spirit. " Put off the old man, who is corrupted ; and be ye renewed in the spirit of your mind ; and put on the new man, created according to God in justice and holiness of truth."[1] " If you live according to the flesh, you shall die; but if by the Spirit you mortify the deeds of the flesh you shall live."[2] " For whosoever are led by the Spirit of God, they are the sons of God."[3] The living according to the flesh and according to the Spirit signify, says S. Austin, the living according to man, or according to God.[4]

The teaching conveyed by these and such-like passages is, that the natural man is not to be allowed to move by an independent principle of his own, which is the principle of his own self-love; but that he is to serve under a higher principle, which is none other than the Holy Spirit of God moving us by His own Divine Love. At the out-set, however, of the spiritual life there is the natural man ready to move. It belongs, then, to Charity at once to take her position, in order that the Spirit of God may from the first have the governance of the soul. By this means the natural principle is put from the commencement under the spiritual ; and as acts make habits, so the spiritual principle

---

[1] Eph. iv. 22.   [2] Rom. viii. 13.   [3] Rom. viii. 14.
[4] "Viventes secundum spiritum, non secundum carnem, hoc est, secundum Deum. non secundum hominem." (S. Aug., " de Civ. Dei," Lib. xiv., C 9.)

gradually gains an ascendency over the natural, and the natural is brought into sweet alliance with the spiritual. Thus we put off the old man, and put on the new man. Courage and fidelity, day by day, in bringing the habit of Charity into action [1] in the midst of occasions, keeping true to the higher principle, and subduing the lower, gradually form and finally develop the full-grown spiritual man, " created according to God, in justice and holiness of truth ".[2] In this way the " one love " does both works : unforming the old man and forming the new man.

If, again, we take perfection as shown forth by a full and faithful exercise of the Christian virtues and counsels, so that the life of a man is seen to be justly balanced, rightly ordered, and adorned with Christ-like virtues, each in its proper time and place, we are obliged to own that the supernatural beauty of such a life is the effect and consequence of a vivifying Charity within the soul. Charity is to be reckoned as the motive-cause of all such virtues, in so far as they are worthy of God and heaven. As S. Thomas says, " Charity, aiming at the ultimate end as its object, moves the other virtues to action. For the virtue which regards the ultimate end always commands the virtues which have regard to the means. And therefore the merit of eternal life first belongs to Charity, then to the other virtues, according as their acts are prompted

---

[1] For the distinction between *habit* and *act*, see note 2, p. 86.
[2] Eph. iv. 23.

by Charity. Hence Charity is the principle of all
good works referred to the last end." [1]

It is true, indeed, that the natural virtues may
exist apart from Charity, at least in an imperfect
degree ; but we are considering ourselves now in
the supernatural order of the Christian life, incor-
porated with Christ, participating, therefore, in His
Spirit, and living in reference to our ultimate end.
As such, Charity becomes 'soul of our soul,' 'life
of our life,'[2] and consequently the principle and
form of the soul's virtues,[3] when we are true, that
is, to the supernatural principle ; for the natural
principle still lives, and often hinders the force of
Charity by moving "præter finem". But if, as true
Christians, we move by the Spirit of Christ,[4] " in
ordine ad finem," Charity hereby becomes our
moving-principle, the life and soul of our actions.[5]
The reason of this is that God is our ultimate end :
and the love of Him as such moves us to acts of

---

[1] " Caritas, inquantum habet ultimum finem pro objecto, movet
alias virtutes ad operandum.　Semper enim habitus ad quem
pertinet finis, imperat habitus ad quos pertinent ea quæ sunt ad
finem.　Et ideo meritum vitæ æternæ primo pertinet ad Caritatem ; ad alias autem virtutes secundario, secundum quod eorum
actus a Caritate imperantur."　Hinc, " Caritas est principium
omnium bonorum operum, quæ in finem ultimum ordinari possunt."　(S. Thom., 1 2, Q 114, Art. 4 ad 1, & in C, & Q 65, Art. 3.)

[2] " Tu, amor meus, Tu vita es animarum, vita vitarum, vita
animæ meæ."　(S. Aug., " Conf.," L iii., C 6.)

[3] " Caritas ad omnes alias virtutes comparatur et ut motor, et
ut forma, et ut finis."　(S. Thom., 3 Sen., D 27, Q 2, A 4, q 3.)

[4] " If we live in the Spirit, let us walk in the Spirit."　(Gal. v.)

[5] " Secundum omnes Sanctos Doctores, Caritas est omnium
virtutum decor et forma, imperatrix ac vita ; ita quod nullius
virtutis actus est meritorius sine Caritate ; idcirco Caritas dicitur
animæ vita."　(Denis Carthus., " de vita Cleric,," Art. 18.)

virtue, as means by which we may advance to Him. This love is Charity.[1] "By Charity," says S. Thomas, "the acts of all other virtues are ordered to their last end ; in virtue of which Charity becomes the form of the other virtues, extending itself as the ruling power ('per modum imperii') to all the actions of human life."[2]

It would seem, however, that, ordinarily speaking, years of faithful practice of the moral virtues as opportunities occur would be required before Charity holds them as with reins in her hand, governing thereby the whole man, and moving him to action promptly, easily, and sweetly. And therefore the majority of those who exhibit in a fair measure the Christian virtues in daily life, would perhaps rather be tending, by the practice of these virtues, towards the perfection of Charity, than enjoying their exercise as the results of such Charity, in calm and sweet possession of the soul. This agrees with the teaching of the Abbot Moses to Cassian : " Fasting, watching, meditation, privation, are not themselves perfection, but the instruments by which we may acquire perfection. They are not the object of our profession, but the means by which we may obtain it. It becomes us, there-

---

[1] " Quia Caritas habet pro objecto ultimum finem humanæ vitæ, scilicet beatitudinem æternam, ideo extendit se ad actus totius humanæ vitæ, per modum imperii." (S. Thom., 2 2, Q 23, Art. 4 ad 2.)

[2] " Per Caritatem ordinantur actus omnium aliarum virtutum ad ultimum finem; et secundum hoc ipsa dat formam actibus omnium aliarum virtutum." " Ideo extendit se ad actus tetius humanæ vitæ, per modum imperii." (S. Thom., 2 2, Q 23, Art. 8, & Art. 4 ad 2.)

fore, to use these means with reference to our end, which is Charity. What will it avail us to perform with punctuality our ordinary exercises, if the main purpose for which we perform them is eluded? To this end, therefore, should be referred our solitude, our fasts, our daily employments,—yea, every penitential exercise, and every virtue, that by these means our hearts may be preserved in calm, and thus we may ascend to the perfection of Charity."[1]

S. Thomas also points to this in his teaching on the active and contemplative life; taking now with S. Gregory the contemplative life for the loving adherence of the soul to God by Charity,[2] and the active life for the exercise of the moral virtues.[3] The Angelic Doctor says: "The active life is a preparation to the contemplative; and therefore until one has attained to perfection in active life, he cannot reach to the contemplative, except in its commencement, and imperfectly. For as long as a man has difficulty in practising the moral virtues, his attention is anxiously engaged with them, which hinders his devotedness to contemplation. But when his active life is perfect, then, having the moral virtues in command, he is able without impediment to give himself to contemplation. And in proportion to his perfection in active life, he is able to unite both action and contemplation to-

---

[1] Cassian, "Conf.," i., C 7.

[2] " Contemplativa vita est Caritatem Dei et proximi tota mente retinere." (S. Greg., Hom. 14 in Ezech.)

[3] S. Thom., 2 2, Q 181, Art. 1.

gether."[1] " In this way we proceed from the active
life to the contemplative ; and from the contemplative life we return to the active, that action may
be directed by contemplation."[2] Hence S. Gregory says that " he who desires to gain the citadel
of contemplation must first prove himself in the
field of action." [3]

From this we see that Charity, while yet imperfect, moves us to the exercise of the Christian
virtues, in order to gain her own perfection ; and
when she has attained to the repose of contemplative love, she returns to the domain of activity in
calm and sweet possession of the soul, to animate,
direct, sustain, and govern the occupations of the
active life. Thus she brings to man both his
essential and accidental perfection, and the beginning of his future beatitude in heaven.[4] Happy is
the soul which thus attains to the habitual union of
its powers in God ! " They now unite to produce .
one harmonious sound," says S. Catherine of Siena,
" like the chords of a musical instrument. The
powers of the soul are the great chords, the senses
of the body the smaller ones. And when all these
are used to the praise of God, and in the service of
our neighbour, they produce one sound, like that of
a harmonious organ. All the saints have touched

---

[1] S. Thom., 3 Sen., D 35, Art. 3, q 3.

[2] S. Thom., 2 2, Q 182, Art. 4 ad 2.

[3] " Qui culmen perfectionis apprehendere nituntur, cum contemplationis arcem tenere desiderant, prius se in campo operis
per exercitium probent." (S. Greg., " Moral.," Lib. vi., C 17.)

[4] ' Godliness is profitable to all things ; having the promise of
the life that now is, and of that which is to come." (1 Tim. iv. 8.)

this organ, and drawn forth musical tones. The
first who sounded it was the sweet and loving Word,
whose Humanity, united to His Divinity, made
sweet music on the wood of the Cross ; and all His
servants have learnt of Him, as of their Master, to
give forth similar music, some in one way and some
in another, Divine Providence giving all the instruments on which to play."[1]

What, now, shall we say to Rodriguez, when
he places our perfection in the ordinary actions
of life ? It is clear when he says this that he
speaks of the *material* of our perfection, and
that he presupposes Charity in our actions as
their *form* or animating spirit. " All our actions,"
says he, " be nothing else but the effects of the
Divine love that animates us. And as in the
temple of Solomon there was nothing but what
was of gold, or covered with gold, so let there be
nothing in you which is not either an act or an
effect of the love of God."[2]

Further, as already said, Charity as a habit,
being our animating principle, has for the gaining
of its own perfection to put itself forth to action ;
and if it act not, it is not true Charity. The perfection of virtue is not its habit, but its act.[3] The
habit is ordained to its act, as the sword to its use.
A man is virtuous, not because he *can* act vir-

[1] S. Cath. Sien., " Dial.," C 147.

[2] Rodriguez, " Christian Perfection," Vol. i., T iii., C 8.

[3] " Unumquodque intantum perfectum est, inquantum est actu :
nam potentia sine actu imperfecta est." (S. Thom., 1 2, Q 3,
Art. 2.)

tuously, but because he *does* so. And the habit of virtue, to insure its perfection, must produce its acts as readily and perfectly as possible. Rightly, therefore, does Rodriguez make perfection reside in our ordinary actions, as the form resides in the matter, the soul in the body, and the kernel in the shell. But the essential constituent of perfection ever remains in the inherent habit of habits, disposed to its acts, viz., Charity uniting with God, and proceeding to action from its principle of love. This is the assimilation of the creature to the Creator, apart from which there can be no perfection. The ordinary works of life are thus the divinely-appointed means and ways by which and in which the habit of love energises and reduces itself to act, thus exercising and expanding its life and power, intensively and extensively, and ·so enabling the soul by repeated acts to develop the habit of love, by means of which it advances to and finally attains its perfection.

Although, therefore, perfection is to be found in our ordinary actions, they depend for this perfection on the Charity that animates them ; and without this it is certain that they are worthless, so far as supernatural worth and merit are concerned. Who teaches this more emphatically than the inspired Apostle ? " If I speak with the tongues of men and angels, and have not Charity, I am become as a sounding brass and a tinkling cymbal. And if I should have prophecy, and should know all mysteries, and all knowledge ; and if I should have all faith, so that I could remove mountains, and have not Charity, I

am nothing. And if I should distribute all my
goods to feed the poor, and if I should deliver
my body to be burned, and have not Charity, it
profiteth me nothing."[1]   Here we see that not only
ordinary actions, but those the most exalted, reckon
for nothing apart from Charity, that is, in supernatural worth and merit ; which is not difficult to
understand, for an action without *love* is a body
without a soul.   Hence S. Augustine said that
" where there is no love, no good work is imputed,
nor is a work rightly called good ";[2] as on the
other hand he says, " Love, and do what you will ;
keep to the root of love ; from this nought but
good springs forth ".[3]   S. Gregory also tells us that
it is not the outer substance of our actions that God
regards, but the inner love that animates them.
" God regards the heart, rather than the external
work.   Nor does He consider how much a man
does, but with how much love he does it."[4]   The
" Imitation " says the same, in the self-same words.[5]

S. Thomas enters carefully into the consideration
of this point, and teaches that the merit of our outward actions wholly depends on the Charity they
contain ; speaking always of supernatural merit, in

---

[1] 1 Cor. xiii. 1.

[2] " Ubi non est dilectio, nullum bonum opus imputatur ; nec
recte bonum opus vocatur." (S. Aug., " de Gratia Christi," C 26.)

[3] " Dilige, et fac quod vis.   Radix sit intus dilectionis.   Non
potest de ista radice nisi bonum existere." (S. Aug., Tract 7 in
Epist. Joan.)

[4] " Cor, et non substantiam pensat Deus ; nec perpendit *quantum* in Ejus sacrificium, sed *ex quanto* proferatur." (S. Greg.,
Hom. 5 in Evang.)

[5] " Imit.," B i., C 15.

reference to the rewards of heaven.[1] It is the inward spirit which is the test and measure of merit in the outward act. So that the active or the contemplative life respectively will be the more meritorious according to the degree of Charity either may contain. A small action done with great Charity is more meritorious than a great action done with small Charity; and the degrees of glory in heaven will be according to the degrees of Charity on earth.[2]

The fact is that our actions are composed of body and soul. They follow our nature, which is the union of matter and spirit. "Operatio sequitur

---

[1] "Radix merendi est Caritas." (S. Thom., 2.2, Q 182, Art. 2.) The influx of Charity into our actions varies indefinitely in degree, according as the habit of Charity is more or less developed and disposed to its acts. In general the influx may be actual or virtual. Actual, when we are directly prompted by Divine love, as our principle and our end; virtual, when Charity's virtue continues in our actions, from the force of its previous act, and practically influences them, from its habitual power ·in the mind and heart. Then, although not adverted to, Charity enters into our actions by a virtual inflow, and is therefore still our principle and our end. So it remains until revoked by any subsequent act incompatible with it, such as a venial sin, which substitutes a natural principle and· end for· Charity; which principle is Cupidity, or self-love, the antagonistic principle to Charity in the soul.

[2] "Actus noster non habet quod sit meritorius ex ipsa substantia actus, sed solum ex habitu virtutis quo informatur. Vis autem merendi est in omnibus virtutibus ex Caritate, quæ habet ipsum finem pro objecto. Et ideo diversitas in merendo tota revertitur ad diversitatem Caritatis. Sic secundum diversos Caritatis gradus erunt diversi gradus in gloria. Unde contingit quandoque quod in activa vita quis plus mereatur quam in contemplativa, vel e converso, secundum quod majorem habet Caritatem, vel minorem. Parvum opus ex magna Caritate factum, magis est meritorium quam magnum opus ex parva Caritate. Principalitas enim meriti est in Caritate: in aliis autem secundum quod Caritate informantur." (S. Thom., 4 Sent., D 49, Q 1, Art. 4; 3 Sent., D 35, A 4, q 2; 3 Sent., D 30, Q 1, A 3, 5.)

esse." There is the outer material, or body of our
actions, and the spirit that animates them. There
is the act produced, and the habit within that
prompts it : the matter, and the form or vivifying
principle. Now, in estimating our actions before
God and placing our perfection in them, we must
know that the one criterion by which to judge
them is their animating spirit, and its influence,
intensively and extensively, within them ; not their
outward magnitude, apart from this. " It is the
Spirit that quickeneth; the flesh profiteth nothing."[1]
And S. Paul has already told us that the grandest
externals, without the inner life of Charity, go for
nothing. Who, indeed, could be so blind as to
imagine that God would be contented with the
outer material of our actions, when after all the
soul is the best part. of our being? God looks at
something more than appearances. " Man seeth
the things that appear ; but God regardeth the
heart."[2]   He is a Spirit ; and our worship of Him
must be " in Spirit and in truth ".[3]   Therefore if a
man's life and actions are to be accounted *truly*
great, and worthy of God and heaven, whatever
their outward appearance may be, they must proceed from a heart animated by the principle of
Divine Charity.[4] The love of God is to be the
soul of our actions. As the soul moves the body,
so Divine Charity is to move the soul. Is it not

---

[1] S. John vi. 64.   [2] 1 Kings xvi. 7.   [3] S. John iv. 24.
[4] " Effectus exterior non pertinet ad Caritatem nisi inquantum
ex affectu procedit." (S. Thom., 3 Sent., D 29, Q 1, A 2.)

the inward love of the heart that God requires before all things? " Thou shalt love the Lord thy God with thy whole heart, and with thy whole soul, and with thy whole strength." And even in His servants of the old law, was it not the "perfect heart" that He looked for? Thus we read that " King Amasias did what was good in the sight of the Lord, yet not with a perfect heart ".[1] And again : " Solomon's heart was not perfect with the Lord ".[2] But "the heart of Asa was perfect with the Lord all his days ".[3] Let us not imagine, then, that God will be satisfied with any amount of customable external service, if we withhold that which He desires more than all. " My son, give me thy heart."[4] How could it be otherwise? Why should God be expected to reward actions which are not done for Him—which flow from a simply human principle? For natural actions there are natural rewards. But if we aim at supernatural rewards, then our principle of action must be in proportion thereto.[5] This supernatural principle we have in Charity, as giving us a participation of God's own Holy Spirit and love. And as we act by it, it communicates its Divine virtue to our actions.

---

[1] 2 Paralip. xxv. 2.   [2] 3 Kings xi. 4.

[3] 3 Kings xv. 14.   [4] Prov. xxiii. 26.

[5] " In merito oportet quod actio æquiparetur mercedi. Actio autem proportionata ad vitam æternam est actio *ex Caritate* facta ; et ideo per eam ex condigno meretur quis ea quæ ad vitam æternam pertinent. Opera autem bona quæ non sunt ex Caritate facta, deficiunt ab ista proportione. Et ideo per ea quis non meretur ex condigno vitam æternam." (S. Thom., 3 Sent., D 18, Art. 2.)

Thus God enters into them, and makes them good,
and worthy of Himself; since He is the only Good,
and we are the recipients of His goodness.

If, then, we live in Charity, let us see that we act
by it. "If we live in the Spirit, let us also walk in
the Spirit."[1] Let us learn to separate the precious
from the vile. If the higher principle of Divine
love has been planted within us, how can we turn
from it to follow instead the biddings of natural and
fleshly love? We ought to beware of withdrawing
ourselves from the action of God and betaking ourselves to independent movements of our own. For
"every plant which My Father hath not planted
shall be rooted up".[2] We ought to fear lest, having
received so great a power, we neglect to use it;
remembering our Lord's impressive teaching and
warning in the parable of the talents, and the con-
demnation of the servant who neglected to turn
his talent to account. "Lord, Thou hast given to
me five talents; behold, I have gained other five."[3]
Grace must gain more grace; light more light;
love must advance to higher love; strength get
greater strength; and progress serve to further
progress. Everything must move according to its
nature. Every power must put forth its proper
operation:[4] the mind by thinking, the eye by

---

[1] "Si spiritu vivimus, spiritu et ambulemus." (Gal. v. 25.) "Si
ergo spiritu vivimus, debemus in omnibus ab Ipso agi. Sicut
enim in vita corporali, corpus non movetur, nisi per animam per
quam vivit, ita in vita spirituali omnis motus noster debet esse a
Spiritu Sancto." (S. Thom., in Pauli Epist. ad Galat. 5.)

[2] S. Matt. xv. 13.   [3] S. Matt. xxv. 20.

[4] "Quælibet res est propter suam operationem."

seeing, the hand by working, the foot by walking. See in like manner the vast power of Charity : the power of loving God and doing great things for Him ; the power of governing our souls, our lives, our actions, according to Him. Do we use this power of love as rightly and readily as our inferior powers? Does it operate? Does it put forth its acts, governing us, leading us on, and moving us according to God? "What more could I do to My vineyard that I have not done to it?" After all that our Lord has done to give us His love ; after planting us in His choice vineyard of Religion : tending, training, nourishing, cultivating our souls, so fitting them to yield to Him sweetly and abundantly the fruits of pure Charity,—are we to be found now bringing forth the "wild grapes" of our own "fleshly loves and fears"?

The power of Charity is for the *act* of Charity, since every power is for its proper act.[1] "A good man, out of a good treasure, bringeth forth good things."[2] Ought we not, then, from the Divine treasure of Charity to bring forth Divine things, viz., Charity's own proper, full, and perfect acts? Thus perfection resides in the ordinary actions of life, in so far as they are animated, prompted, and regulated by the principle of Charity. And when in due time, by great fidelity to the lights and movements of the Holy Spirit, Charity has attained her full sway within the soul, and moves the faculties and bodily

---

[1] "Ratio potentiæ est ut sit principium actus." (S. Thom., I 2, Q 49, Art. 3.)

[2] S. Matt. xii. 35.

25

powers to act promptly, easily, and sweetly, then is brought about that happy harmony within, whereby the natural man is subdued to the spiritual, and the spirit is subdued to God, and we live and act no longer according to man, but according to God. Then shine forth the gifts and the fruits of the Holy Spirit in the soul wherein the Divine Image is now restored. It has given "all for all"; and God delights to manifest again the life of Christ in mortal flesh. Wisdom, Understanding, Knowledge, Counsel, Fortitude, Peace, Joy, Patience, and all other virtues follow as the effects of perfect Charity.[1] They belong by right to a life which is Divine. "How hath He not also with Him given us all things ? "[2]

Wisdom shows all things in the light of God, teaching the soul to judge of them, "ex altissima causa ; et secundum rationes divinas,"[3] *i.e.*, from their highest cause, and by Divine principles. And this on account of the soul's *nearness* to God, and its relation to Divine things.[4] For since Charity unites the soul to the source of all light, it naturally and necessarily throws light upon the mind in

---

[1] "In Caritate proficere est in omni virtute incrementum accipere, atque in septem donis Sancti Spiritus augmentum sortiri. Nam Caritas est virtus dignissima, omniumque virtutum forma, vita, vertex, finis, regina, ac motrix. Nec aliqua virtus tam efficaciter et valenter movet ac incitat ad omnem actum virtutum, nec ita celeriter et potenter retrahit a peccatis, ut amor Dei." (Denis Carth., "Inflammat. Div. amor.," A 1.)

[2] Rom. viii. 32.

[3] S. Thom., 2 2, Q 45, Art. 1 & 2.

[4] "Propter connaturalitatem quandam ad ea de quibus est judicandum." (S. Thom, 2 2, Q 45, Art. 2.)

its choice and use of the means leading to the end.[1] " For what man knoweth the things of a man but the spirit of a man that is in him ? So the things also that are of God no man knoweth but the Spirit of God." By contact with the Spirit of God man knows the things that are of God, and thus judges and orders the works of life according to Him.[2] From this light of love ·shining in the mind proceeds the Divine virtue of *Discretion*,[3] which is the discernment of the mind in regard to the operations of the will ;[4] or the light of God, showing the soul what to do ; or the recognition of the " Divine call"; rightly ordering Charity, and enabling the soul to walk " according to God," not "according to man," and to follow the instincts of the Divine, not the human, spirit.[5] " He who has not this discretion" (said Abbot Moses) "will have the eye of his mind, as well as of his actions, involved in obscurity, and he will grope on in the darkness of a vexed and troubled spirit. Discretion is the guide

---

[1] " Ad sapientem pertinet considerare causam altissimam, per quam certissime de aliis judicatur, et secundum quam omnia ordinare oportet. Ille qui cognoscit causam altissimam in aliquo genere, dicitur esse sapiens in illo genere. Ille autem qui cognoscit causam altissimam simpliciter, quæ est Deus, dicitur sapiens simpliciter, inquantum per regulas divinas omnia potest judicare et ordinare." (S. Thom., 2 2, Q 45, Art. 1 & 2.)

[2] " Ad sapientiam prius pertinet contemplatio divinorum, quæ est visio principii : et posterius dirigere actus humanos secundum rationes divinas." (S. Thom., 2 2, Q 45, Art. 3 ad 3.)

[3] " Love is a fire, burning and shining. When it burns in the will, it shines in the understanding." (Card. Bona, " Via Comp.," C 9.)

[4] " Recta ratio agibilium." (Arist.)

[5] " Dona Spiritus Sancti faciunt nos bene sequentes instinctum ipsius." (S. Thom., 1 2, Q 68, Art. 2 ad 3.)

of life, the mistress and the counsellor of all virtues, without which no virtue can be brought to perfection."[1]   Nor does it consist only in *seeing* the right thing, but in *doing* it also, as S. Thomas carefully notes.[2]   From which we see that Divine Wisdom and Discretion presuppose the formed habit of Charity in the soul.   Indeed, Wisdom · is Charity *perfected*, by being rightly developed, ordered, and applied to action ; as the inspired Word itself teaches : " The love of God is honourable wisdom ".[3] Thus Wisdom must be loving, and love must be wise.   Hence the word " ordinata " in the diagram, p. 359, points to Discretion as Charity ordered and perfected.[4]

Understanding enables the soul to penetrate the truths of faith, the meaning of Holy Scripture, and the sense of spiritual books.   Those whose Charity is weak, and whose hearts are consequently unpurified, believe Divine things without realising them, and read holy books without understanding them.[5]   Even S. Teresa tells us that for

[1] Cassian, " Conf.," ii., C 2 and 4.

[2] " Laus prudentiæ non consistit in sola consideratione, sed in applicatione ad opus, quod est finis practicæ rationis.   Et ideo si in hoc defectus accidat, maxime est contrarium prudentiæ. Quia sicut finis est potissimus in unoquoque, ita et defectus qui est circa finem est pessimus." (S. Thom., 2 2, Q 47, Art. 1 ad 3.)

[3] Ecclus. i. 14.   S. Augustine also says, " Summa sapientia est Caritas Dei ".   (S. Aug., Epist. 140 ad Honorat., C 18.)

[4] " Ordinavit in me Caritatem." (Cant. ii. 4.)   " Omnino necessarie.   Et quo zelus fervidior, ac vehementior spiritus, profusiorque Caritas, eo vigilantiori opus scientia est, quæ zelum supprimat, spiritum temperet, ordinat Caritatem."   (S. Bern., Serm. 49 in Cant.)

[5] " Nisi legentium mentes ad alta profecerint, Divina' dicta velut in imis non intellecta jacent." (S. Greg., Hom. 7 in Ezech.)

many years she "read much, and understood nothing";[1] that is, until her spiritual eye had been
opened. The gift of Divine understanding enlightens
the soul in proportion to its Charity, this being the
bond of union with the Holy Spirit, by means
whereof He communicates His light.[2] Hence the
Apostle says, "Being rooted and founded in
Charity, you may be able to comprehend".[3] If,
therefore, we wish for much light let us have much
love. Then by means of Divine love we shall
understand Divine things. " His unction teacheth
you of all things."[4] The Spirit of God dwelling in
the soul, and working there by Charity, teaches us
to see and understand things in His own Divine
light.[5] "God hath given wisdom to them that love
Him."[6] " But," says Lallemant, " these lights come
to us by degrees, according to our interior disposition, and depart also in the same manner, leaving
us in darkness, so that we have an alternation of
day and night within our souls. We ought to
aspire after a perpetual day; nor will it fail to

---

[1] S. Teresa, " Life by herself," C 12.

[2] Let it be remembered we are now considering Understanding,
not as an intellectual virtue, but as a *gift*, disposing the soul to
move by the instinct of the Holy Spirit, in its knowledge of Divine
things; as S. Thomas says, " Secundum quod operatur ex instinctu
Divino." (S. Thom., 1 2, Q 68, A 1 ad 4.) As such, understanding
is in the soul as an infusion of the Holy Ghost, in virtue of the
union of Charity, and is thus in proportion to the diffusion of
Charity : " propter quandam connaturalitatem ".

[3] Eph. iii. 17.   [4] 1 John ii. 27.

[5] " Spiritus Sanctus mentem inhabitans, doceat quid oporteat
fieri, intellectum illuminando de agendis : et affectum inclinat ad
recte agendum." (S. Thom., in Pauli Epist. ad Rom. viii.)

[6] Ecclus. i. 10.

shine in our soul when, having thoroughly purified
it, we shall continually follow the guidance of the
Holy Spirit."[1]

Knowledge illuminates the mind with Divine
Light in human things,[2] enabling us to judge of
them in reference to God, as the last end of all;
showing us what we ought to believe, the views we
ought to take, the course we ought to pursue; and
this both in regard to our own souls and those of
others.[3]   By this gift we see readily and clearly the
state of our own interior; our habits of mind and
heart; our acts, with their principles, qualities, and
ends.   We get our views of the work of the Church,
of the world, of society, of the souls of others.   We
form a prompt judgment in the midst of our duties,
seeing the right thing to be said and done.   In the
whole work of our perfection, and in the guidance
of souls, much knowledge is needed—the knowledge that comes from love.   "Amor ipse notitia
est:"[4] the light that is diffused in the mind by the
presence of the Divine Spirit.   "We have received
the Spirit that is of God, that we may know the
things that are given us from God.   Which things
also we speak; not in the learned words of human
wisdom, but in the doctrine of the Spirit.   But the
sensual man perceiveth not these things that are of
the Spirit of God; for it is foolishness to him, and

---

[1] Lallemant, "Sp. Doct.," P 4, C 2, A 1, § 8.
[2] "Donum scientiæ est solum circa res humanas vel creatas."
(S. Thom., 2 2, Q 9, A 2.)
[3] "Spiritualis omnia judicat." (1 Cor. ii. 15.)
[4] S. Greg., Hom. 27 in Evang.

he cannot understand. But the spiritual man judgeth all things, and himself is judged of no man."[1]

Counsel points to the use of right means in particular circumstances. "And it is easy to perceive its necessity ; since it is not enough to know that a thing is good in itself. We have also to judge whether it is good under actual circumstances: whether it is better than something else, and more suited to the object we are aiming at. This knowledge we acquire by the gift of counsel."[2] Love, uniting the soul with God, tells us in these circumstances the things that please Him. For who knows better than a lover the things that please the Beloved? The constant regard which a loving soul has to the Divine Presence enables it to see the course to take. And God on His part governs the soul that is faithful to Him, and manifests Himself to it ; as our Lord assures us, "We will come to him, and make Our abode with him ; and I will manifest Myself to him".[3] "I will give thee understanding, and instruct thee in the way in which thou shouldst go : I will fix mine eyes upon thee."[4] In the continual variety of circumstances in which we find ourselves, it concerns us to aim consistently at acting by Divine, not human, principles. Those who are not governed by Charity are necessarily moving under lower influences, such

[1] 1 Cor. ii. 12.
[2] Lallemant, " Sp. Doctr.," P 4, A 4.
[3] S. John xiv. 23.   [4] Ps. xxxi.

as selfish interest, or "fleshly loves and fears".[1]
All this is averse to true counsel, which tells us that
the right principle of action is always that of
Divine Charity ; and this in its turn supplies a
constant light to the soul by means of Discretion,
showing it how to discern, decide, and move amidst
the continually-changing scenes and surroundings
of daily life.

Piety gives a filial affection towards God, and a
love for all things that regard Him and His service.
By this gift we experience a delight in holy things ;
and a corresponding disrelish for those which are
profane and frivolous.   How could it be otherwise
with a soul that makes the Divine Lover its one
love, and His Charity its one object?   Whatever
speaks to it of God quickens its love; as though
the chord of its heart within vibrated to the sound
without.   Whatever leads it from Him comes as a
discord, grating on its spiritual sense.[2]   Hence its
constant tendency is to *simplicity* in spiritual life,
that is, *oneness* of aim, by drawing all things to the
"one Good," and living by the principle of the
"one love".[3]   And all the good things of separate
creatures are seen as the belongings of the "one

---

[1] " Quicunque avertitur a fine debito, necesse est quod aliquem
finem indebitum sibi præstituat, quia omne agens agit propter
finem." (S. Thom., 2 2, Q 45, A 1 ad 1.)

[2] " Sancti viri valde intolerabile æstimant quidquid illud non
sonat quod intus amant." (S. Greg., " Moral.," Lib. vii., C 6.)

[3] " He to whom all things are one, who sees all things in one,
who draws all things to one, may be steady in heart, and peaceably repose in God.   O Truth, my God, make me one with Thee
in everlasting love." (" Imit.," B i., C 3.)

Good," and all the works of life are done as the operations of the "one love". For although there are "diversities of graces" there is but "one Lord"; although "diversities of operations," but one Spirit.[1] The loving soul, therefore, keeps to unity in diversity; knowing, as S. Teresa says, that it is the property of the one love to work in a thousand different ways.[2] It therefore loves good things as the overflowings of God's goodness, and as the belongings of the "one love". Holy Scripture it loves as the very voice of the Beloved; holy books as the echo of His voice; holy souls as His own image and abode and "homeliest home";[3] holy places and things, as drawing both itself and others to the renewed thought and love of Him.[4] But put it into the world of externals—leave it with those whose conversation is vain and profitless—invite it to while away its time in idle gratification—and its spirit saddens and wearies. It says: " Caritas non est hic"; and it " cries that we are to be pitied, who content ourselves with so little. God" (it saith) "hath infinite treasure to bestow; and we take up with a little devotion that passes in a moment. Blind as we are, we hinder God, and stop the current of His graces." But when He finds a loving soul, " He pours into it His graces

---

[1] I Cor. xii. 4.

[2] " It is the property of love to be always working in a thousand different ways." (S. Teresa, " Int. Castle," M 6, C 9.)

[3] "In us is His homeliest home, and His endless dwelling." (M. Juliana of Norw., " Revel.," C 67.)

[4] " Similis simili gaudet—quasi formæ suæ conveniens."

and favours plentifully.   There they flow like a torrent which, after being stopped against its ordinary course, when it has found a passage spreads itself with impetuosity and abundance.   Let us stop the torrent no more.   Let us break down the barriers which hinder it.   Let us make way for Grace."[1]   Far too little for a soul that has found the Creator are the perishable gratifications of creatures.[2]   God alone, and the things of God, are satisfaction for such a soul.   Hence S. Augustine said that " the abundance of everything apart from God, to him was want";[3] and that the "loss of creatures was sweetness," now that he found his joy in the Divine Presence and love.[4]   For " as it is easy for a powerful monarch who has superb mansions to despise the poor cottage of a labourer, and for a rich man to be heedless of a crown-piece, so when once the soul has found God she freely bids adieu to created things.   The possession of God quenches her hunger and thirst, and hinders her from wandering after creatures, in search of the wretched content they give.   For she is united to Him who is a torrent of delights, and an inex-

---

[1] B. Lawrence Carm., Lett. 4.

[2] " Animæ videnti Creatorem, angusta est omnis creatura." (S. Greg., " Dialog.," L ii., C 35.)

[3] " Omnis copia quæ Deus non est, mihi egestas est."   (S. Aug., " Conf.," Lib. xiii., C 8.

[4] "Quam suave mihi subito factum est carere suavitatibus nugarum ! et quas amittere metus fuerat, jam dimittere gaudium erat.   Ejiciebas enim eas a me, vera Tu et summa suavitas ; ejiciebas, et intrabas pro eis omni voluptate dulcior." (S. Aug., " Conf.," Lib. ix., C 1.)

haustible source of beauty and sweetness, and all that can rejoice the human heart." [1]

Fortitude strengthens and sustains the soul in the labours it undertakes and the sufferings it endures in the service of God. " Without this gift no notable progress can be made in the spiritual life. Mortification and prayer, which are its principal exercises, demand a generous determination to overcome all the difficulties to be encountered in the way of the Spirit, which is so opposed to our natural inclinations." [2] No power is equal to that of love in carrying us through our duties and supporting us in difficulties. It is "as strong as death".[3] It softens the hardest things, and sweetens those that are bitterest. As the " Imitation " says, " It spurs us on to do great things, and makes all that is bitter sweet and savoury ".[4] The ardent desire of love to please and serve God by our labours and trials at once infuses an element of sweetness into them. This desire of love it is that spurs us on and sustains us, even to death itself. And thus we see how fortitude springs from love.

The *fear of God* maintains the soul in reverence and submission to Him. By this gift the soul has a profound regard to the overwhelming majesty of God above it, with a corresponding horror of sin and of everything opposed to the Divine Will ;

---

[1] Saint-Jure, " Spir. Man," Vol. ii., C 3, § 13.
[2] Lallemant, " Sp. Doctr.," P 4, C 4, Art. 6.
[3] Cant. viii. 6.　　　　　　　[4] " Imit.," B iii., C 5.

desiring constantly in all things to render to God a
faithful service.   It knows that the soul of man is
the domain of God, and that He alone must reign
therein.   Its aim, therefore, is to drive from its
interior all elements that are opposed or unlike to
God.   With a view to this it renounces all sins,
great and small, deliberate imperfections, unruly
movements, and even the least irregularity in its
operations ; knowing that " in the matter of love
the want of perfection is a notable fault ".[1]   The
soul must become like to God.   " We know that
when He shall appear, we shall be like to Him."[2]
Therefore anything short of perfection is insufficient.

These heavenly gifts, then, and all other
virtues follow as the effects of perfect Charity.
They belong by right to a life which is Divine ;
for " he who is joined to the Lord is one Spirit ".[3]
With the Spirit of God all virtues belong to the
soul.   They are the fruits and accompaniments of
this Divine Spirit.   Hence Charity, as the first-fruit
of the Spirit, is the life of such a soul, because the
spirit lives by love ; and love diffused within flows
out of its abundance into the souls of others.   As
a good tree brings forth good fruits, and as " a
good man from a good treasure bringeth forth
good things,"[4] so a loving soul from a loving heart
brings forth loving actions as its own proper fruits.[5]

---

[1] Words recorded in the life of Sister Benigne, lay-Sister of
the Visitation, as spoken to her by the " Divine Love".
[2] 1 John iii. 2.   [3] 1 Cor. vi. 17.   [4] S. Matt. xii. 35.
[5] " Quasi formæ suæ conveniens."

Joy necessarily follows—the joy of the Spirit, which results from living by one consistent principle, whereby the soul is established in an unchanging disposition of friendship with God, enjoying "the grace of a delightful familiarity" with Him;[1] God loving, and drawing, and moving the soul, and the soul sweetly responding to His love and movement.[2] Such as these attain to a happy equality, in the midst of the inequalities of life. They find the Divine Presence and love in all around them. They have come to the Fountain of Living Water, which "makes glad the city of God" within them,[3] and their souls are cleansed in the profusion of its heavenly streams, which flow around them as a ceaseless torrent, in all the beauties of nature and grace.[4] Before the living waters of this Fountain around them and within them, faults, and fleshly loves and fears, and scruples, all give way. "If we drink of it only once," says S. Teresa, "I am certain it leaves the soul pure, and cleansed from all her faults."[5] "And the Spirit and the Bride say, Come ; and he that thirsteth, let him come ;

---

[1] "Imit.," B iii., C 37.

[2] "Regard thy call; that's all in all." (D. Gertrude More.)

[3] "Fluminis impetus lætificat civitatem Dei." (Ps. xlv. 4.)

[4] S. Bonaventure, in his life of S. Francis of Assisi, says of the Seraphic Patriarch : " He rejoiced in all the works of God's hands, and by the glory and beauty of that mirror he rose to the principle and cause of them all. In all things fair he beheld Him who is most fair ; finding the way to the Beloved by His footsteps in created things. With unspeakable devotion he enjoyed that Fountain of goodness, flowing forth through all creatures, as in so many streams." (S. Bonav., " Life of S. Francis," C 9.)

[5] S. Teresa, " Way of Perf.," C 19.

and he that will, let him take the water of life freely."[1]

Peace, patience, benignity, and the rest all follow in this Divine life, because the disturbing elements have been removed from the soul. The power of love has brought the whole man into order under God; the lower powers serving the spiritual powers, and the spirit loving and serving God. Peace therefore being, as S. Augustine says, the "tranquillity of order"[2] follows as a natural result; and patience, benignity, and the other fruits of the Holy Ghost are as the offspring of Charity, accompanying her train as children following their mother.[3]

S. Thomas expresses in chosen words this perfect union of the soul with God, and the perfection with which it consequently operates. He considers the

[1] Apoc. xxii. 17. "Whosoever drinks of the Fountain of living water shall not thirst: that is, shall not thirst for earthly things; for when God satisfies the soul she always has a desire to drink again of this water. And the mercy of God is so great that He forbids no one to strive to come and drink at this Fountain of life. Rather He calls us aloud, though He does not force us. Do not, therefore, loiter on the way. I do not say, however, that it is in your power to arrive at contemplation, but that you should use all your exertions to attain it. It is not your choice, but our Lord's. But if you do what lies in you, and dispose yourselves for contemplation, I believe He will not fail to give it you, if you have true humility and mortification. I consider it certain that all those who do not loiter by the way shall not want this Living Water. May our Lord give us grace to seek it as it should be sought. And whether we will or no, we all travel towards this Fountain, though by different ways." (S. Teresa, "Way of Perf.," C 19, 17, 20, 21.)

[2] "Pax est tranquillitas ordinis." (S. Aug., "de Civ. Dei," L xix., C 13.)

[3] "Caritas mater est, custosque omnium virtutum." (S. Greg., "de cura Past.," P 3, a 10.)

union as a transformation in God, in which God is as the "form" of the soul. "Love," he says, "is a union, or transformation, by which the lover is transformed in the Beloved, and in a certain sense changed into Him. So that the union of love is as the union of form and matter, which makes simply one. And inasmuch as that which becomes the form of another is made one with it, therefore by love the lover is made one with the Beloved, and the Beloved becomes the form of the lover. Hence the Apostle says that 'he who is joined to the Lord is one Spirit'." [1]

The soul, being thus informed with Divine life and love, moves to the works of its life under the Divine influence. It becomes a fit instrument in the hands of God, who moves it according to Himself and His pure will and good pleasure. "For everyone," says the Angelic Doctor, "acts according to his form, which is the principle of his movement." [2] The Divine Spirit, therefore, as the form and principle of the soul, moves it according to Himself, since "the loving soul is ever inclined to act according to the requirements of the Beloved;

---

[1] "Amor est ipsa unio, vel transformatio, qua amans in amatum transformatur, et quodammodo convertitur in Ipsum. Unde unio amoris est sicut unio formæ et materiæ, quæ facit unum simpliciter. Et quia omne quod efficitur forma alicujus, efficitur unum cum illo, ideo per amorem amans fit unum cum amato, quod factum est forma amantis. Et ideo dicit Apostolus, 'Qui adhæret Domino, unus spiritus est'." (S. Thom., 3 Sent., D 27, Q 1, Art. 1 ad 2 & 4, & in C.)

[2] "Unumquodque agit secundum exigentiam suæ formæ, quæ est principium agendi, et regula operis." (S. Thom., 3 Sent., D 27, Q 1, Art. 1.)

and this with readiness and delight, as agreeing with its inmost nature. So that whatever the loving soul now does or suffers, all is sweet and savoury to it, and helps to increase its love, by drawing it more and more to the Beloved in the things it does and suffers for His sake. And as fire cannot be restrained from its natural movement, except by violence, so neither can the lover from moving according to love. And as violence is repugnant to nature, so to a lover it would be painful to act against his love, or even beside it. But to act according to it is ever pleasing to him. For the lover and the Beloved being as one, they ever work in harmony together."[1]

What shall we say after this but that the soul enters even now the regions of heavenly beatitude, becoming already an attendant before the throne of God, being associated with the angels and saints in their life of ceaseless love, and placed by God here below as portion of

---

[1] "Ita amans, cujus affectus est informatus ipso bono, inclinatur per amorem ad operandum secundum exigentiam amati. Et talis operatio est maxime sibi delectabilis, quasi formæ suæ conveniens. Unde amans, quidquid facit vel patitur pro amato, totum est sibi delectabile; et semper magis accenditur in amatum, inquantum majorem delectationem in amato experitur in his quæ propter ipsum facit vel patitur. Et sicut ignis non potest retineri a motu qui competit sibi secundum exigentiam suæ formæ, nisi per violentiam, ita neque amans quin agat secundum amorem. Et quia omne violentum est tristabile, quasi voluntati repugnans, ideo etiam est pænosum contra inclinationem amoris operari, vel etiam præter eam. Operari autem secundum eam est operari ea quæ amato competunt. Cum enim amans amatum assumpserit quasi idem sibi, oportet ut quasi personam amati amans gerat in omnibus quæ ad amatum spectant." (S. Thom., 3 Sent., D 27, Q 1, A 1.)

His paradise on earth,[1] wherein He may dwell and display the beauty of His presence and the richness of His gifts, and receive in return the constant homage of an unreserved and faithful love? It has given "all for all," and found "all in all".[2] And being "rooted and founded in Charity," it is "able to comprehend with all the saints what is the breadth, and length, and height, and depth; to know also the Charity of Christ, and to be filled unto all the fulness of God ".[3]

"See, Lord, how everything vanishes in me but the one treasure of Thy love."[4]

Ah! Divine Loveliness! take Thou my soul for time and eternity. Be Thou my life, my form, my moving-principle. Rid me of my fleshly loves and fears; and let me move by Thee and according to Thee, with all the promptitude, ease, and sweetness that belong to the life of perfect Charity. "O Sweetness of my heart! O Life of my soul! most bright Light! my Origin and my first Principle! all-sufficient One! mortify in me whatever displeases Thee, and make me according to Thine own heart. When shall I perfectly please Thee in all things? When shall I be free from

---

[1] "The soul of the just man is a paradise wherein God dwells. What a room, then, ought that to be, in which a King so powerful, so wise, so pure, so full of every perfection, delights Himself! Since, then, we may in some degree enjoy heaven on earth, let us earnestly beseech our Lord to grant us His grace and show us the way, lest through our own fault we miss it." (S. Teresa, "Int. Castle," C 1, and M 5, C 1.)

[2] "The lover gives all for all, and has all in all." ("Imit.," B iii., C 5.)

[3] Eph. iii. 17. [4] Suso, "Etern. Wisd.," C 23.

everything apart from Thee? When shall I be all Thine, and cease to be mine own? When will there be nothing in me but what is Thine? When wilt Thou inflame and consume me with the fire of Thy love? When wilt Thou penetrate me with Thy sweetness? When wilt Thou perfectly unite, absorb, and transform me in Thyself? O my God, my Love, my sweet Friend, my Joy, my Life! Immense Goodness! too late have I known Thee, too late have I loved Thee! O Beauty, ancient and ever new, I implore Thy clemency—suffer me never more to be separated from Thee."[1]

[1] S. Peter of Alcantara, "Libell. de Oratione," P 1, C 11.